Shojo Beat

Skip·Beat!

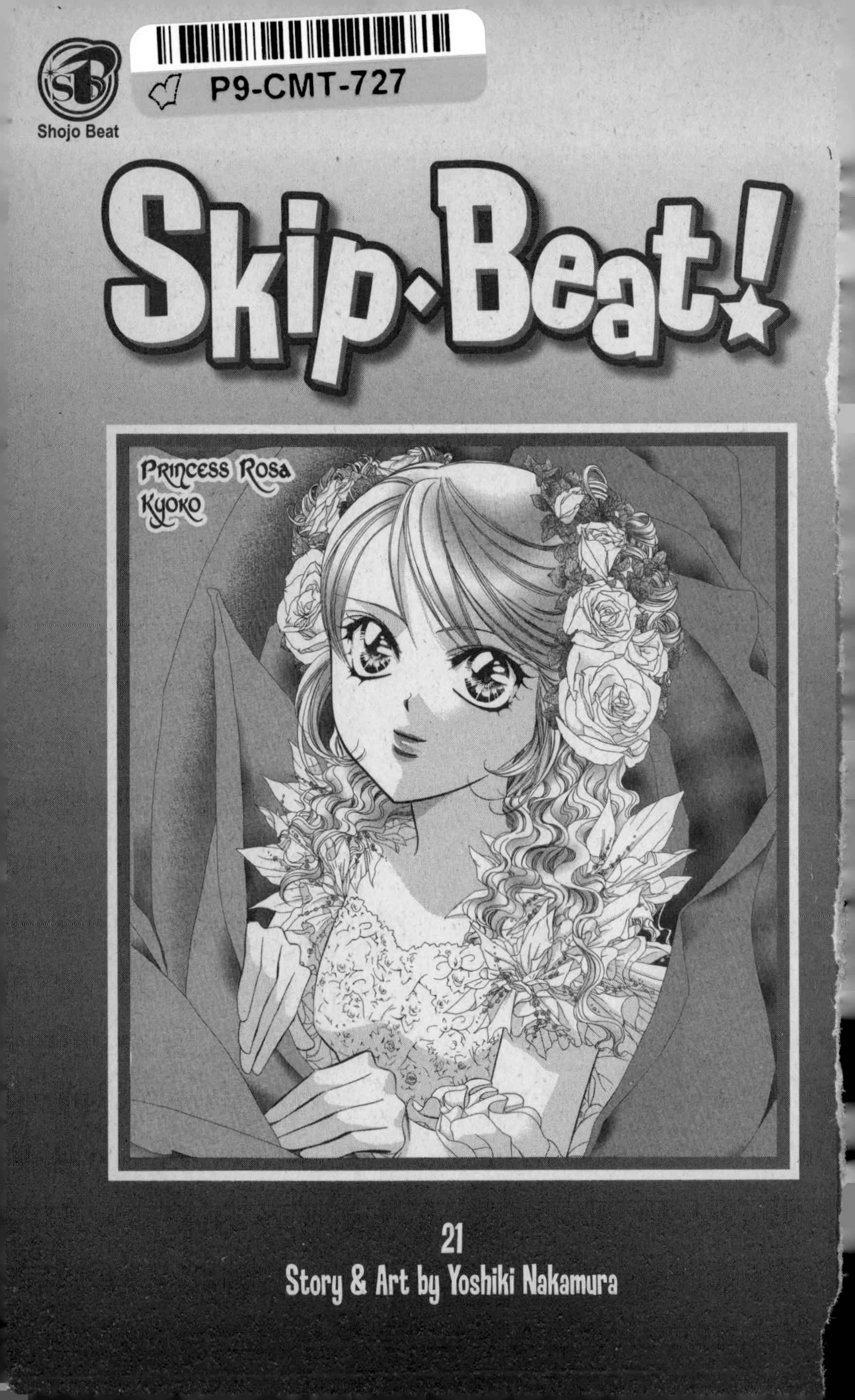
Princess Rosa
Kyoko

21

Story & Art by Yoshiki Nakamura

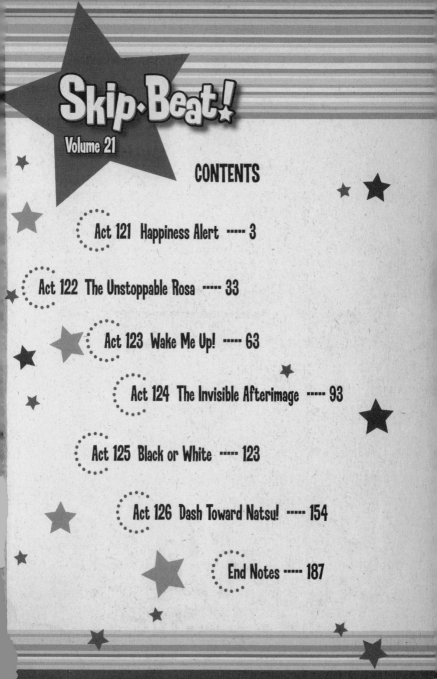

Skip·Beat!

Volume 21

CONTENTS

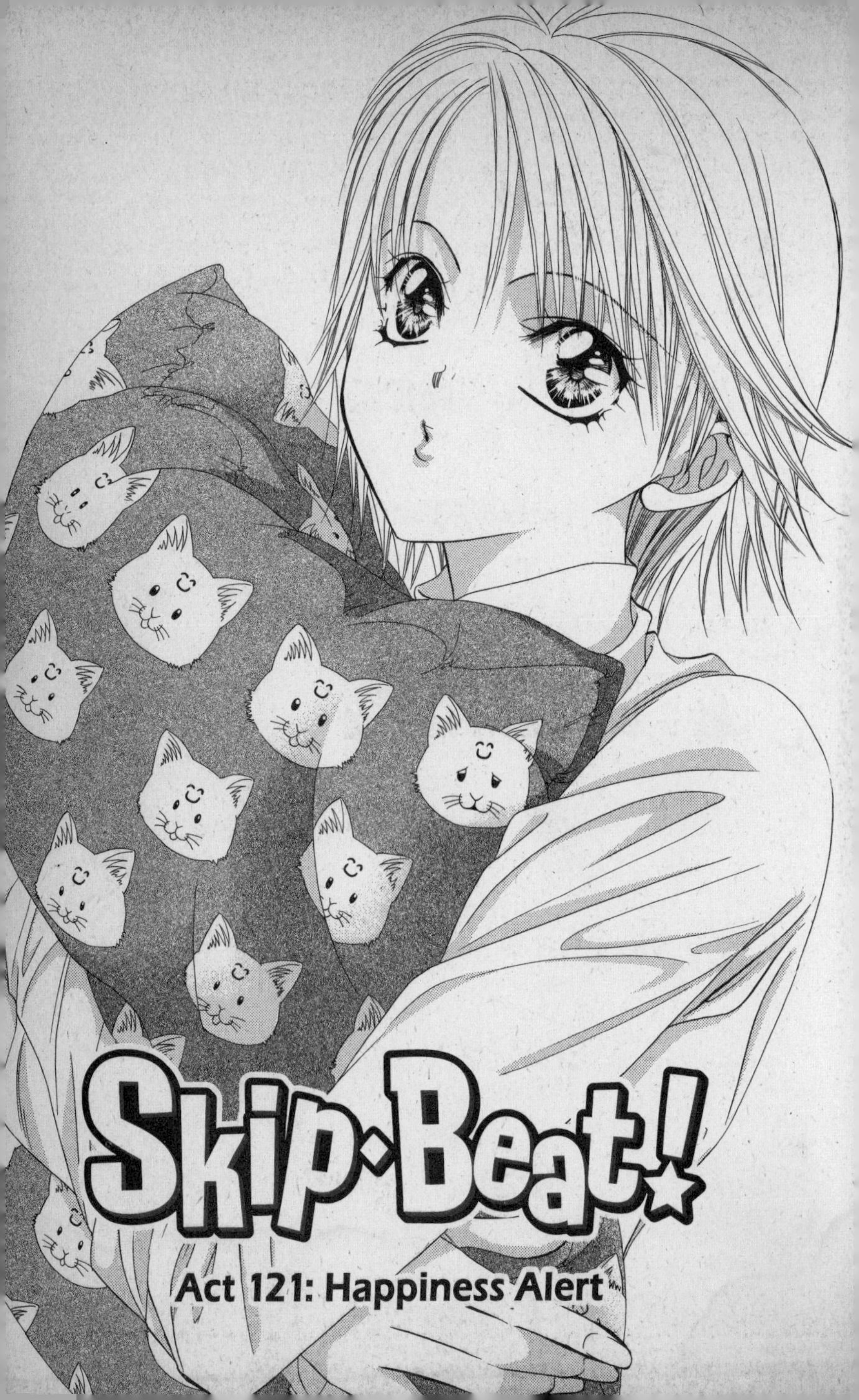
Skip·Beat!
Act 121: Happiness Alert

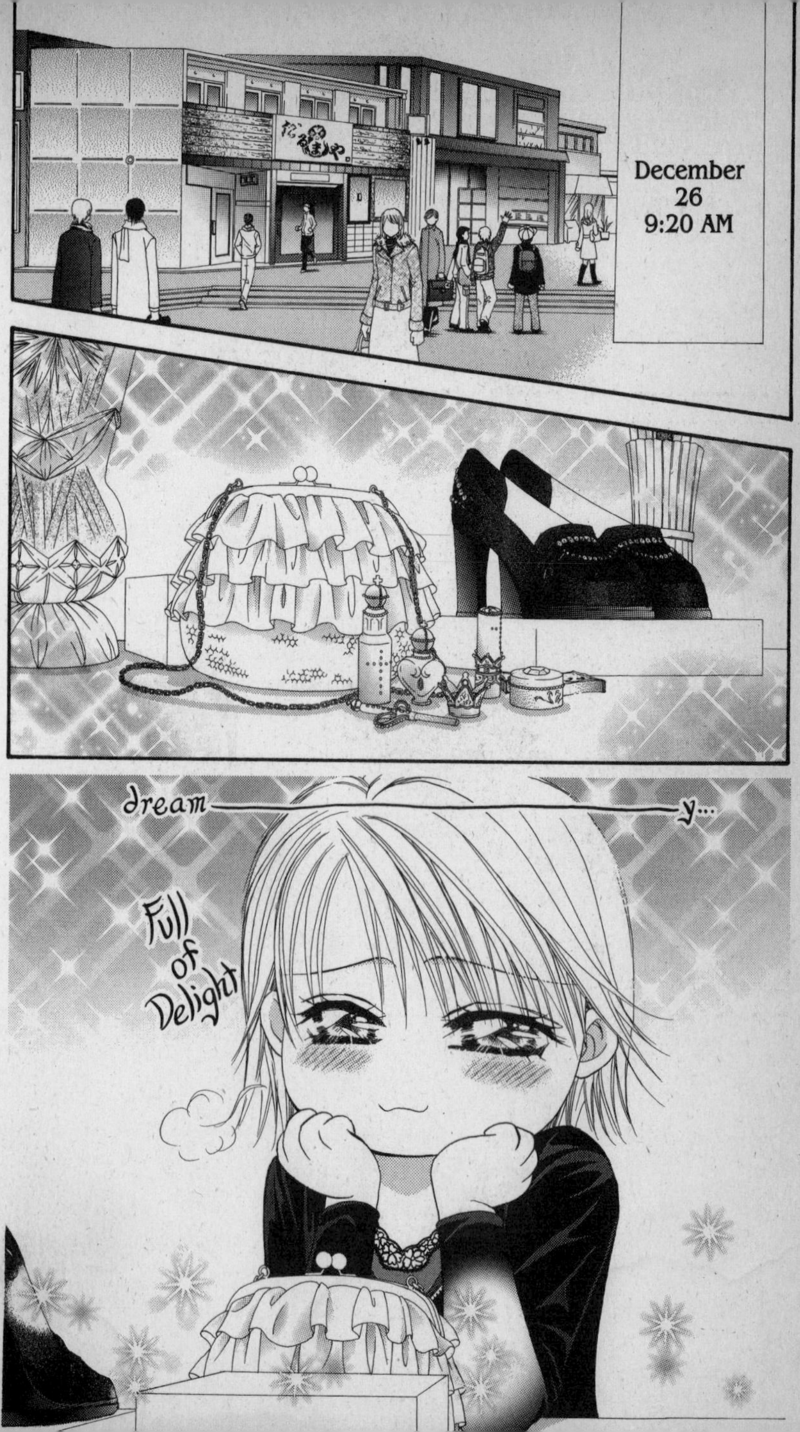
December 26 9:20 AM
dream————y...
Full of Delight

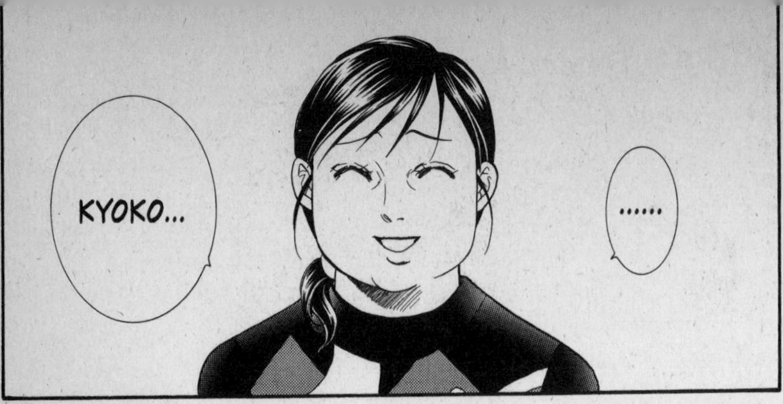
......
KYOKO...
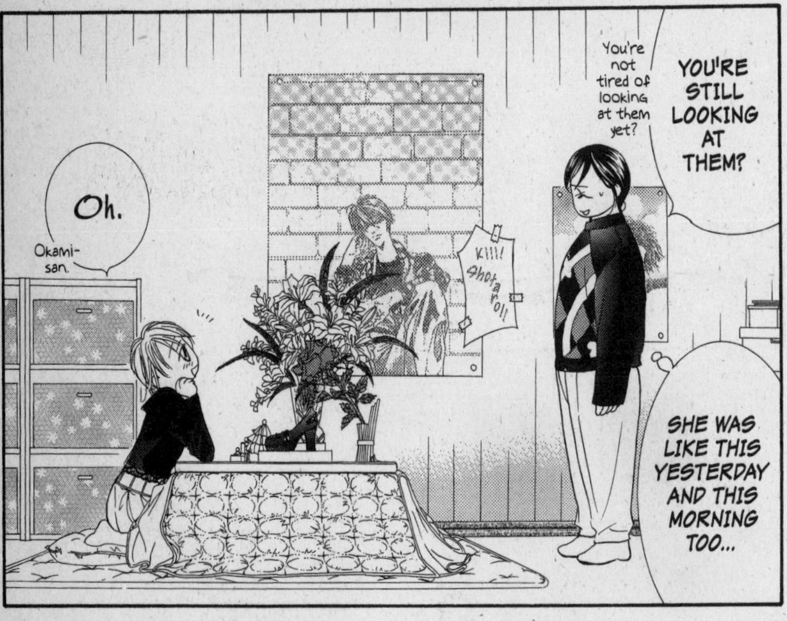
YOU'RE STILL LOOKING AT THEM?
You're not tired of looking at them yet?
SHE WAS LIKE THIS YESTERDAY AND THIS MORNING TOO...
Kill! Shotaro!!
Oh.
Okami-san.
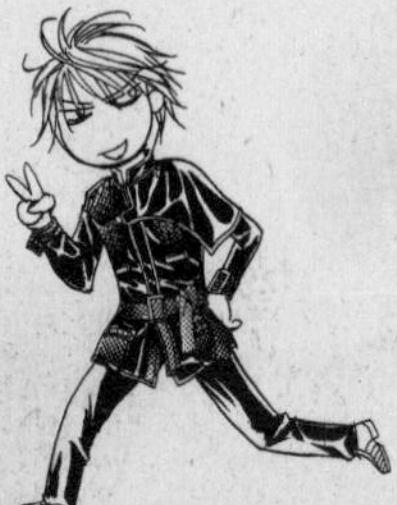

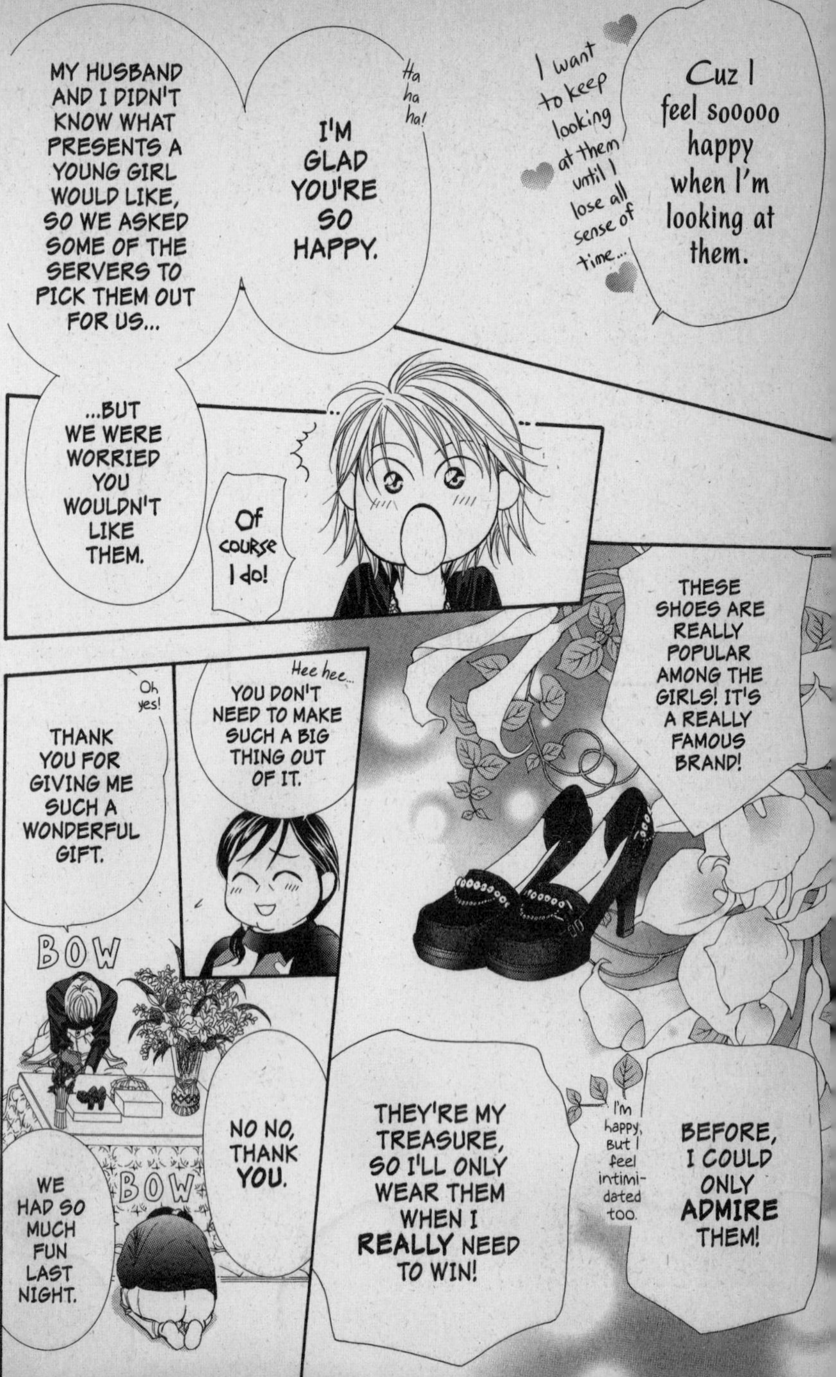
Cuz I feel sooooo happy when I'm looking at them.
I want to keep looking at them until I lose all sense of time...
Ha ha ha!
I'M GLAD YOU'RE SO HAPPY.
MY HUSBAND AND I DIDN'T KNOW WHAT PRESENTS A YOUNG GIRL WOULD LIKE, SO WE ASKED SOME OF THE SERVERS TO PICK THEM OUT FOR US...
...BUT WE WERE WORRIED YOU WOULDN'T LIKE THEM.
Of course I do!
THESE SHOES ARE REALLY POPULAR AMONG THE GIRLS! IT'S A REALLY FAMOUS BRAND!
BEFORE, I COULD ONLY ADMIRE THEM!
I'm happy, but I feel intimidated too.
THEY'RE MY TREASURE, SO I'LL ONLY WEAR THEM WHEN I REALLY NEED TO WIN!
Hee hee...
YOU DON'T NEED TO MAKE SUCH A BIG THING OUT OF IT.
Oh yes!
THANK YOU FOR GIVING ME SUCH A WONDERFUL GIFT.
BOW
NO NO, THANK YOU.
BOW
WE HAD SO MUCH FUN LAST NIGHT.

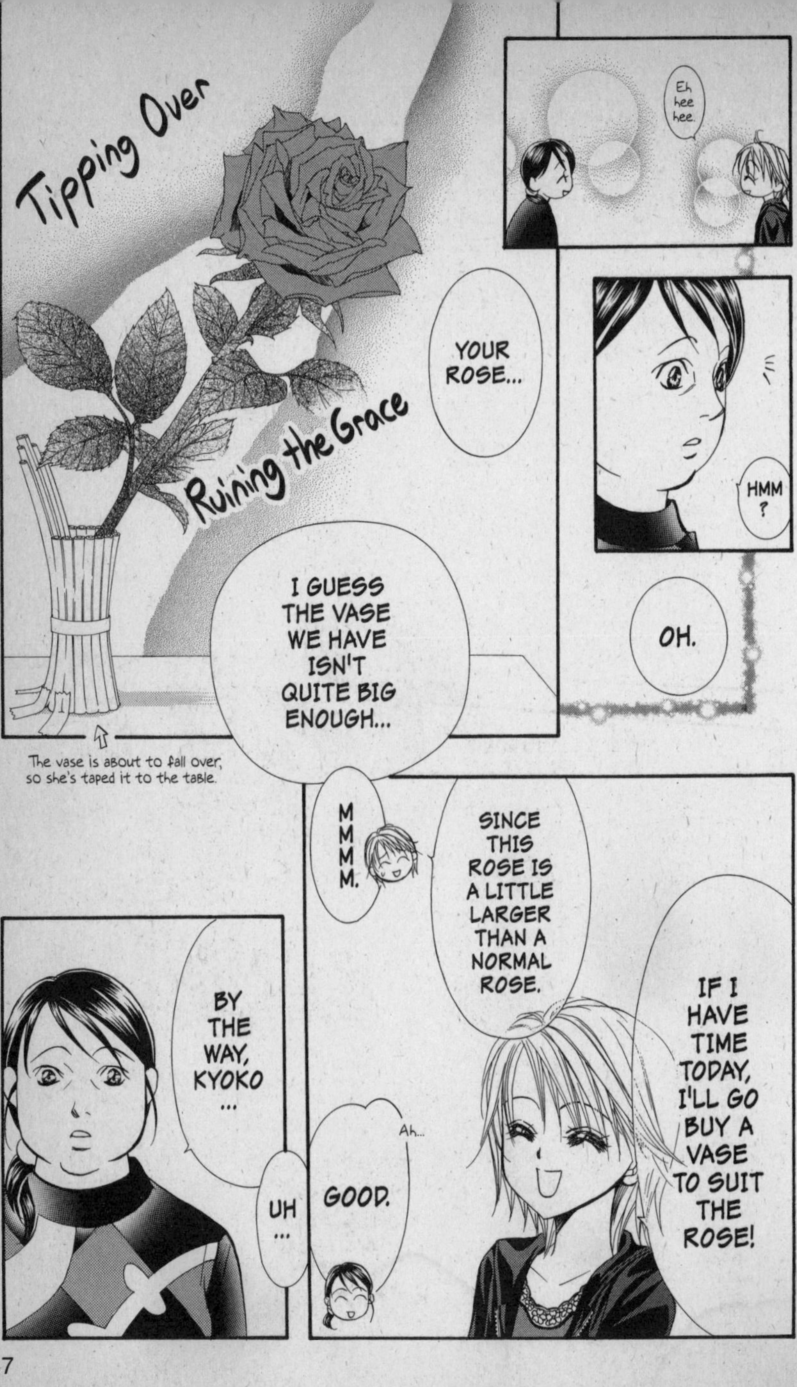
Tipping Over
Ruining the Grace
Eh hee hee.
YOUR ROSE...
HMM ?
OH.
I GUESS THE VASE WE HAVE ISN'T QUITE BIG ENOUGH...
MMMM.
SINCE THIS ROSE IS A LITTLE LARGER THAN A NORMAL ROSE.
IF I HAVE TIME TODAY, I'LL GO BUY A VASE TO SUIT THE ROSE!
Ah...
GOOD.
BY THE WAY, KYOKO ...
UH ...
The vase is about to fall over, so she's taped it to the table.

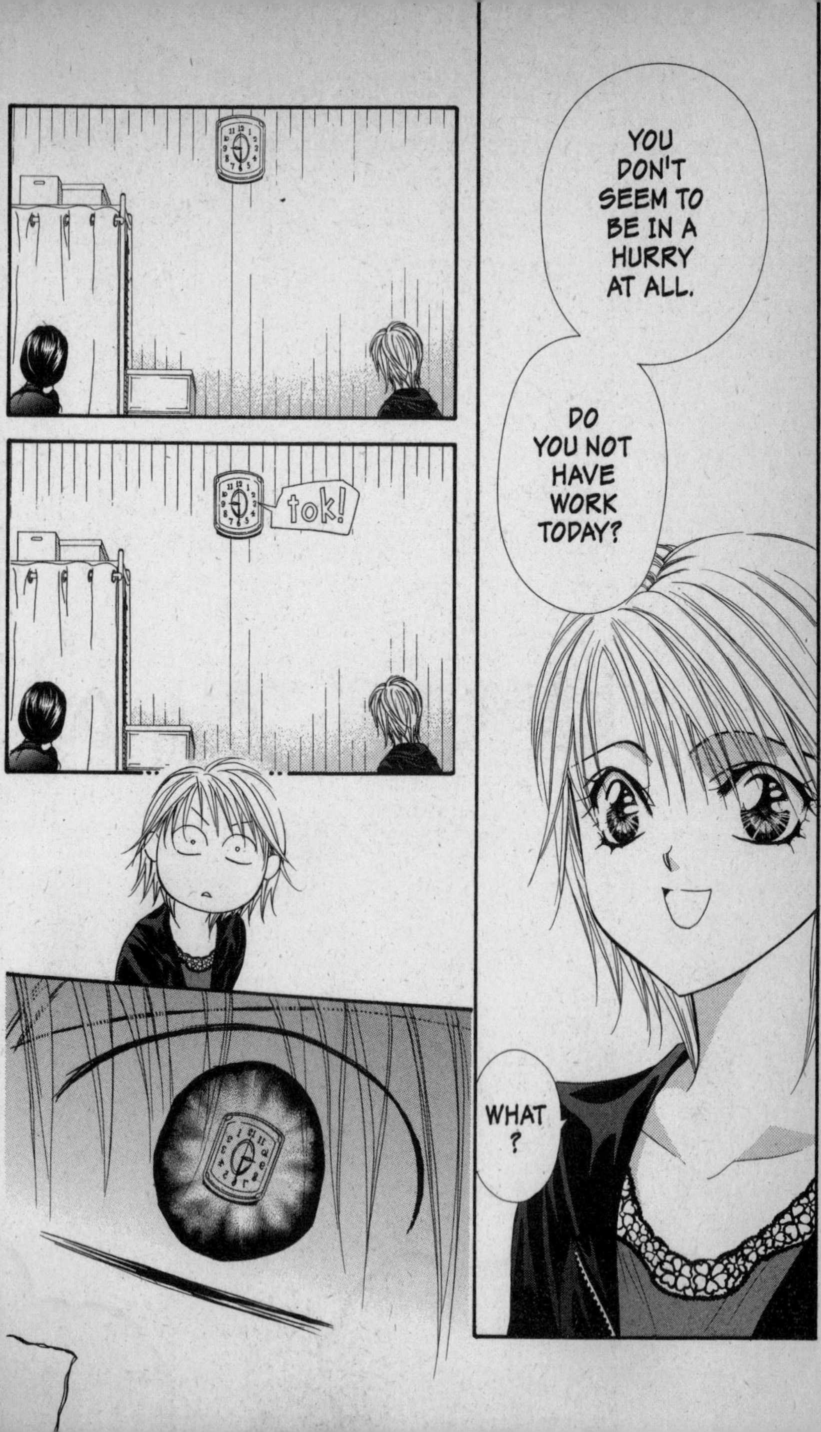
YOU DON'T SEEM TO BE IN A HURRY AT ALL.
DO YOU NOT HAVE WORK TODAY?
WHAT ?
tok!

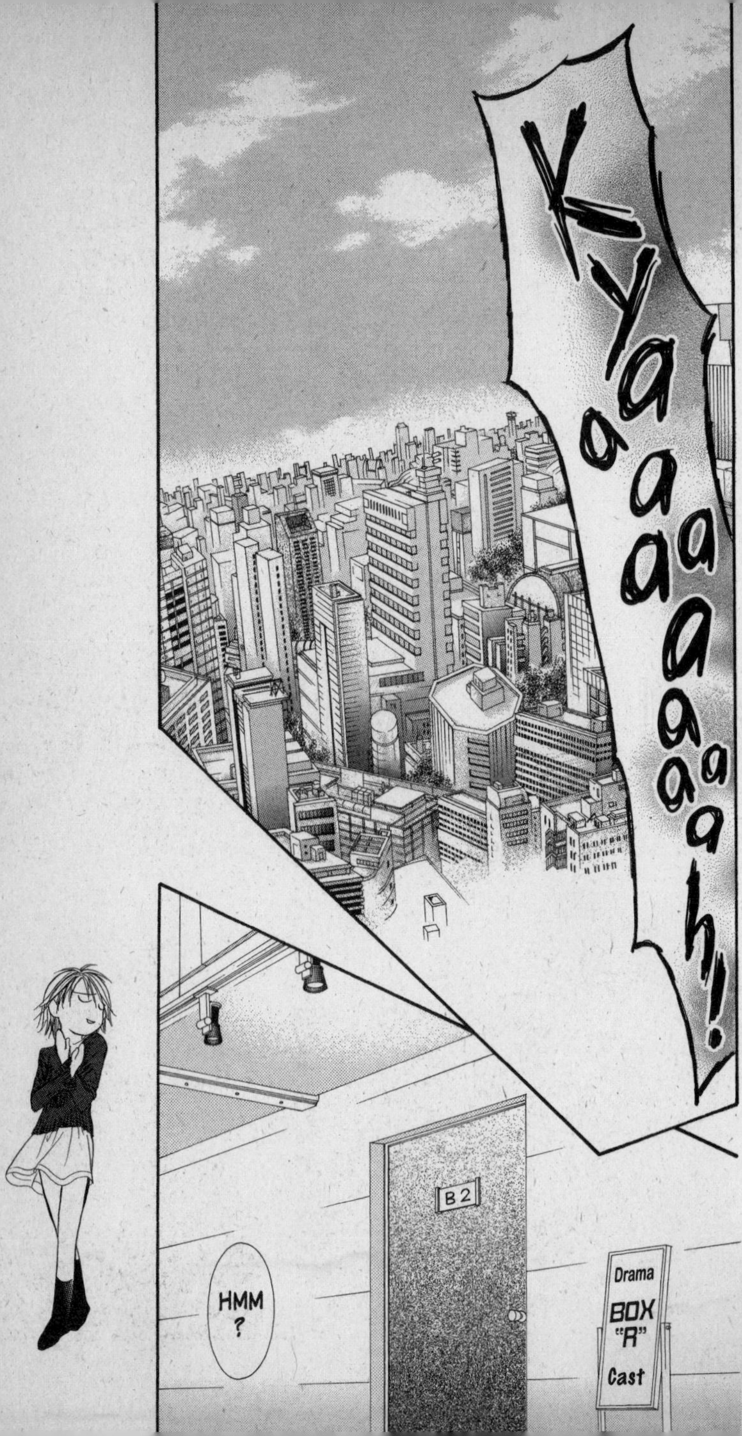
Kyaaaaaaaaaaah!!
Drama
BOX
"R"
Cast
B2
HMM
?

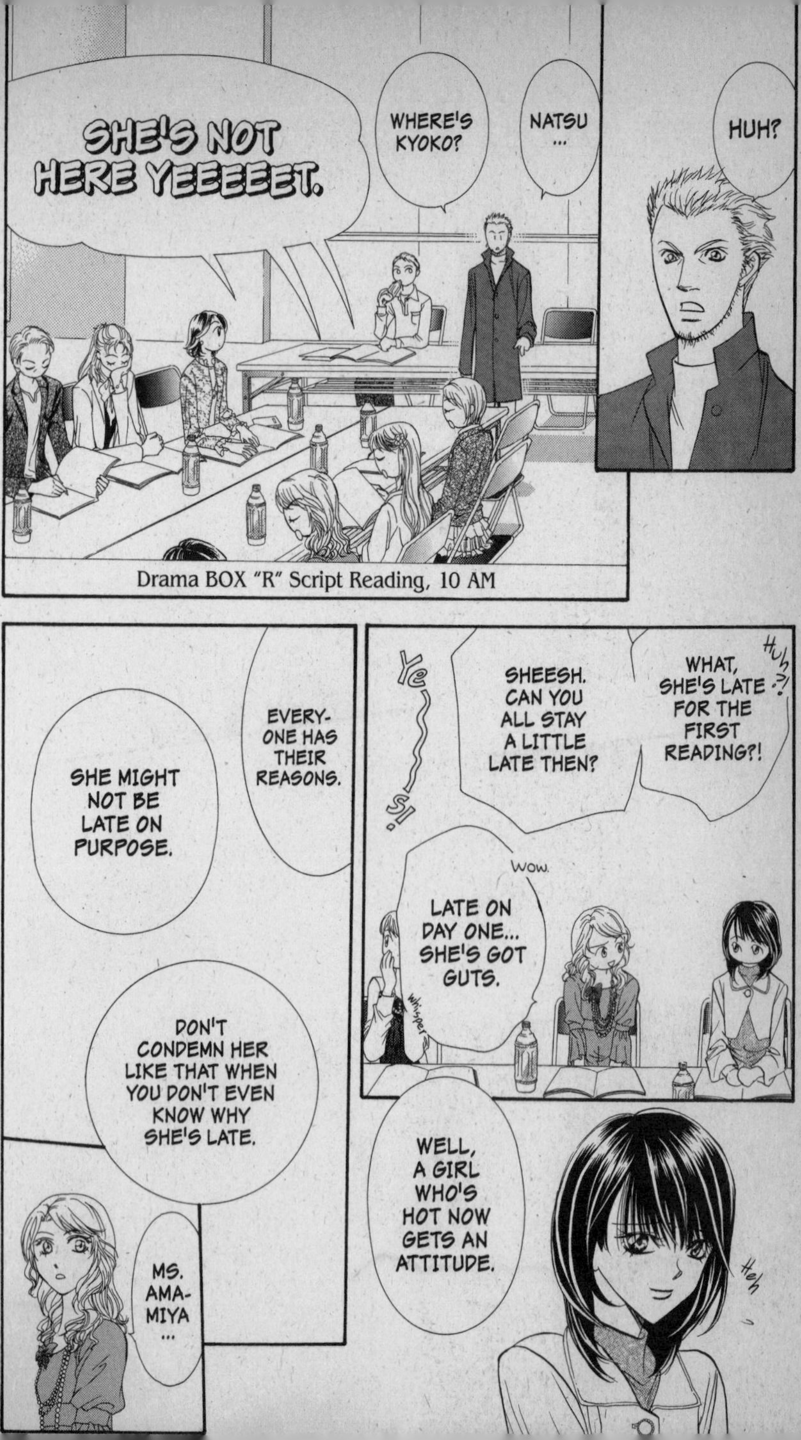
HUH?
NATSU ...
WHERE'S KYOKO?
SHE'S NOT HERE YEEEEEET.
Drama BOX "R" Script Reading, 10 AM
Huh?!
WHAT, SHE'S LATE FOR THE FIRST READING?!
SHEESH. CAN YOU ALL STAY A LITTLE LATE THEN?
Ye---s!
WOW.
LATE ON DAY ONE... SHE'S GOT GUTS.
whisper
WELL, A GIRL WHO'S HOT NOW GETS AN ATTITUDE.
Heh
EVERY-ONE HAS THEIR REASONS.
SHE MIGHT NOT BE LATE ON PURPOSE.
DON'T CONDEMN HER LIKE THAT WHEN YOU DON'T EVEN KNOW WHY SHE'S LATE.
MS. AMA-MIYA ...

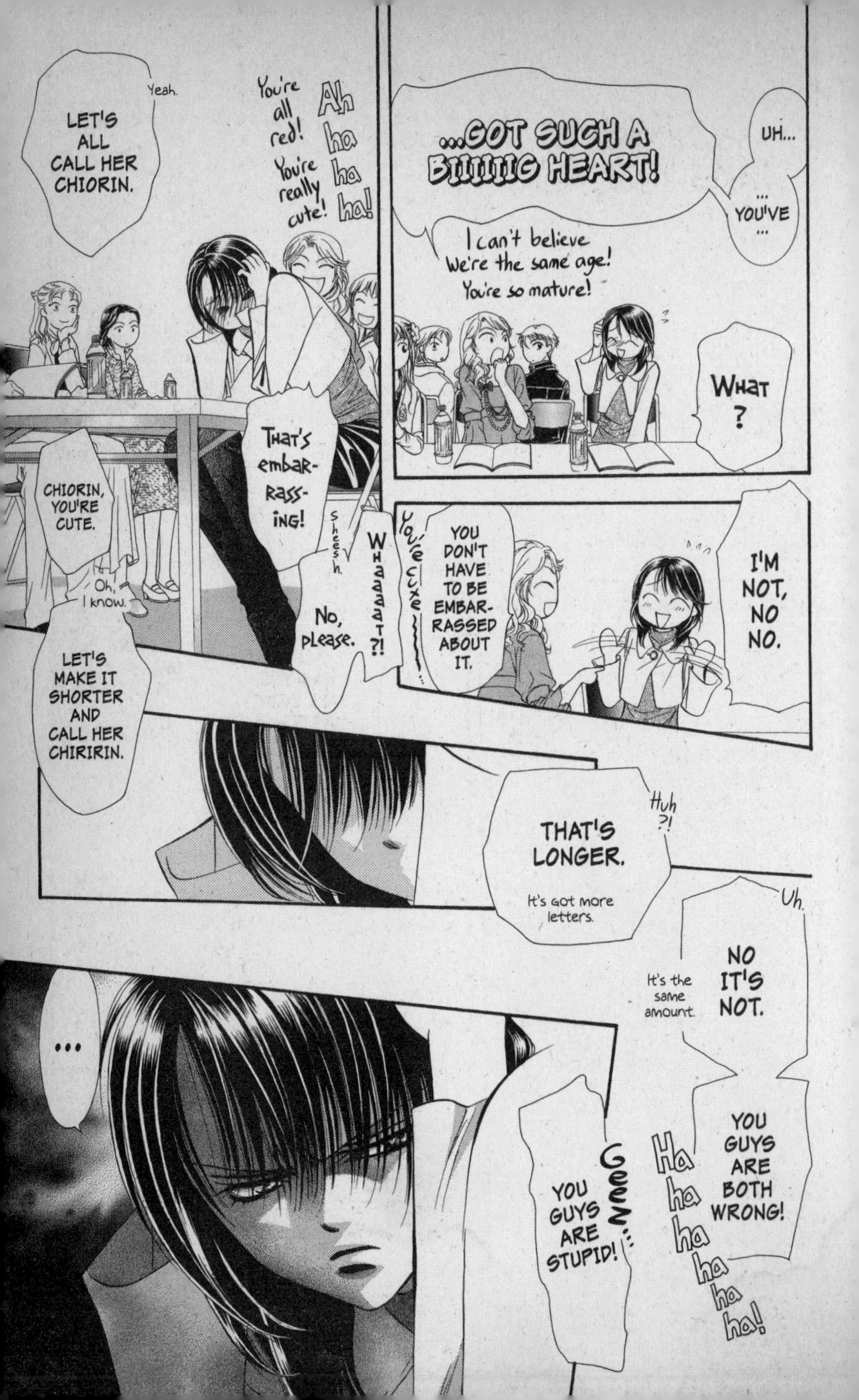
UH...
...YOU'VE...
...GOT SUCH A BIIIIIG HEART!
WHAT?
I can't believe we're the same age! You're so mature!
I'M NOT, NO NO.
YOU DON'T HAVE TO BE EMBARRASSED ABOUT IT.
You're cute~...
Whaaaaat?!
Ah ha ha ha!
You're all red! You're really cute!
Yeah.
LET'S ALL CALL HER CHIORIN.
That's embarrassing!
Sheesh.
No, please.
CHIORIN, YOU'RE CUTE.
Oh, I know.
LET'S MAKE IT SHORTER AND CALL HER CHIRIRIN.
Huh?!
THAT'S LONGER.
It's got more letters.
Uh.
NO IT'S NOT.
It's the same amount.
YOU GUYS ARE BOTH WRONG!
Ha ha ha ha ha ha!
Geez...
YOU GUYS ARE STUPID!
...

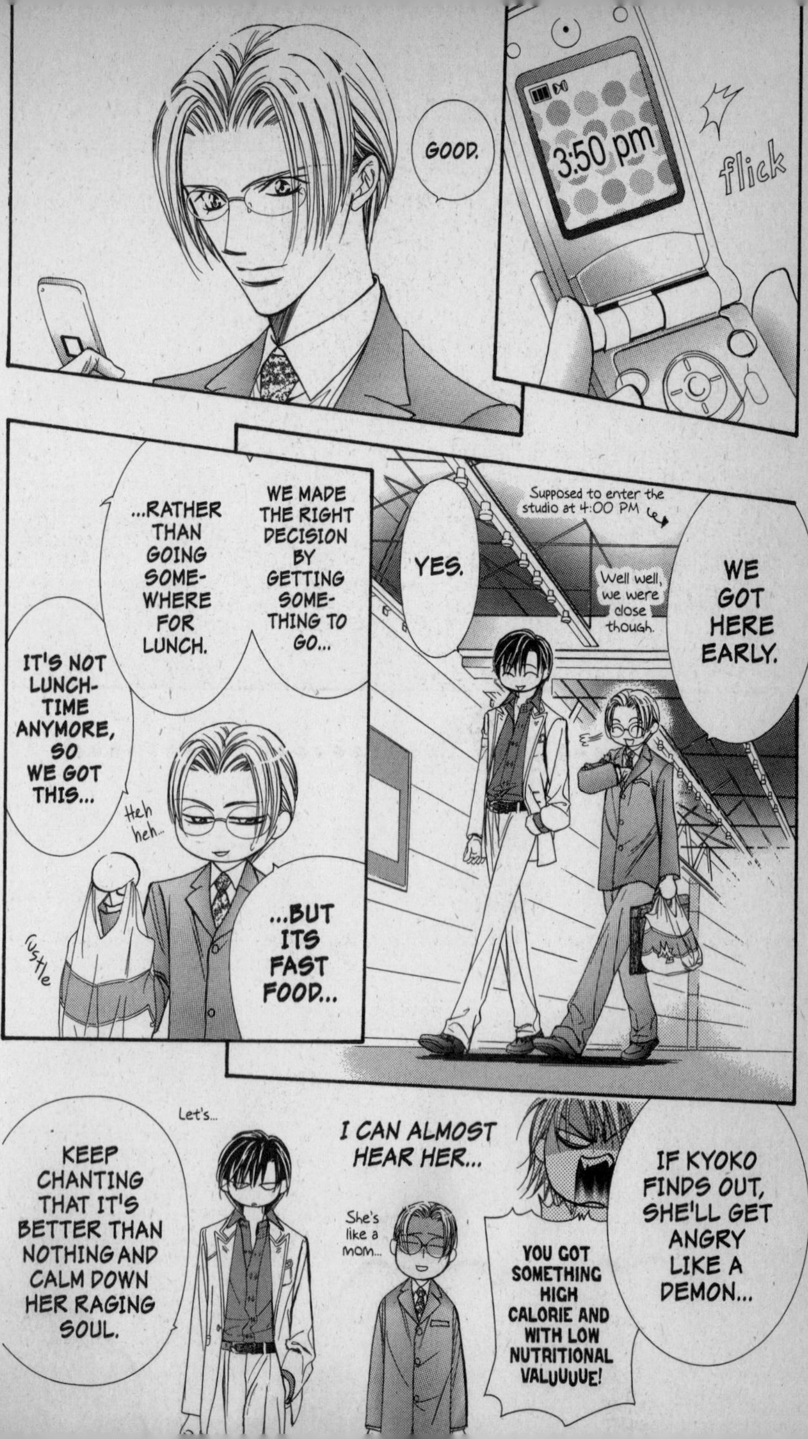
3:50 pm
flick
GOOD.
Supposed to enter the studio at 4:00 PM
WE GOT HERE EARLY.
Well well, we were close though.
YES.
WE MADE THE RIGHT DECISION BY GETTING SOMETHING TO GO...
...RATHER THAN GOING SOMEWHERE FOR LUNCH.
IT'S NOT LUNCHTIME ANYMORE, SO WE GOT THIS...
Heh heh...
...BUT ITS FAST FOOD...
rustle
IF KYOKO FINDS OUT, SHE'LL GET ANGRY LIKE A DEMON...
YOU GOT SOMETHING HIGH CALORIE AND WITH LOW NUTRITIONAL VALUUUUE!
I CAN ALMOST HEAR HER...
She's like a mom...
Let's...
KEEP CHANTING THAT IT'S BETTER THAN NOTHING AND CALM DOWN HER RAGING SOUL.

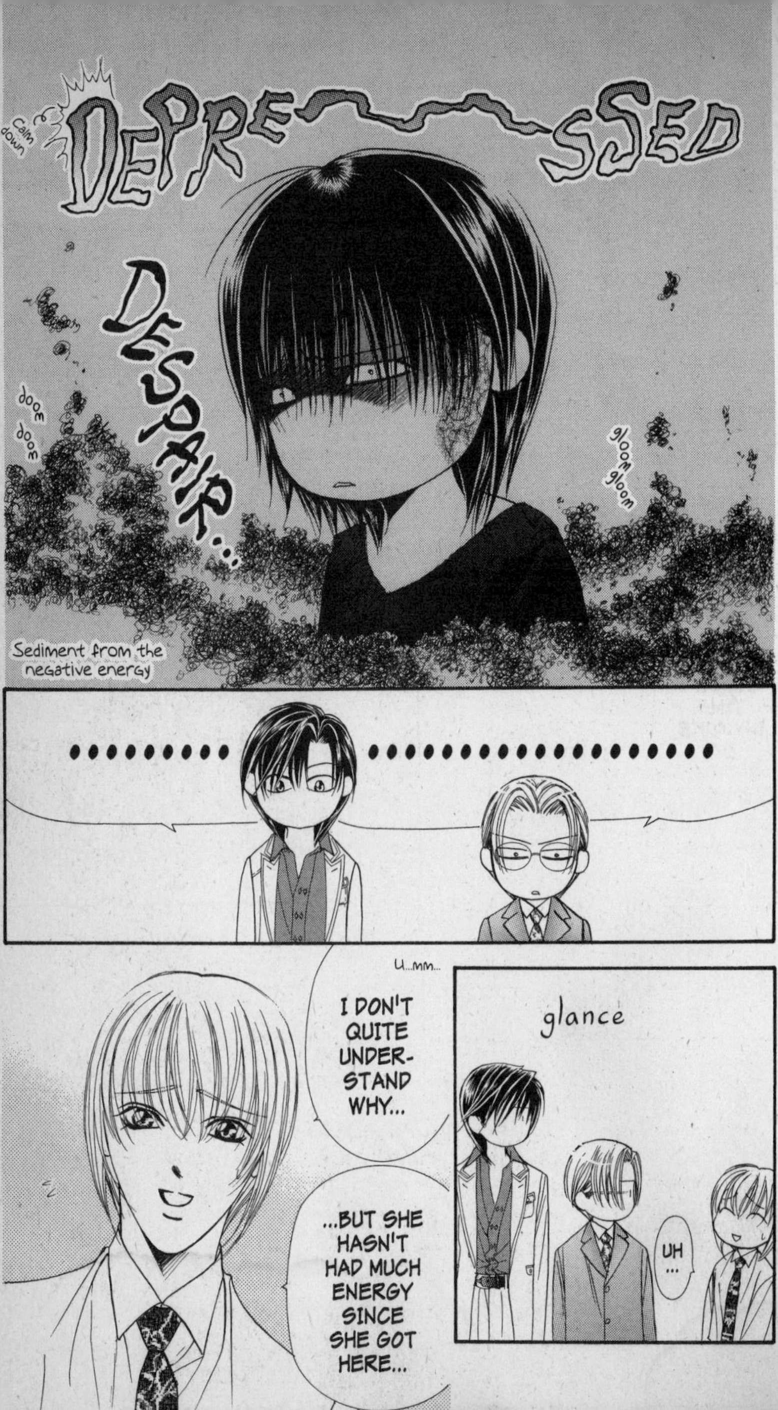
DEPRE~~~SSED
calm down
gloom gloom
DESPAIR...
doom doom
Sediment from the negative energy
....
....
glance
UH ...
U...MM...
I DON'T QUITE UNDER-STAND WHY...
...BUT SHE HASN'T HAD MUCH ENERGY SINCE SHE GOT HERE...

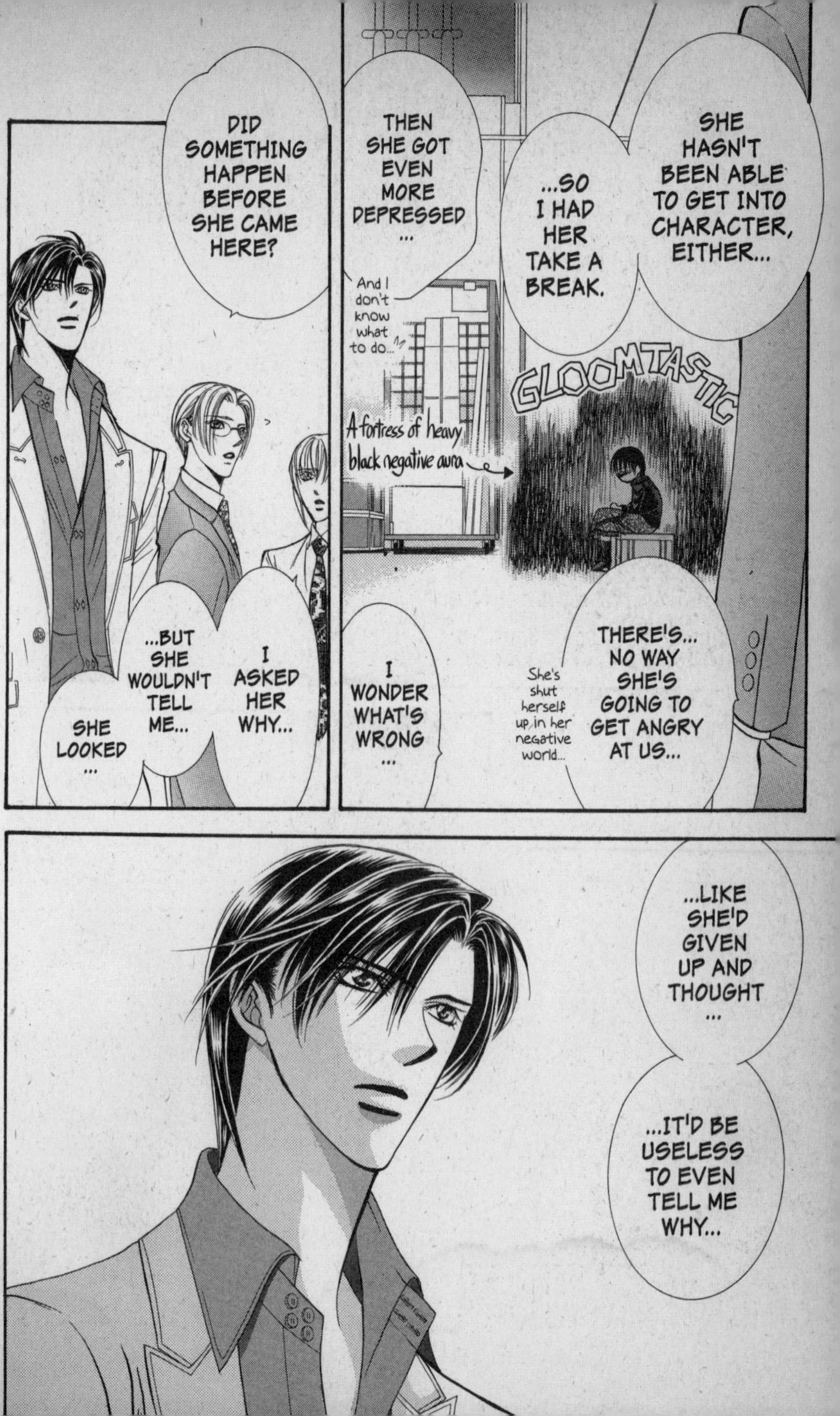
SHE HASN'T BEEN ABLE TO GET INTO CHARACTER, EITHER...
...SO I HAD HER TAKE A BREAK.
THEN SHE GOT EVEN MORE DEPRESSED...
And I don't know what to do...
GLOOMTASTIC
A fortress of heavy black negative aura
THERE'S... NO WAY SHE'S GOING TO GET ANGRY AT US...
She's shut herself up in her negative world...
I WONDER WHAT'S WRONG...
DID SOMETHING HAPPEN BEFORE SHE CAME HERE?
I ASKED HER WHY...
...BUT SHE WOULDN'T TELL ME...
SHE LOOKED...
...LIKE SHE'D GIVEN UP AND THOUGHT...
...IT'D BE USELESS TO EVEN TELL ME WHY...

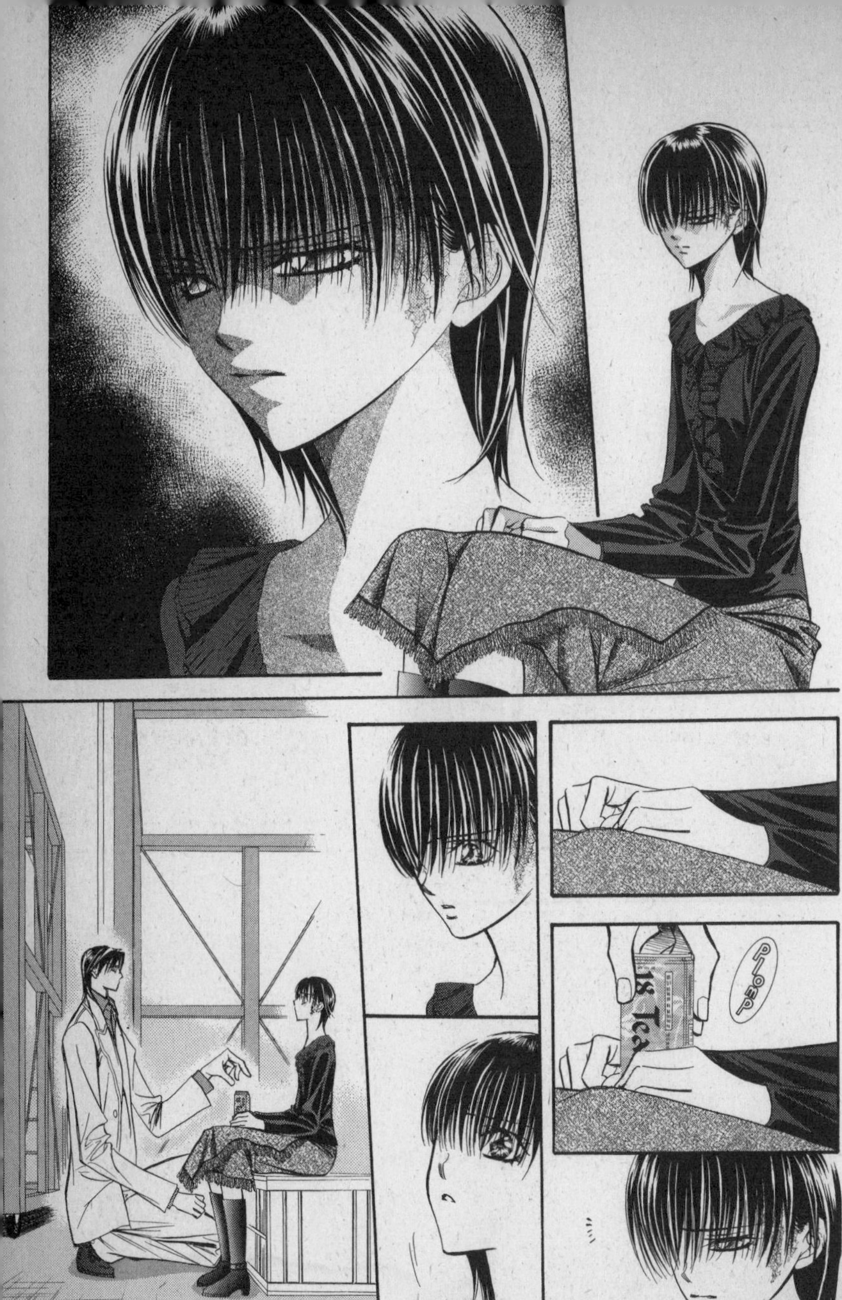
PLOMP
18 Tea
...

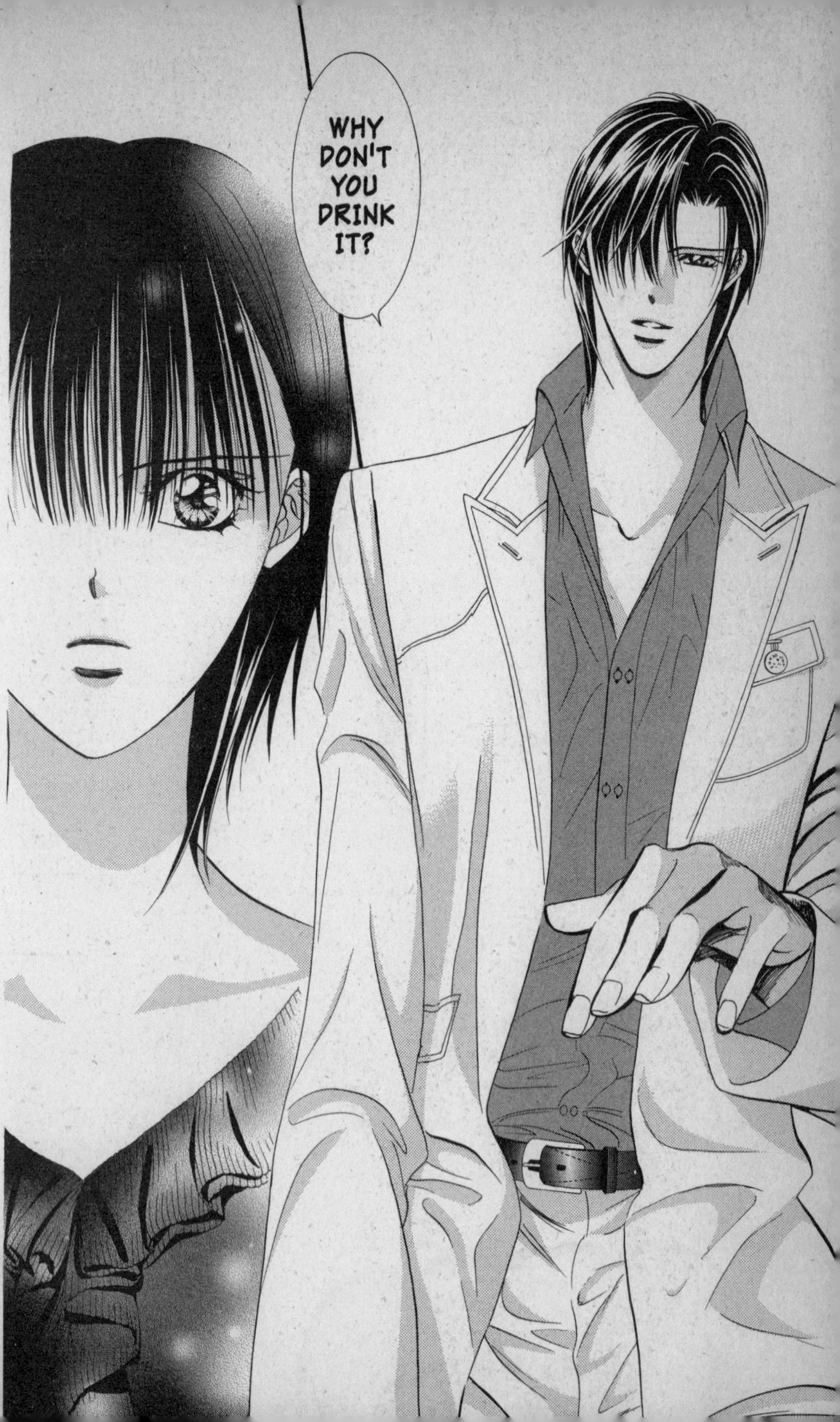
WHY DON'T YOU DRINK IT?

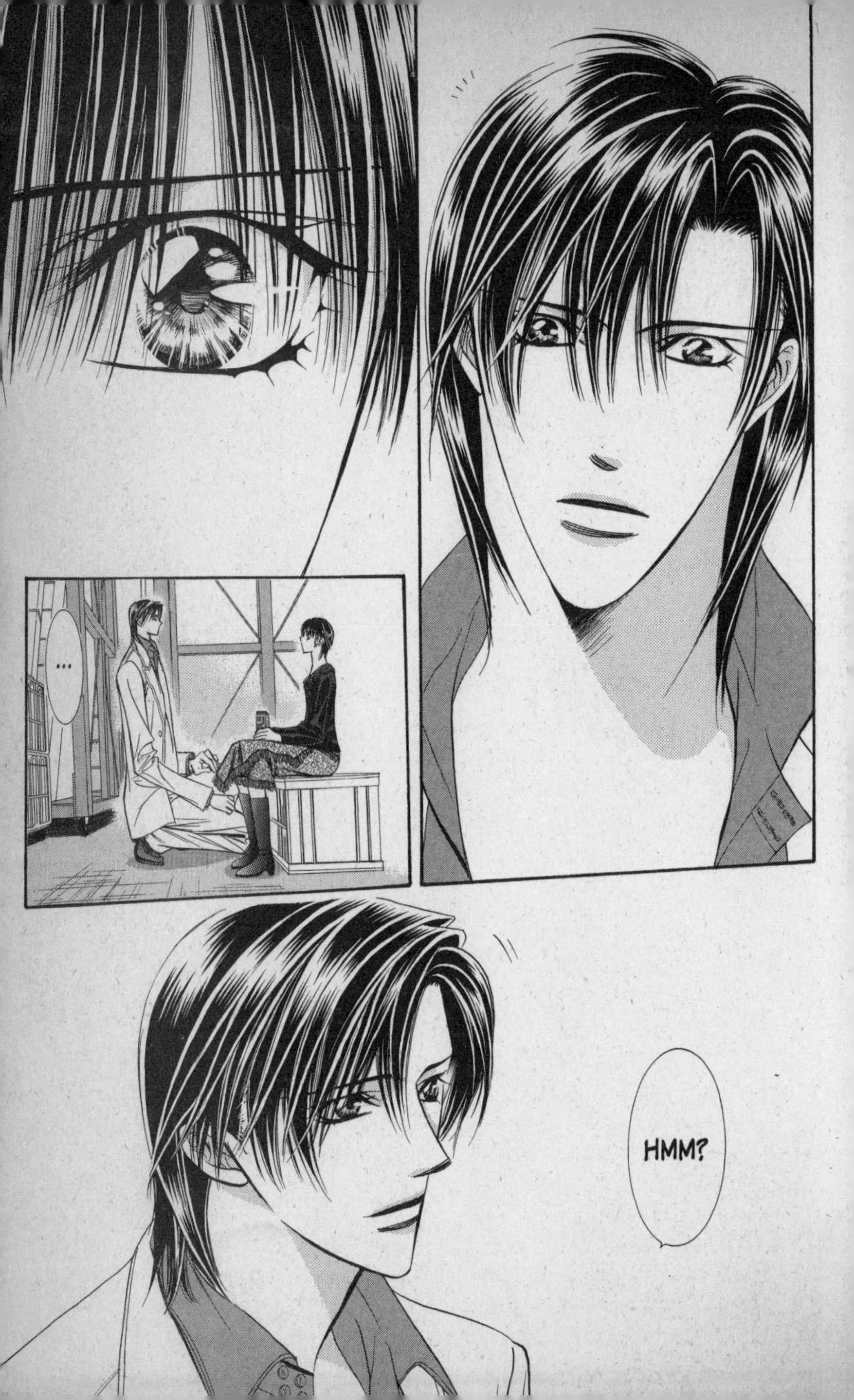
...
HMM?

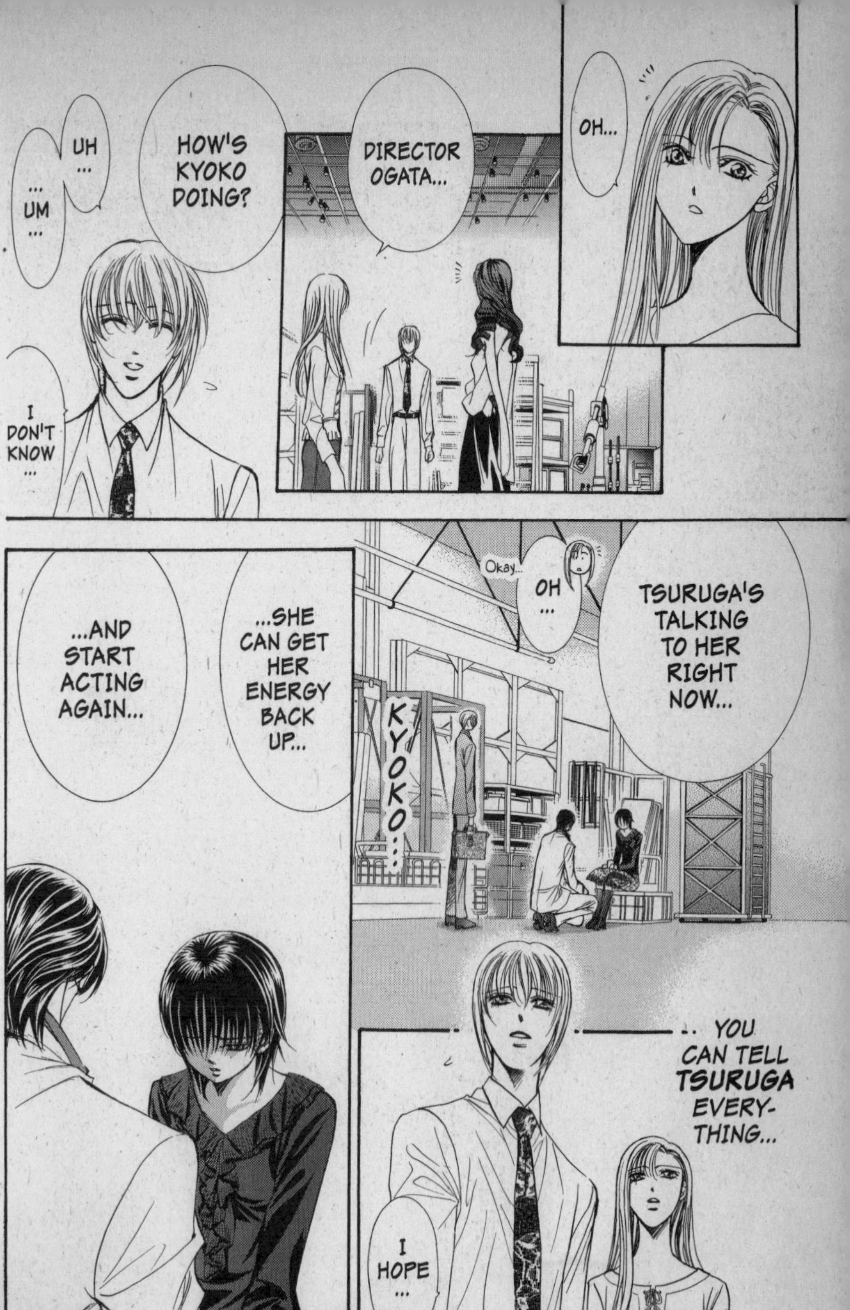
OH...
DIRECTOR OGATA...
HOW'S KYOKO DOING?
UH... ...UM...
I DON'T KNOW...
TSURUGA'S TALKING TO HER RIGHT NOW...
OH...
Okay...
KYOKO...
...YOU CAN TELL TSURUGA EVERYTHING...
I HOPE...
...SHE CAN GET HER ENERGY BACK UP...
...AND START ACTING AGAIN...

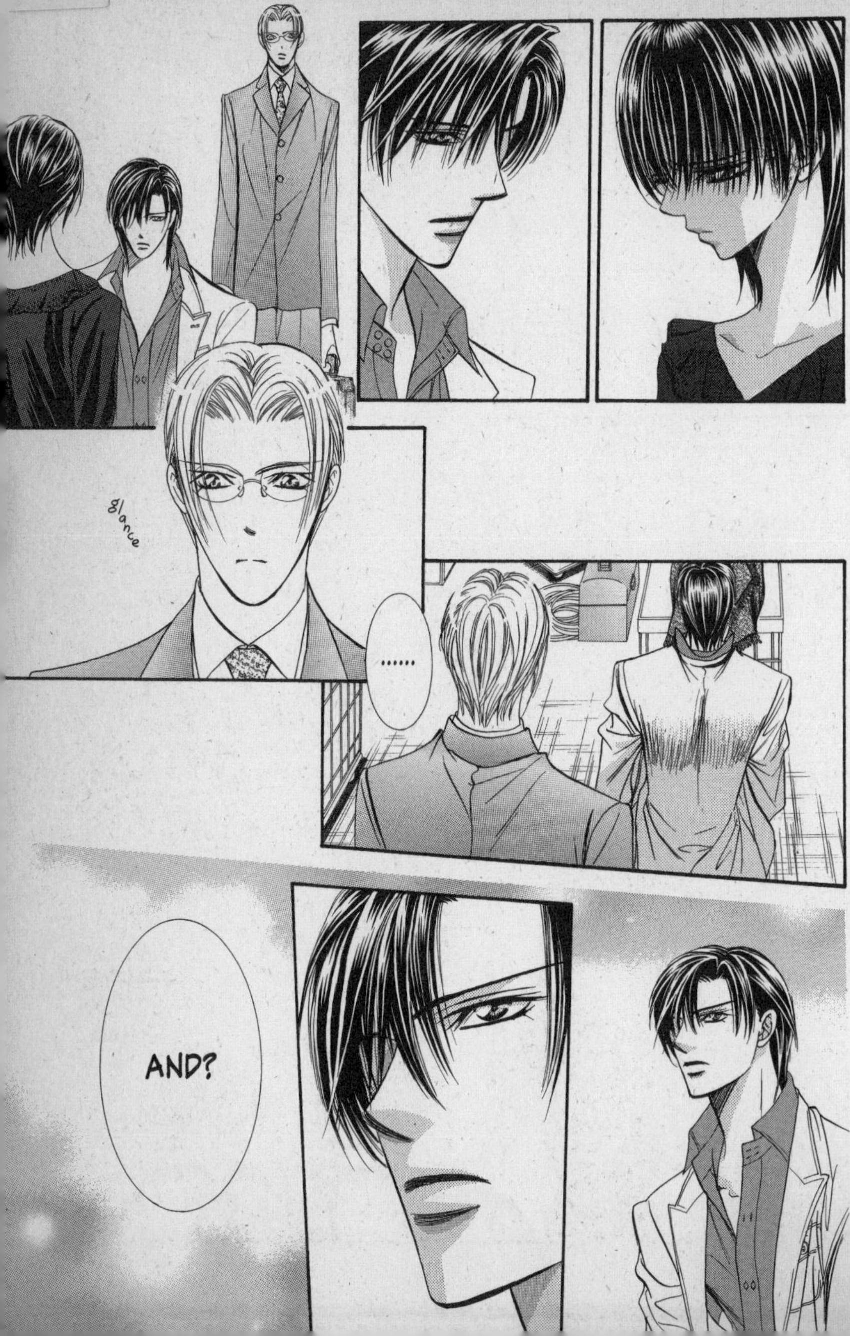
glance
......
AND?

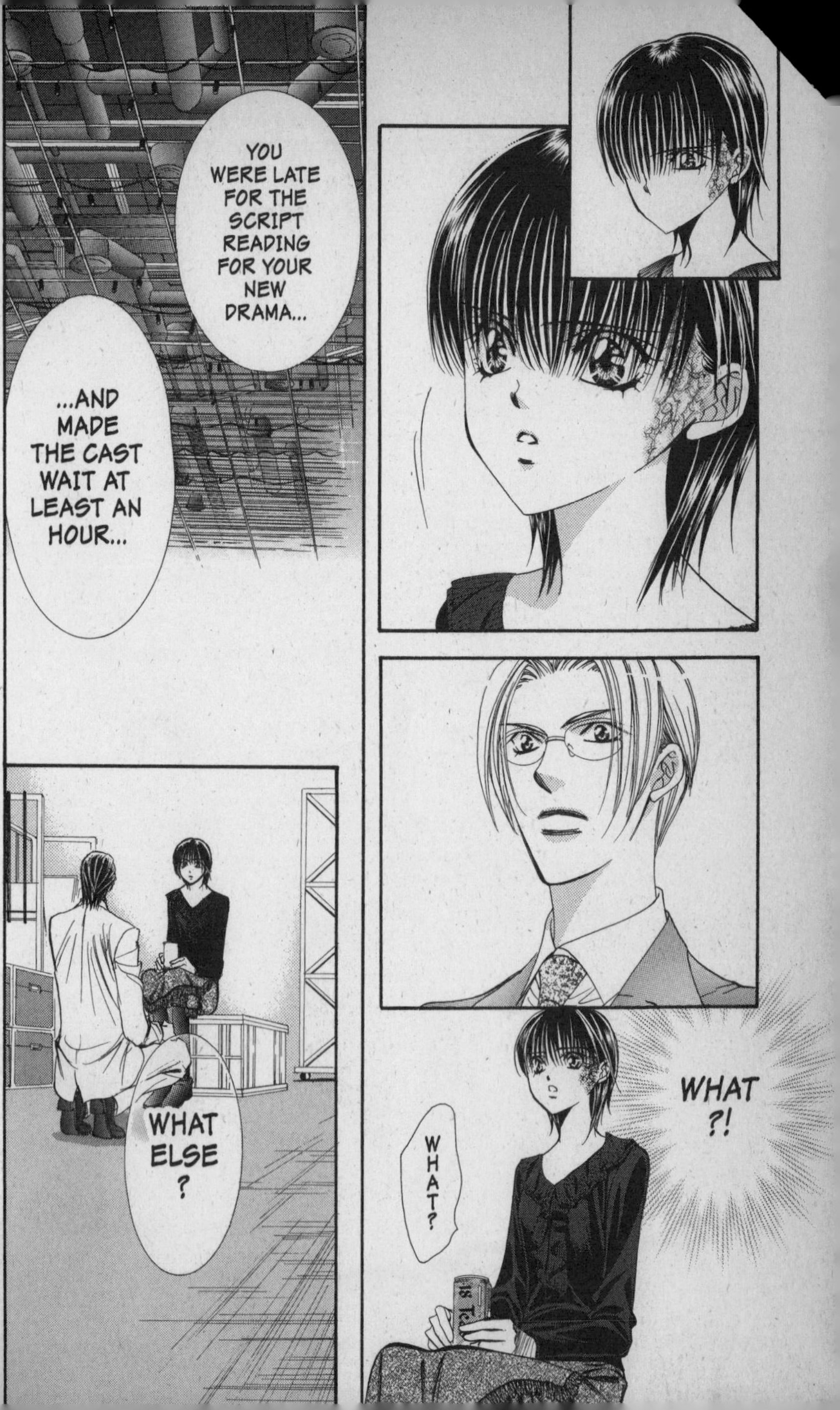
WHAT?
WHAT?!
YOU WERE LATE FOR THE SCRIPT READING FOR YOUR NEW DRAMA...
...AND MADE THE CAST WAIT AT LEAST AN HOUR...
WHAT ELSE?

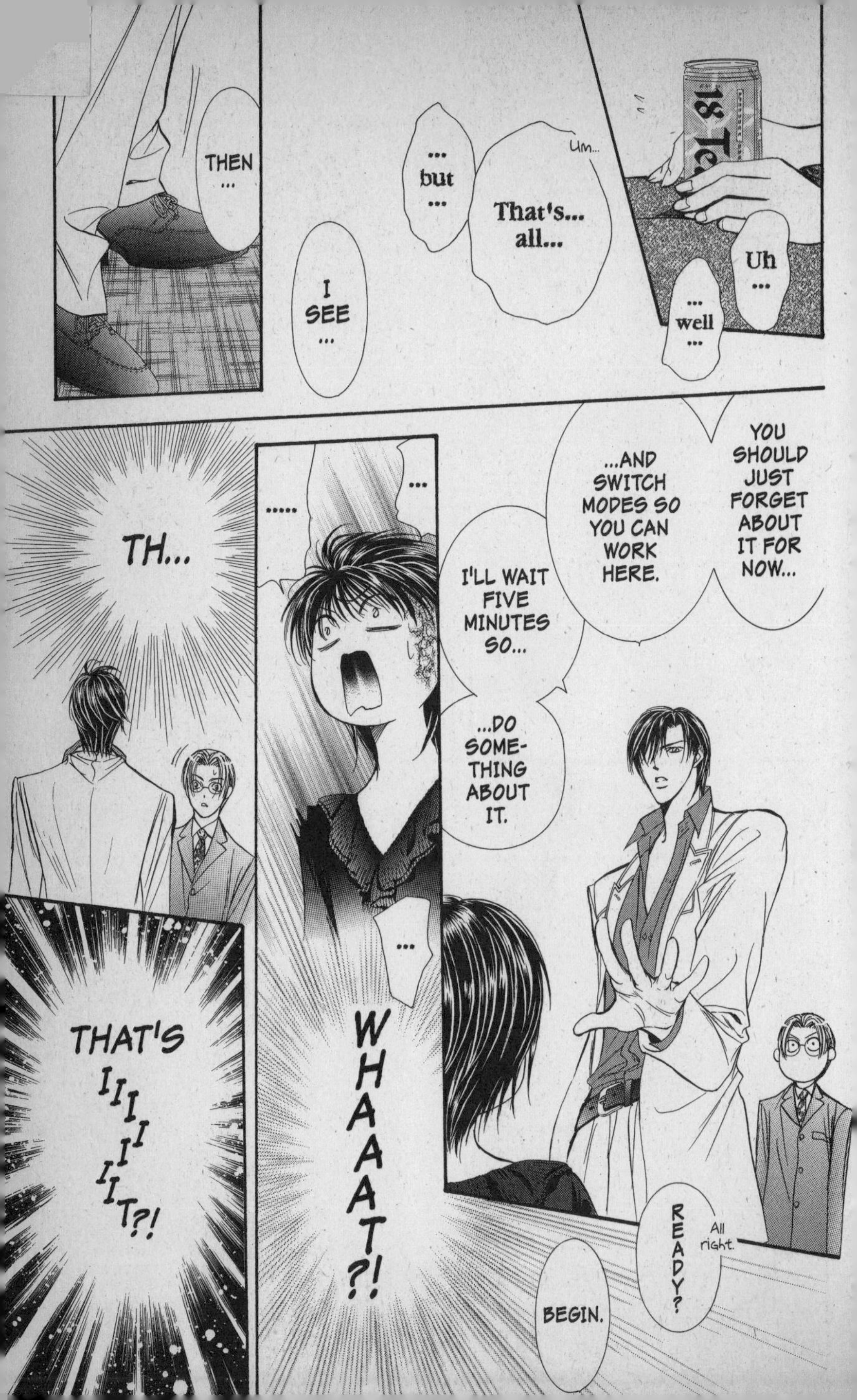

Uh...
...well...
Um...
That's... all...
...but...
I SEE...
THEN...
YOU SHOULD JUST FORGET ABOUT IT FOR NOW...
...AND SWITCH MODES SO YOU CAN WORK HERE.
I'LL WAIT FIVE MINUTES SO...
...DO SOMETHING ABOUT IT.
READY?
All right.
BEGIN.
...
.....
...
WHAAAT?!
TH...
THAT'S IIIIIIIT?!

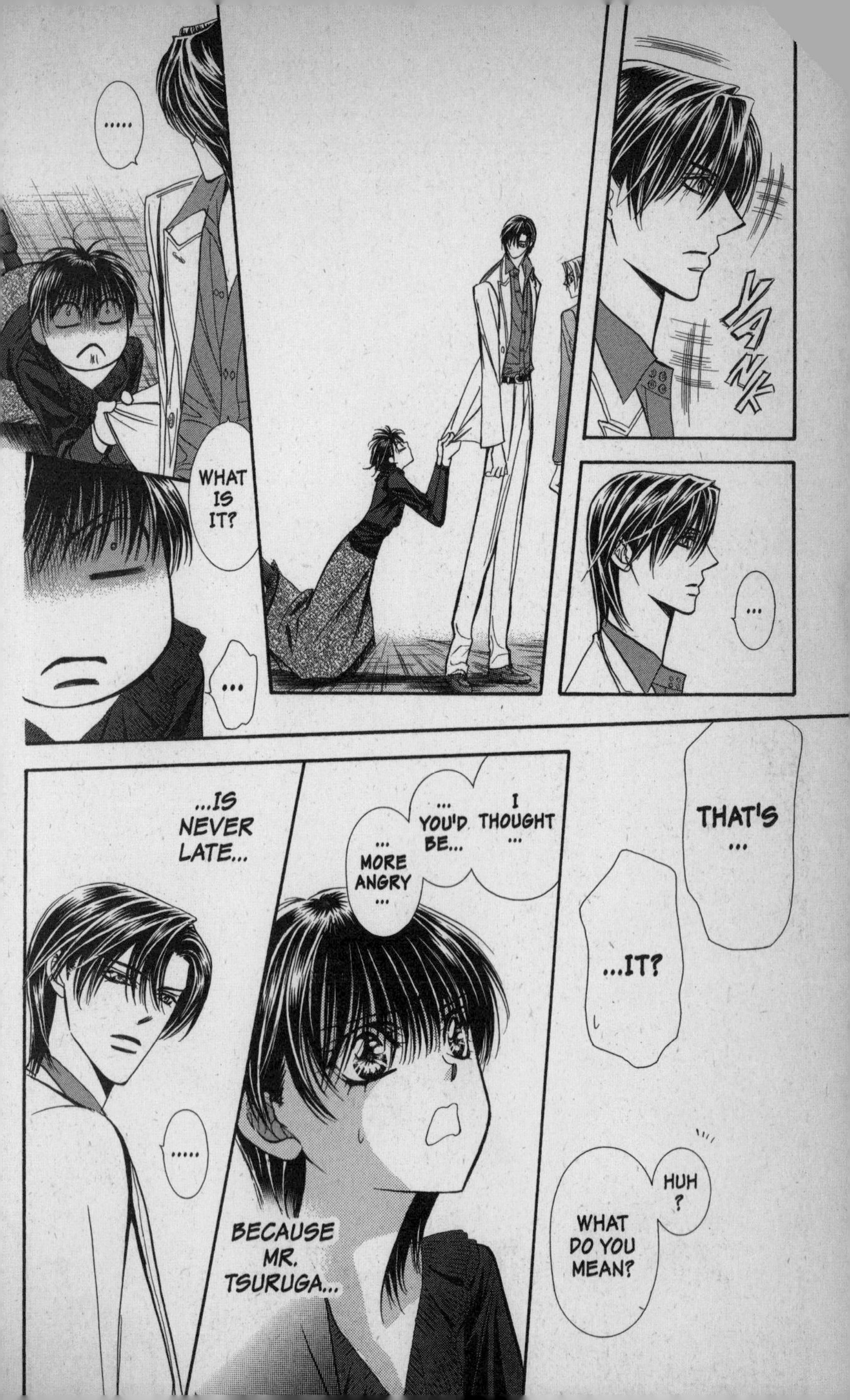
YANK
...
.....
WHAT IS IT?
...
THAT'S ...
...IT?
HUH?
WHAT DO YOU MEAN?
I THOUGHT ...
... YOU'D BE...
... MORE ANGRY ...
BECAUSE MR. TSURUGA...
...IS NEVER LATE...
.....

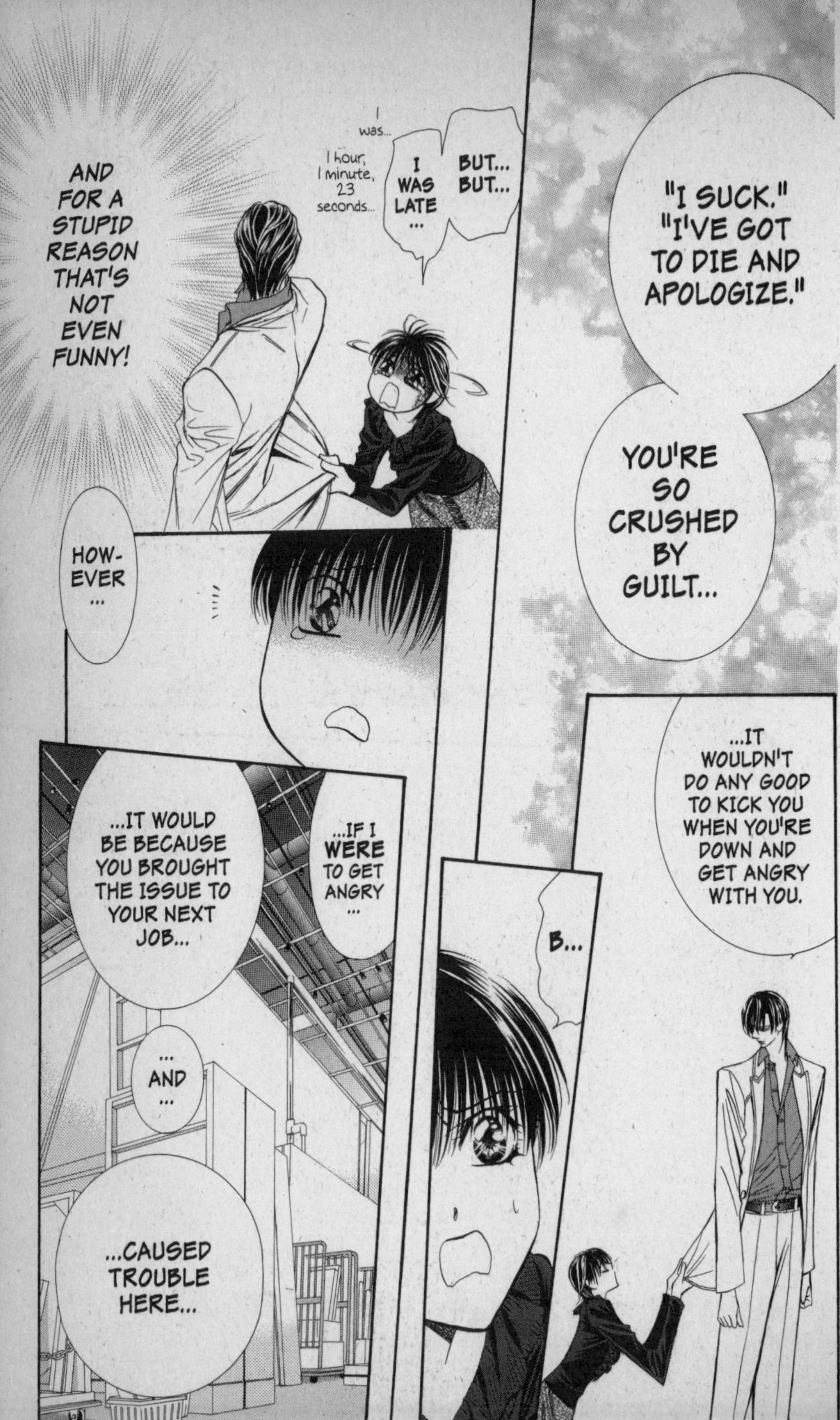
"I SUCK." "I'VE GOT TO DIE AND APOLOGIZE."
YOU'RE SO CRUSHED BY GUILT...
BUT... BUT...
I WAS LATE...
I was... 1 hour, 1 minute, 23 seconds...
AND FOR A STUPID REASON THAT'S NOT EVEN FUNNY!
HOW-EVER...
...IT WOULDN'T DO ANY GOOD TO KICK YOU WHEN YOU'RE DOWN AND GET ANGRY WITH YOU.
B...
...IF I WERE TO GET ANGRY...
...IT WOULD BE BECAUSE YOU BROUGHT THE ISSUE TO YOUR NEXT JOB...
...AND...
...CAUSED TROUBLE HERE...

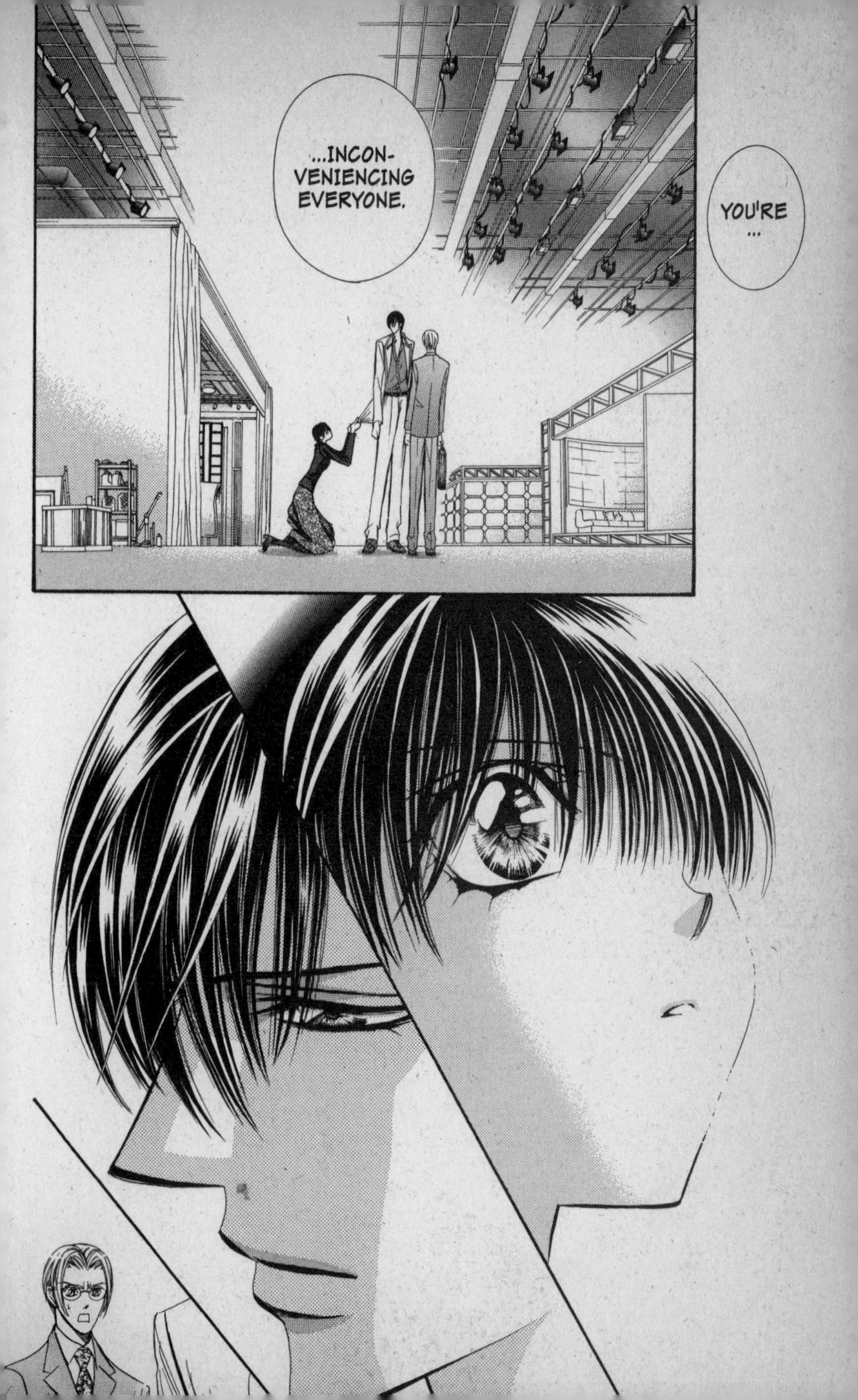
YOU'RE ...
...INCON-VENIENCING EVERYONE.

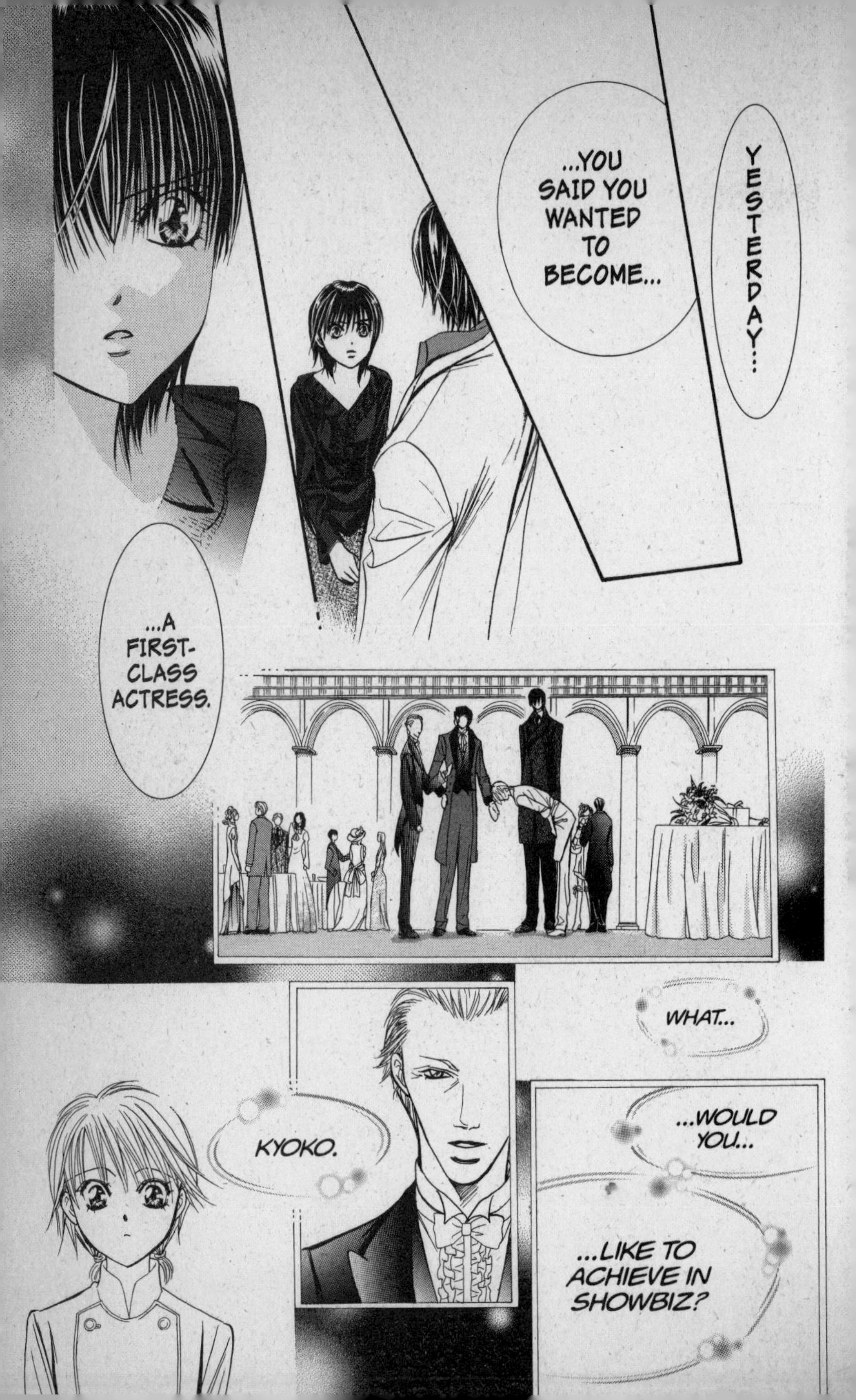
YESTERDAY...
...YOU SAID YOU WANTED TO BECOME...
...A FIRST-CLASS ACTRESS.
WHAT...
...WOULD YOU...
...LIKE TO ACHIEVE IN SHOWBIZ?
KYOKO.

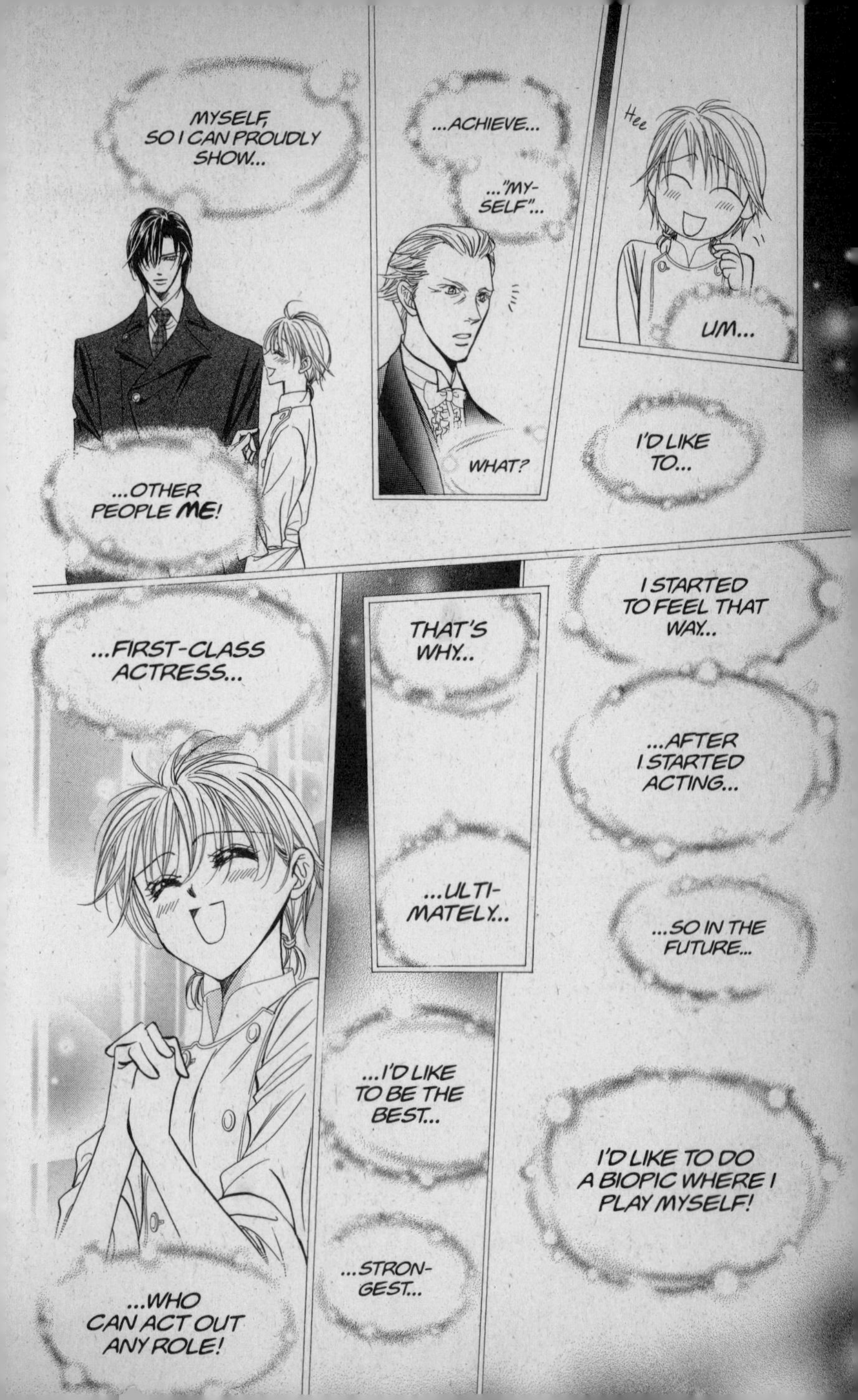
Hee
UM...
I'D LIKE TO...
...ACHIEVE...
..."MY-SELF"...
WHAT?
MYSELF, SO I CAN PROUDLY SHOW...
...OTHER PEOPLE ME!
I STARTED TO FEEL THAT WAY...
...AFTER I STARTED ACTING...
...SO IN THE FUTURE...
I'D LIKE TO DO A BIOPIC WHERE I PLAY MYSELF!
THAT'S WHY...
...ULTIMATELY...
...I'D LIKE TO BE THE BEST...
...STRONGEST...
...FIRST-CLASS ACTRESS...
...WHO CAN ACT OUT ANY ROLE!

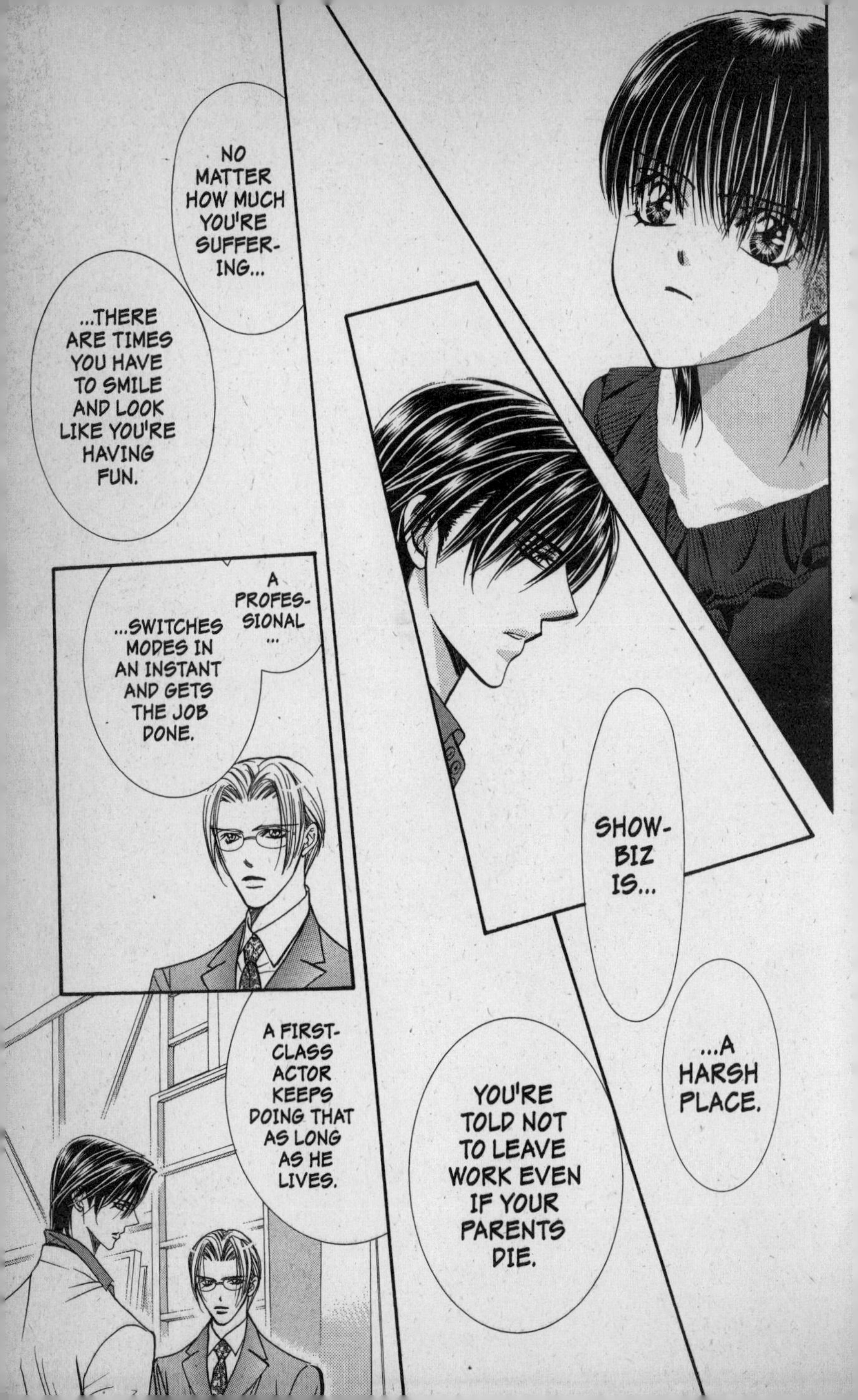
SHOW-BIZ IS...
...A HARSH PLACE.
YOU'RE TOLD NOT TO LEAVE WORK EVEN IF YOUR PARENTS DIE.
NO MATTER HOW MUCH YOU'RE SUFFER-ING...
...THERE ARE TIMES YOU HAVE TO SMILE AND LOOK LIKE YOU'RE HAVING FUN.
A PROFES-SIONAL...
...SWITCHES MODES IN AN INSTANT AND GETS THE JOB DONE.
A FIRST-CLASS ACTOR KEEPS DOING THAT AS LONG AS HE LIVES.

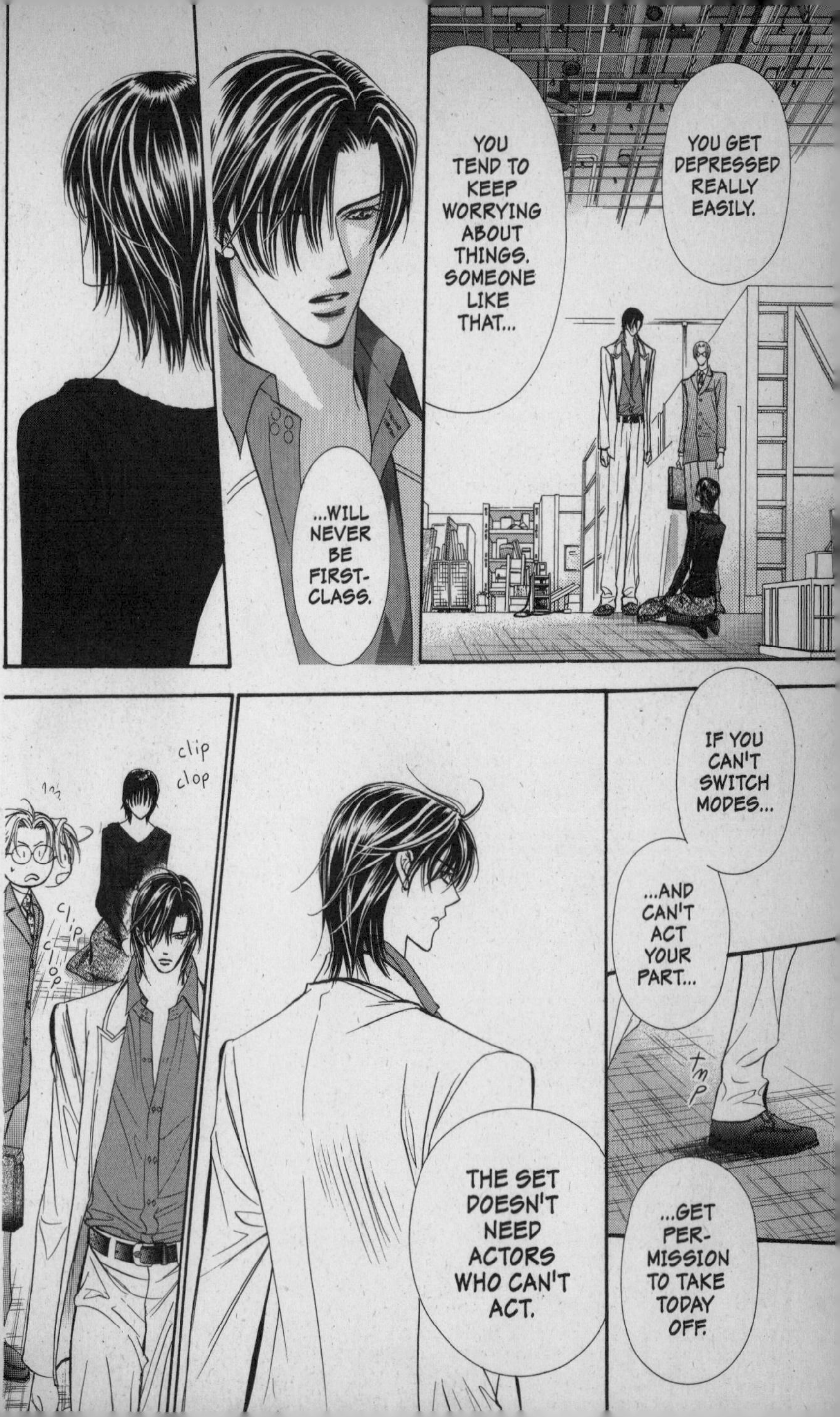

YOU GET DEPRESSED REALLY EASILY.
YOU TEND TO KEEP WORRYING ABOUT THINGS. SOMEONE LIKE THAT...
...WILL NEVER BE FIRST-CLASS.
IF YOU CAN'T SWITCH MODES...
...AND CAN'T ACT YOUR PART...
tmp
...GET PERMISSION TO TAKE TODAY OFF.
THE SET DOESN'T NEED ACTORS WHO CAN'T ACT.
clip clop
clip clop

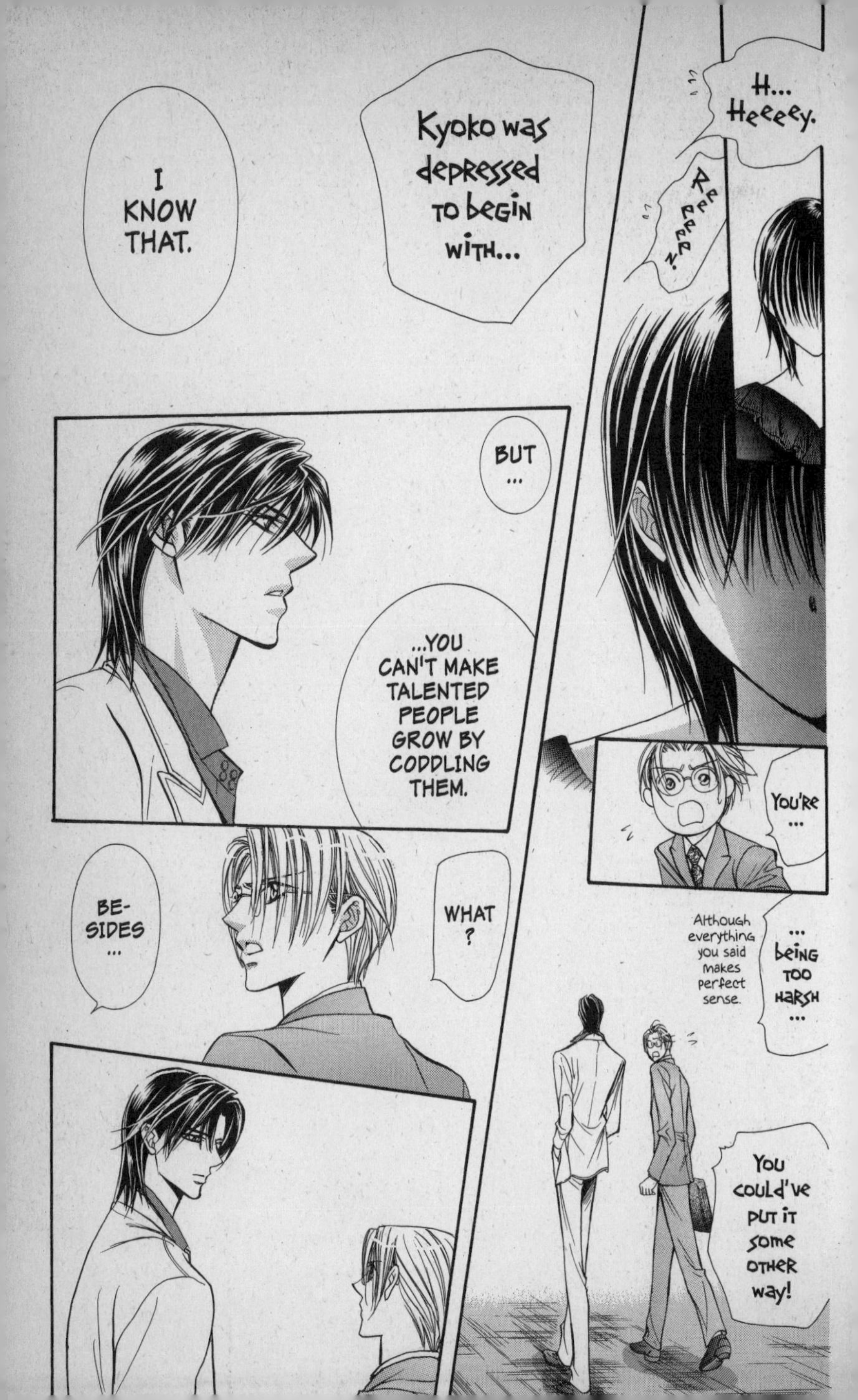
H... Heeeey.
Reeeeen!
You're...
...being too harsh...
Although everything you said makes perfect sense.
You could've put it some other way!
Kyoko was depressed to begin with...
I KNOW THAT.
BUT...
...YOU CAN'T MAKE TALENTED PEOPLE GROW BY CODDLING THEM.
WHAT?
BE-SIDES...

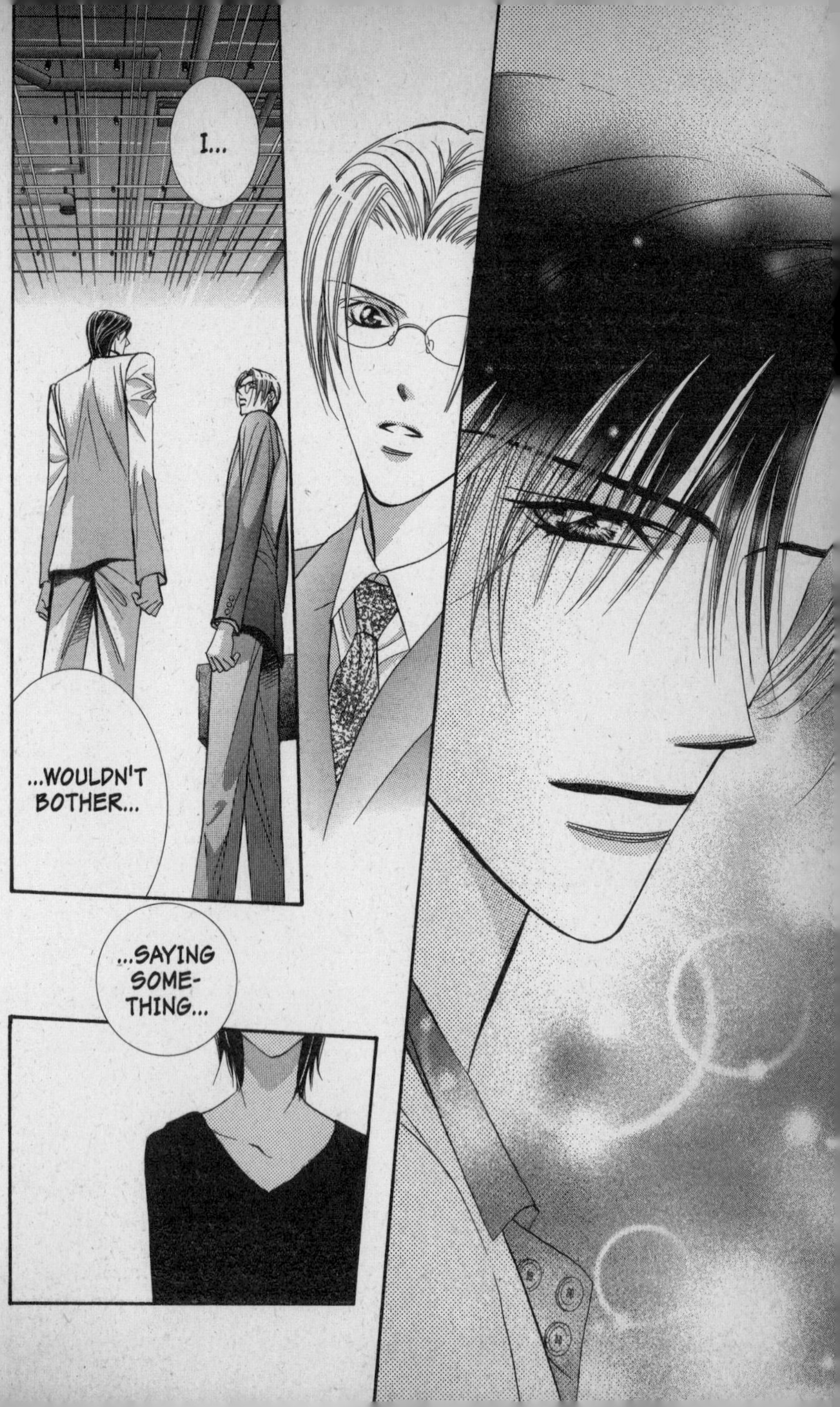
I...
...WOULDN'T BOTHER...
...SAYING SOME-THING...

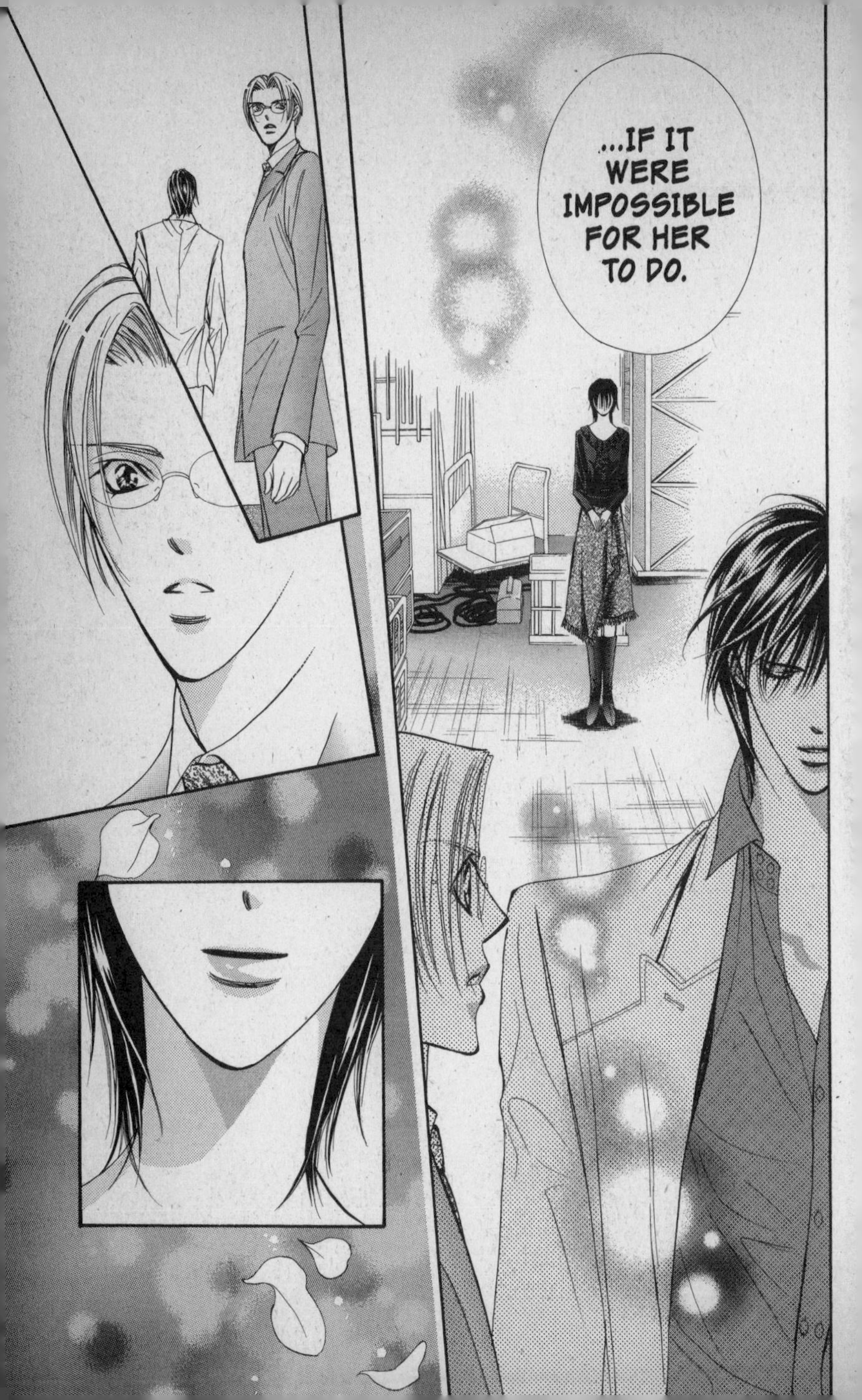
...IF IT WERE IMPOSSIBLE FOR HER TO DO.

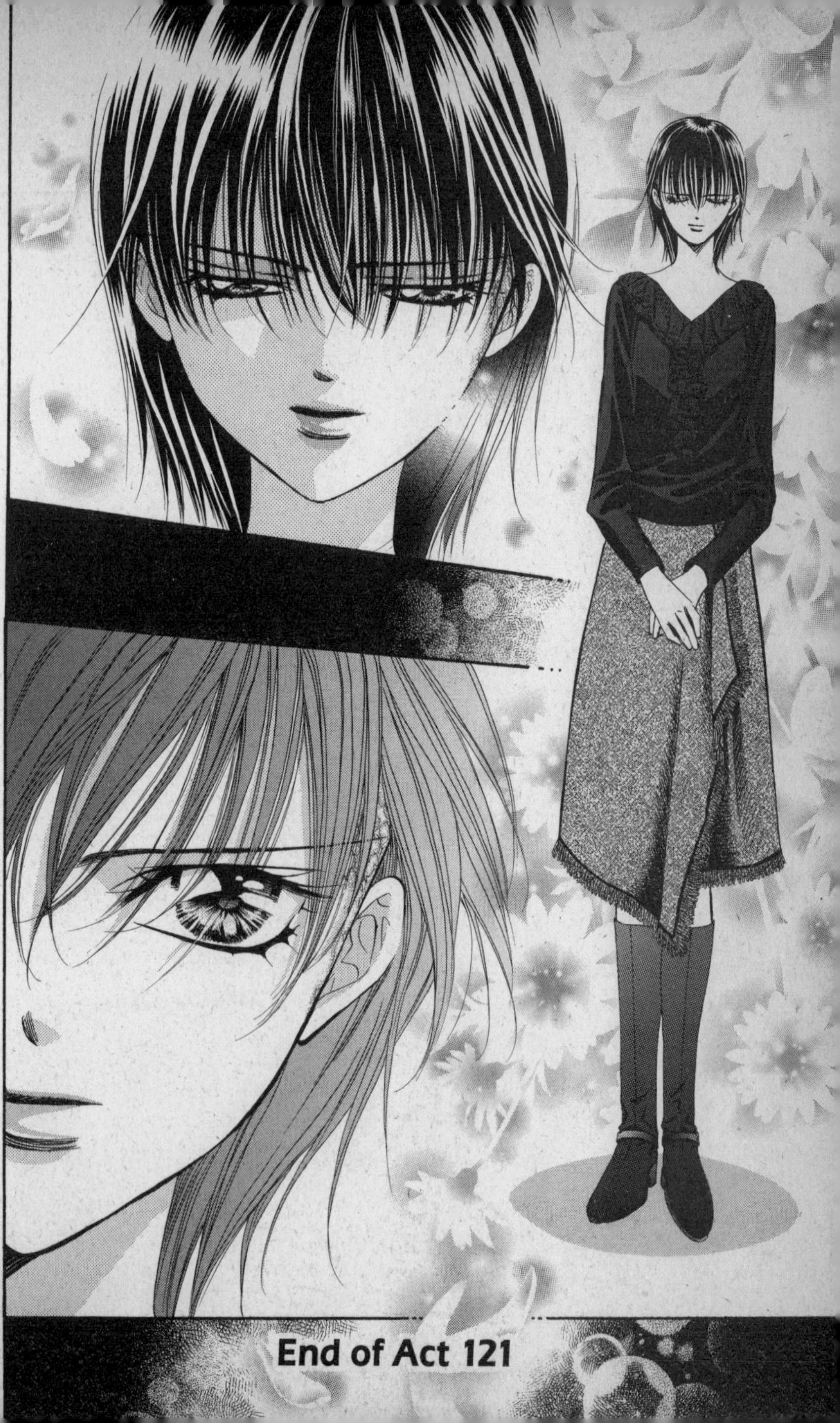
End of Act 121

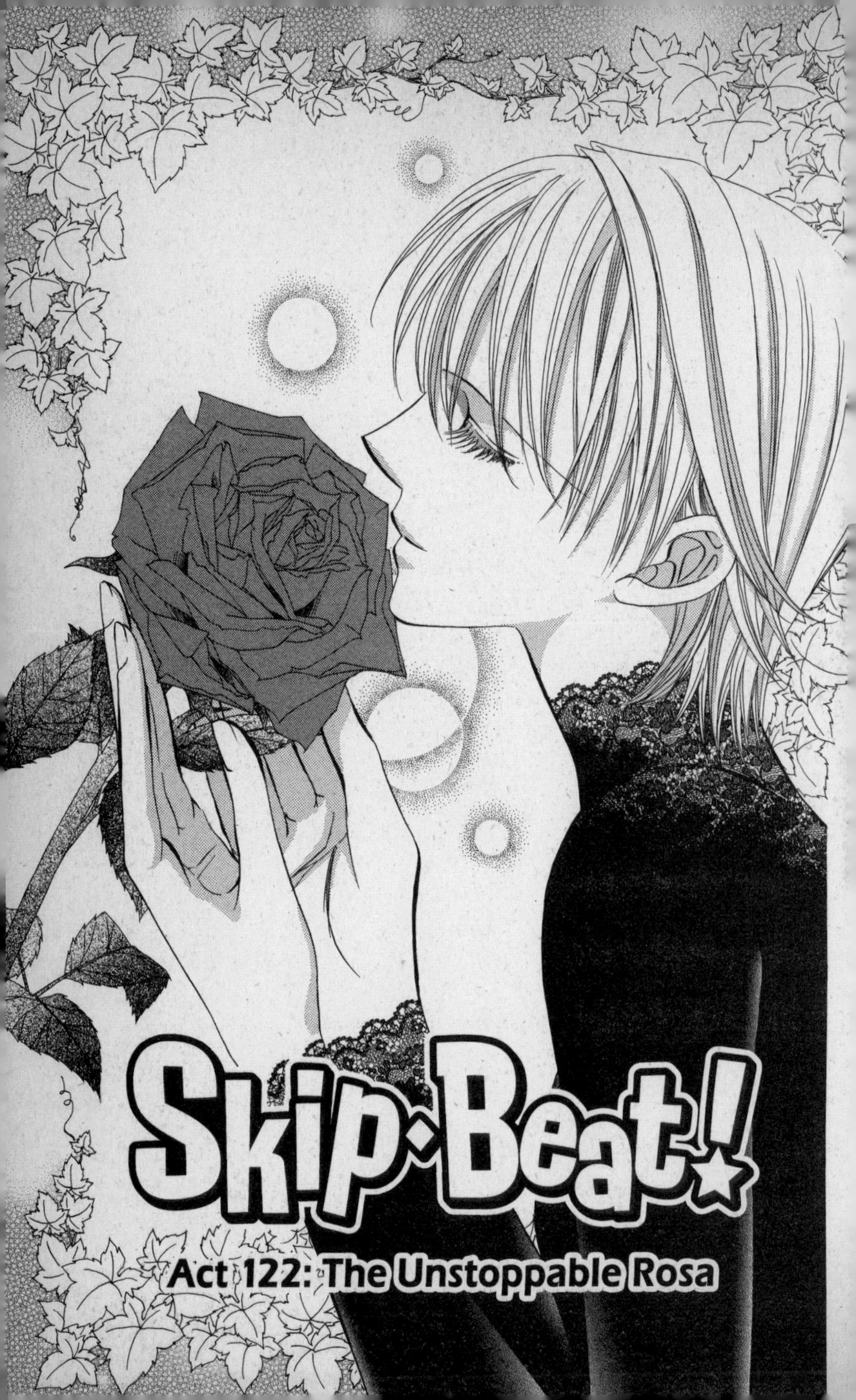
Skip·Beat!
Act 122: The Unstoppable Rosa

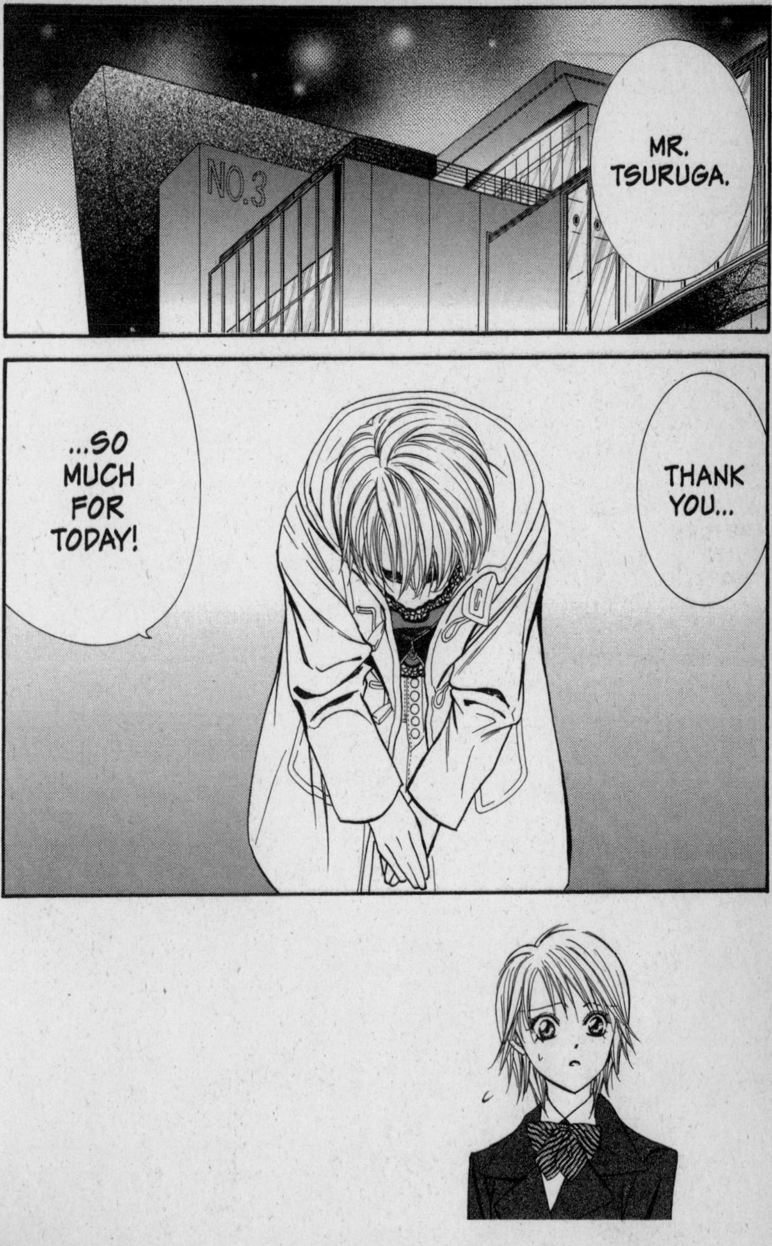
MR. TSURUGA.
THANK YOU...
...SO MUCH FOR TODAY!

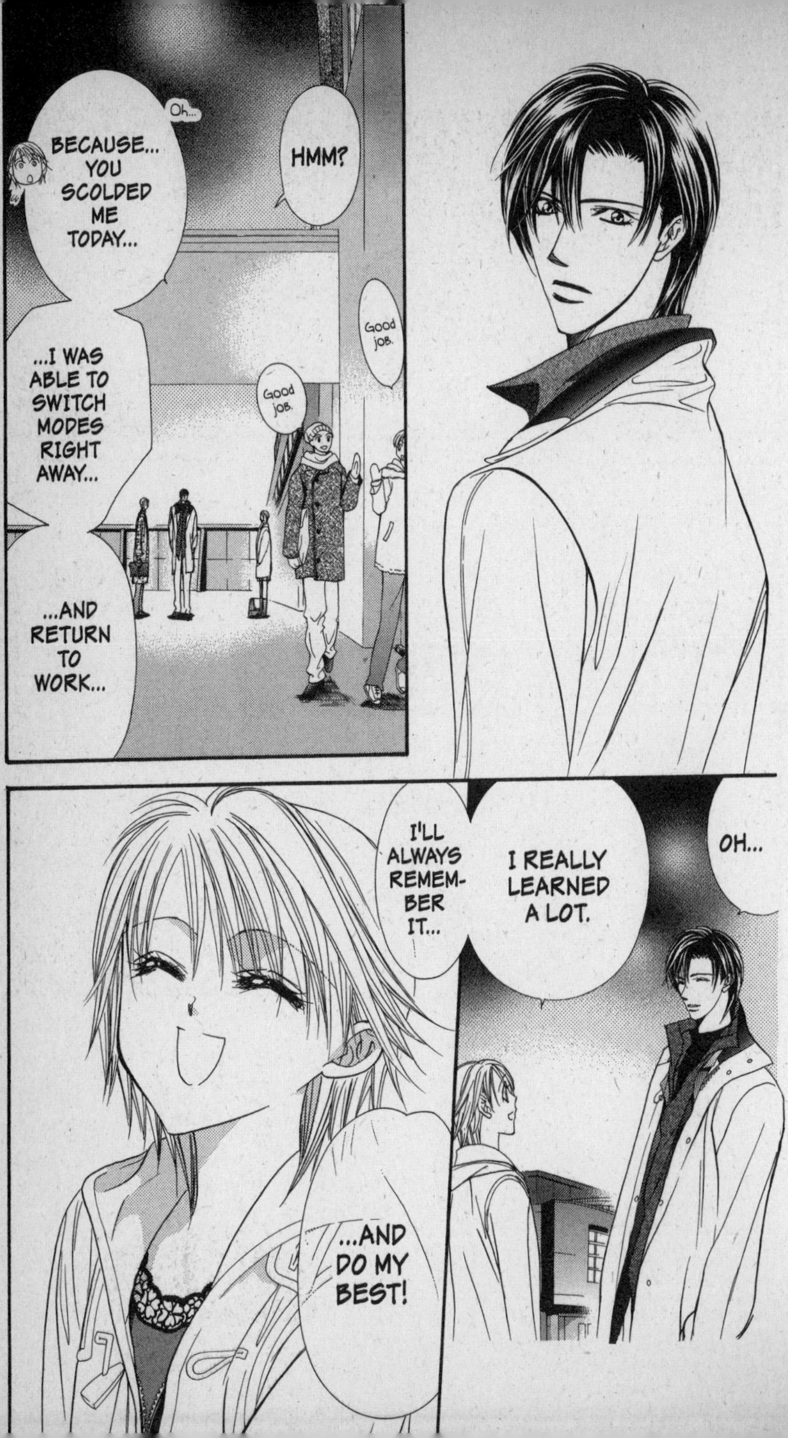
HMM?
Oh...
BECAUSE... YOU SCOLDED ME TODAY...
Good job.
Good job.
...I WAS ABLE TO SWITCH MODES RIGHT AWAY...
...AND RETURN TO WORK...
OH...
I REALLY LEARNED A LOT.
I'LL ALWAYS REMEMBER IT...
...AND DO MY BEST!

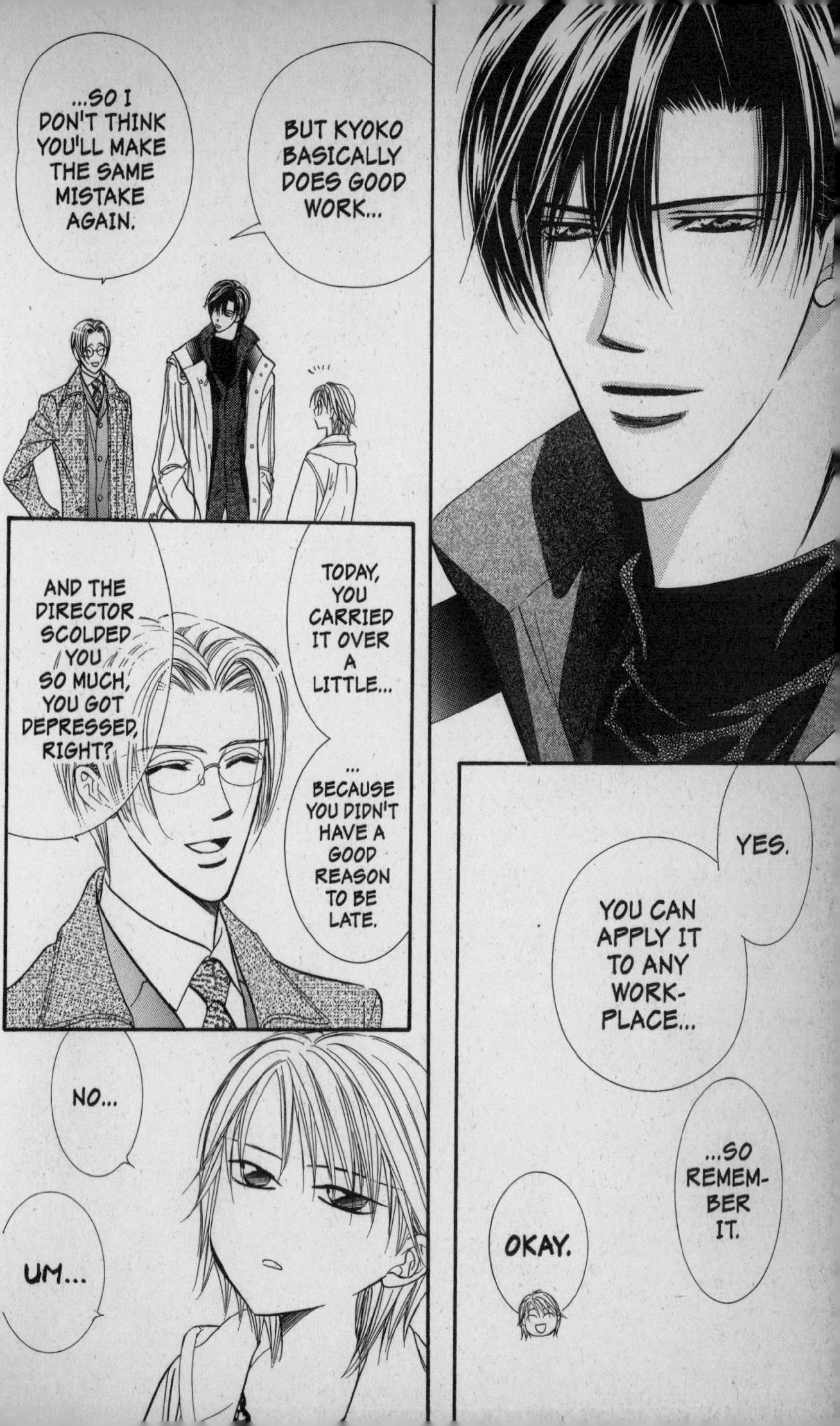
YES.
YOU CAN APPLY IT TO ANY WORK-PLACE...
...SO REMEMBER IT.
OKAY.
BUT KYOKO BASICALLY DOES GOOD WORK...
...SO I DON'T THINK YOU'LL MAKE THE SAME MISTAKE AGAIN.
TODAY, YOU CARRIED IT OVER A LITTLE...
...BECAUSE YOU DIDN'T HAVE A GOOD REASON TO BE LATE.
AND THE DIRECTOR SCOLDED YOU SO MUCH, YOU GOT DEPRESSED, RIGHT?
NO...
UM...

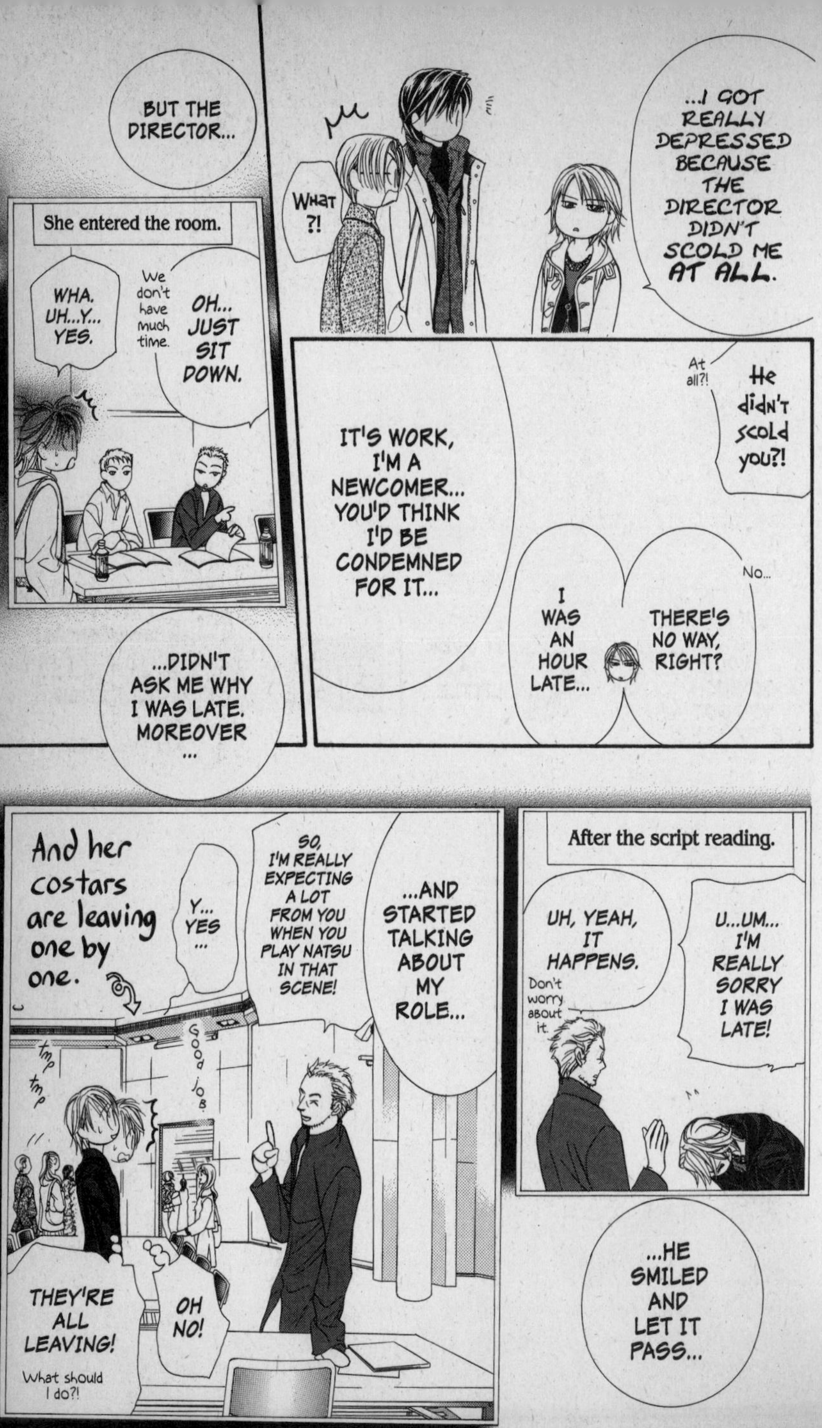
...I GOT REALLY DEPRESSED BECAUSE THE DIRECTOR DIDN'T SCOLD ME AT ALL.
WHAT?!
At all?!
He didn't scold you?!
No...
THERE'S NO WAY, RIGHT?
I WAS AN HOUR LATE...
IT'S WORK, I'M A NEWCOMER... YOU'D THINK I'D BE CONDEMNED FOR IT...
BUT THE DIRECTOR...
She entered the room.
OH... JUST SIT DOWN.
We don't have much time.
WHA. UH...Y... YES.
...DIDN'T ASK ME WHY I WAS LATE. MOREOVER...
After the script reading.
U...UM... I'M REALLY SORRY I WAS LATE!
UH, YEAH, IT HAPPENS.
Don't worry about it.
...HE SMILED AND LET IT PASS...
...AND STARTED TALKING ABOUT MY ROLE...
SO, I'M REALLY EXPECTING A LOT FROM YOU WHEN YOU PLAY NATSU IN THAT SCENE!
Y... YES...
And her costars are leaving one by one.
Good job
tmp tmp
OH NO!
THEY'RE ALL LEAVING!
What should I do?!

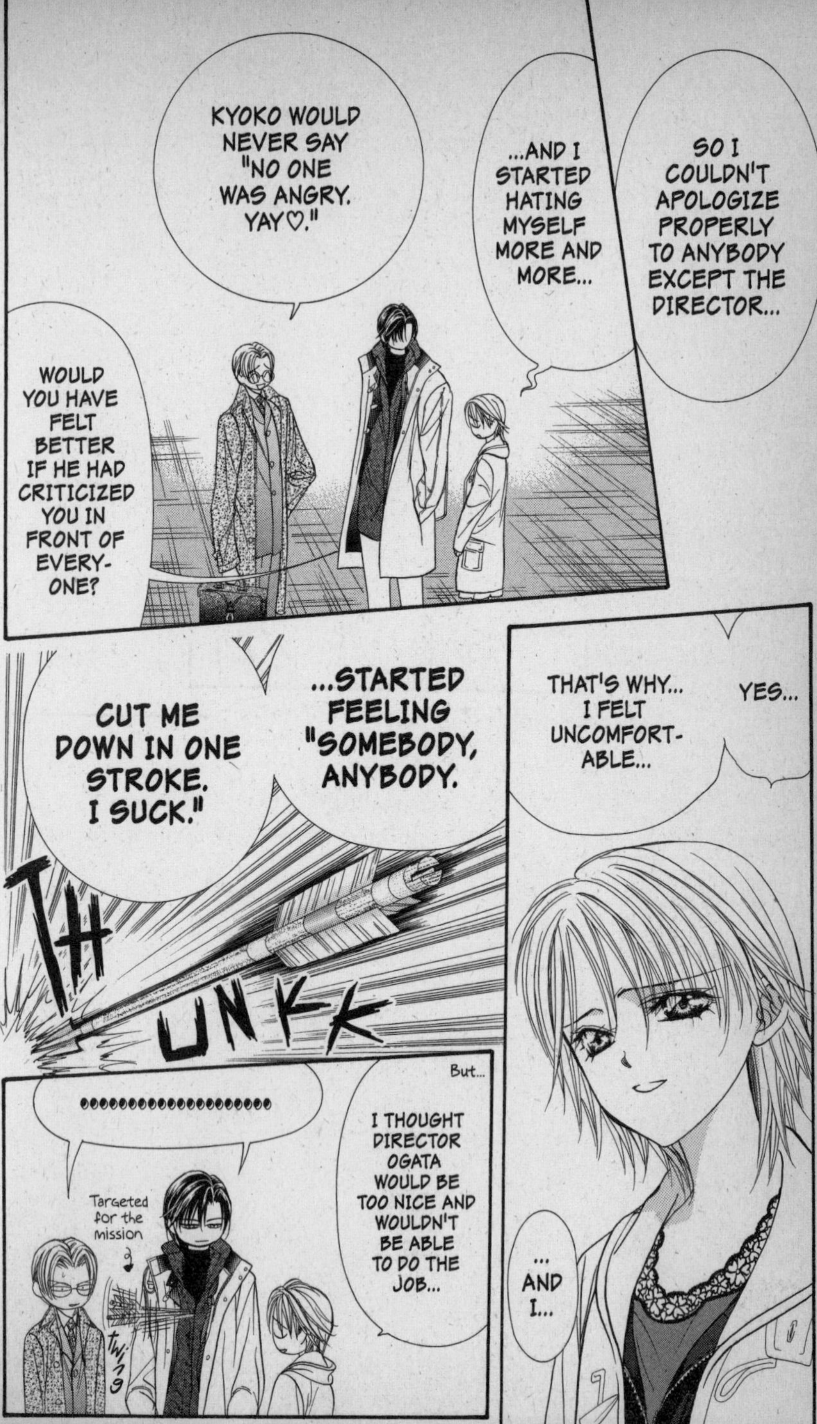
SO I COULDN'T APOLOGIZE PROPERLY TO ANYBODY EXCEPT THE DIRECTOR...
...AND I STARTED HATING MYSELF MORE AND MORE...
KYOKO WOULD NEVER SAY "NO ONE WAS ANGRY. YAY♡."
WOULD YOU HAVE FELT BETTER IF HE HAD CRITICIZED YOU IN FRONT OF EVERY-ONE?
YES...
THAT'S WHY... I FELT UNCOMFORT-ABLE...
... AND I...
...STARTED FEELING "SOMEBODY, ANYBODY.
CUT ME DOWN IN ONE STROKE. I SUCK."
THUNKK
But...
I THOUGHT DIRECTOR OGATA WOULD BE TOO NICE AND WOULDN'T BE ABLE TO DO THE JOB...
oooooooooooooooooooo
Targeted for the mission
twing

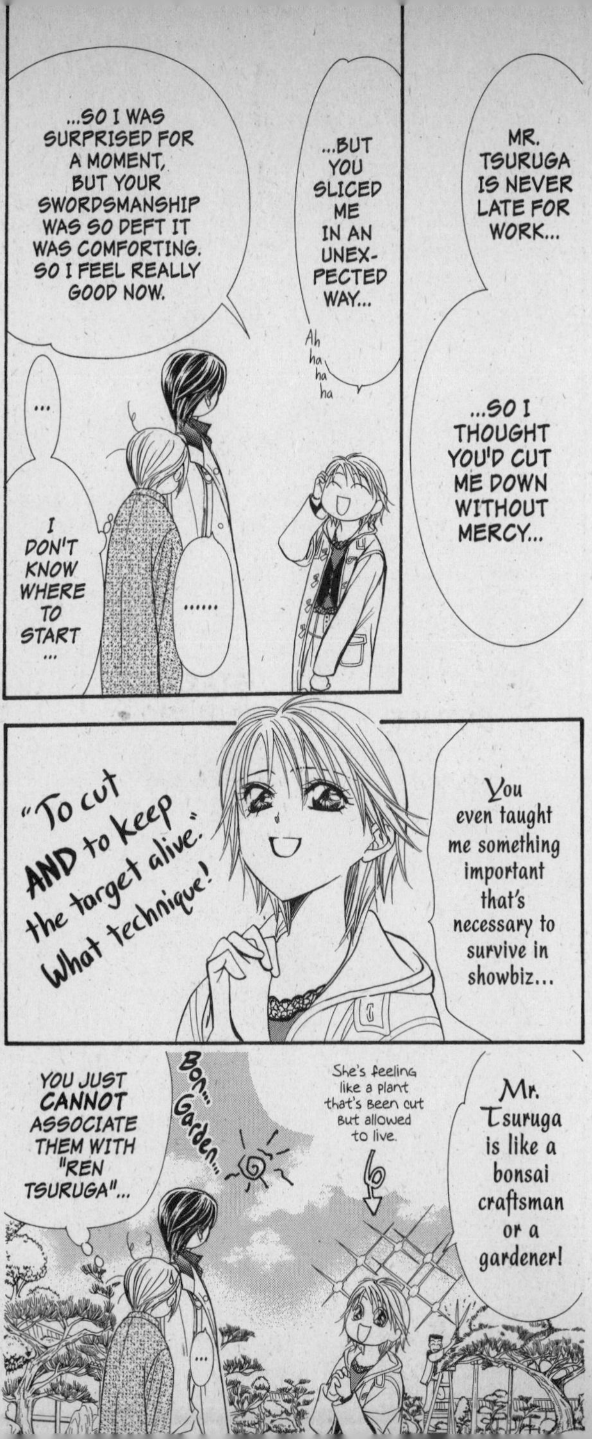
MR. TSURUGA IS NEVER LATE FOR WORK...
...SO I THOUGHT YOU'D CUT ME DOWN WITHOUT MERCY...
...BUT YOU SLICED ME IN AN UNEXPECTED WAY...
Ah ha ha ha
...SO I WAS SURPRISED FOR A MOMENT, BUT YOUR SWORDSMANSHIP WAS SO DEFT IT WAS COMFORTING. SO I FEEL REALLY GOOD NOW.
......
...
I DON'T KNOW WHERE TO START ...
You even taught me something important that's necessary to survive in showbiz...
"To cut AND to keep the target alive." What technique!
Mr. Tsuruga is like a bonsai craftsman or a gardener!
She's feeling like a plant that's been cut but allowed to live.
Bon... Garden...
YOU JUST CANNOT ASSOCIATE THEM WITH "REN TSURUGA"...
...
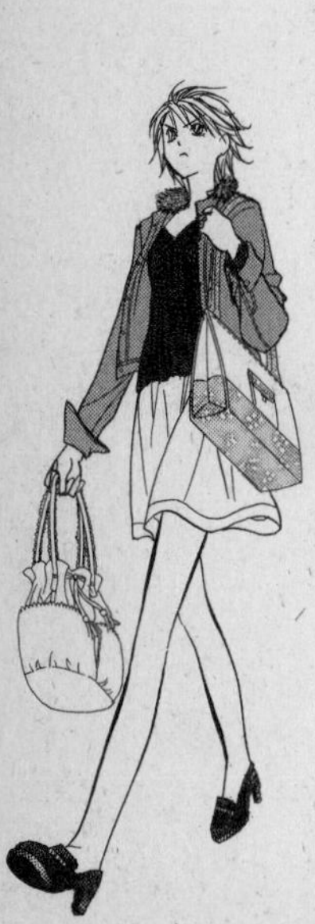

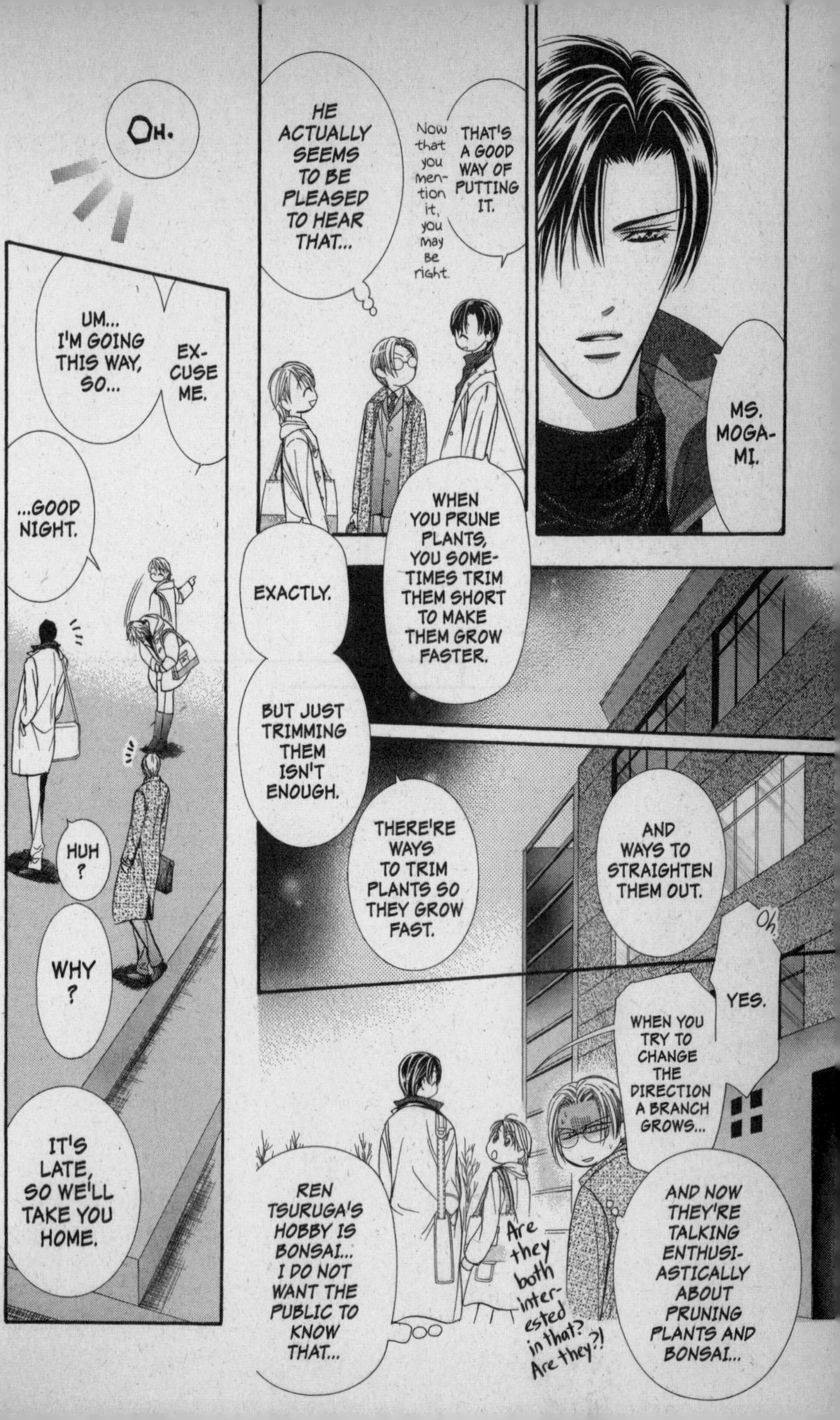
MS. MOGA-MI.
THAT'S A GOOD WAY OF PUTTING IT.
Now that you mention it, you may be right.
HE ACTUALLY SEEMS TO BE PLEASED TO HEAR THAT...
WHEN YOU PRUNE PLANTS, YOU SOMETIMES TRIM THEM SHORT TO MAKE THEM GROW FASTER.
EXACTLY.
BUT JUST TRIMMING THEM ISN'T ENOUGH.
THERE'RE WAYS TO TRIM PLANTS SO THEY GROW FAST.
AND WAYS TO STRAIGHTEN THEM OUT.
Oh.
YES.
WHEN YOU TRY TO CHANGE THE DIRECTION A BRANCH GROWS...
AND NOW THEY'RE TALKING ENTHUSI-ASTICALLY ABOUT PRUNING PLANTS AND BONSAI...
Are they both inter-ested in that? Are they?!
REN TSURUGA'S HOBBY IS BONSAI... I DO NOT WANT THE PUBLIC TO KNOW THAT...
OH.
UM... I'M GOING THIS WAY, SO...
EX-CUSE ME.
...GOOD NIGHT.
HUH?
WHY?
IT'S LATE, SO WE'LL TAKE YOU HOME.

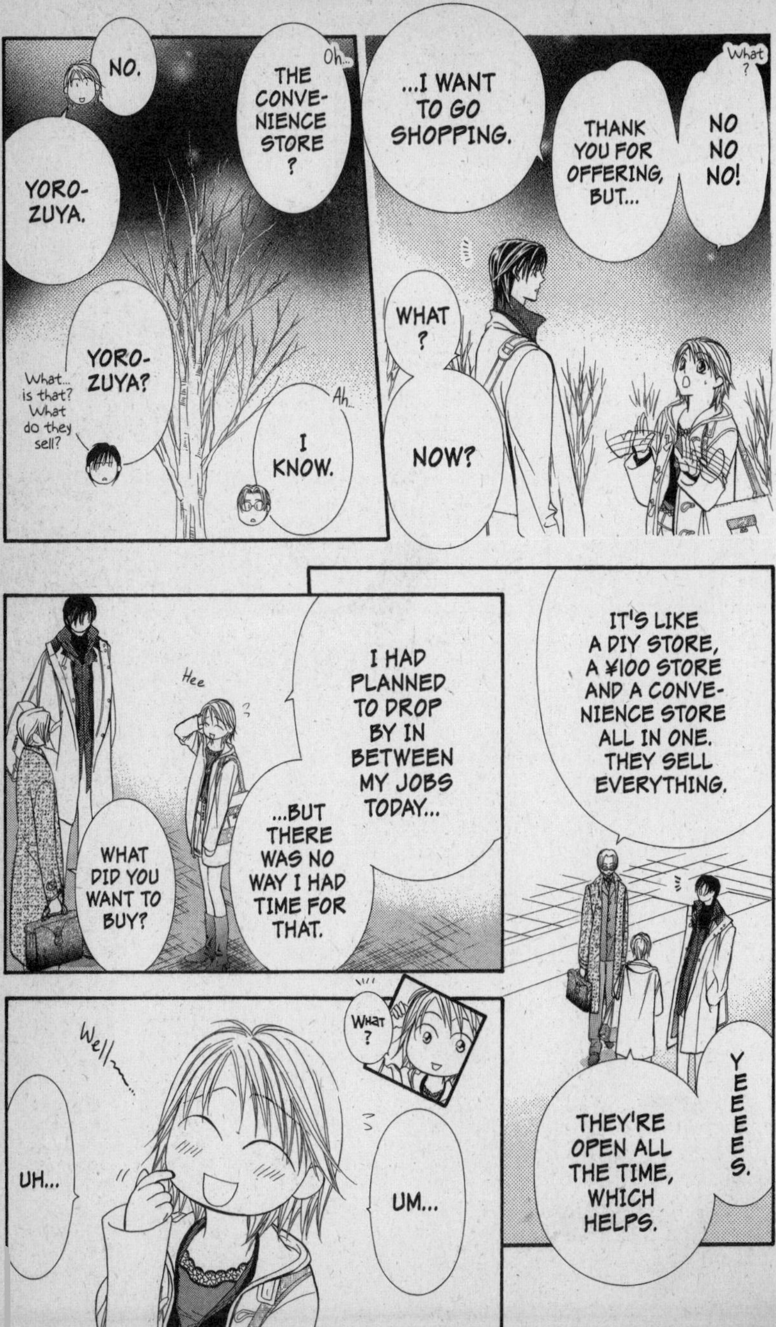
What?
NO NO NO!
THANK YOU FOR OFFERING, BUT...
...I WANT TO GO SHOPPING.
WHAT?
NOW?
Oh...
THE CONVENIENCE STORE?
NO.
YORO-ZUYA.
YORO-ZUYA?
What... is that? What do they sell?
Ah...
I KNOW.
IT'S LIKE A DIY STORE, A ¥100 STORE AND A CONVENIENCE STORE ALL IN ONE. THEY SELL EVERYTHING.
YEEEES.
THEY'RE OPEN ALL THE TIME, WHICH HELPS.
I HAD PLANNED TO DROP BY IN BETWEEN MY JOBS TODAY...
...BUT THERE WAS NO WAY I HAD TIME FOR THAT.
Hee
WHAT DID YOU WANT TO BUY?
WHAT?
UM...
Well~...
UH...

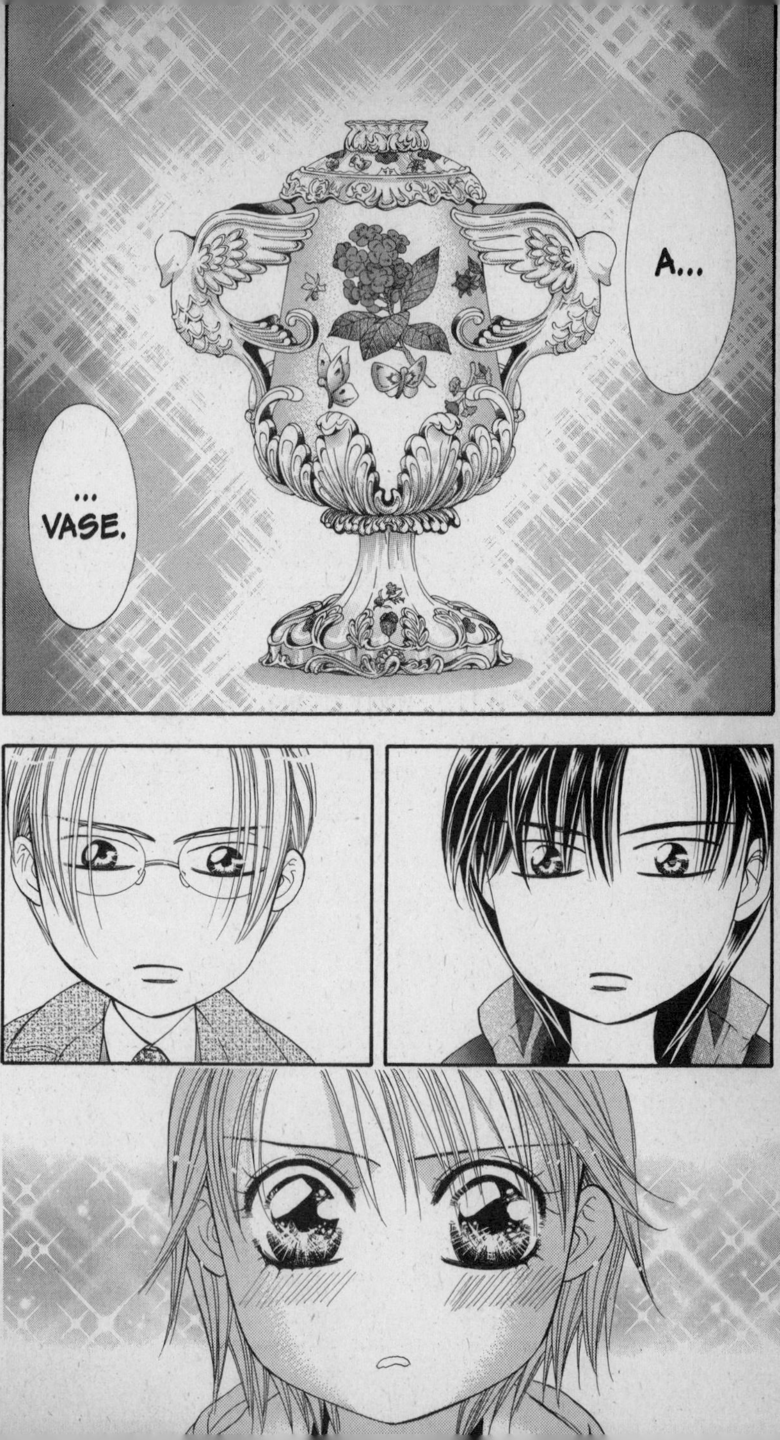
A...
... VASE.

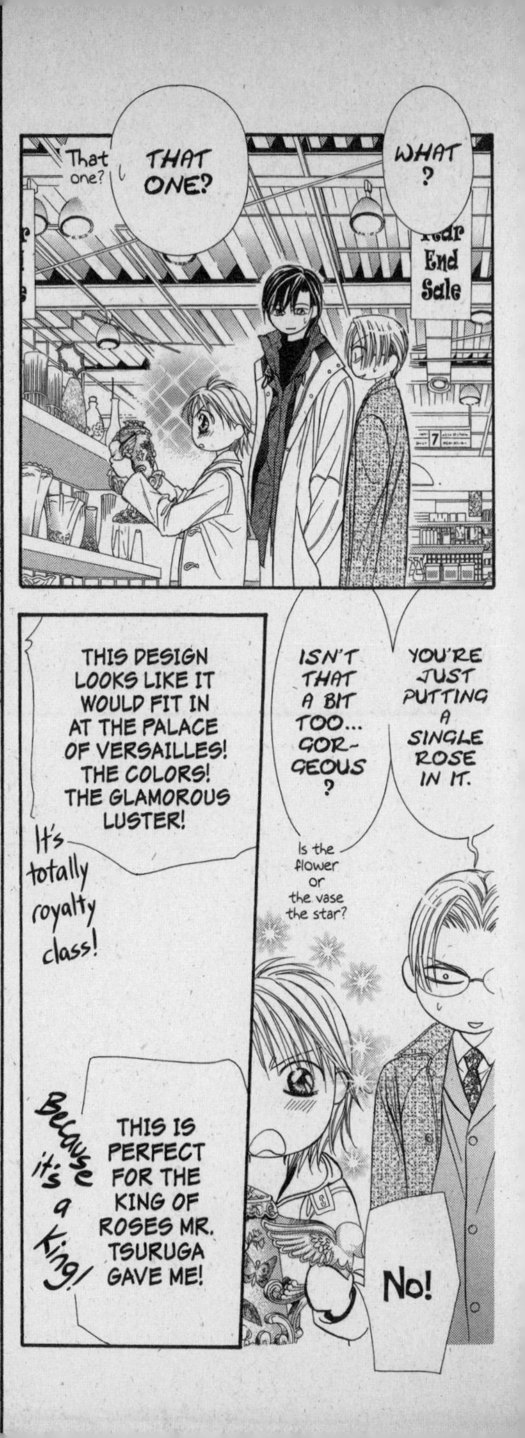
WHAT?
THAT ONE?
That one?
End Sale
YOU'RE JUST PUTTING A SINGLE ROSE IN IT.
ISN'T THAT A BIT TOO... GORGEOUS?
Is the flower or the vase the star?
THIS DESIGN LOOKS LIKE IT WOULD FIT IN AT THE PALACE OF VERSAILLES! THE COLORS! THE GLAMOROUS LUSTER!
It's totally royalty class!
No!
THIS IS PERFECT FOR THE KING OF ROSES MR. TSURUGA GAVE ME!
Because it's a king!
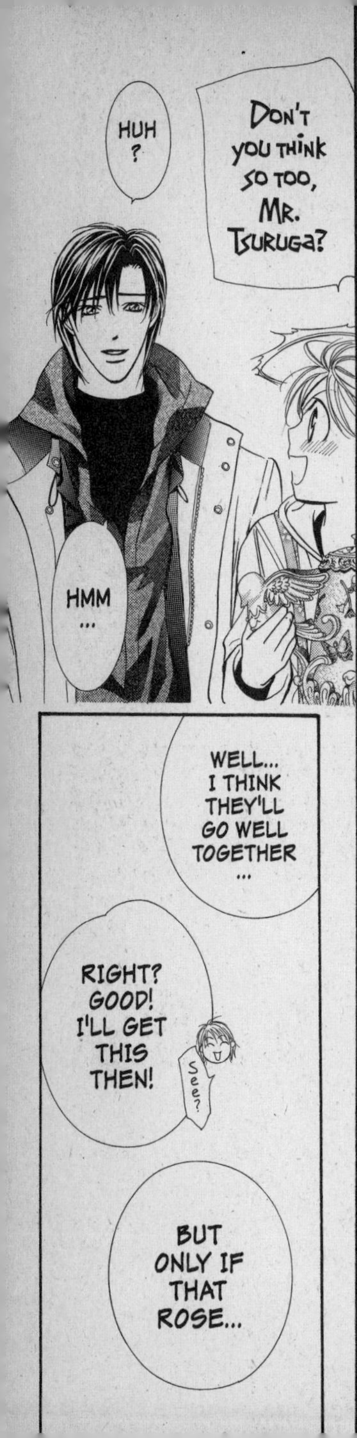
DON'T YOU THINK SO TOO, MR. TSURUGA?
HUH?
HMM...
WELL... I THINK THEY'LL GO WELL TOGETHER...
RIGHT? GOOD! I'LL GET THIS THEN!
See?
BUT ONLY IF THAT ROSE...

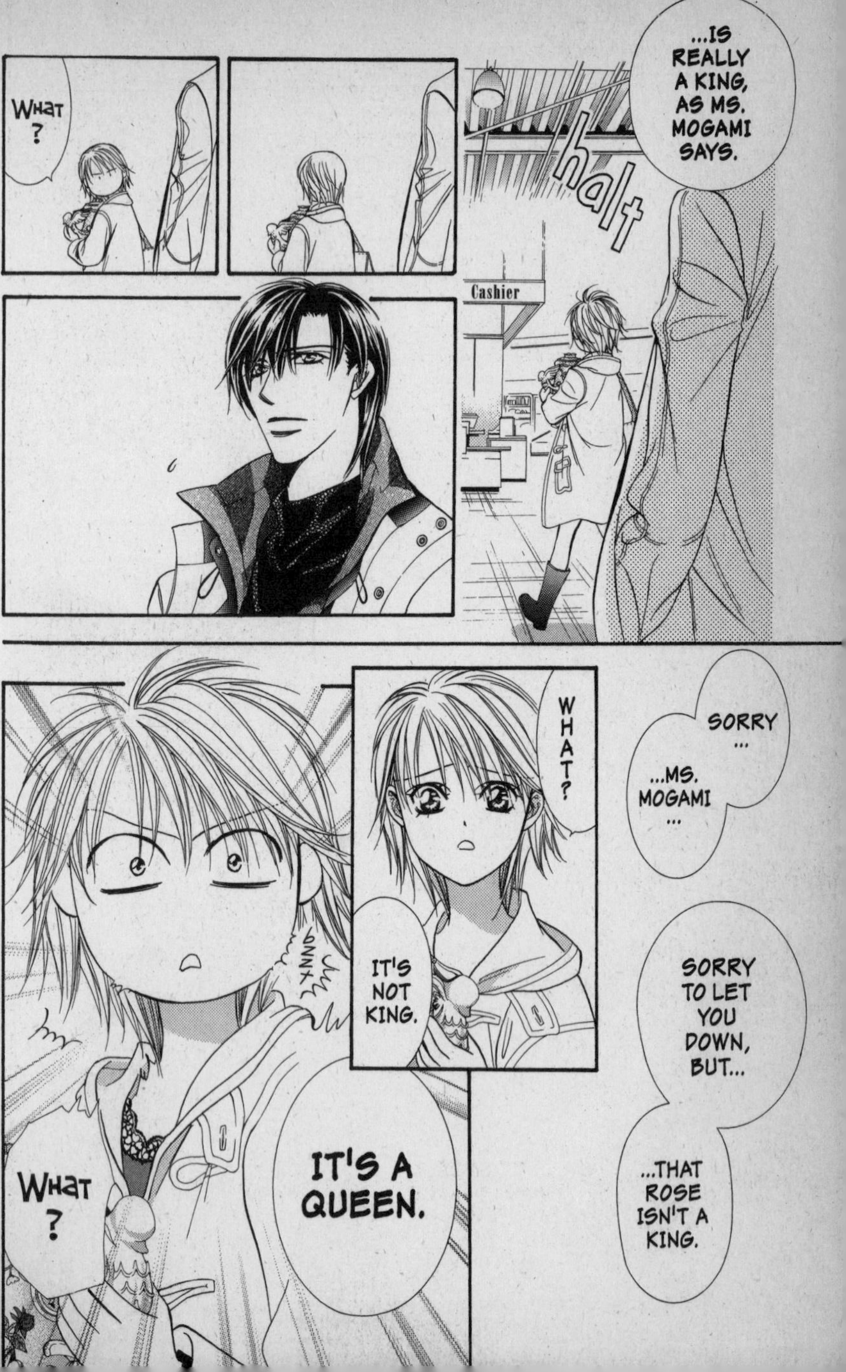
...IS REALLY A KING, AS MS. MOGAMI SAYS.
halt
Cashier
WHAT ?
SORRY ...
...MS. MOGAMI ...
SORRY TO LET YOU DOWN, BUT...
...THAT ROSE ISN'T A KING.
WHAT?
IT'S NOT KING.
WHAT ?
IT'S A QUEEN.

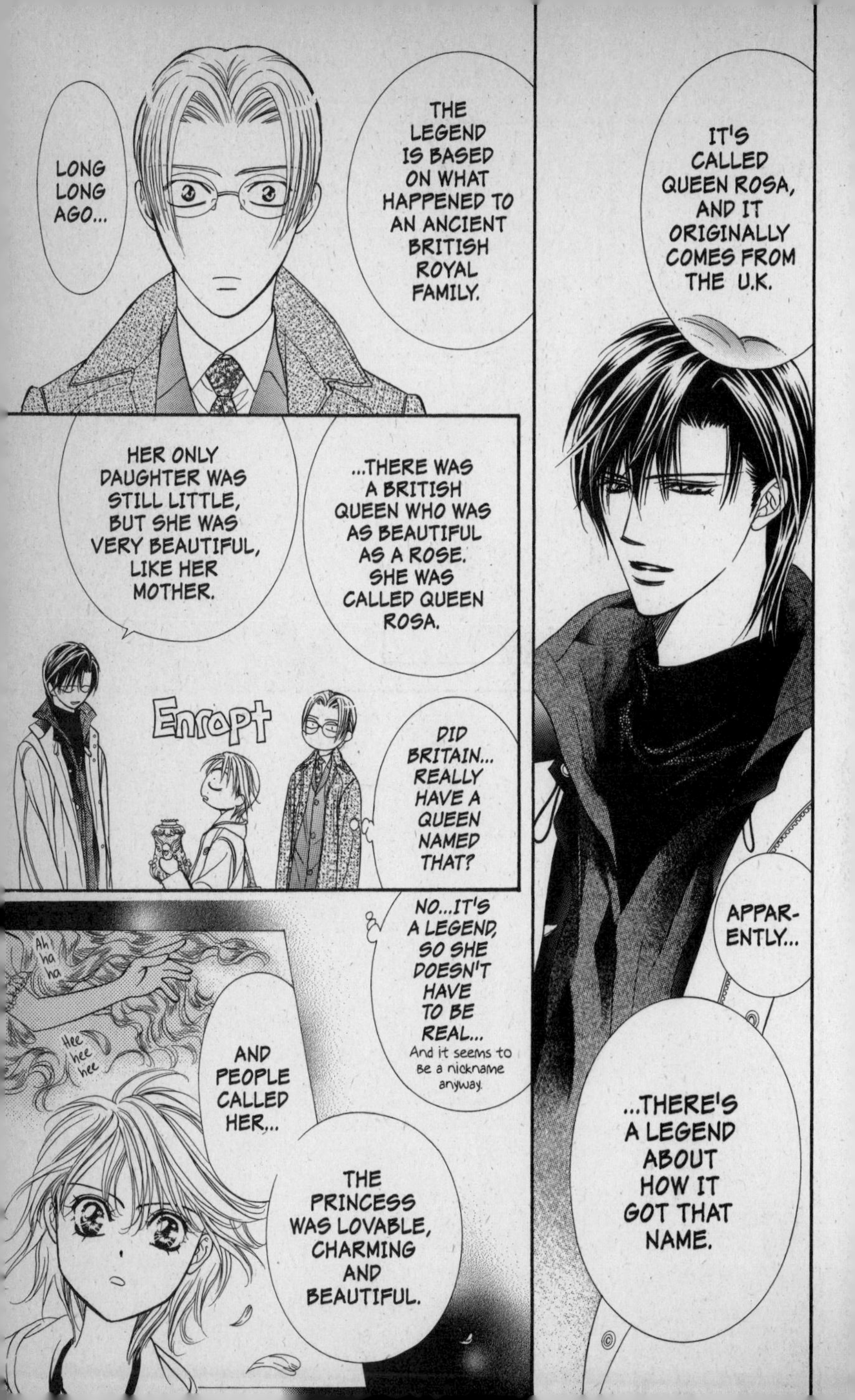
IT'S CALLED QUEEN ROSA, AND IT ORIGINALLY COMES FROM THE U.K.
APPAR-ENTLY...
...THERE'S A LEGEND ABOUT HOW IT GOT THAT NAME.
THE LEGEND IS BASED ON WHAT HAPPENED TO AN ANCIENT BRITISH ROYAL FAMILY.
LONG LONG AGO...
...THERE WAS A BRITISH QUEEN WHO WAS AS BEAUTIFUL AS A ROSE. SHE WAS CALLED QUEEN ROSA.
HER ONLY DAUGHTER WAS STILL LITTLE, BUT SHE WAS VERY BEAUTIFUL, LIKE HER MOTHER.
DID BRITAIN... REALLY HAVE A QUEEN NAMED THAT?
Enropt
NO...IT'S A LEGEND, SO SHE DOESN'T HAVE TO BE REAL...
And it seems to be a nickname anyway.
AND PEOPLE CALLED HER...
THE PRINCESS WAS LOVABLE, CHARMING AND BEAUTIFUL.
Ah ha ha
Hee hee hee

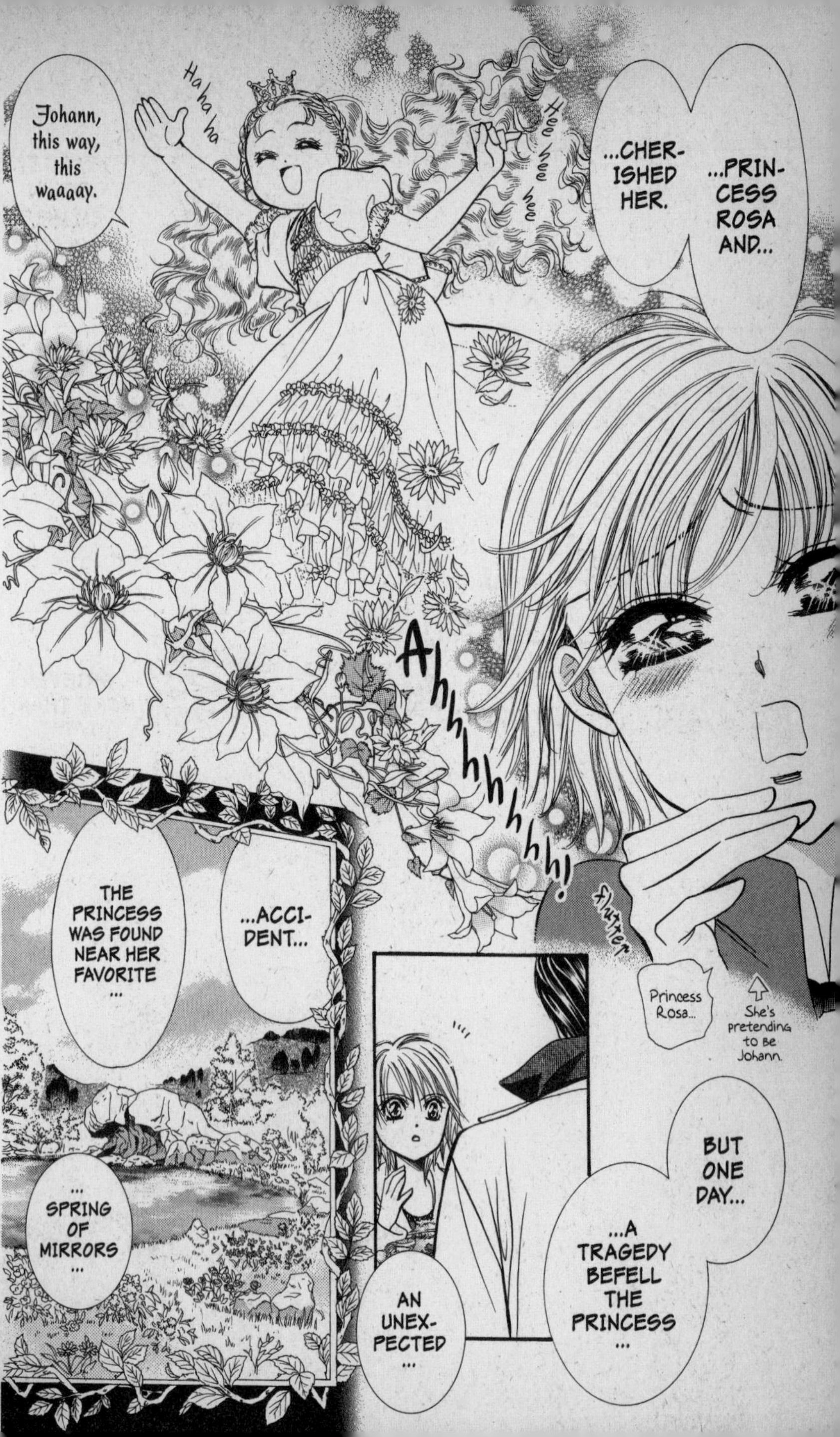
...PRIN-CESS ROSA AND...
...CHER-ISHED HER.
Hee hee hee
Ha ha ha
Johann, this way, this waaaay.
Ahhhhhhhhhh!
flutter
Princess Rosa...
She's pretending to be Johann.
BUT ONE DAY...
...A TRAGEDY BEFELL THE PRINCESS...
AN UNEX-PECTED...
...ACCI-DENT...
THE PRINCESS WAS FOUND NEAR HER FAVORITE...
...SPRING OF MIRRORS...

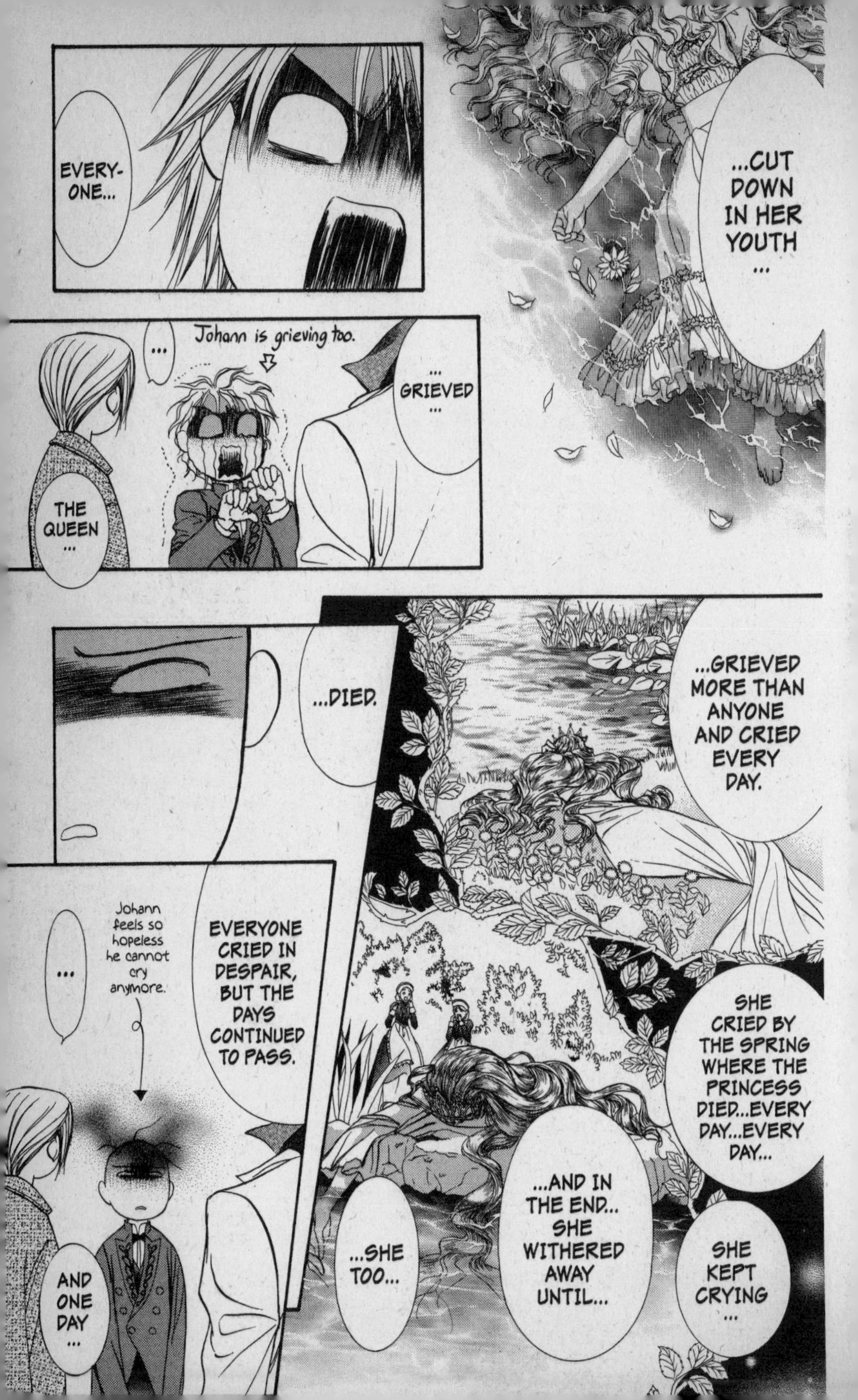
...CUT DOWN IN HER YOUTH ...
EVERY-ONE...
... GRIEVED ...
Johann is grieving too.
...
THE QUEEN ...
...GRIEVED MORE THAN ANYONE AND CRIED EVERY DAY.
SHE CRIED BY THE SPRING WHERE THE PRINCESS DIED...EVERY DAY...EVERY DAY...
SHE KEPT CRYING ...
...AND IN THE END... SHE WITHERED AWAY UNTIL...
...SHE TOO...
...DIED.
EVERYONE CRIED IN DESPAIR, BUT THE DAYS CONTINUED TO PASS.
Johann feels so hopeless he cannot cry anymore.
...
AND ONE DAY ...

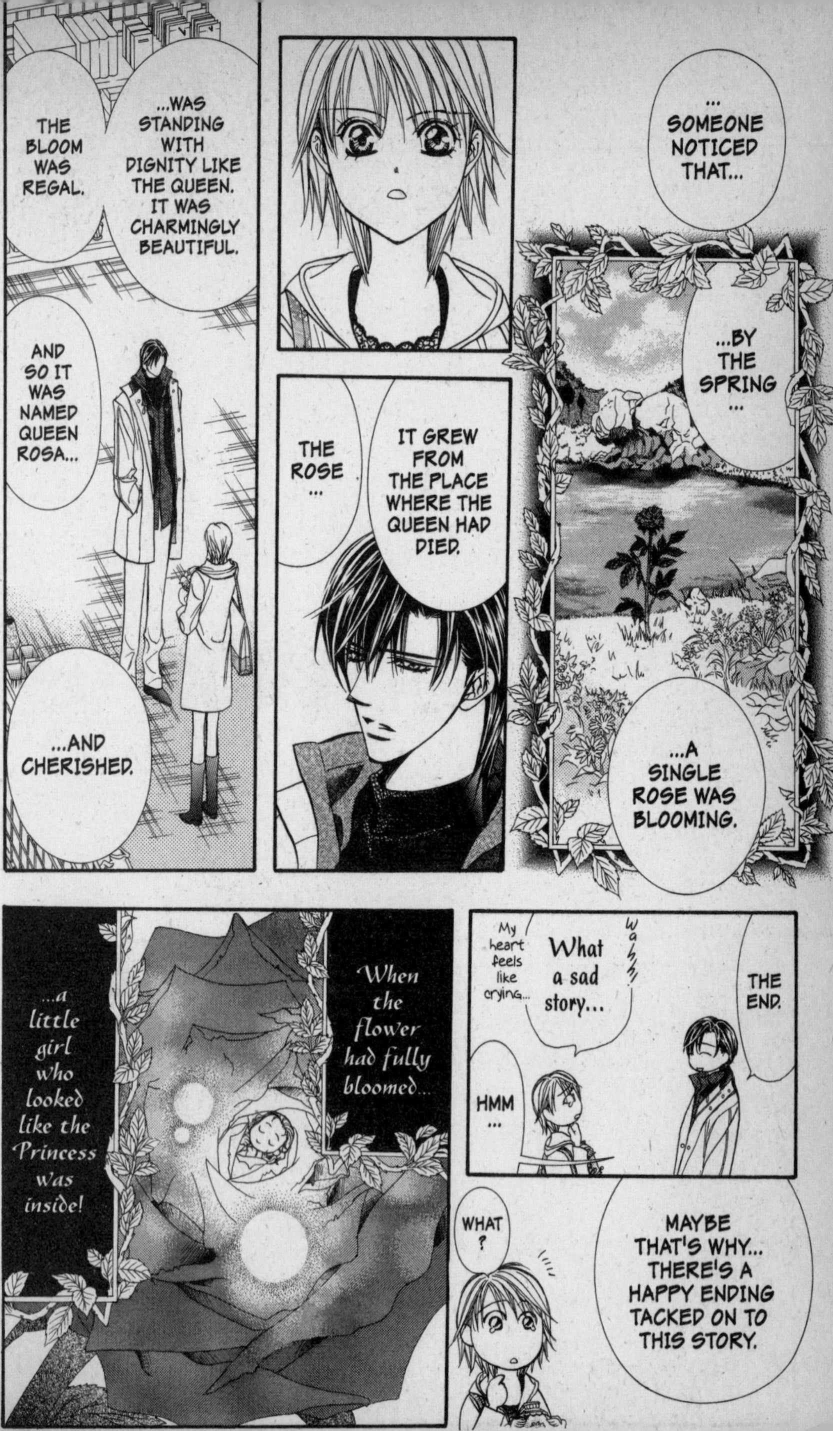

... SOMEONE NOTICED THAT...
...BY THE SPRING...
...A SINGLE ROSE WAS BLOOMING.
IT GREW FROM THE PLACE WHERE THE QUEEN HAD DIED.
THE ROSE...
...WAS STANDING WITH DIGNITY LIKE THE QUEEN. IT WAS CHARMINGLY BEAUTIFUL.
THE BLOOM WAS REGAL.
AND SO IT WAS NAMED QUEEN ROSA...
...AND CHERISHED.
THE END.
Wahh!
What a sad story...
My heart feels like crying...
HMM...
MAYBE THAT'S WHY... THERE'S A HAPPY ENDING TACKED ON TO THIS STORY.
WHAT?
When the flower had fully bloomed...
...a little girl who looked like the Princess was inside!

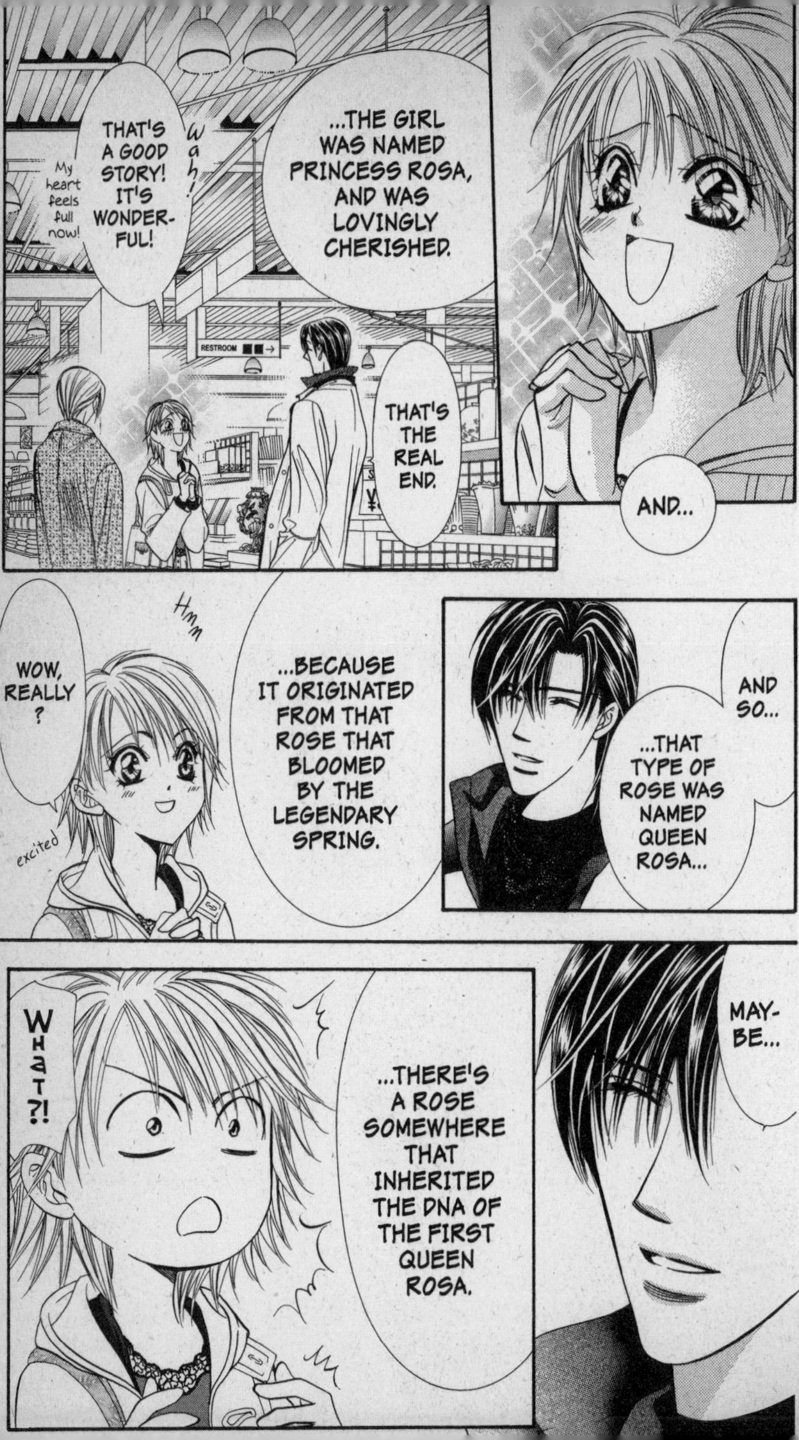
...THE GIRL WAS NAMED PRINCESS ROSA, AND WAS LOVINGLY CHERISHED.
Wah!
THAT'S A GOOD STORY! IT'S WONDER-FUL!
My heart feels full now!
RESTROOM
THAT'S THE REAL END.
AND...
AND SO...
...THAT TYPE OF ROSE WAS NAMED QUEEN ROSA...
...BECAUSE IT ORIGINATED FROM THAT ROSE THAT BLOOMED BY THE LEGENDARY SPRING.
Hmm
WOW, REALLY?
excited
MAY-BE...
...THERE'S A ROSE SOMEWHERE THAT INHERITED THE DNA OF THE FIRST QUEEN ROSA.
WHAT?!

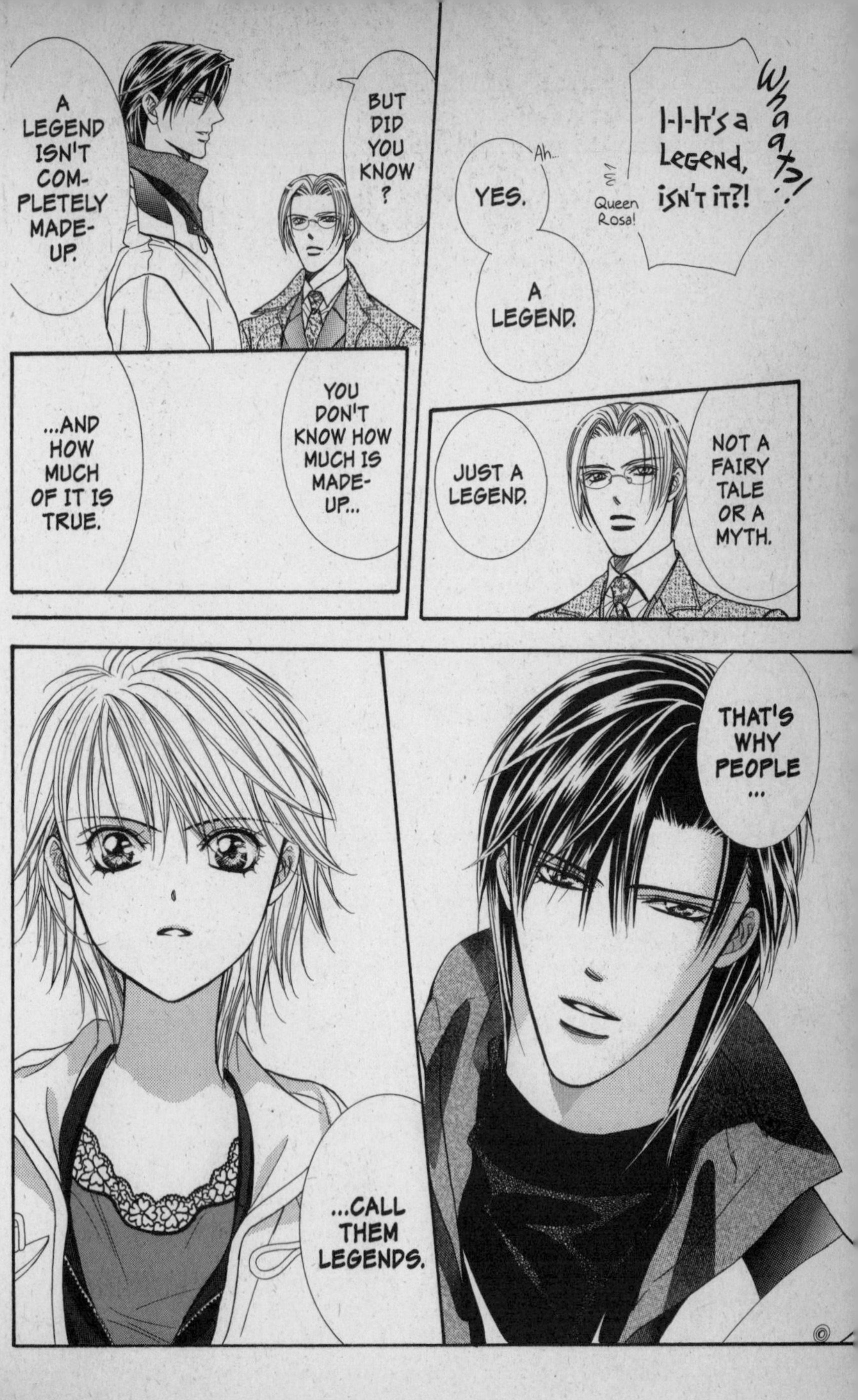
Whaat?!
I-I-It's a Legend, isn't it?!
Queen Rosa!
Ah...
YES.
A LEGEND.
BUT DID YOU KNOW?
A LEGEND ISN'T COMPLETELY MADE-UP.
NOT A FAIRY TALE OR A MYTH.
JUST A LEGEND.
YOU DON'T KNOW HOW MUCH IS MADE-UP...
...AND HOW MUCH OF IT IS TRUE.
THAT'S WHY PEOPLE...
...CALL THEM LEGENDS.

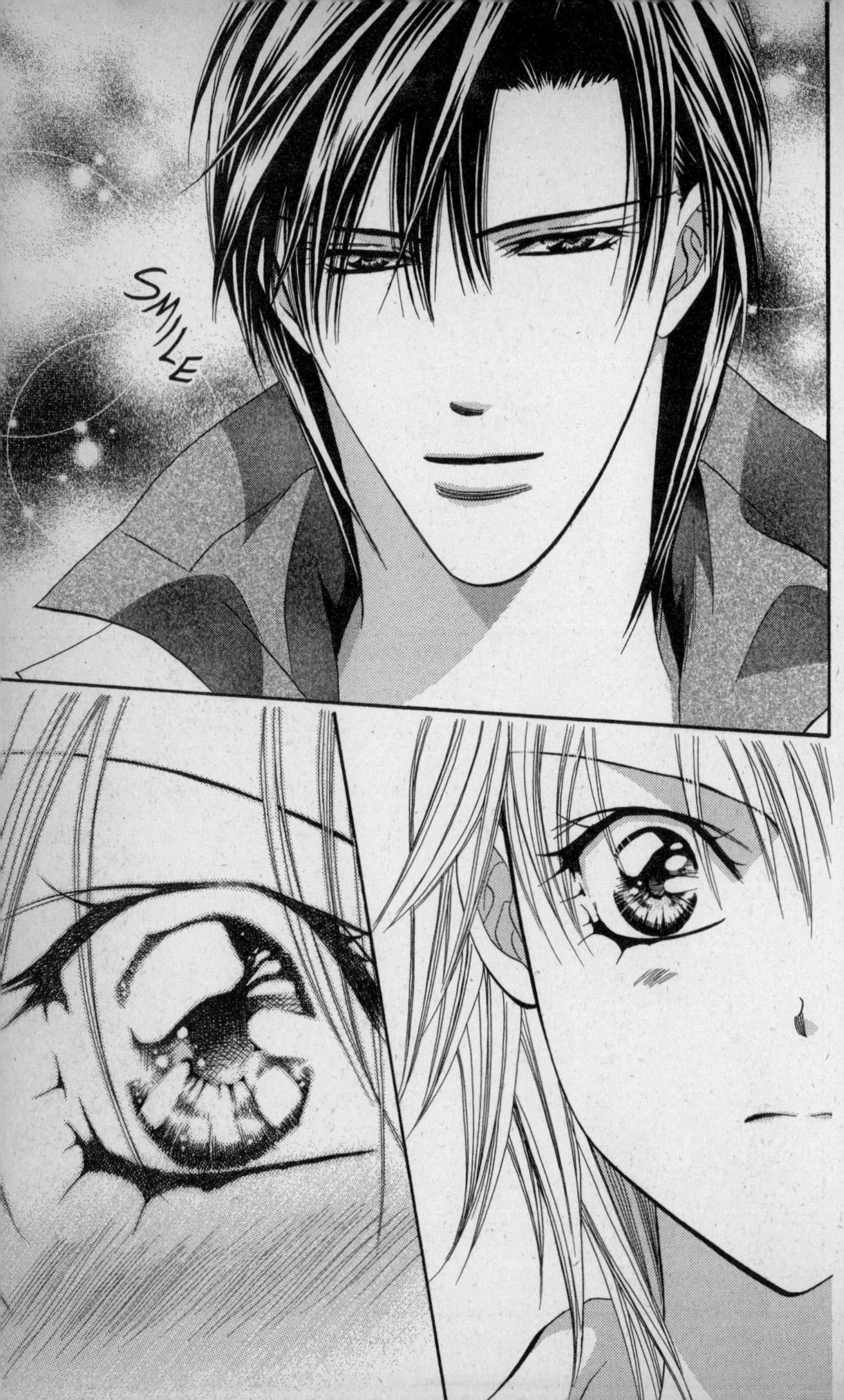
SMILE

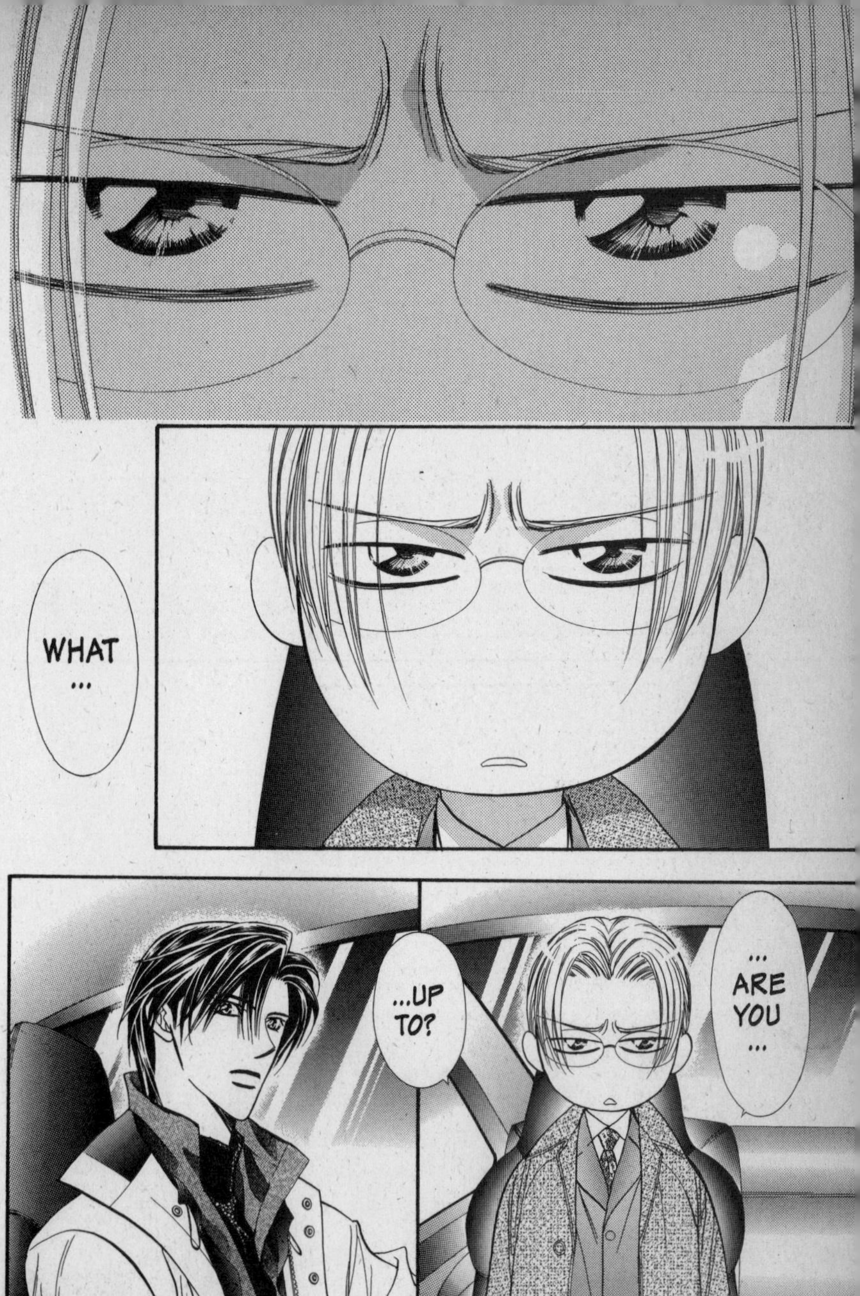
WHAT ...
... ARE YOU ...
...UP TO?

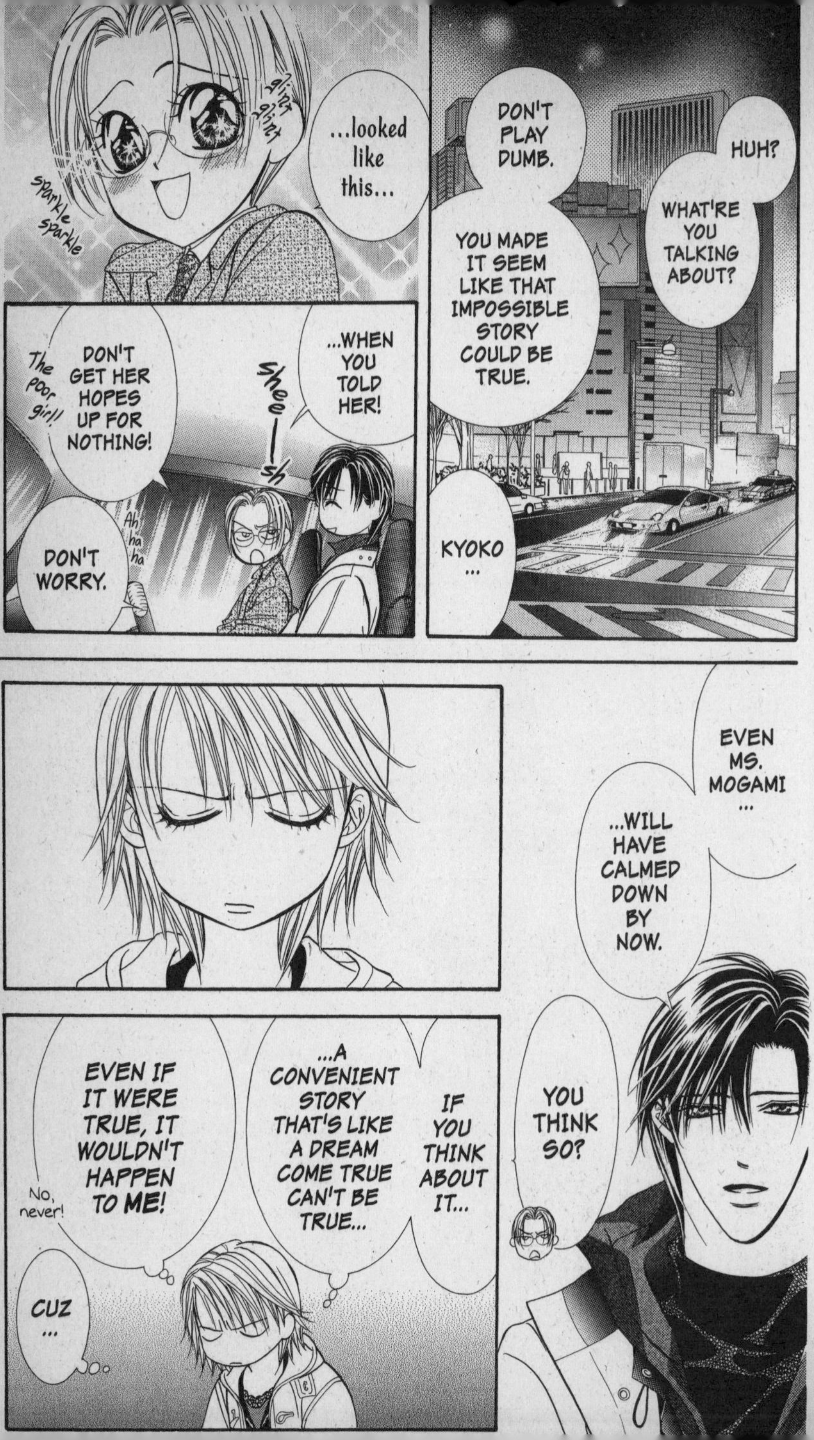
HUH?
WHAT'RE YOU TALKING ABOUT?
DON'T PLAY DUMB.
YOU MADE IT SEEM LIKE THAT IMPOSSIBLE STORY COULD BE TRUE.
KYOKO ...
glint glint
...looked like this...
sparkle sparkle
...WHEN YOU TOLD HER!
shee-ish
DON'T GET HER HOPES UP FOR NOTHING!
The poor girl!!
Ah ha ha
DON'T WORRY.
EVEN MS. MOGAMI ...
...WILL HAVE CALMED DOWN BY NOW.
YOU THINK SO?
IF YOU THINK ABOUT IT...
...A CONVENIENT STORY THAT'S LIKE A DREAM COME TRUE CAN'T BE TRUE...
EVEN IF IT WERE TRUE, IT WOULDN'T HAPPEN TO ME!
No, never!
CUZ ...

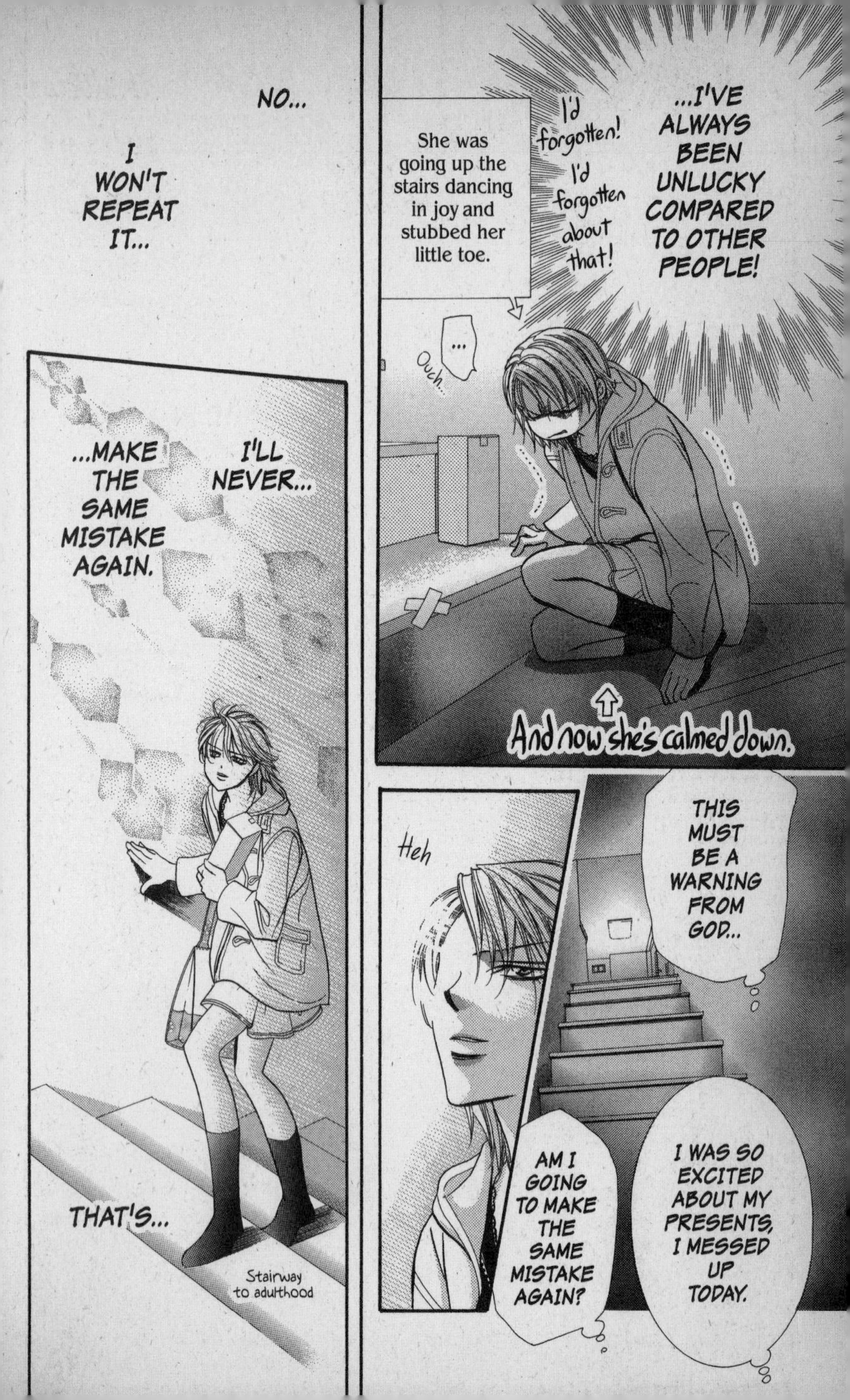
...I'VE ALWAYS BEEN UNLUCKY COMPARED TO OTHER PEOPLE!
I'd forgotten! I'd forgotten about that!
She was going up the stairs dancing in joy and stubbed her little toe.
...
Ouch...
And now she's calmed down.
THIS MUST BE A WARNING FROM GOD...
Heh
I WAS SO EXCITED ABOUT MY PRESENTS, I MESSED UP TODAY.
AM I GOING TO MAKE THE SAME MISTAKE AGAIN?
NO...
I WON'T REPEAT IT...
I'LL NEVER...
...MAKE THE SAME MISTAKE AGAIN.
THAT'S...
Stairway to adulthood

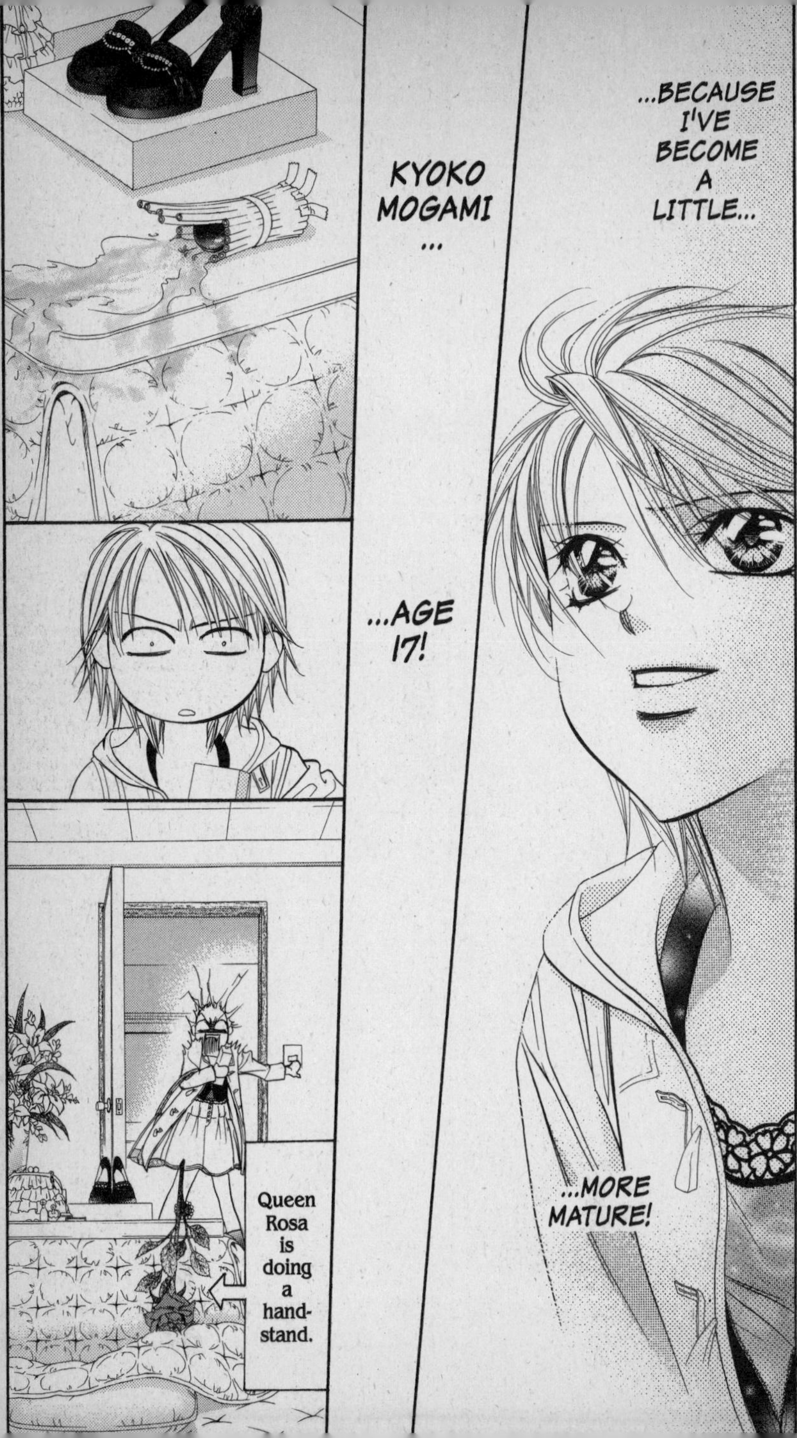
...BECAUSE I'VE BECOME A LITTLE...
...MORE MATURE!
KYOKO MOGAMI ...
...AGE 17!
Queen Rosa is doing a hand-stand.

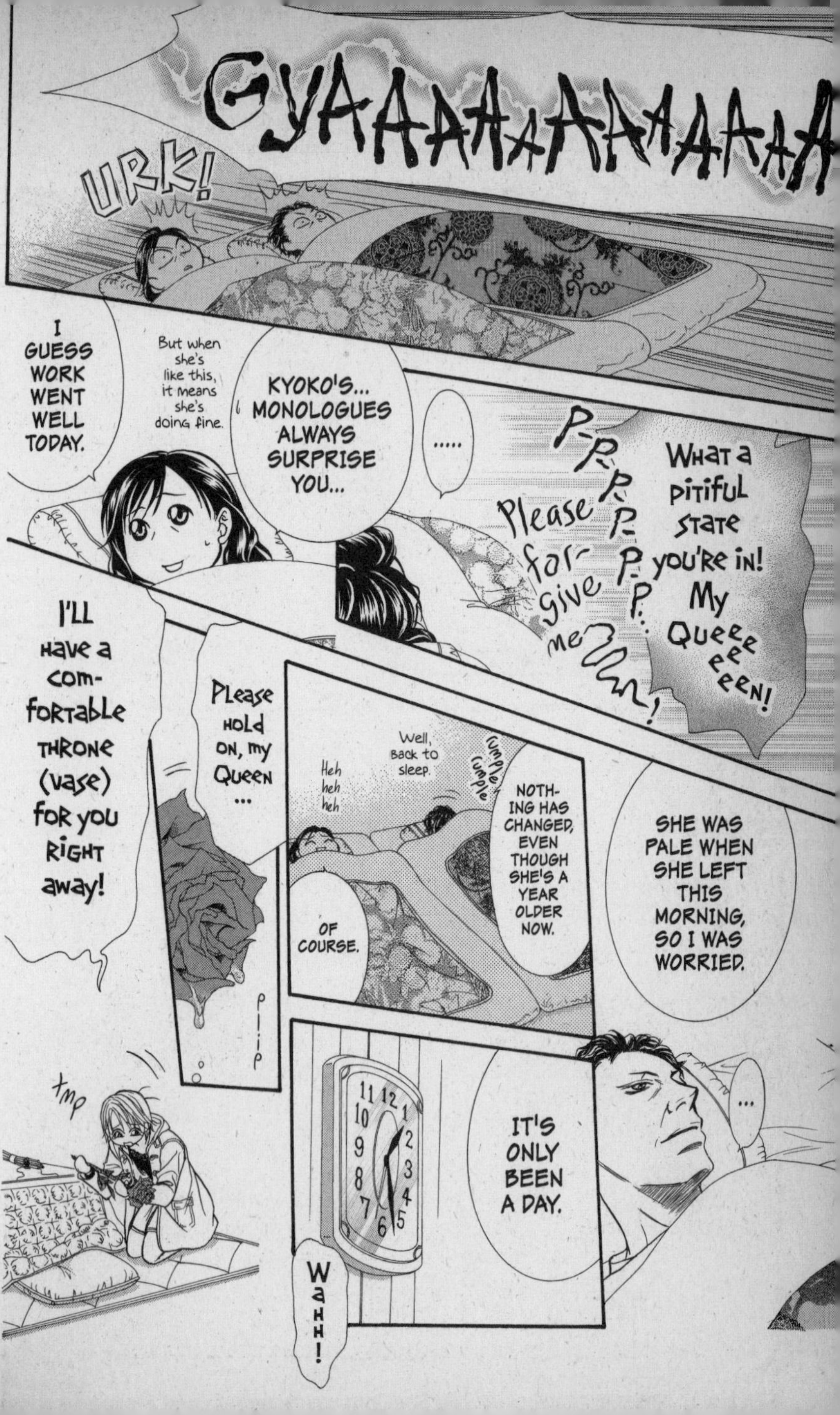
GYAAAAAAAAAAAA
URK!
What a pitiful state you're in! My Queeeeeen!
P-P-P-P-P-P...
Please forgive meeee!
.....
KYOKO'S... MONOLOGUES ALWAYS SURPRISE YOU...
But when she's like this, it means she's doing fine.
I GUESS WORK WENT WELL TODAY.
SHE WAS PALE WHEN SHE LEFT THIS MORNING, SO I WAS WORRIED.
NOTHING HAS CHANGED, EVEN THOUGH SHE'S A YEAR OLDER NOW.
OF COURSE.
Well, back to sleep.
cumple cumple
Heh heh heh
Please hold on, my Queen...
plip
I'LL have a comfortable THRONE (vase) for you RIGHT away!
...
IT'S ONLY BEEN A DAY.
Wahh!

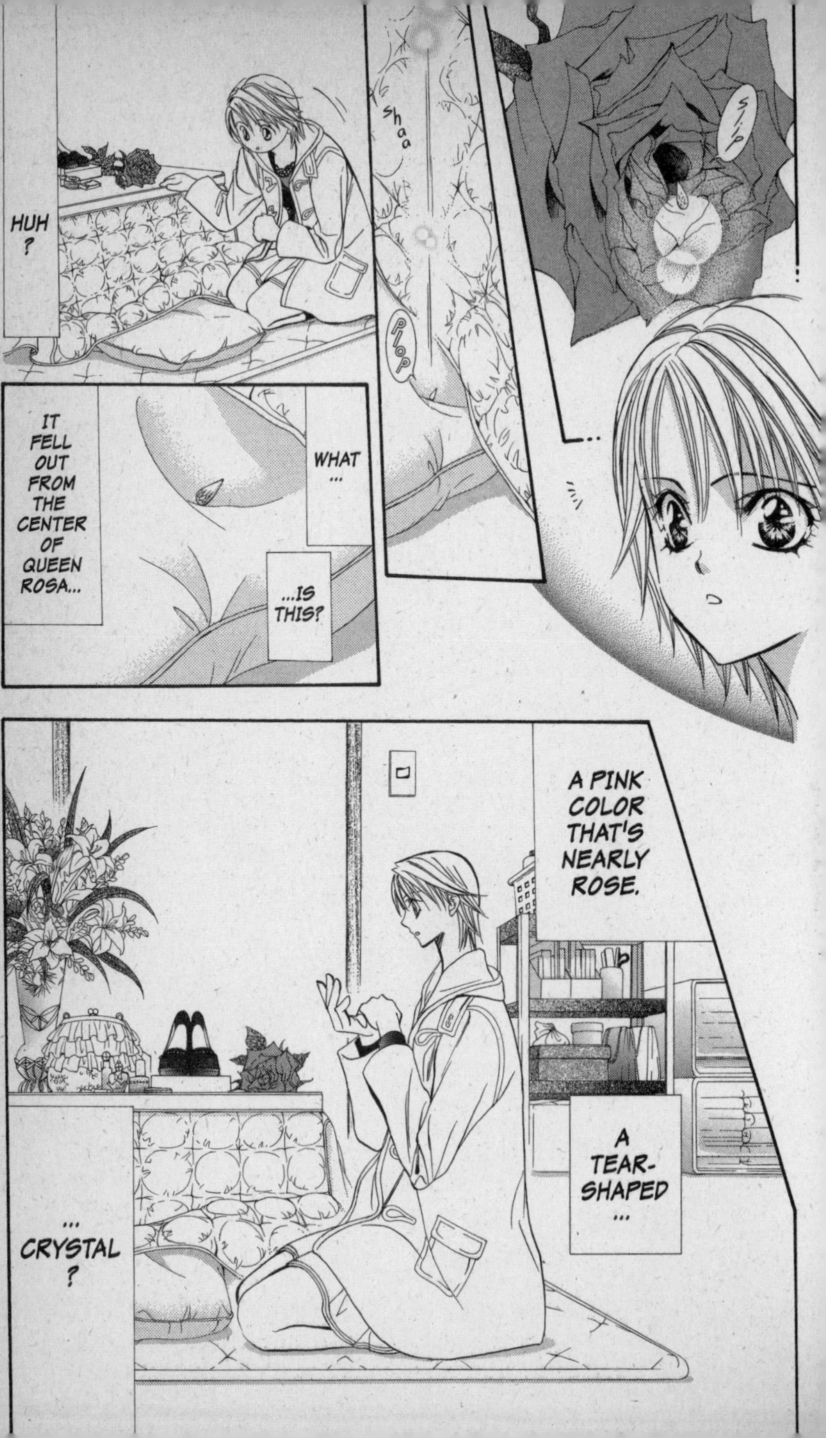

slip
...
shaa
PLOP
HUH?
WHAT...
...IS THIS?
IT FELL OUT FROM THE CENTER OF QUEEN ROSA...
A PINK COLOR THAT'S NEARLY ROSE.
A TEAR-SHAPED...
...CRYSTAL?

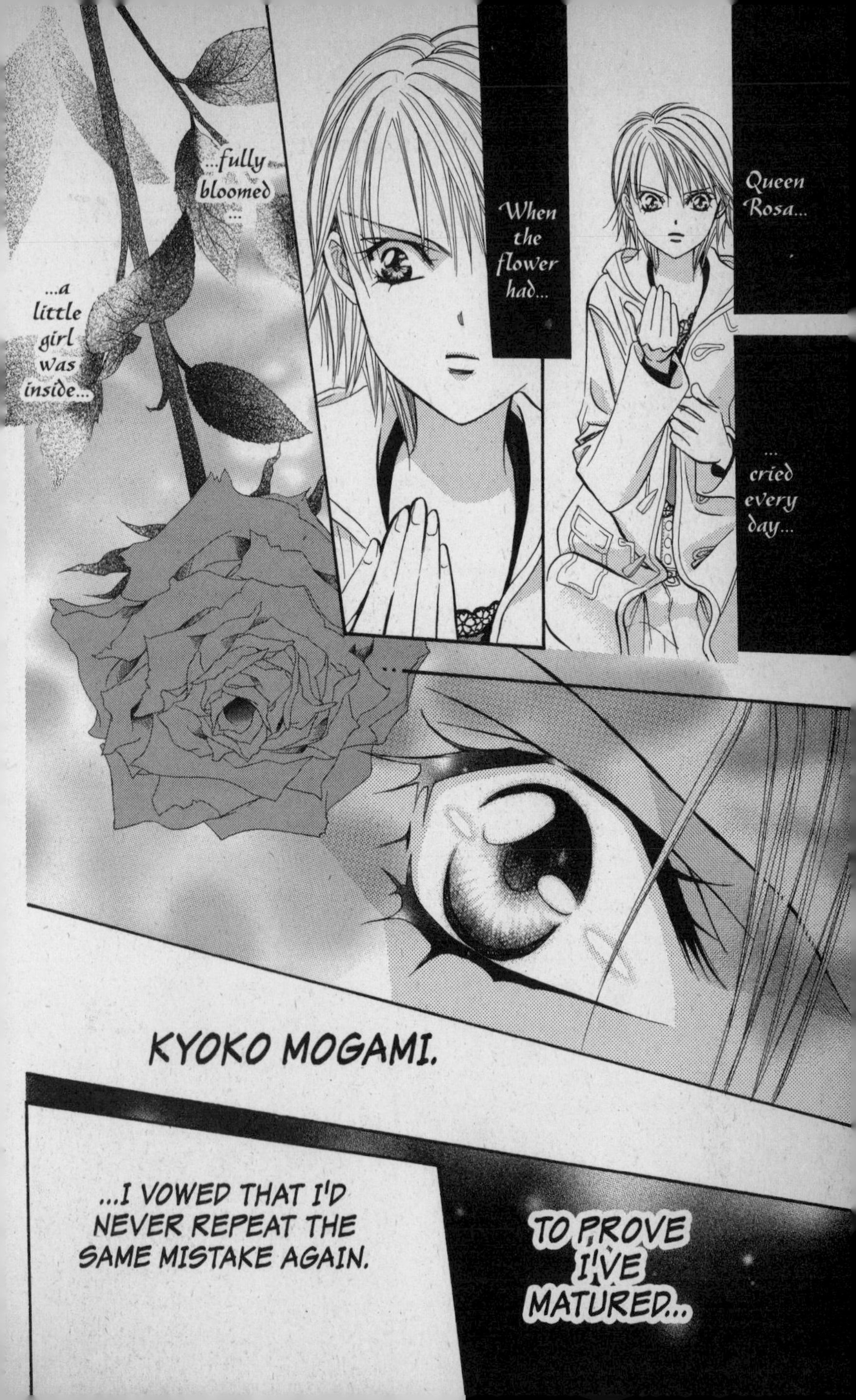

Queen Rosa...
...cried every day...
When the flower had...
...fully bloomed...
...a little girl was inside...
...
KYOKO MOGAMI.
TO PROVE I'VE MATURED...
...I VOWED THAT I'D NEVER REPEAT THE SAME MISTAKE AGAIN.

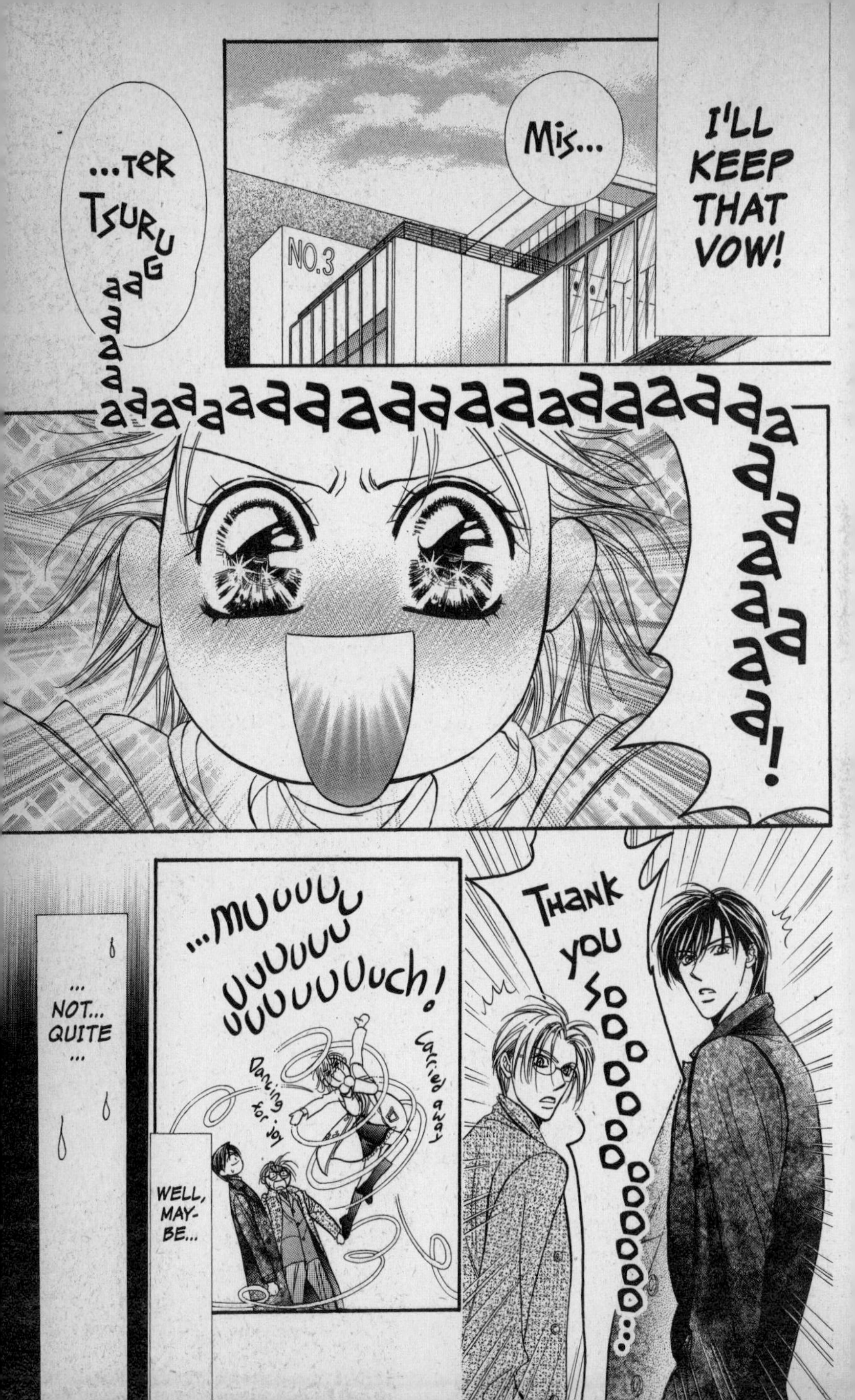
I'LL KEEP THAT VOW!
Mis...
...TER TSURUGAaaaaaaaaaaaaaaaaaaaaaaaaaaaaaaaaaaaaaaa!
THANK YOU SOOOOOOOOOOOOOO...
...MUUUUUUUUUUUUUUUUUUUUUCH!
Carried away
Dancing for joy
WELL, MAY-BE...
...NOT... QUITE...

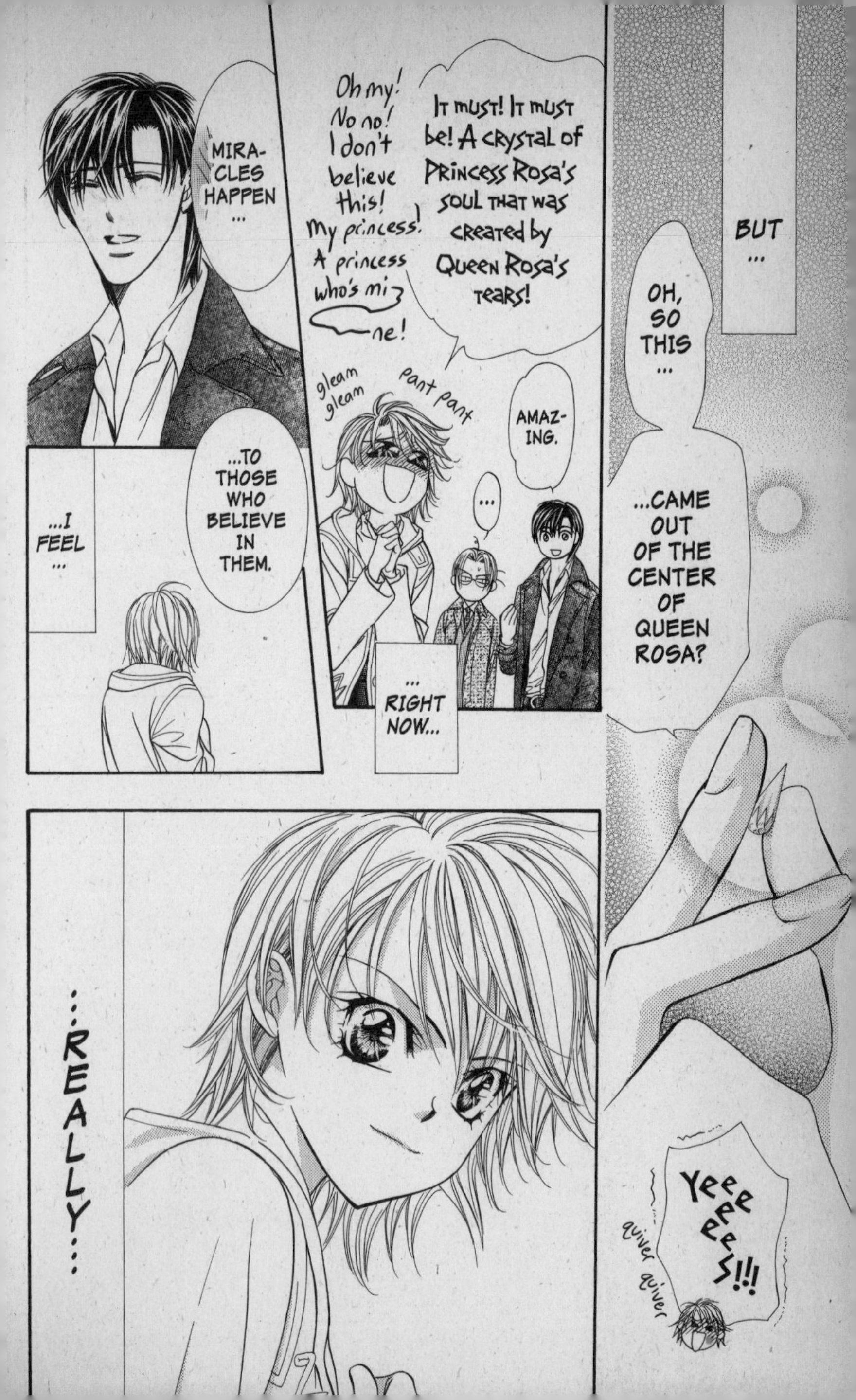
BUT...
OH, SO THIS...
...CAME OUT OF THE CENTER OF QUEEN ROSA?
Yeeeeees!!!
quiver quiver
It must! It must be! A crystal of Princess Rosa's soul that was created by Queen Rosa's tears!
Oh my! No no! I don't believe this! My princess! A princess who's mi ne!
AMAZ-ING.
pant pant
gleam gleam
...
...RIGHT NOW...
MIRA-CLES HAPPEN...
...TO THOSE WHO BELIEVE IN THEM.
...I FEEL...
...REALLY...

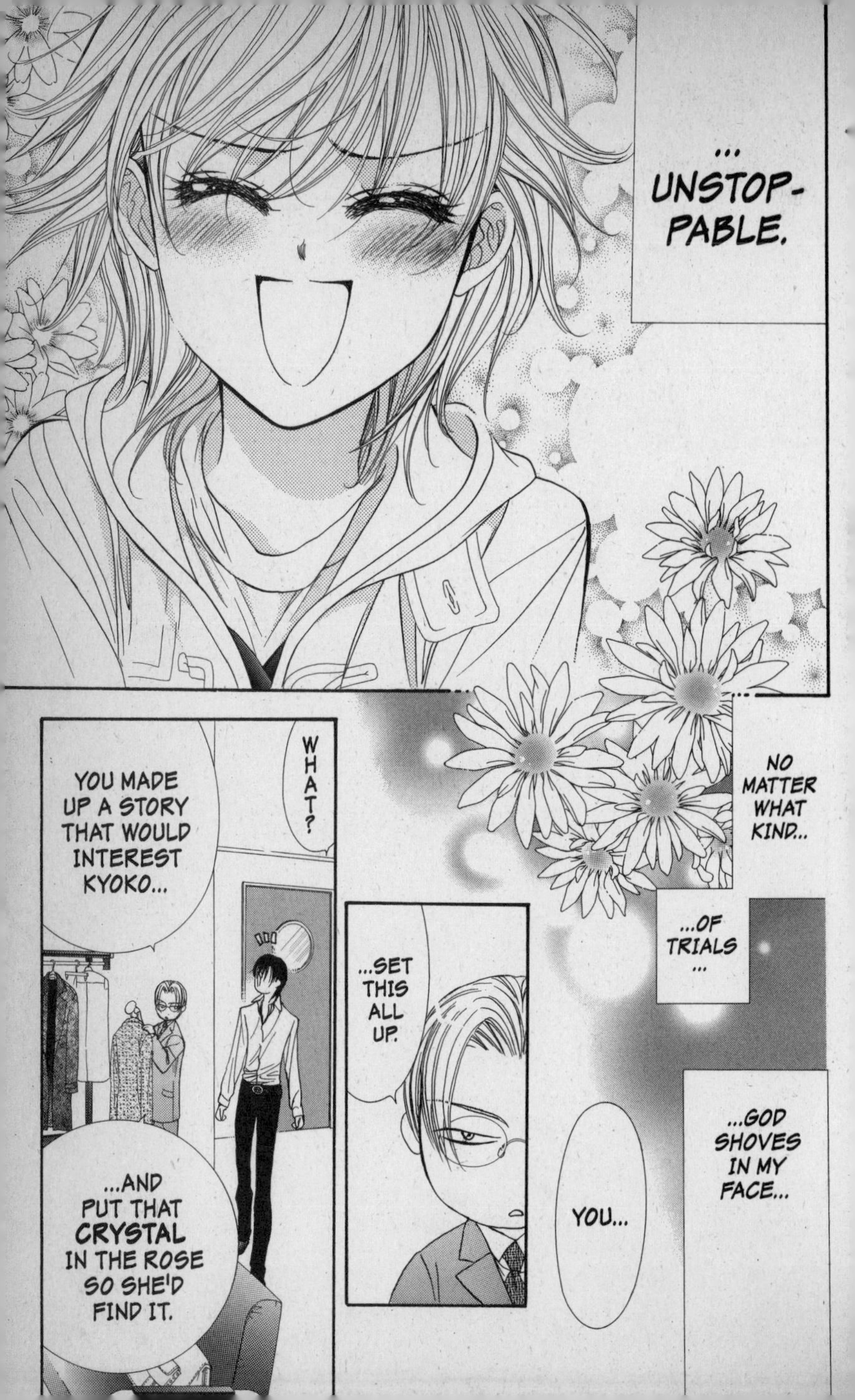
... UNSTOP-PABLE.
NO MATTER WHAT KIND...
...OF TRIALS ...
...GOD SHOVES IN MY FACE...
YOU...
...SET THIS ALL UP.
WHAT?
YOU MADE UP A STORY THAT WOULD INTEREST KYOKO...
...AND PUT THAT CRYSTAL IN THE ROSE SO SHE'D FIND IT.

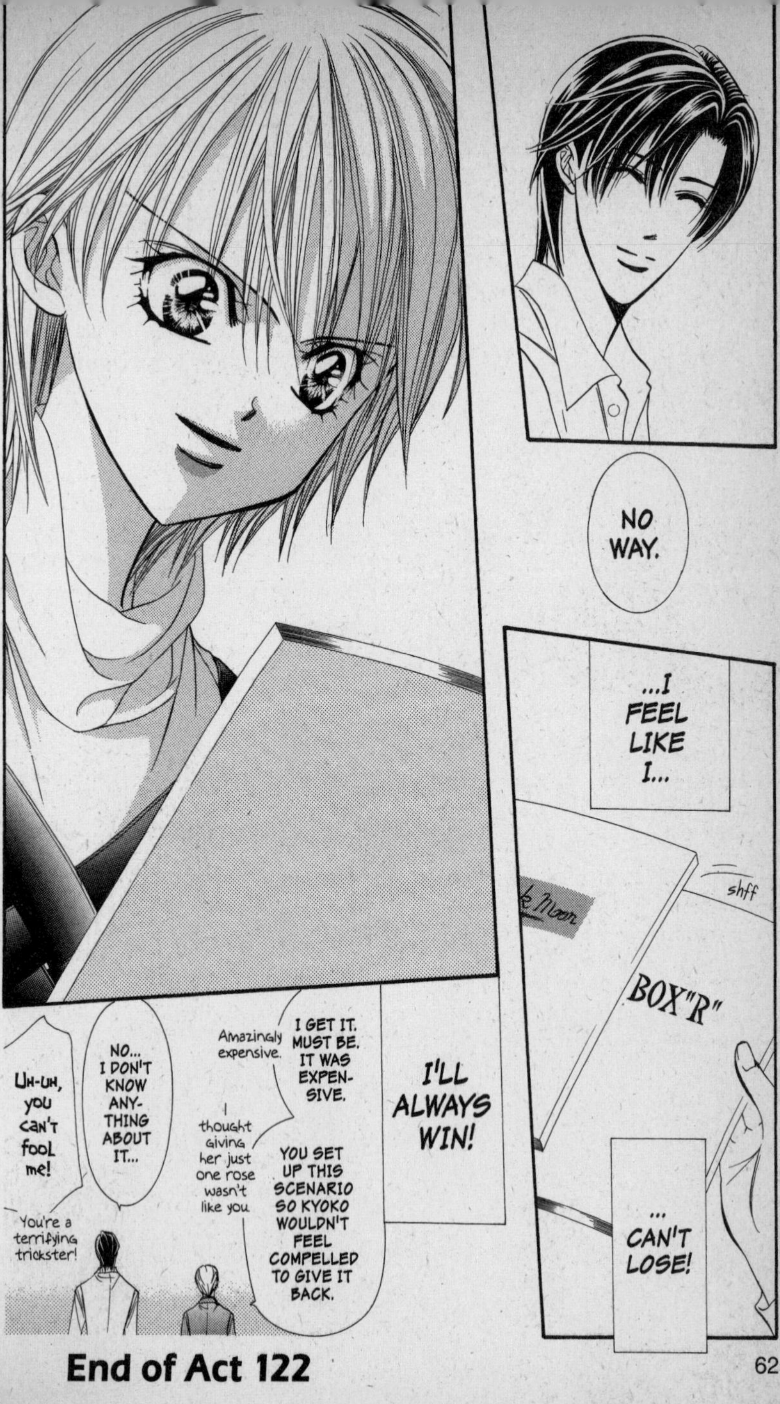
NO WAY.
...I FEEL LIKE I...
shff
BOX"R"
...CAN'T LOSE!
I'LL ALWAYS WIN!
I GET IT. MUST BE. IT WAS EXPENSIVE.
Amazingly expensive.
YOU SET UP THIS SCENARIO SO KYOKO WOULDN'T FEEL COMPELLED TO GIVE IT BACK.
I thought giving her just one rose wasn't like you
NO... I DON'T KNOW ANYTHING ABOUT IT...
UH-UH, you can't fool me!
You're a terrifying trickster!

End of Act 122

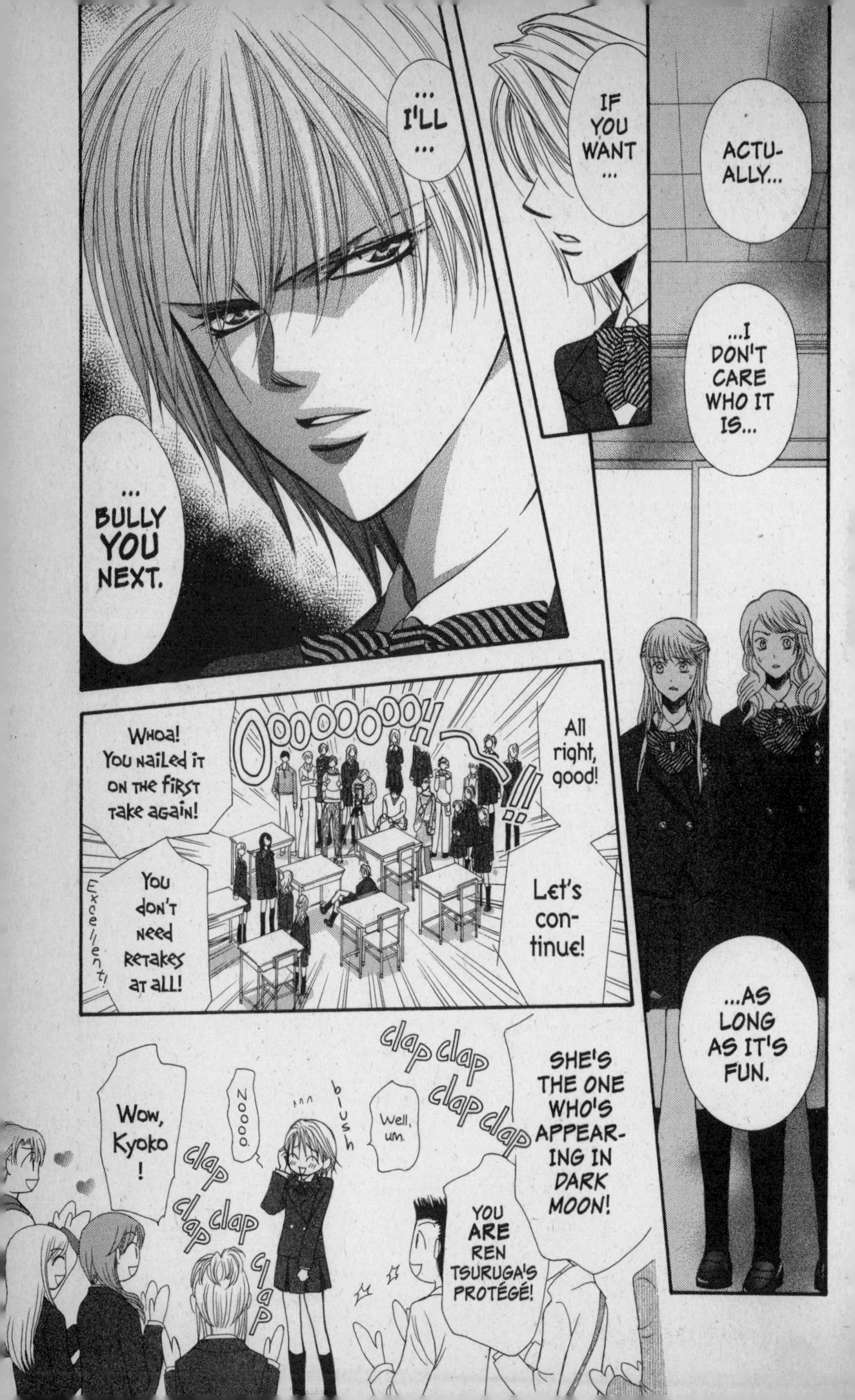
ACTU-ALLY...
...I DON'T CARE WHO IT IS...
...AS LONG AS IT'S FUN.
IF YOU WANT...
...I'LL...
...BULLY YOU NEXT.
All right, good!
Let's continue!
OOOOOOOOH!!
Whoa! You nailed it on the first take again!
You don't need retakes at all!
Excellent!
SHE'S THE ONE WHO'S APPEARING IN DARK MOON!
YOU ARE REN TSURUGA'S PROTÉGÉ!
clap clap clap clap
Well, um.
blush
Noooo.
clap clap clap clap
Wow, Kyoko!

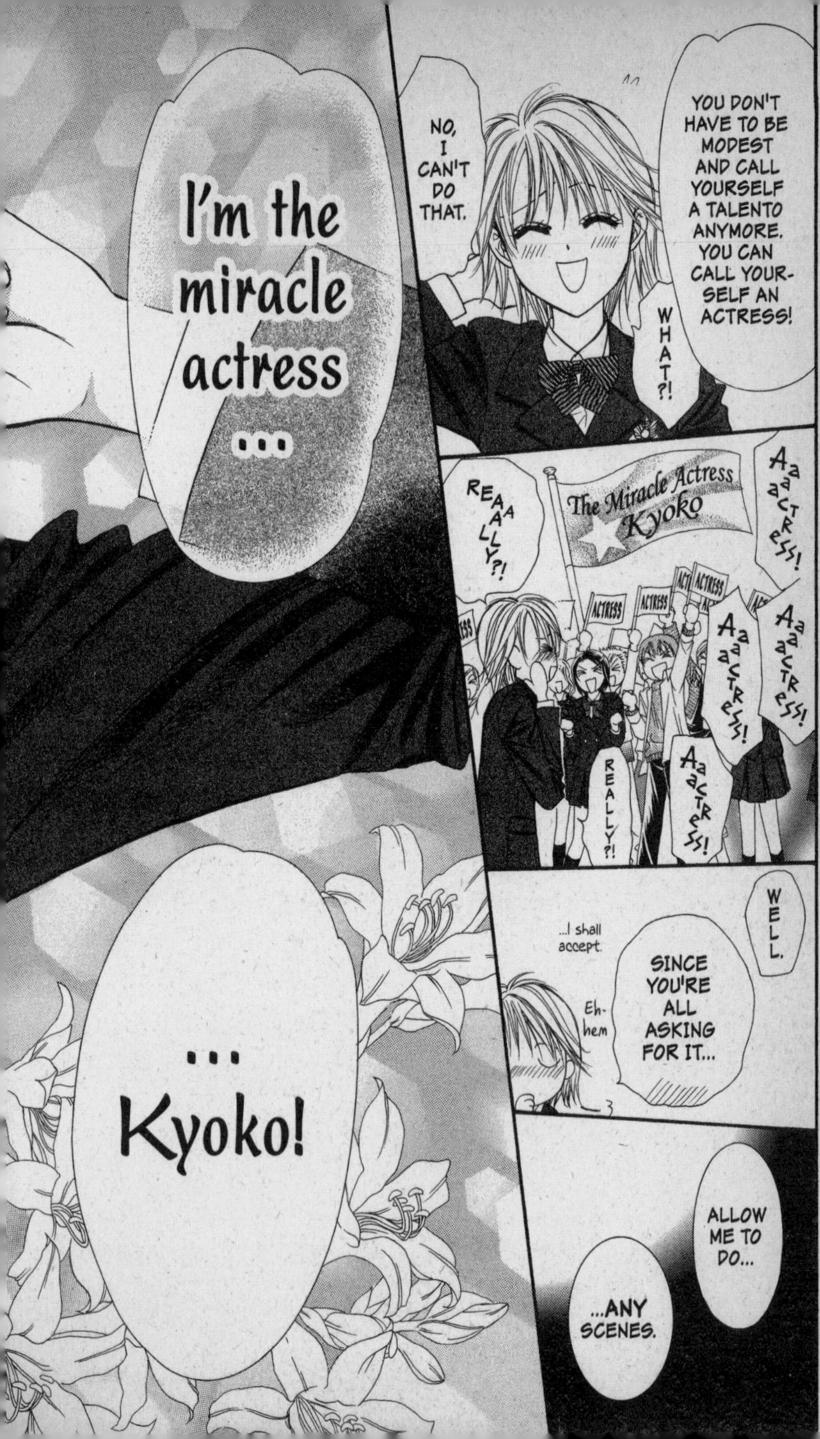

YOU DON'T HAVE TO BE MODEST AND CALL YOURSELF A TALENTO ANYMORE. YOU CAN CALL YOURSELF AN ACTRESS!
WHAT?!
NO, I CAN'T DO THAT.
Aaactress!
The Miracle Actress Kyoko
REAAALLY?!
ACTRESS
Aaactress!
Aaactress!
REALLY?!
Aaactress!
WELL.
SINCE YOU'RE ALL ASKING FOR IT...
...I shall accept.
Eh-hem
ALLOW ME TO DO...
...ANY SCENES.
I'm the miracle actress...
...Kyoko!

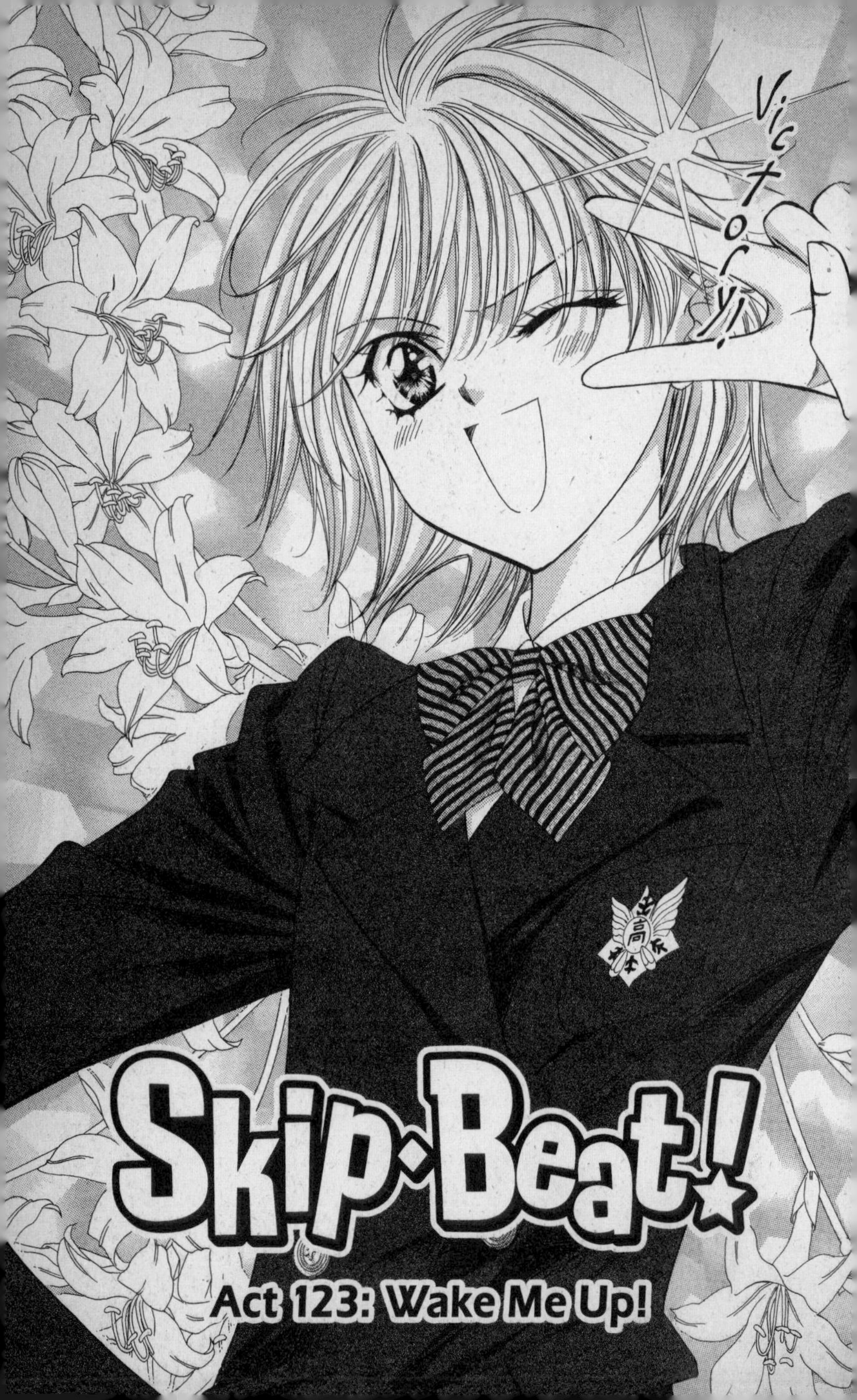
Victory!
Skip·Beat!
Act 123: Wake Me Up!

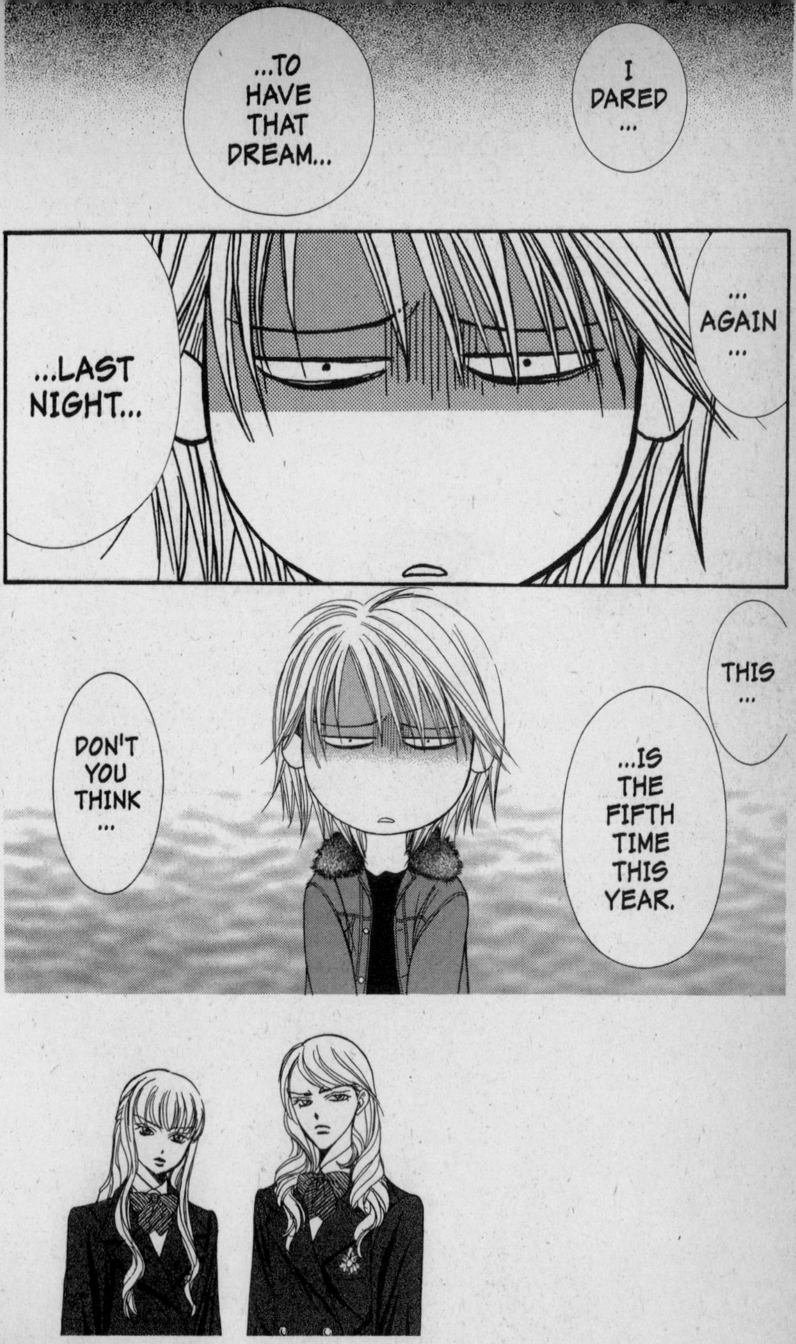
I DARED ...
...TO HAVE THAT DREAM...
... AGAIN ...
...LAST NIGHT...
THIS ...
...IS THE FIFTH TIME THIS YEAR.
DON'T YOU THINK ...

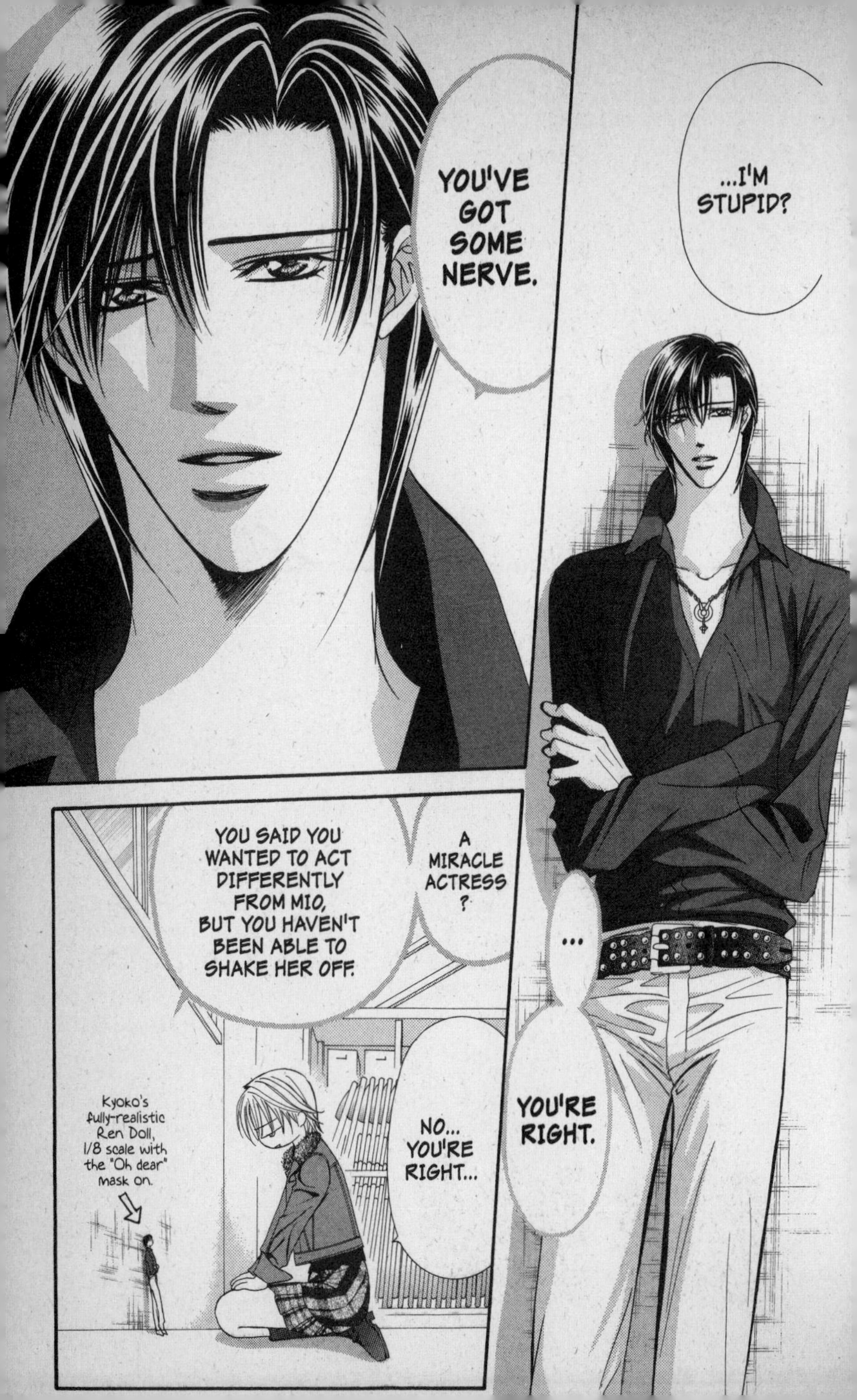
...I'M STUPID?
...
YOU'RE RIGHT.
YOU'VE GOT SOME NERVE.
A MIRACLE ACTRESS?
YOU SAID YOU WANTED TO ACT DIFFERENTLY FROM MIO, BUT YOU HAVEN'T BEEN ABLE TO SHAKE HER OFF.
NO... YOU'RE RIGHT...
Kyoko's fully-realistic Ren Doll, 1/8 scale with the "Oh dear" mask on.

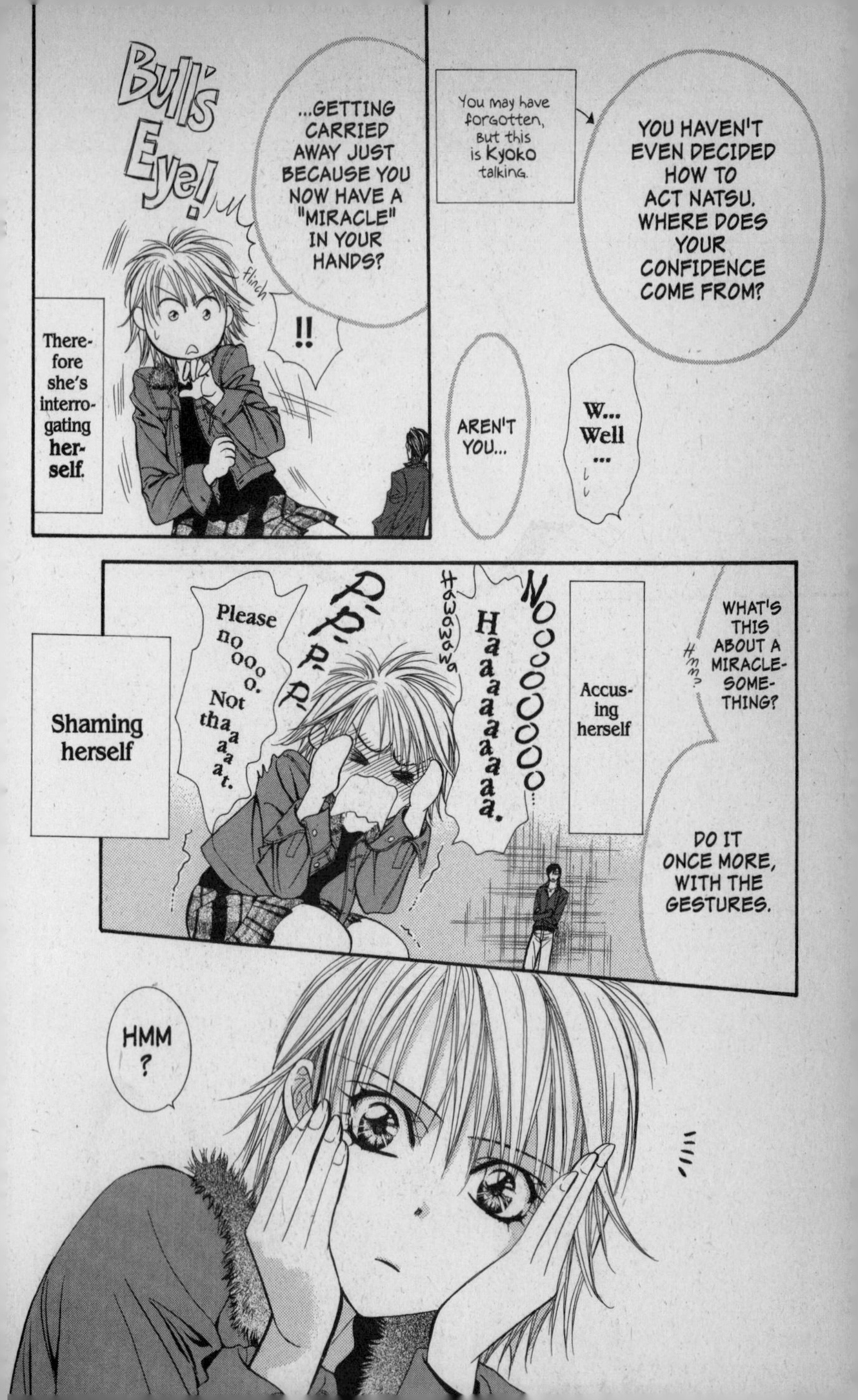
You may have forgotten, but this is Kyoko talking.
YOU HAVEN'T EVEN DECIDED HOW TO ACT NATSU. WHERE DOES YOUR CONFIDENCE COME FROM?
W... Well ...
AREN'T YOU...
...GETTING CARRIED AWAY JUST BECAUSE YOU NOW HAVE A "MIRACLE" IN YOUR HANDS?
!!
Bull's Eye!
flinch
There-fore she's interro-gating her-self.
WHAT'S THIS ABOUT A MIRACLE-SOMETHING?
Hmm?
Accus-ing herself
NOOOOOOOO...
Haaaaaaaaaa.
Hawawawa
P.P.P.P.
Please noooooo. Not thaaaaat.
Shaming herself
DO IT ONCE MORE, WITH THE GESTURES.
HMM?

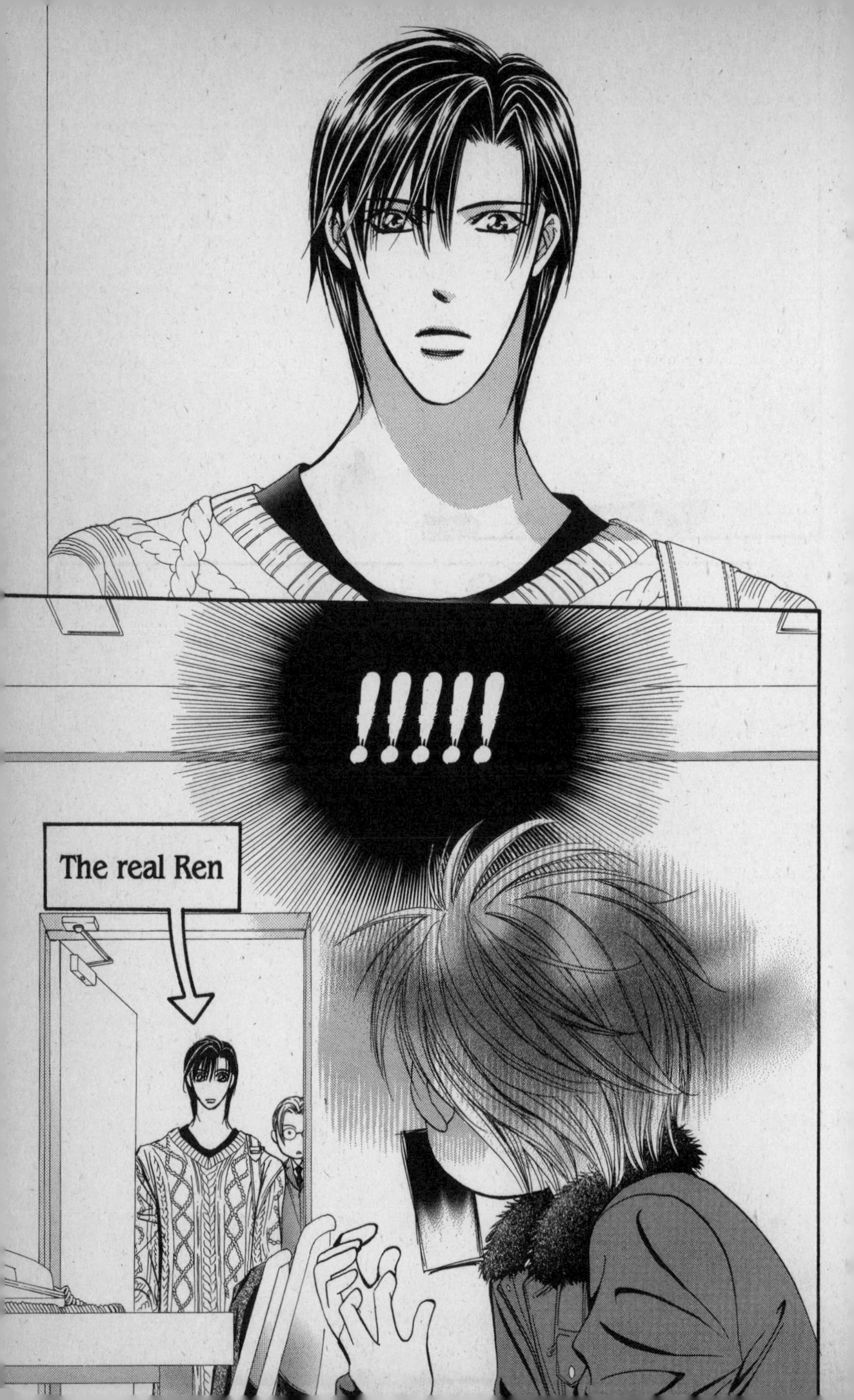
!!!!!
The real Ren

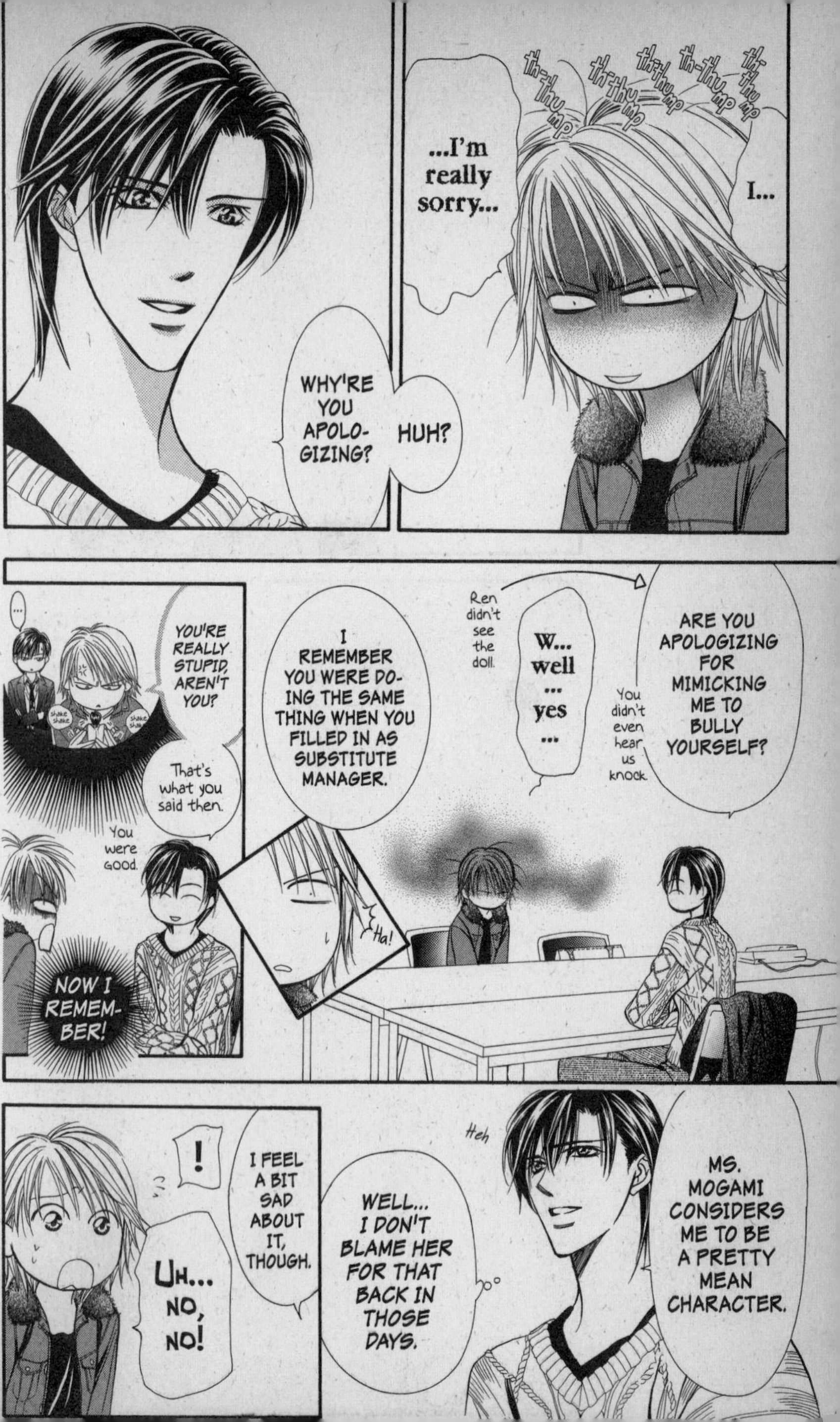
th-thump th-thump th-thump th-thump th-thump
I...
...I'm really sorry...
HUH?
WHY'RE YOU APOLO-GIZING?
ARE YOU APOLOGIZING FOR MIMICKING ME TO BULLY YOURSELF?
You didn't even hear us knock.
Ren didn't see the doll.
W... well... yes...
I REMEMBER YOU WERE DO-ING THE SAME THING WHEN YOU FILLED IN AS SUBSTITUTE MANAGER.
...
YOU'RE REALLY STUPID, AREN'T YOU?
shake shake
shake shake
That's what you said then.
You were good.
Ha!
NOW I REMEM-BER!
MS. MOGAMI CONSIDERS ME TO BE A PRETTY MEAN CHARACTER.
Heh
WELL... I DON'T BLAME HER FOR THAT BACK IN THOSE DAYS.
I FEEL A BIT SAD ABOUT IT, THOUGH.
!
UH... NO, NO!

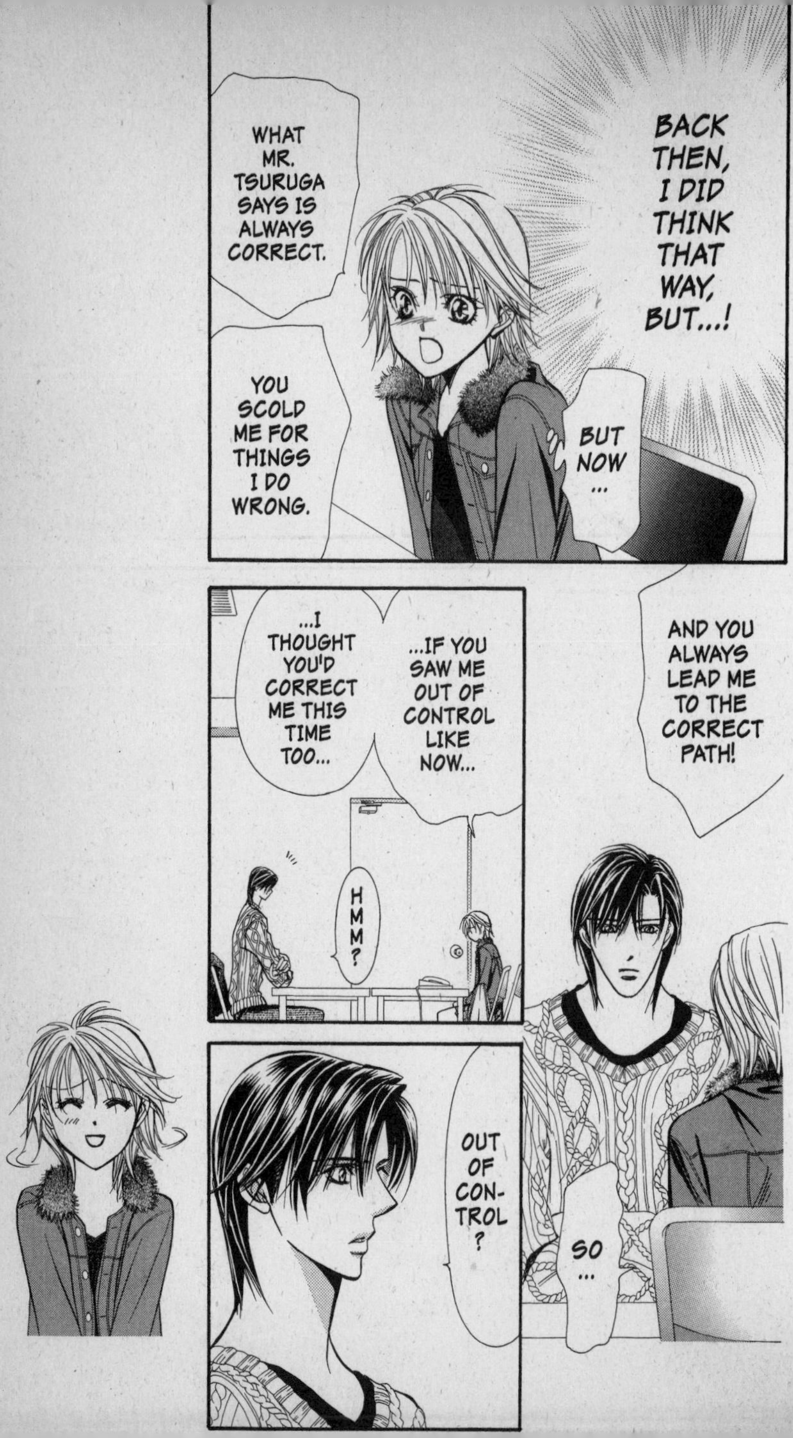
BACK THEN, I DID THINK THAT WAY, BUT...!
WHAT MR. TSURUGA SAYS IS ALWAYS CORRECT.
BUT NOW...
YOU SCOLD ME FOR THINGS I DO WRONG.
AND YOU ALWAYS LEAD ME TO THE CORRECT PATH!
SO...
...IF YOU SAW ME OUT OF CONTROL LIKE NOW...
...I THOUGHT YOU'D CORRECT ME THIS TIME TOO...
HMM?
OUT OF CON-TROL?

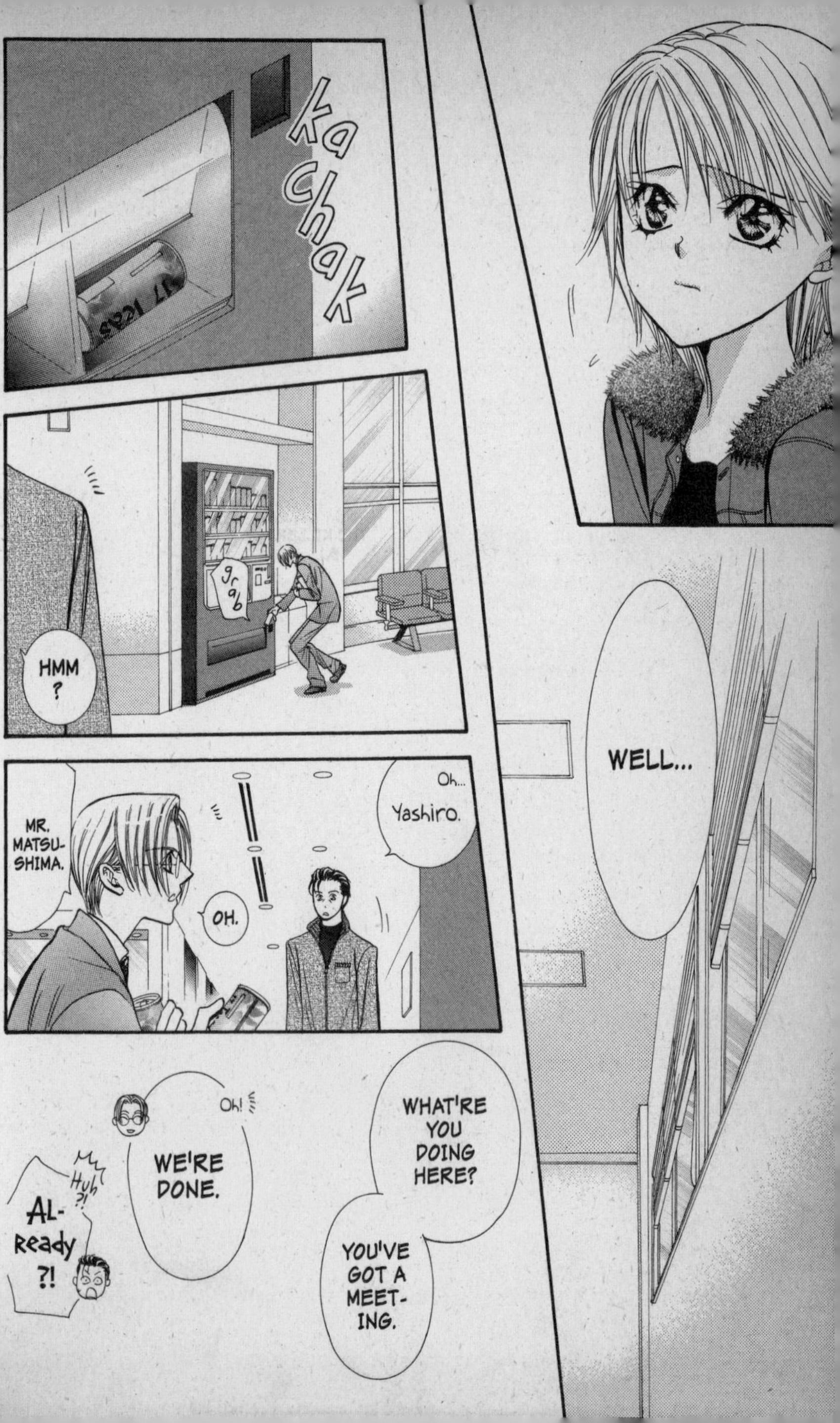
WELL...
ka chak
grab
HMM ?
Oh... Yashiro.
MR. MATSU-SHIMA.
OH.
WHAT'RE YOU DOING HERE?
YOU'VE GOT A MEET-ING.
Oh!
WE'RE DONE.
Huh ?!
AL-ready ?!

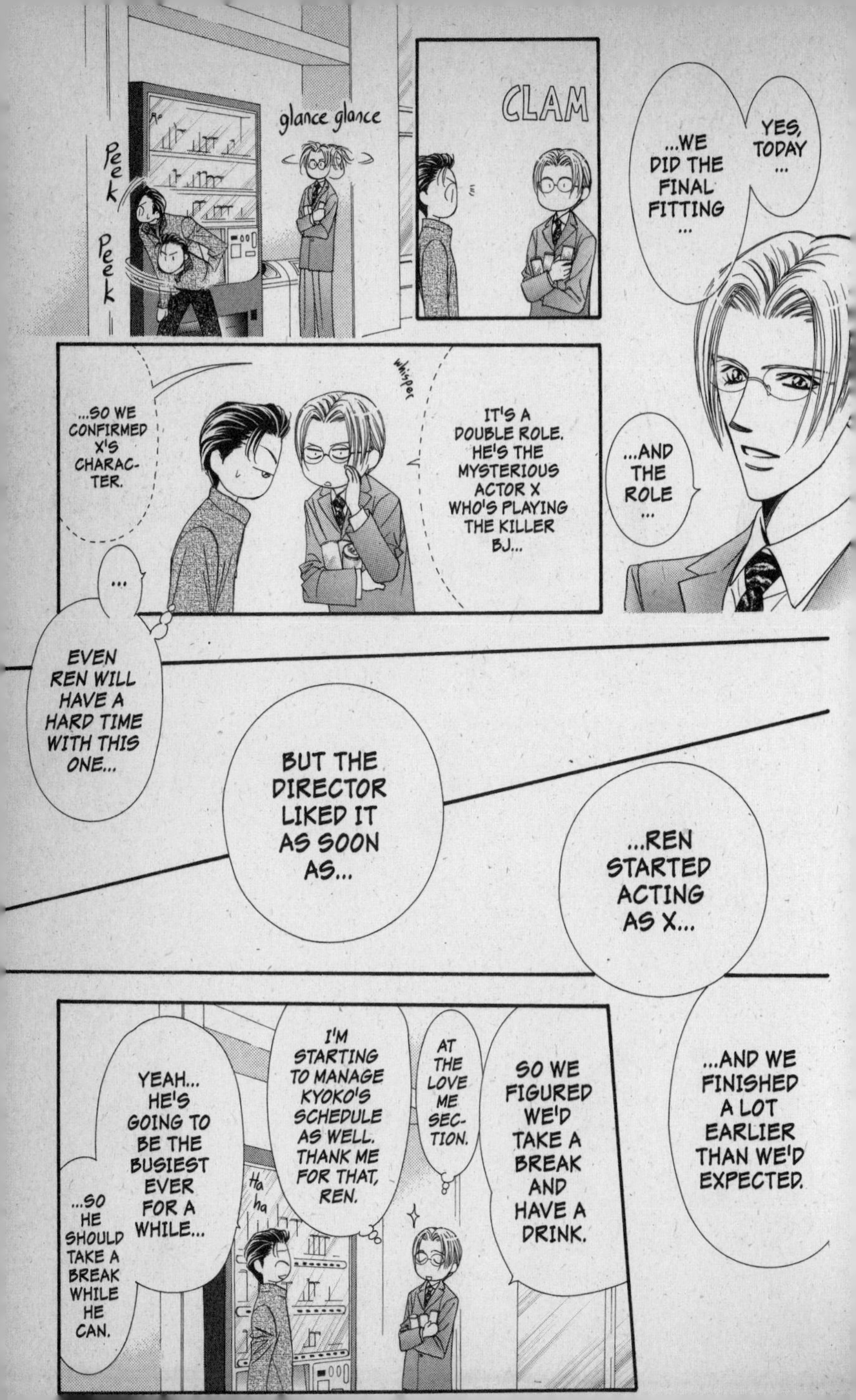
YES, TODAY...
...WE DID THE FINAL FITTING...
...AND THE ROLE...
CLAM
glance glance
Peek Peek
IT'S A DOUBLE ROLE. HE'S THE MYSTERIOUS ACTOR X WHO'S PLAYING THE KILLER BJ...
whisper
...SO WE CONFIRMED X'S CHARACTER.
...
EVEN REN WILL HAVE A HARD TIME WITH THIS ONE...
BUT THE DIRECTOR LIKED IT AS SOON AS...
...REN STARTED ACTING AS X...
...AND WE FINISHED A LOT EARLIER THAN WE'D EXPECTED.
SO WE FIGURED WE'D TAKE A BREAK AND HAVE A DRINK.
AT THE LOVE ME SECTION.
I'M STARTING TO MANAGE KYOKO'S SCHEDULE AS WELL. THANK ME FOR THAT, REN.
YEAH... HE'S GOING TO BE THE BUSIEST EVER FOR A WHILE...
...SO HE SHOULD TAKE A BREAK WHILE HE CAN.
Ha ha

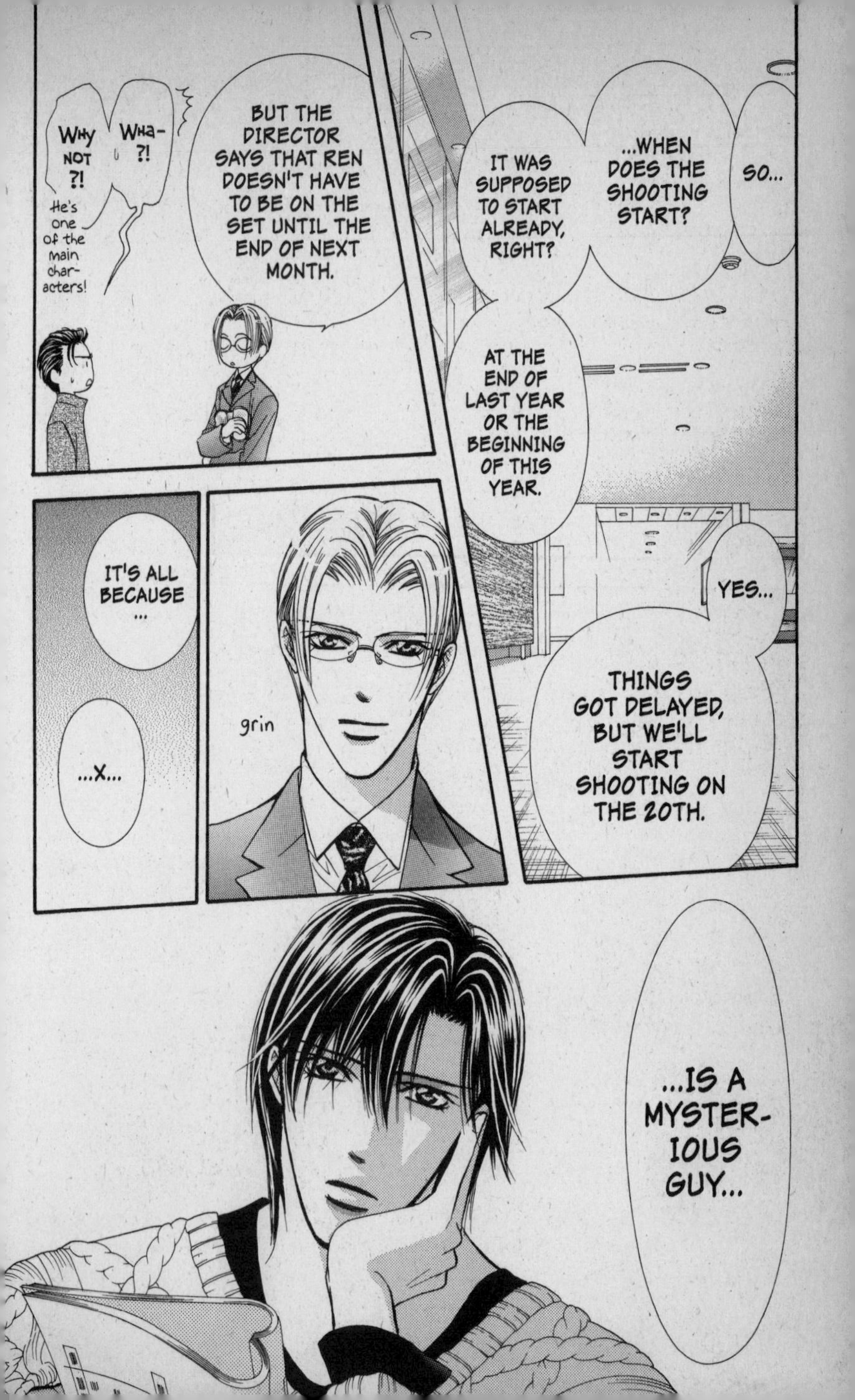
SO...
...WHEN DOES THE SHOOTING START?
IT WAS SUPPOSED TO START ALREADY, RIGHT?
AT THE END OF LAST YEAR OR THE BEGINNING OF THIS YEAR.
YES...
THINGS GOT DELAYED, BUT WE'LL START SHOOTING ON THE 20TH.
BUT THE DIRECTOR SAYS THAT REN DOESN'T HAVE TO BE ON THE SET UNTIL THE END OF NEXT MONTH.
WHA- ?!
WHY NOT ?!
He's one of the main characters!
grin
IT'S ALL BECAUSE ...
...X...
...IS A MYSTERIOUS GUY...

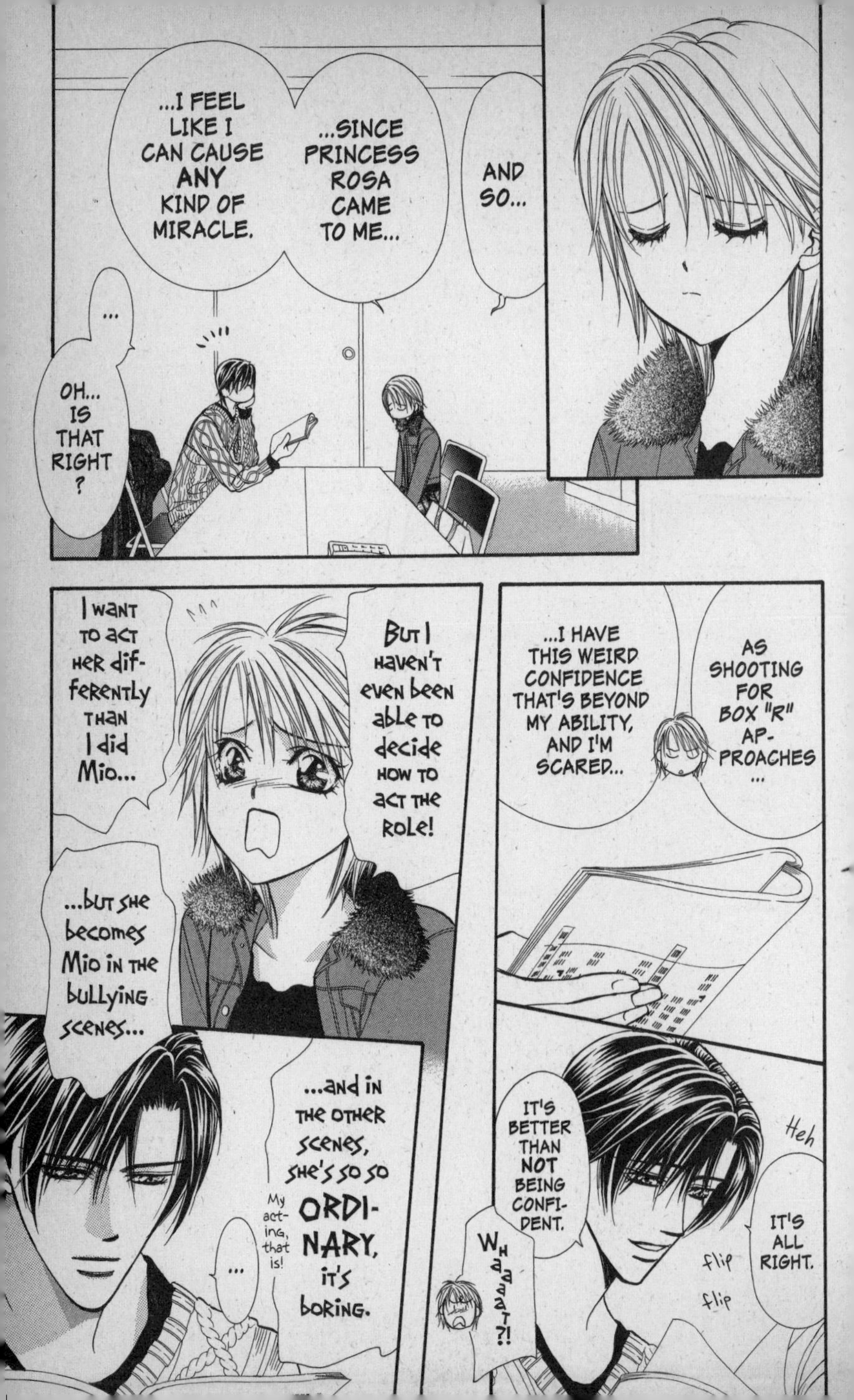
AND SO...
...SINCE PRINCESS ROSA CAME TO ME...
...I FEEL LIKE I CAN CAUSE ANY KIND OF MIRACLE.
...
OH... IS THAT RIGHT?
AS SHOOTING FOR BOX "R" APPROACHES...
...I HAVE THIS WEIRD CONFIDENCE THAT'S BEYOND MY ABILITY, AND I'M SCARED...
But I haven't even been able to decide how to act the role!
I want to act her differently than I did Mio...
...but she becomes Mio in the bullying scenes...
Heh
IT'S ALL RIGHT.
flip
flip
IT'S BETTER THAN NOT BEING CONFIDENT.
Whaaaat?!
...and in the other scenes, she's so so ORDINARY, it's boring.
My acting, that is!
...

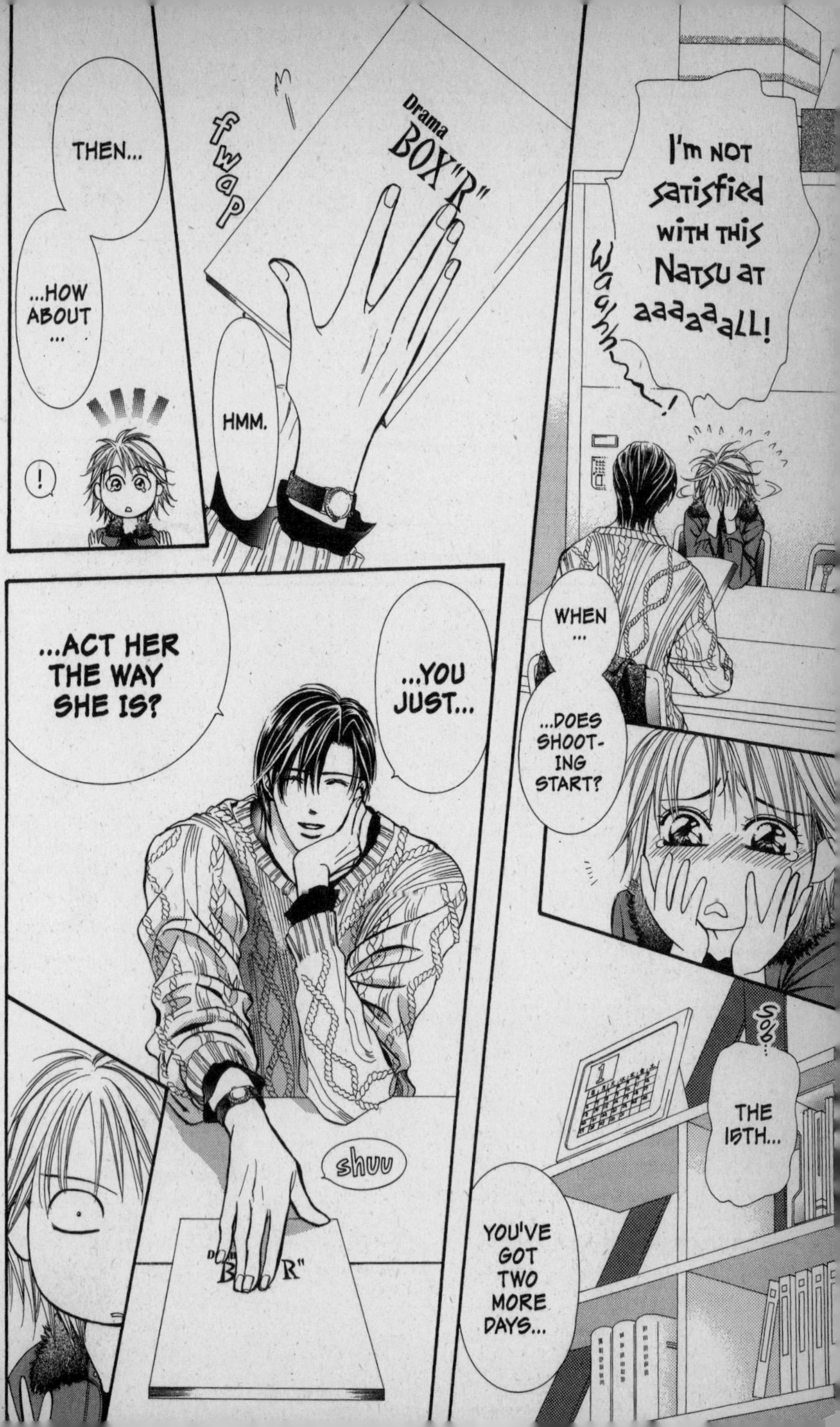
I'm NOT satisfied with THIS Natsu at aaaaaaLL!
Waahh~~!
WHEN...
...DOES SHOOTING START?
Sob...
THE 15TH...
YOU'VE GOT TWO MORE DAYS...
Drama BOX"R"
fwap
HMM.
THEN...
...HOW ABOUT...
!
...YOU JUST...
...ACT HER THE WAY SHE IS?
shuu

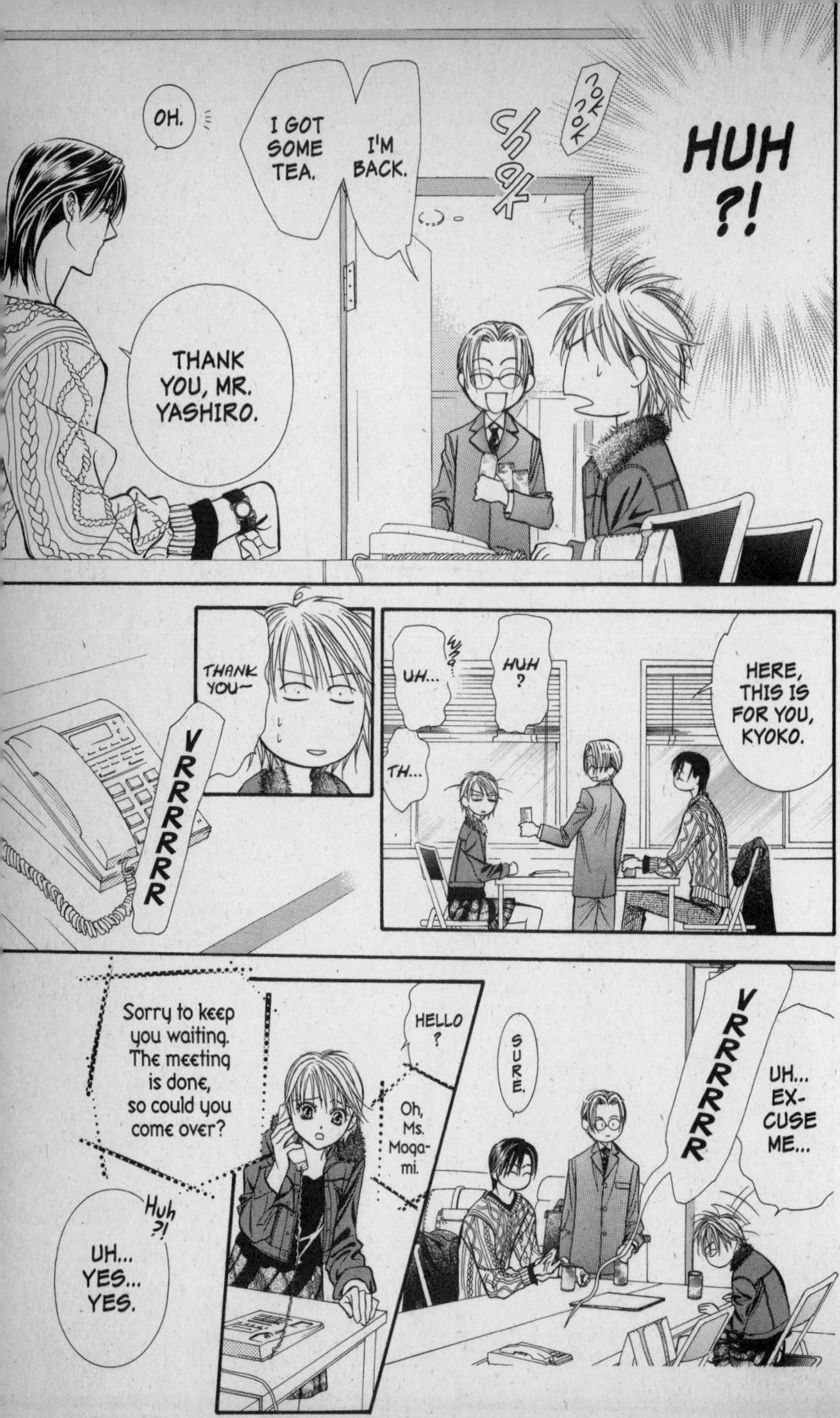
HUH ?!
nok nok
chak
I'M BACK.
I GOT SOME TEA.
OH.
THANK YOU, MR. YASHIRO.
HERE, THIS IS FOR YOU, KYOKO.
HUH ?
UH...
TH...
THANK YOU~
VRRRRRR
VRRRRRR
UH... EX- CUSE ME...
SURE.
HELLO ?
Oh, Ms. Moga- mi.
Sorry to keep you waiting. The meeting is done, so could you come over?
Huh ?!
UH... YES... YES.

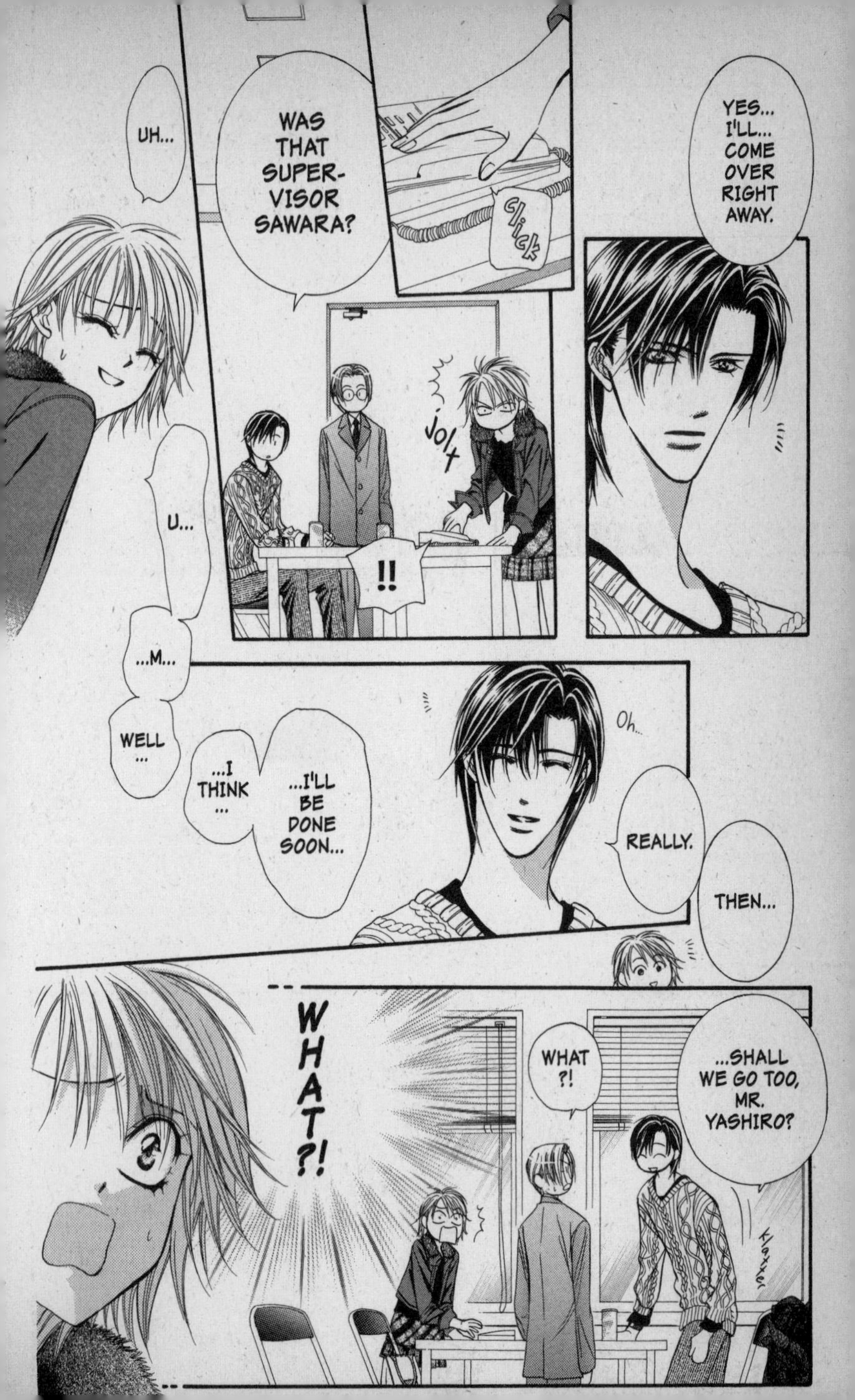

click
YES... I'LL... COME OVER RIGHT AWAY.
WAS THAT SUPER-VISOR SAWARA?
jolt
!!
UH...
U...
...M...
WELL...
...I THINK...
...I'LL BE DONE SOON...
Oh..
REALLY.
THEN...
...SHALL WE GO TOO, MR. YASHIRO?
WHAT ?!
WHAT ?!

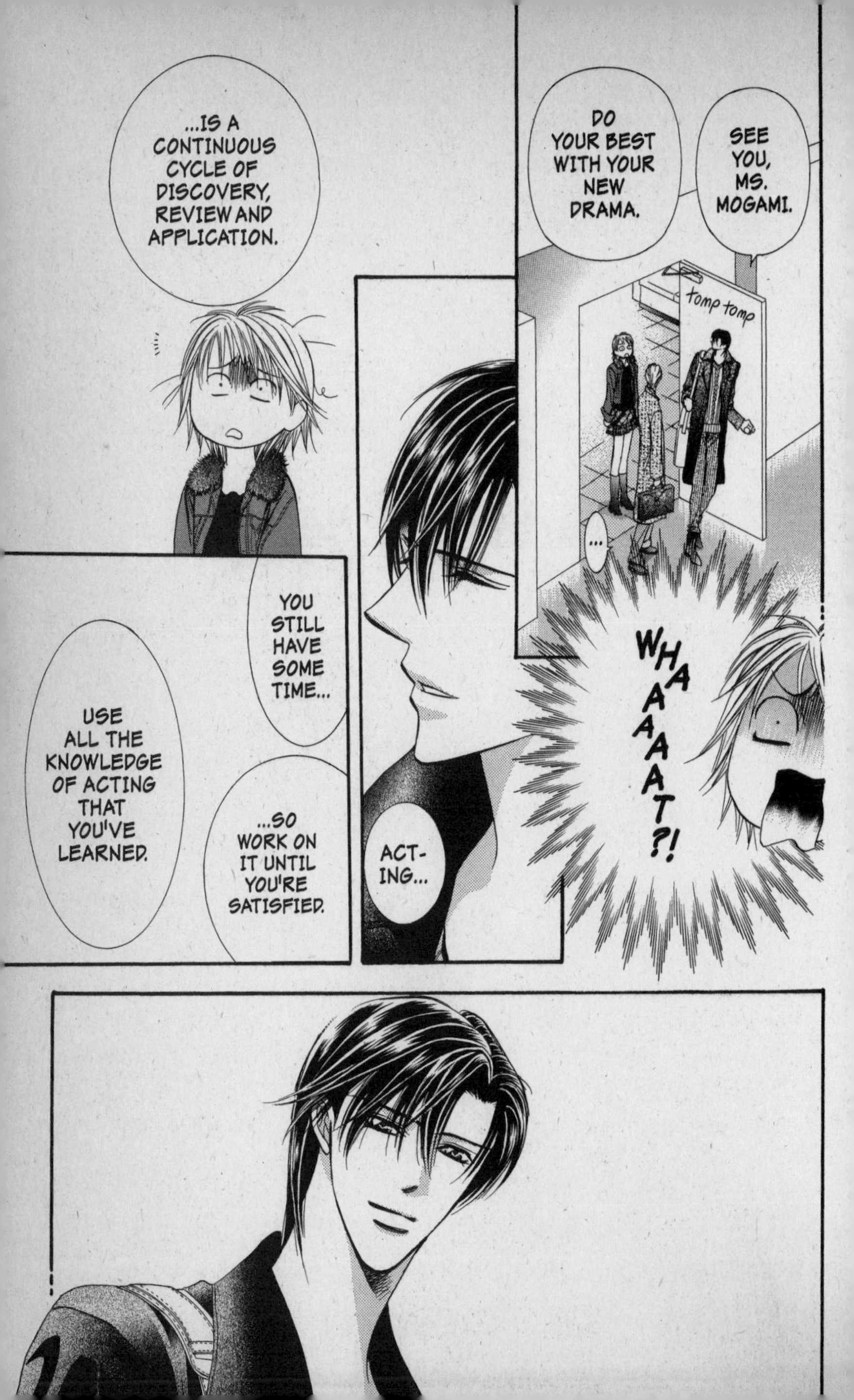
...IS A CONTINUOUS CYCLE OF DISCOVERY, REVIEW AND APPLICATION.
YOU STILL HAVE SOME TIME...
USE ALL THE KNOWLEDGE OF ACTING THAT YOU'VE LEARNED.
...SO WORK ON IT UNTIL YOU'RE SATISFIED.
ACT-ING...
DO YOUR BEST WITH YOUR NEW DRAMA.
SEE YOU, MS. MOGAMI.
tomp tomp
...
WHAAAAAT?!

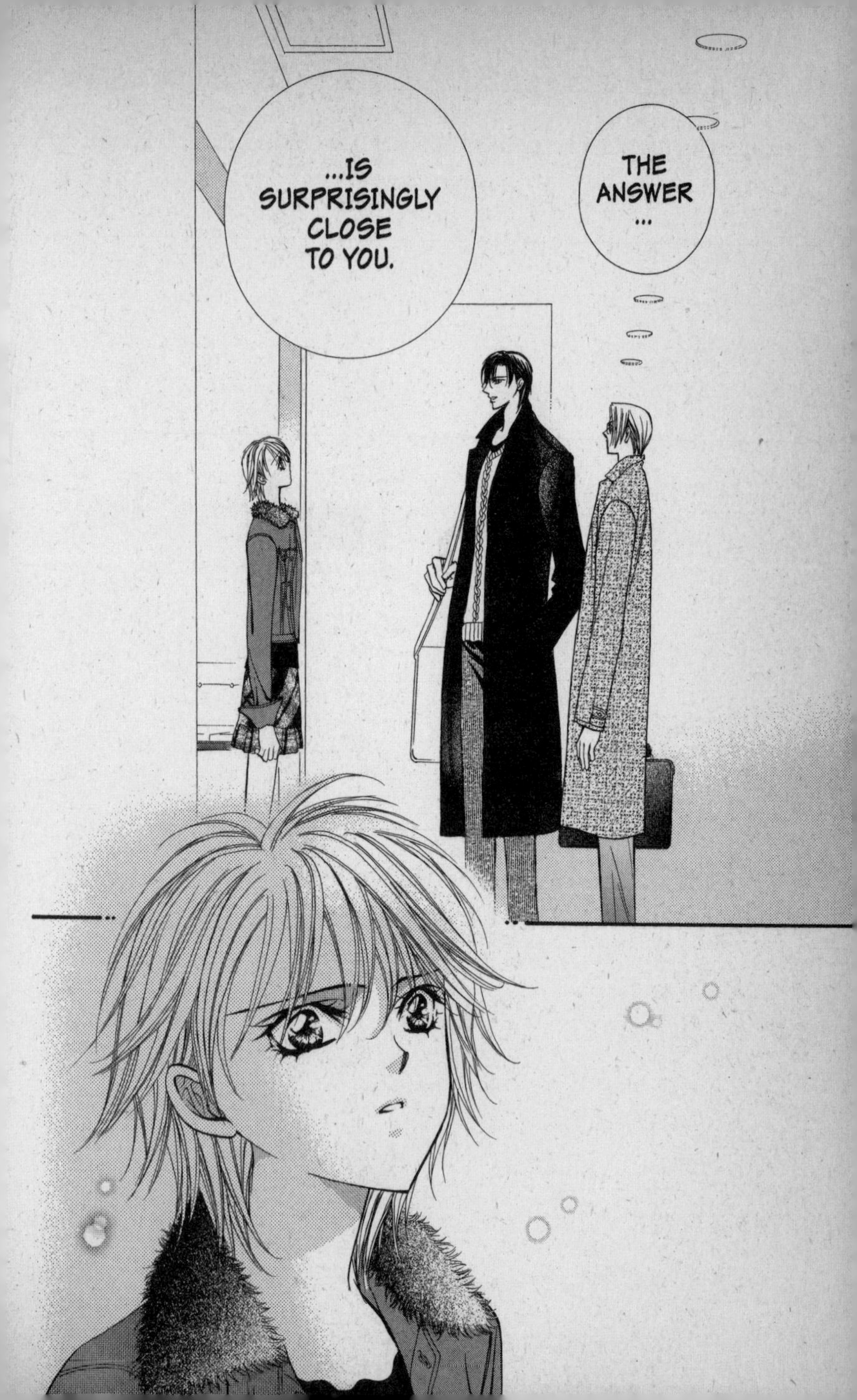
THE ANSWER ...
...IS SURPRISINGLY CLOSE TO YOU.

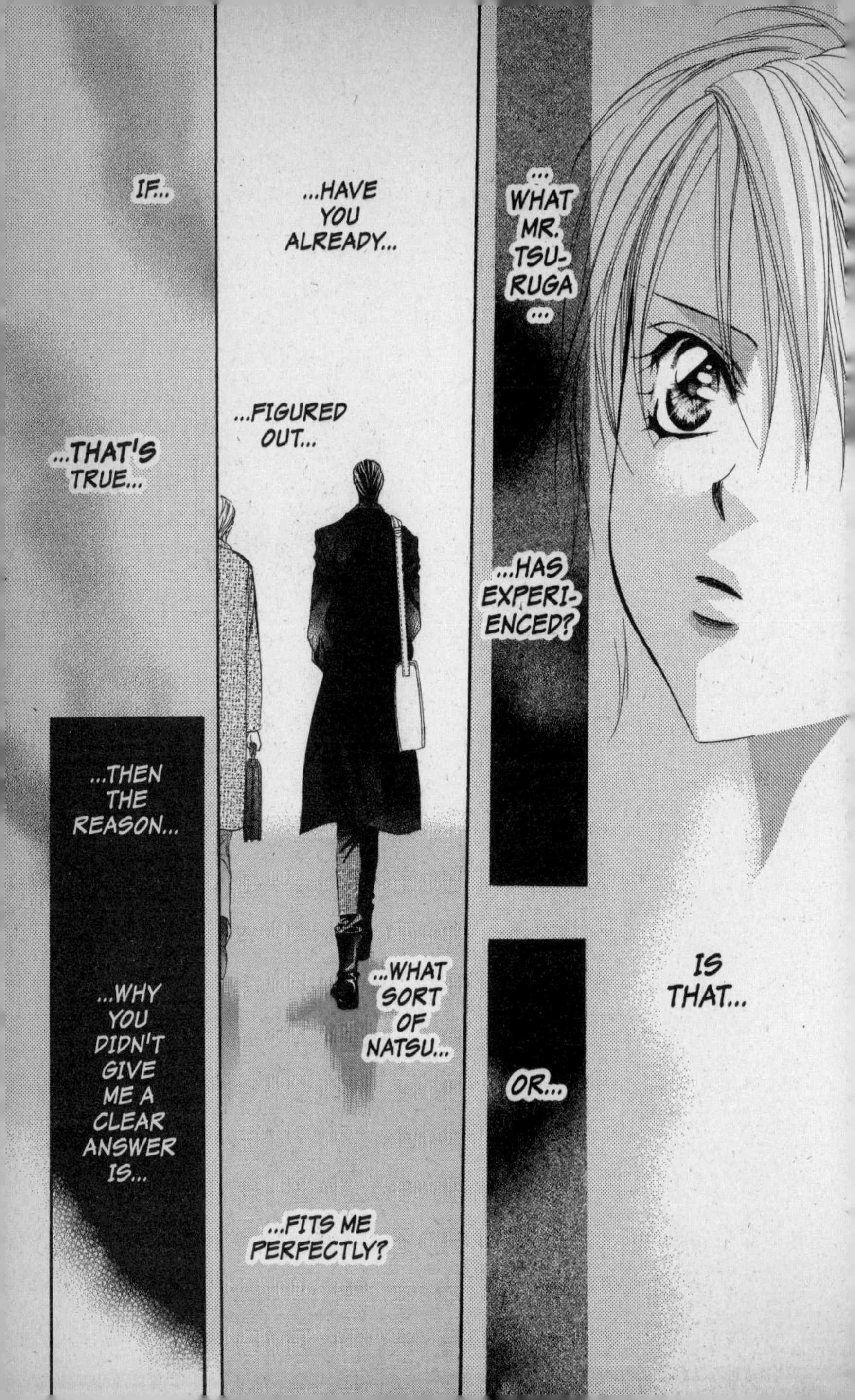

...WHAT MR. TSURUGA...
...HAS EXPERIENCED?
IS THAT...
OR...
...HAVE YOU ALREADY...
...FIGURED OUT...
...WHAT SORT OF NATSU...
...FITS ME PERFECTLY?
IF...
...THAT'S TRUE...
...THEN THE REASON...
...WHY YOU DIDN'T GIVE ME A CLEAR ANSWER IS...

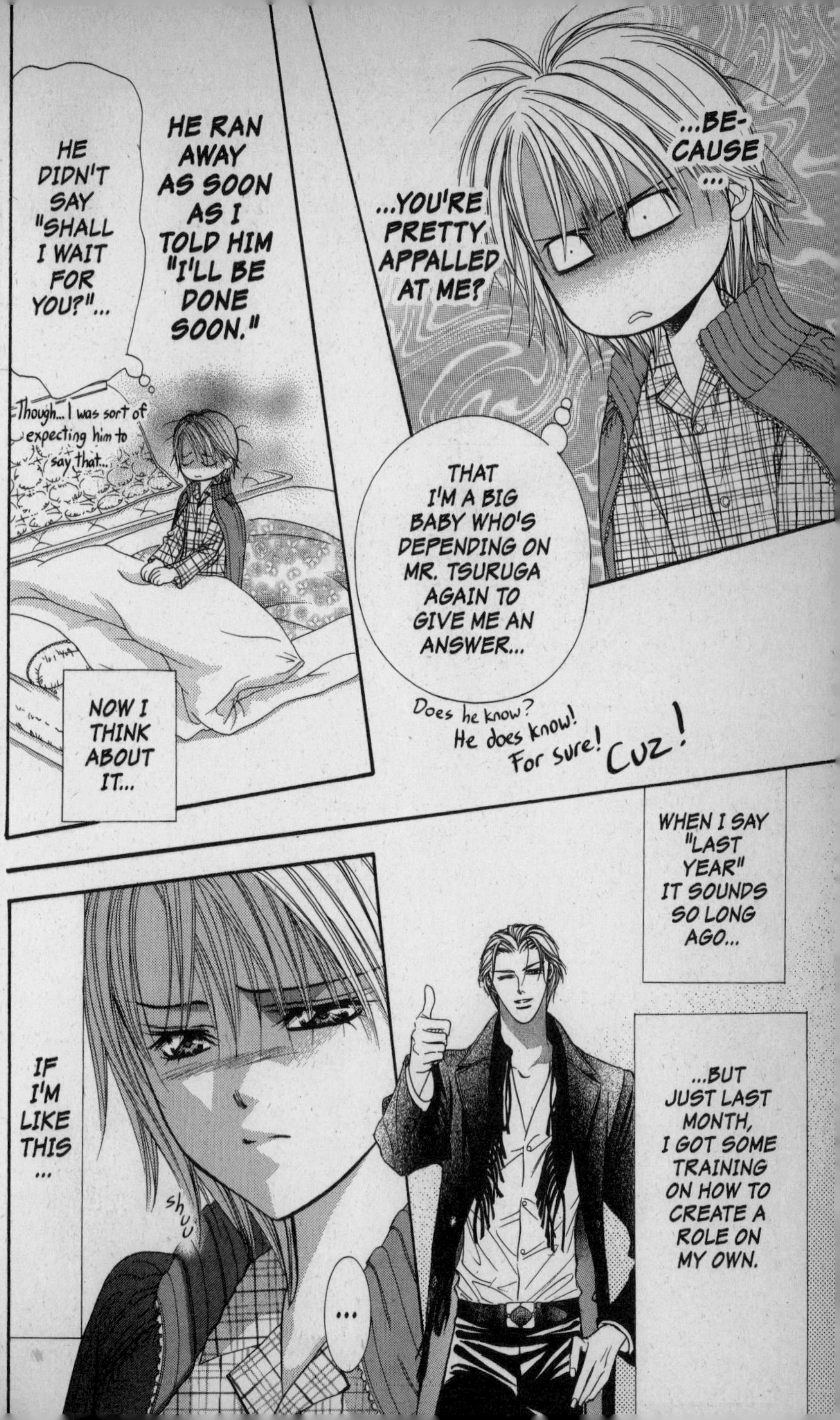
...BE-CAUSE...
...YOU'RE PRETTY APPALLED AT ME?
THAT I'M A BIG BABY WHO'S DEPENDING ON MR. TSURUGA AGAIN TO GIVE ME AN ANSWER...
Does he know? He does know! For sure!
CUZ!
HE RAN AWAY AS SOON AS I TOLD HIM "I'LL BE DONE SOON."
HE DIDN'T SAY "SHALL I WAIT FOR YOU?"...
Though... I was sort of expecting him to say that...
NOW I THINK ABOUT IT...
WHEN I SAY "LAST YEAR" IT SOUNDS SO LONG AGO...
...BUT JUST LAST MONTH, I GOT SOME TRAINING ON HOW TO CREATE A ROLE ON MY OWN.
IF I'M LIKE THIS...
SHUU
...

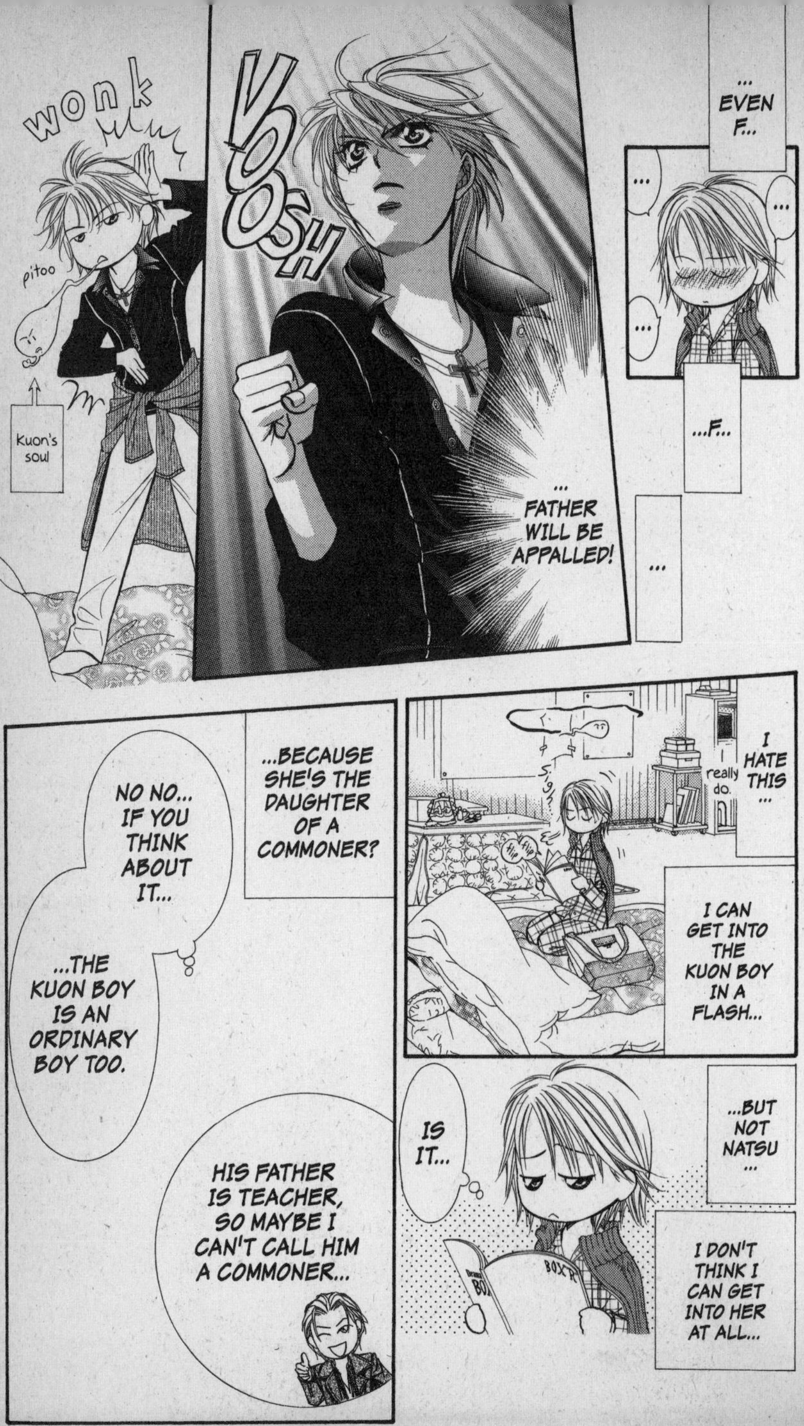

...EVEN F...
...
...
...
...F...
...
VOOSH
...FATHER WILL BE APPALLED!
wonk
pitoo
Kuon's soul
I HATE THIS...
I really do.
I CAN GET INTO THE KUON BOY IN A FLASH...
...BUT NOT NATSU...
I DON'T THINK I CAN GET INTO HER AT ALL...
IS IT...
BOX R
...BECAUSE SHE'S THE DAUGHTER OF A COMMONER?
NO NO... IF YOU THINK ABOUT IT...
...THE KUON BOY IS AN ORDINARY BOY TOO.
HIS FATHER IS TEACHER, SO MAYBE I CAN'T CALL HIM A COMMONER...

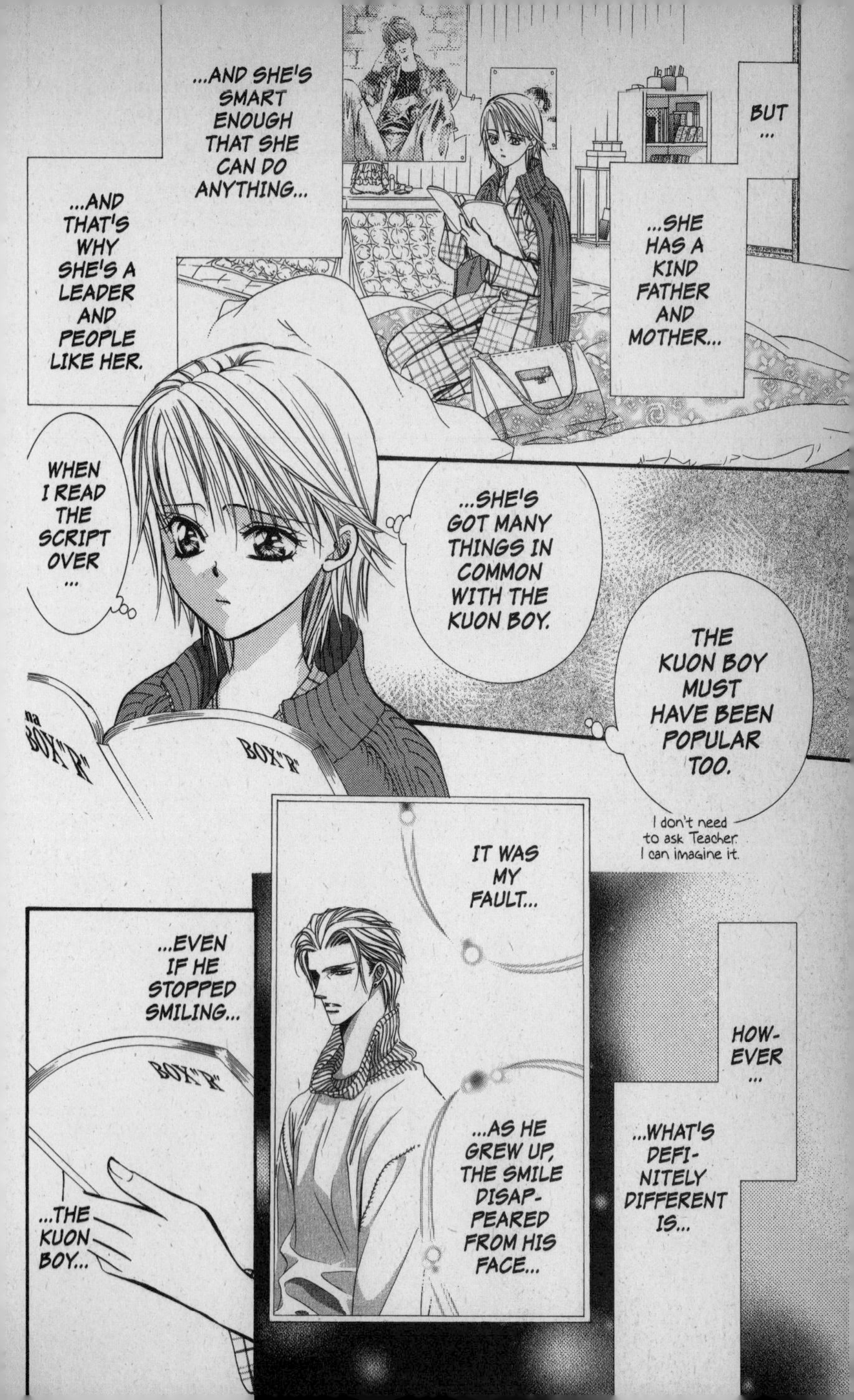
BUT ...
...SHE HAS A KIND FATHER AND MOTHER...
...AND SHE'S SMART ENOUGH THAT SHE CAN DO ANYTHING...
...AND THAT'S WHY SHE'S A LEADER AND PEOPLE LIKE HER.
WHEN I READ THE SCRIPT OVER ...
...SHE'S GOT MANY THINGS IN COMMON WITH THE KUON BOY.
THE KUON BOY MUST HAVE BEEN POPULAR TOO.
I don't need to ask Teacher. I can imagine it.
BOX"R"
HOW-EVER ...
...WHAT'S DEFI-NITELY DIFFERENT IS...
IT WAS MY FAULT...
...AS HE GREW UP, THE SMILE DISAP-PEARED FROM HIS FACE...
...EVEN IF HE STOPPED SMILING...
...THE KUON BOY...

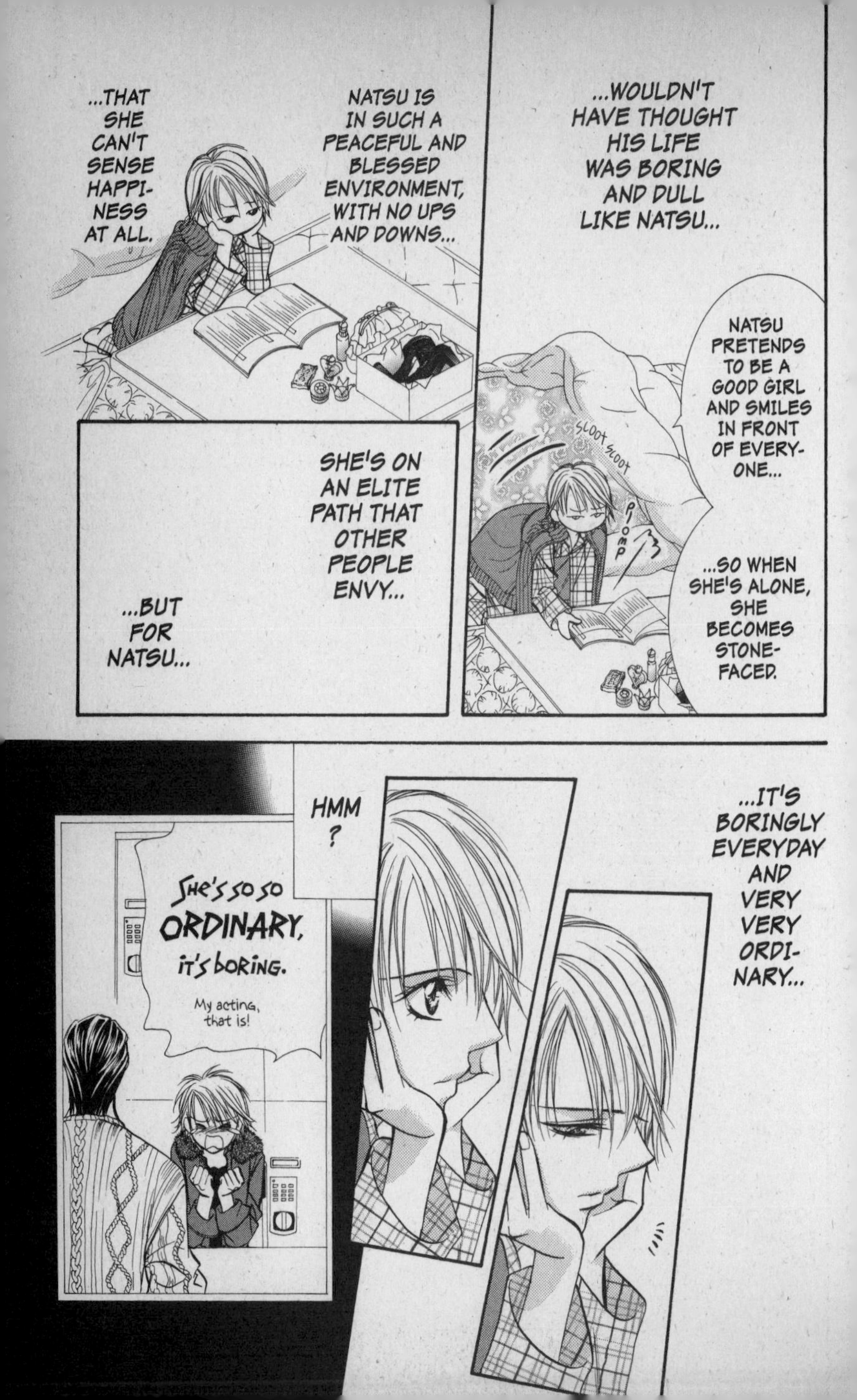
...WOULDN'T HAVE THOUGHT HIS LIFE WAS BORING AND DULL LIKE NATSU...
NATSU PRETENDS TO BE A GOOD GIRL AND SMILES IN FRONT OF EVERY-ONE...
SCOOT SCOOT
PLOMP
...SO WHEN SHE'S ALONE, SHE BECOMES STONE-FACED.
NATSU IS IN SUCH A PEACEFUL AND BLESSED ENVIRONMENT, WITH NO UPS AND DOWNS...
...THAT SHE CAN'T SENSE HAPPI-NESS AT ALL.
SHE'S ON AN ELITE PATH THAT OTHER PEOPLE ENVY...
...BUT FOR NATSU...
...IT'S BORINGLY EVERYDAY AND VERY VERY ORDI-NARY...
HMM ?
She's so so ORDINARY, it's boring.
My acting, that is!

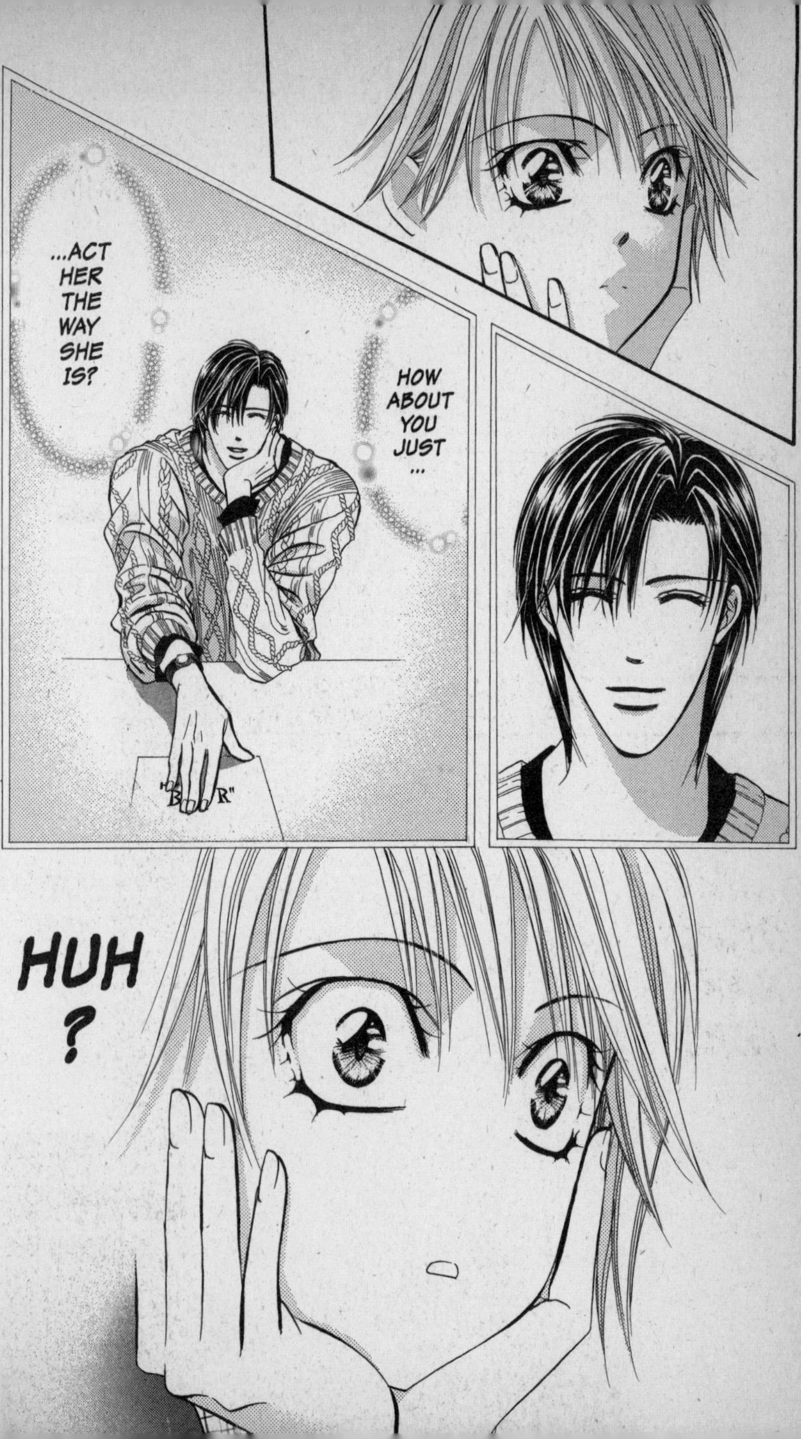
HOW ABOUT YOU JUST ...
...ACT HER THE WAY SHE IS?
HUH ?

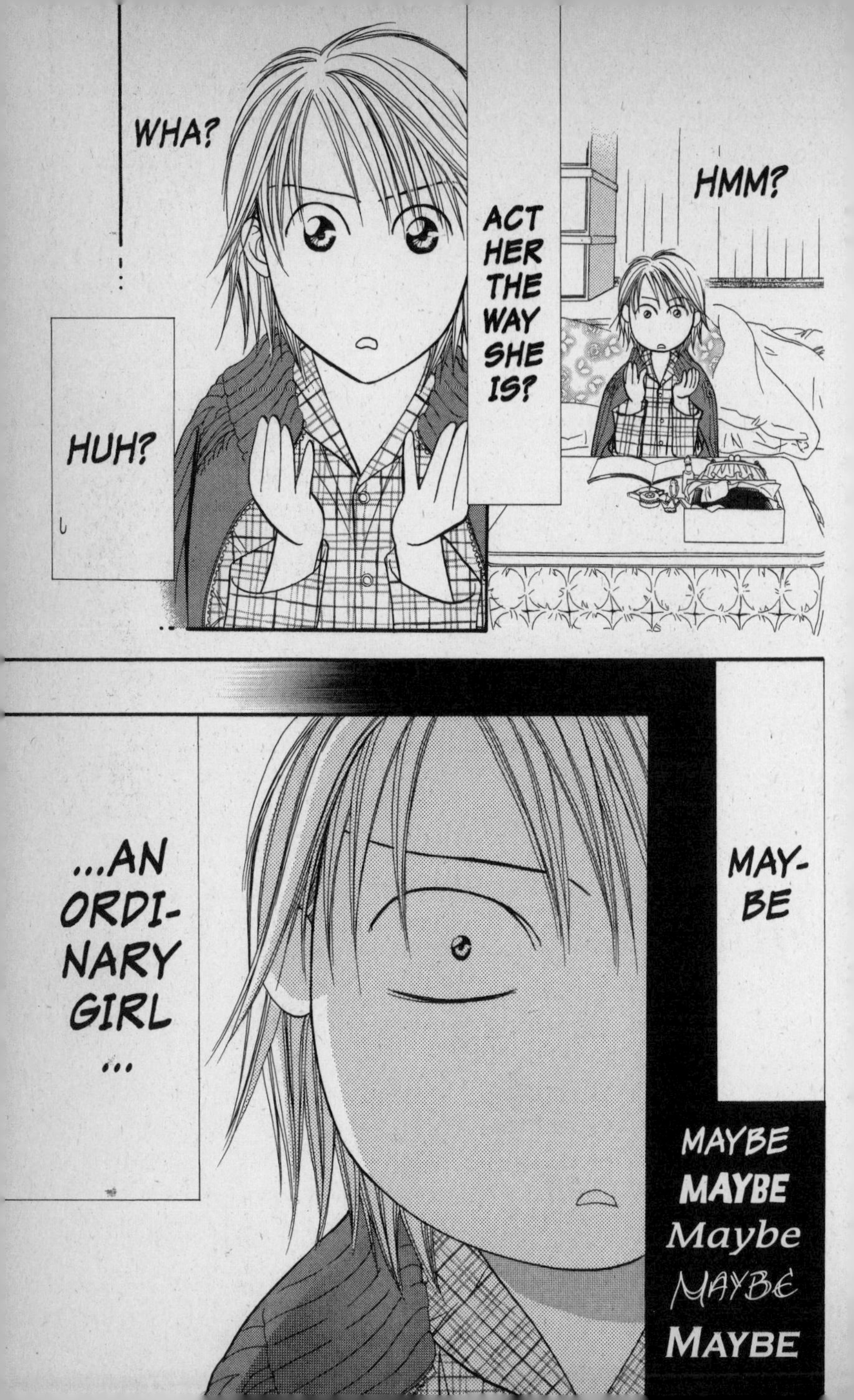
HMM?
ACT HER THE WAY SHE IS?
WHA? ...
HUH?
MAY-BE
...AN ORDINARY GIRL ...
MAYBE MAYBE Maybe MAYBE MAYBE

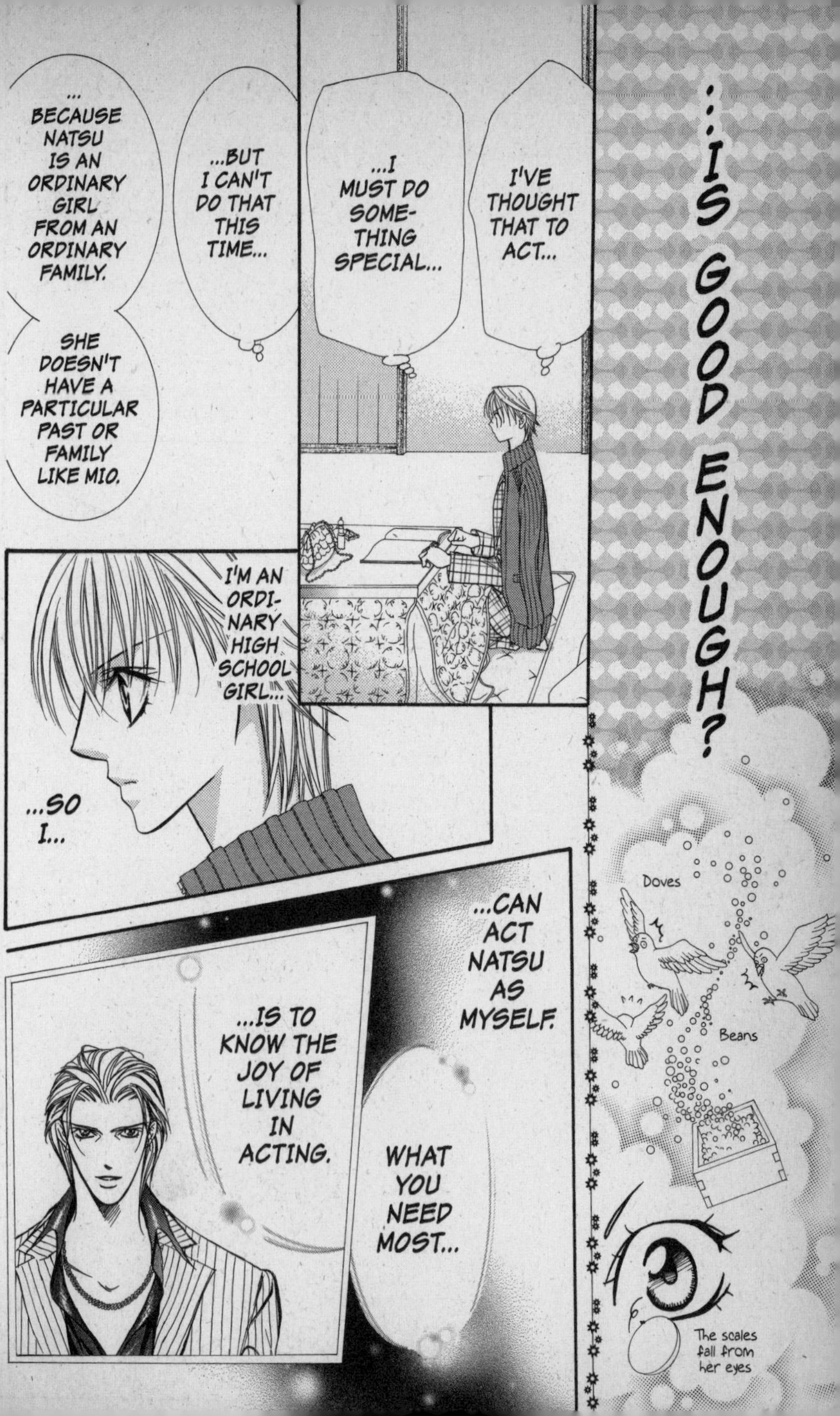
I'VE THOUGHT THAT TO ACT...
...I MUST DO SOME-THING SPECIAL...
...BUT I CAN'T DO THAT THIS TIME...
...BECAUSE NATSU IS AN ORDINARY GIRL FROM AN ORDINARY FAMILY.
SHE DOESN'T HAVE A PARTICULAR PAST OR FAMILY LIKE MIO.
I'M AN ORDI-NARY HIGH SCHOOL GIRL...
...SO I...
...CAN ACT NATSU AS MYSELF.
WHAT YOU NEED MOST...
...IS TO KNOW THE JOY OF LIVING IN ACTING.
...IS GOOD ENOUGH?
Doves
Beans
The scales fall from her eyes

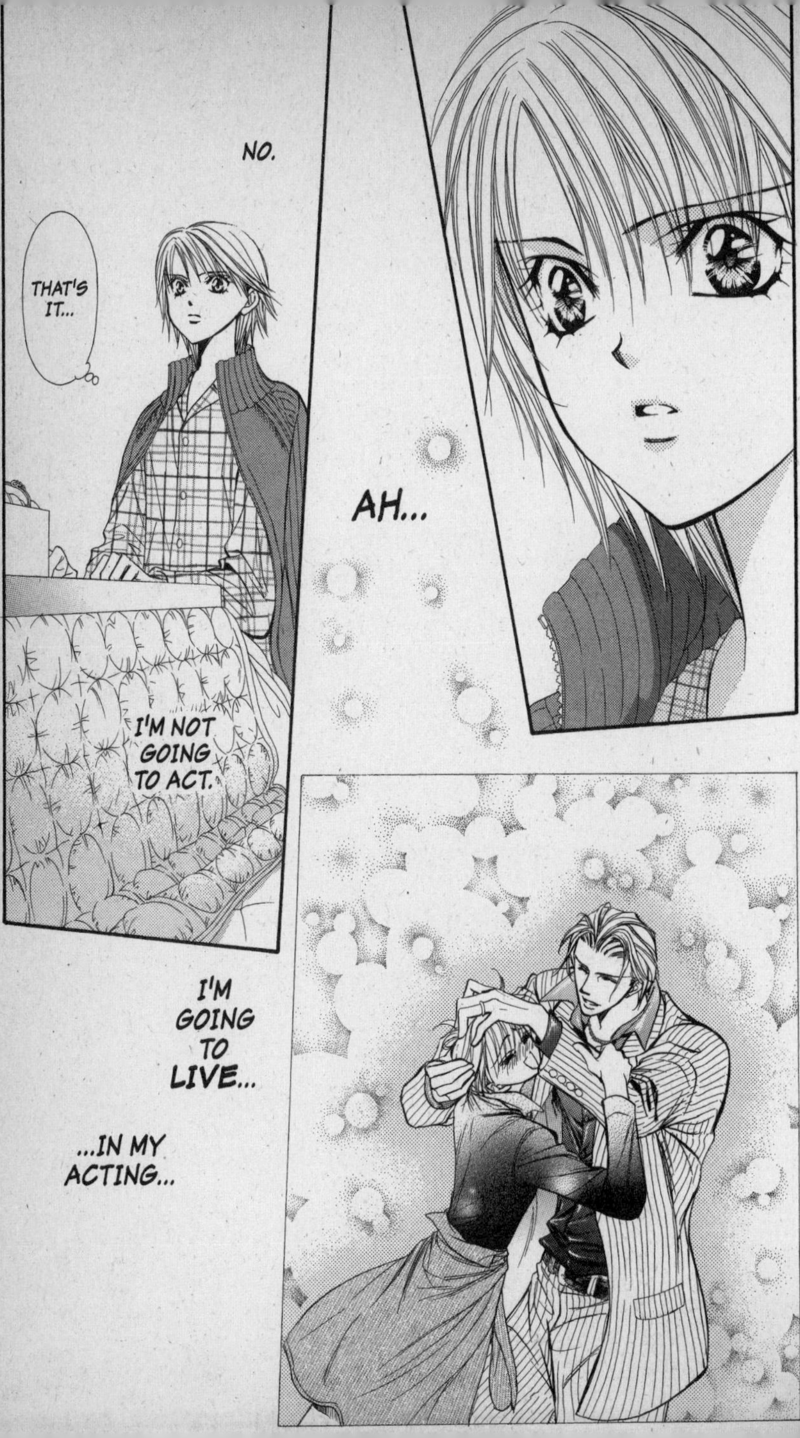
AH...
NO.
THAT'S IT...
I'M NOT GOING TO ACT.
I'M GOING TO LIVE...
...IN MY ACTING...

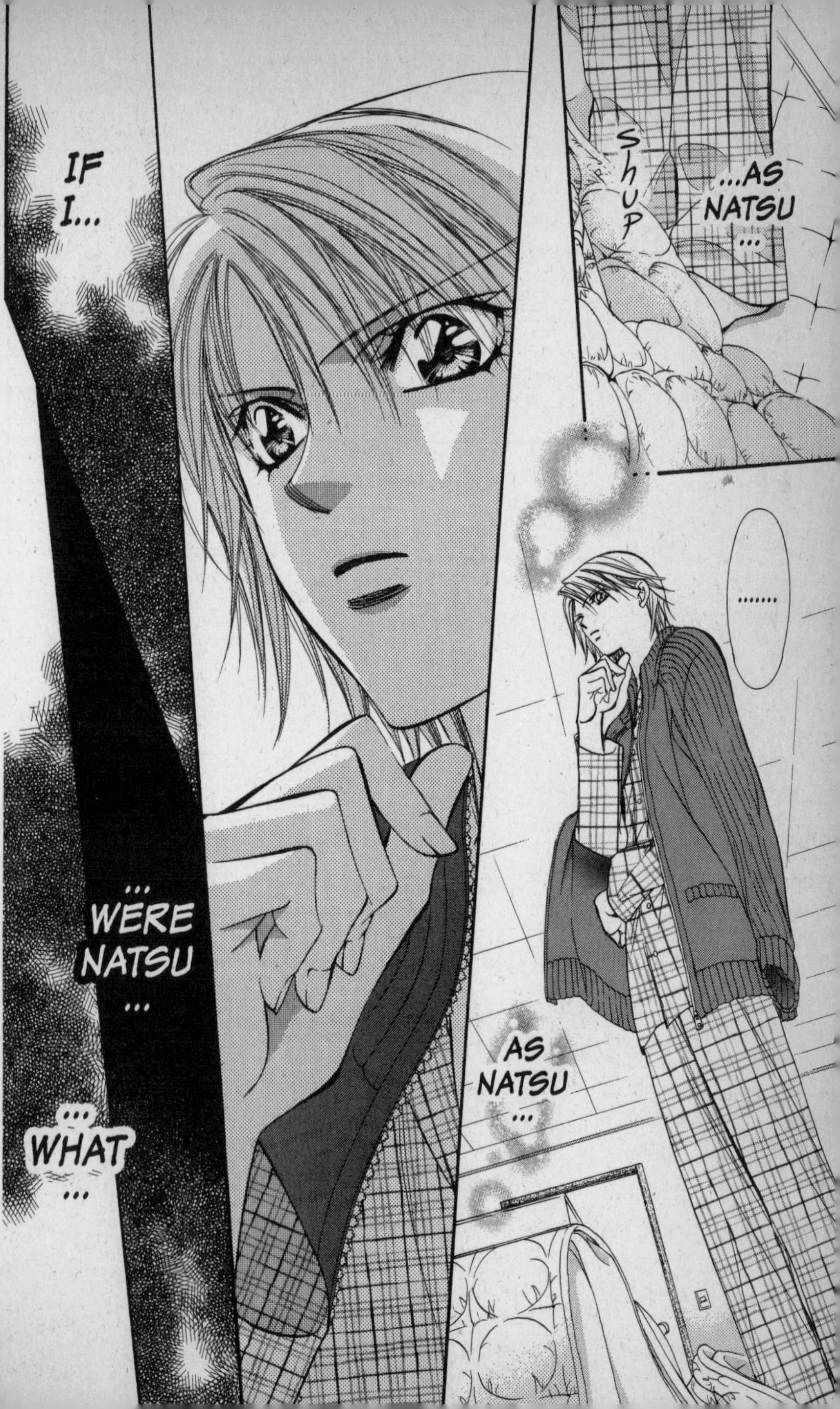
...AS NATSU ...
SHUP
......
AS NATSU ...
IF I...
...WERE NATSU ...
...WHAT ...

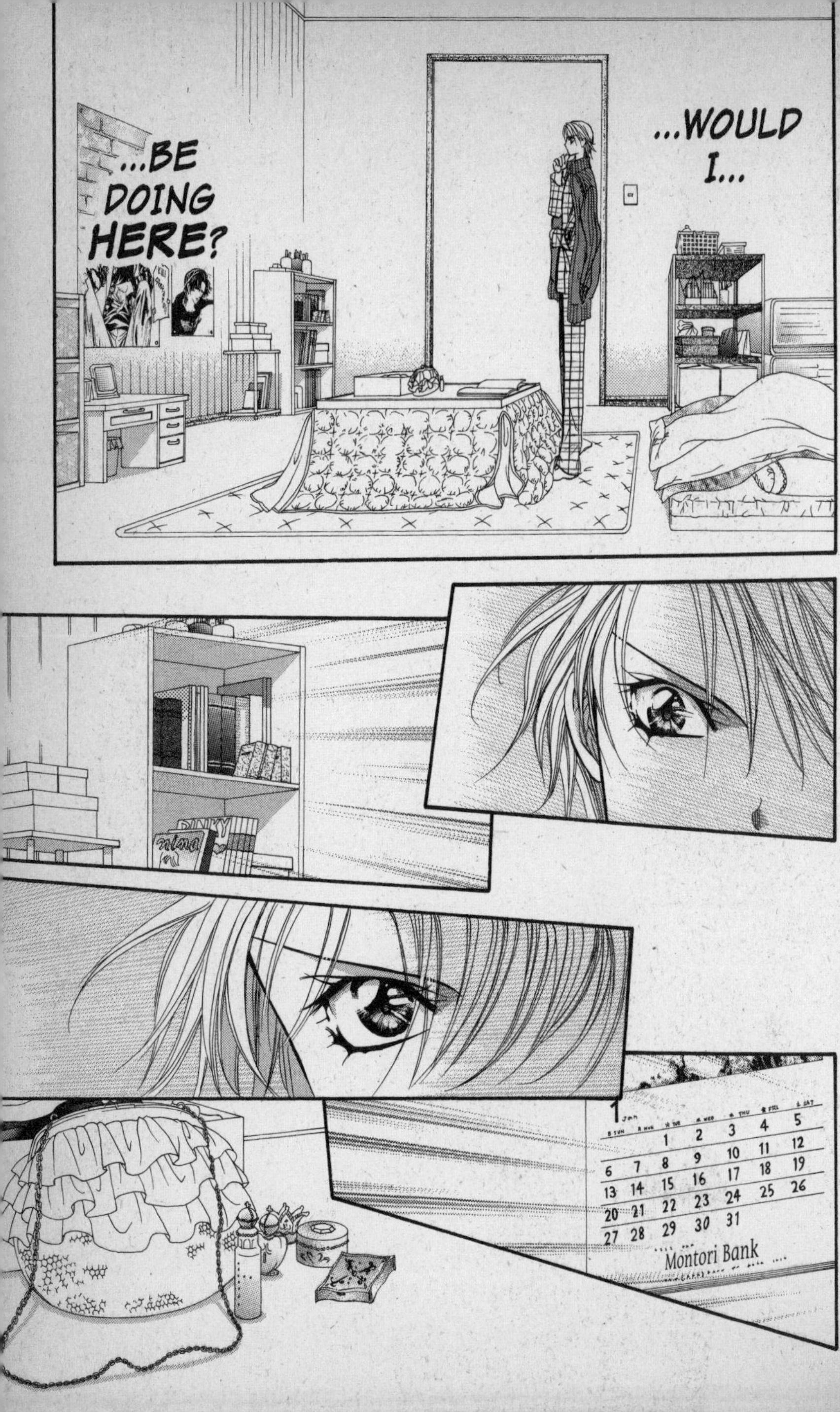
...WOULD I...
...BE DOING HERE?
Montori Bank

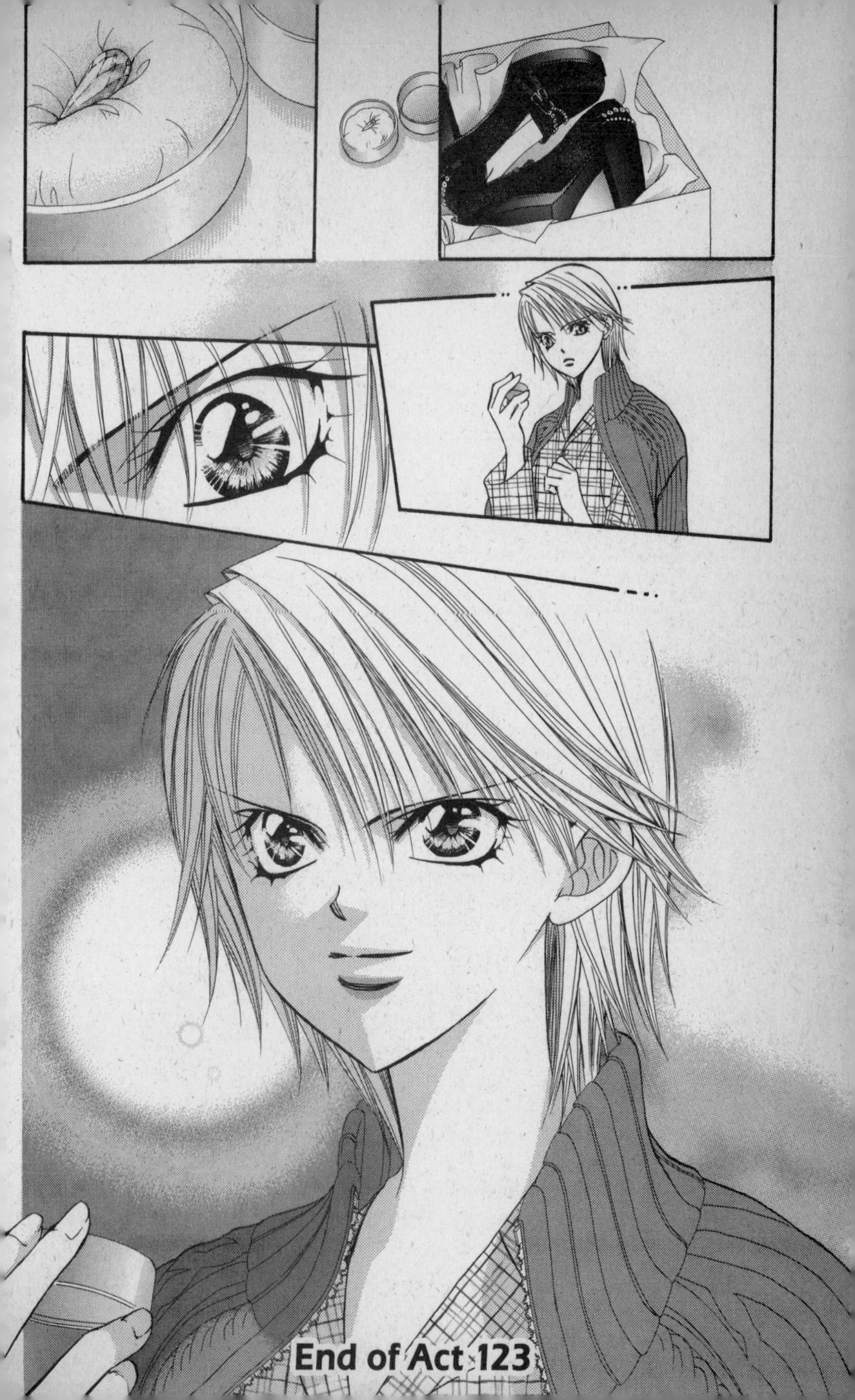
...
...
End of Act 123

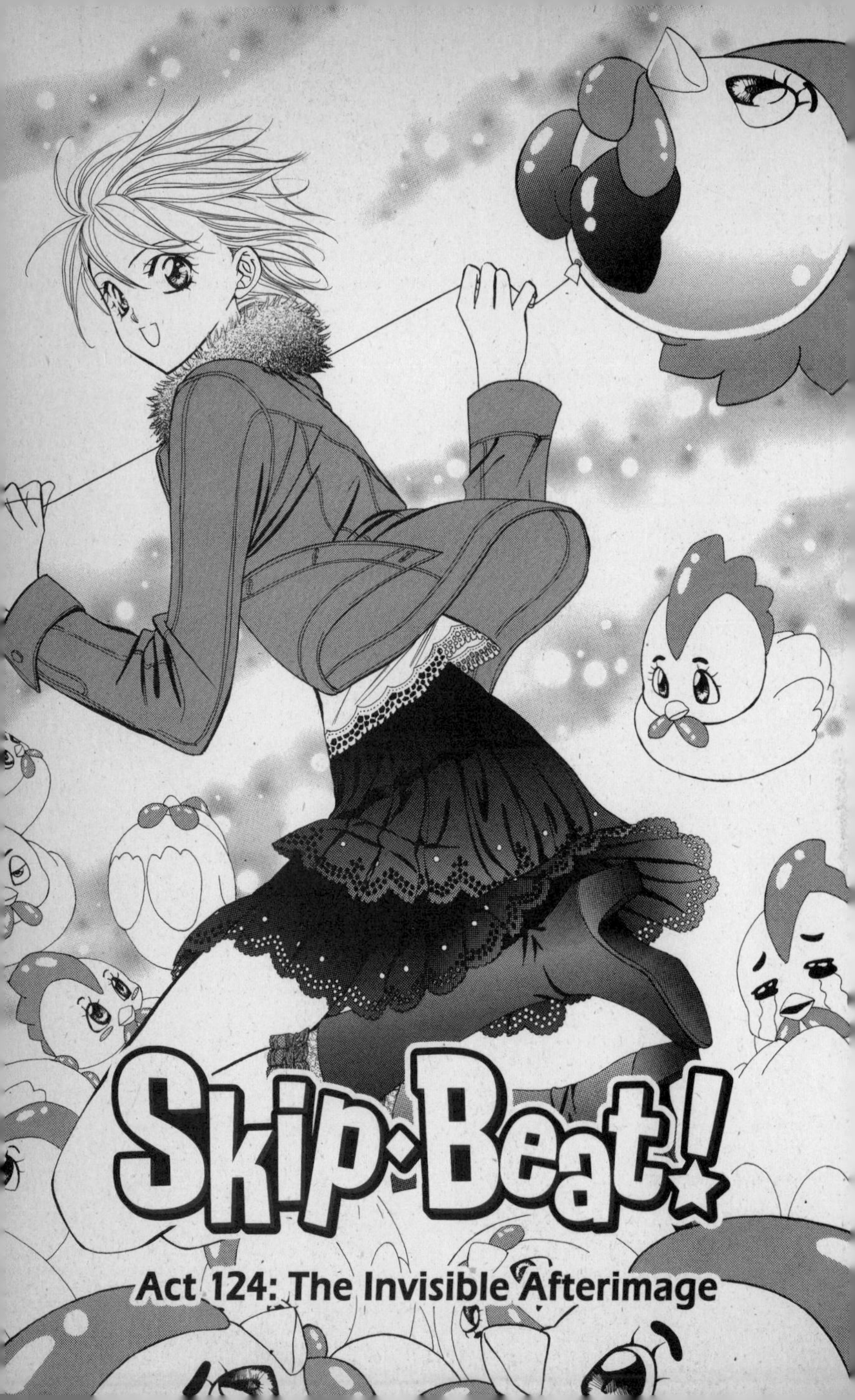

Skip·Beat!
Act 124: The Invisible Afterimage

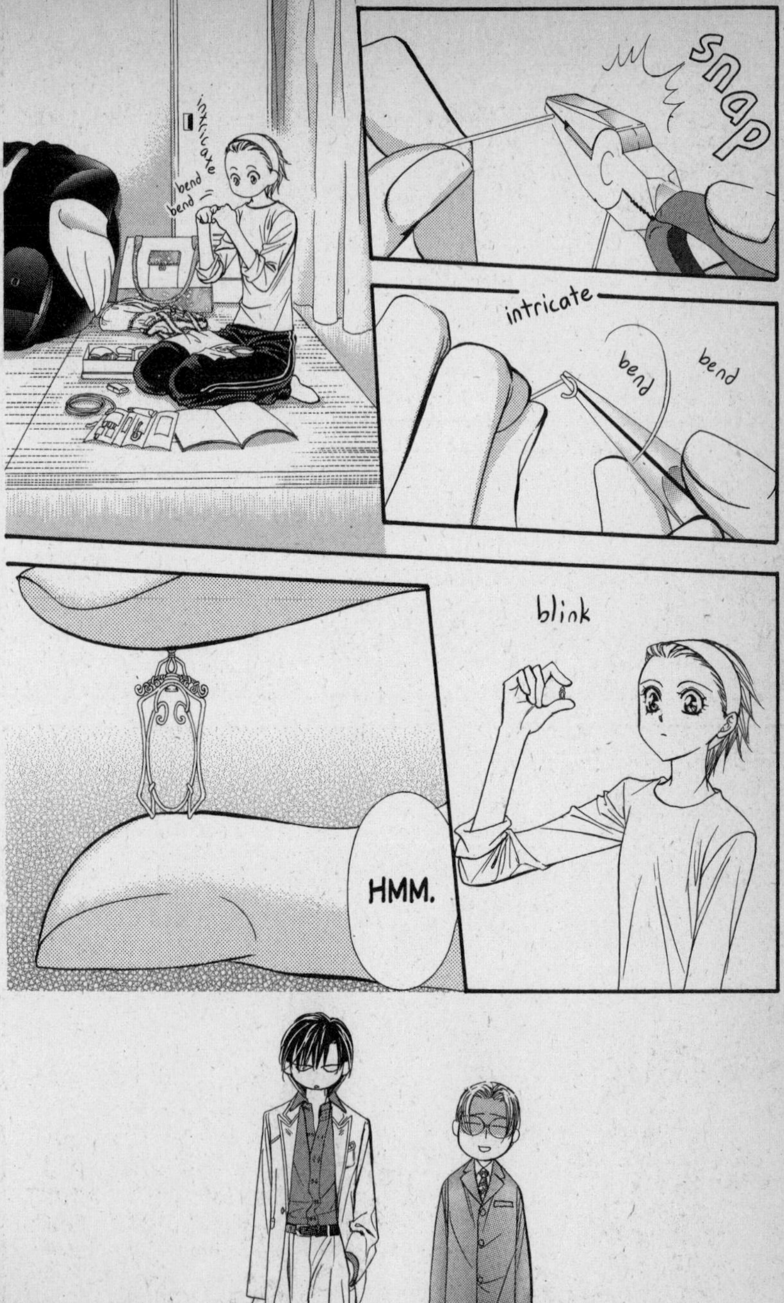
snap
intricate
bend
bend
intricate
bend
bend
blink
HMM.

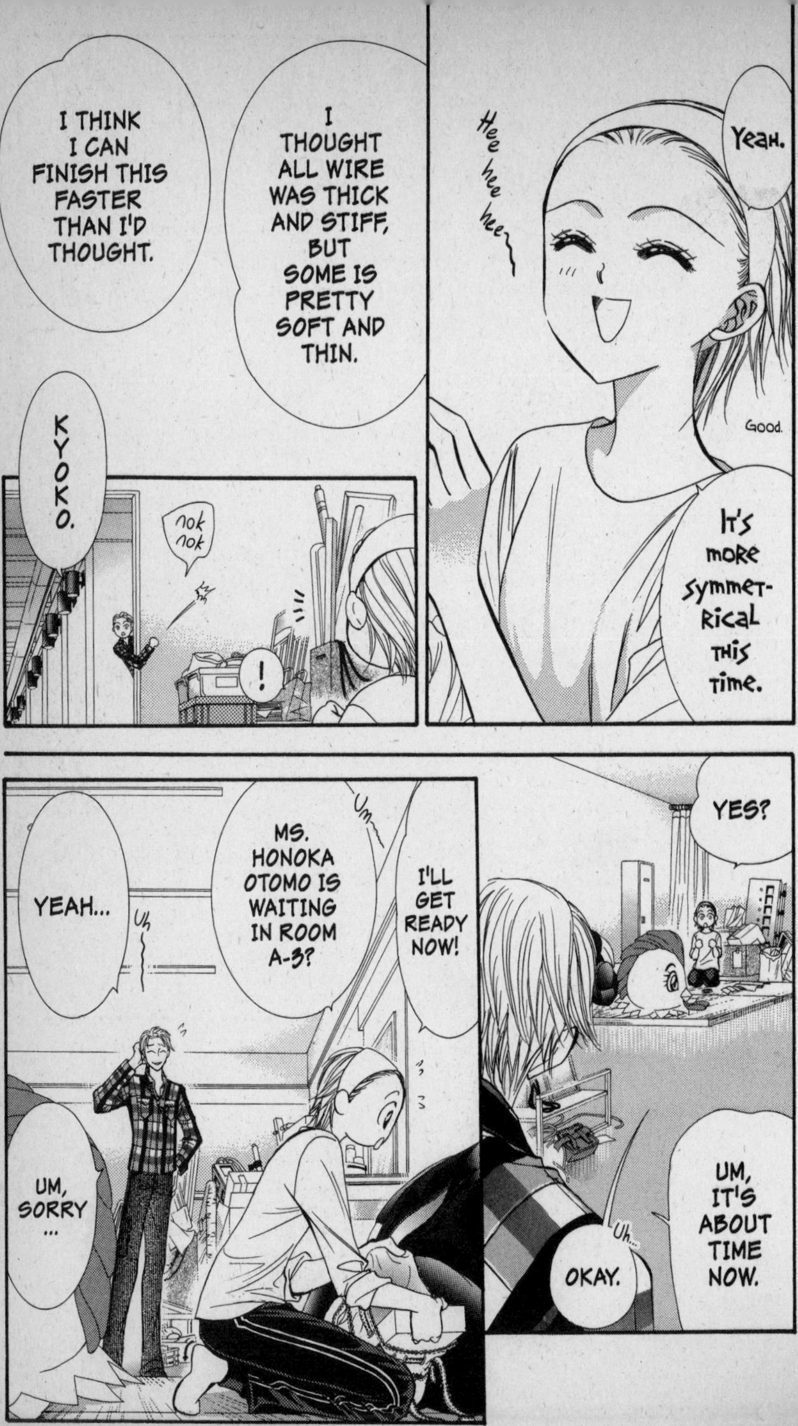
Yeah.
Hee hee hee
Good.
It's more symmetrical this time.
I thought all wire was thick and stiff, but some is pretty soft and thin.
I think I can finish this faster than I'd thought.
Kyoko.
nok nok
!
Yes?
Um, it's about time now.
Uh...
Okay.
Um
Ms. Honoka Otomo is waiting in room A-3?
I'll get ready now!
Yeah...
Uh
Um, sorry...

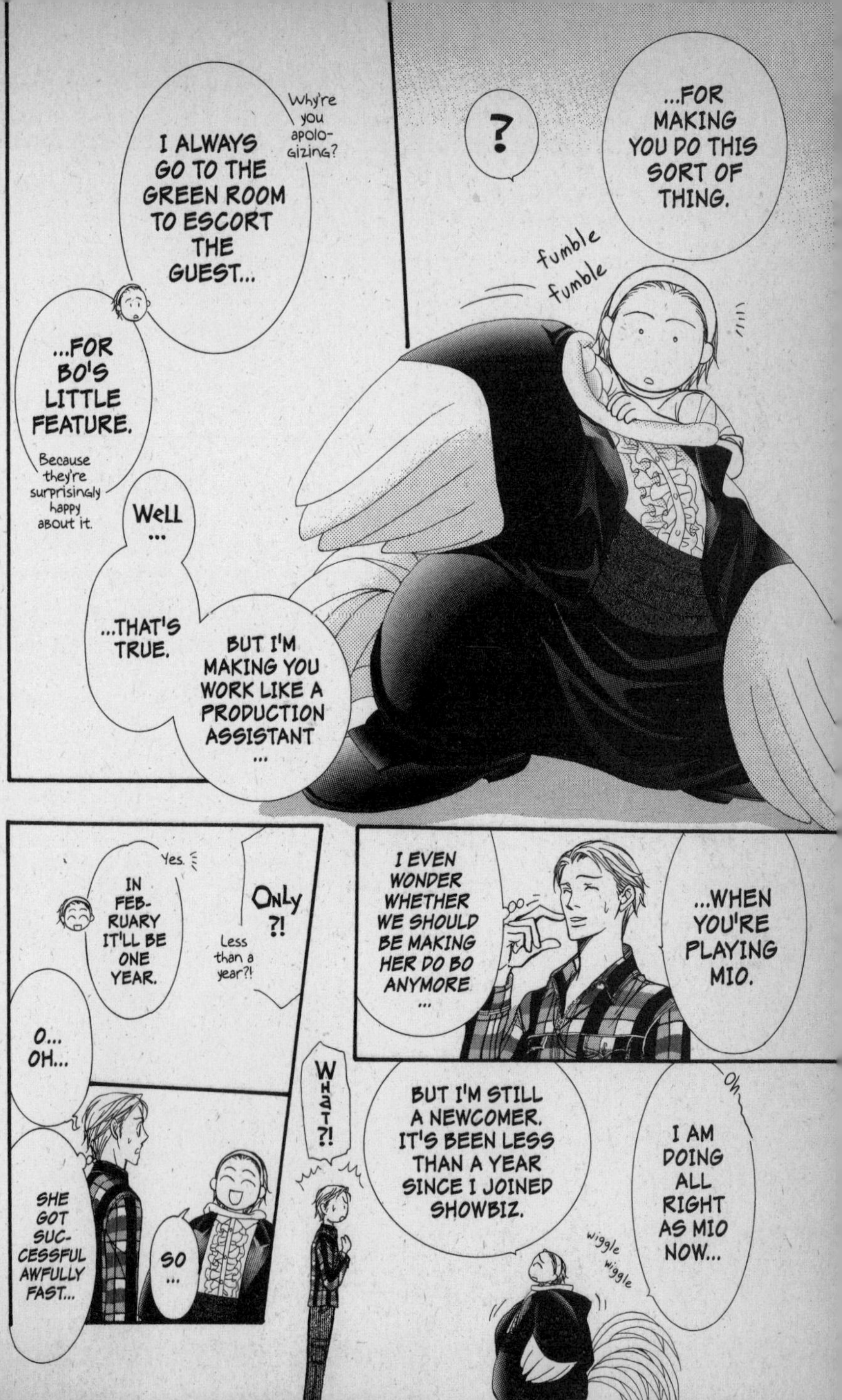
...FOR MAKING YOU DO THIS SORT OF THING.
?
fumble fumble
I ALWAYS GO TO THE GREEN ROOM TO ESCORT THE GUEST...
Why're you apolo-gizing?
...FOR BO'S LITTLE FEATURE.
Because they're surprisingly happy about it.
Well...
...THAT'S TRUE.
BUT I'M MAKING YOU WORK LIKE A PRODUCTION ASSISTANT...
...WHEN YOU'RE PLAYING MIO.
I EVEN WONDER WHETHER WE SHOULD BE MAKING HER DO BO ANYMORE...
Oh
I AM DOING ALL RIGHT AS MIO NOW...
wiggle wiggle
BUT I'M STILL A NEWCOMER. IT'S BEEN LESS THAN A YEAR SINCE I JOINED SHOWBIZ.
WHAT?!
Only?!
Less than a year?!
Yes.
IN FEB-RUARY IT'LL BE ONE YEAR.
O... OH...
SO...
SHE GOT SUC-CESSFUL AWFULLY FAST...

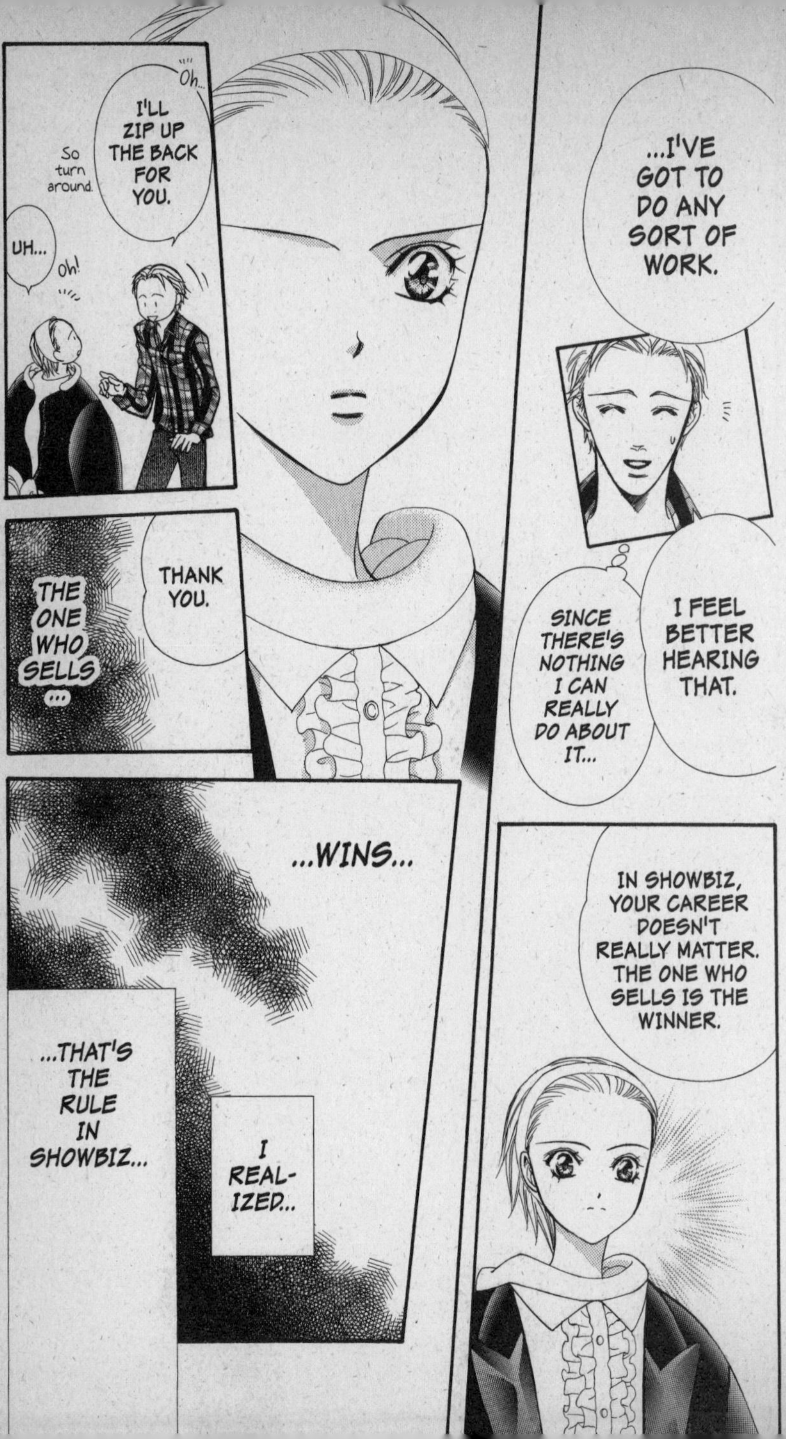
...I'VE GOT TO DO ANY SORT OF WORK.
I FEEL BETTER HEARING THAT.
SINCE THERE'S NOTHING I CAN REALLY DO ABOUT IT...
IN SHOWBIZ, YOUR CAREER DOESN'T REALLY MATTER. THE ONE WHO SELLS IS THE WINNER.
Oh...
I'LL ZIP UP THE BACK FOR YOU.
So turn around.
UH...
Oh!
THANK YOU.
THE ONE WHO SELLS...
...WINS...
...THAT'S THE RULE IN SHOWBIZ...
I REALIZED...

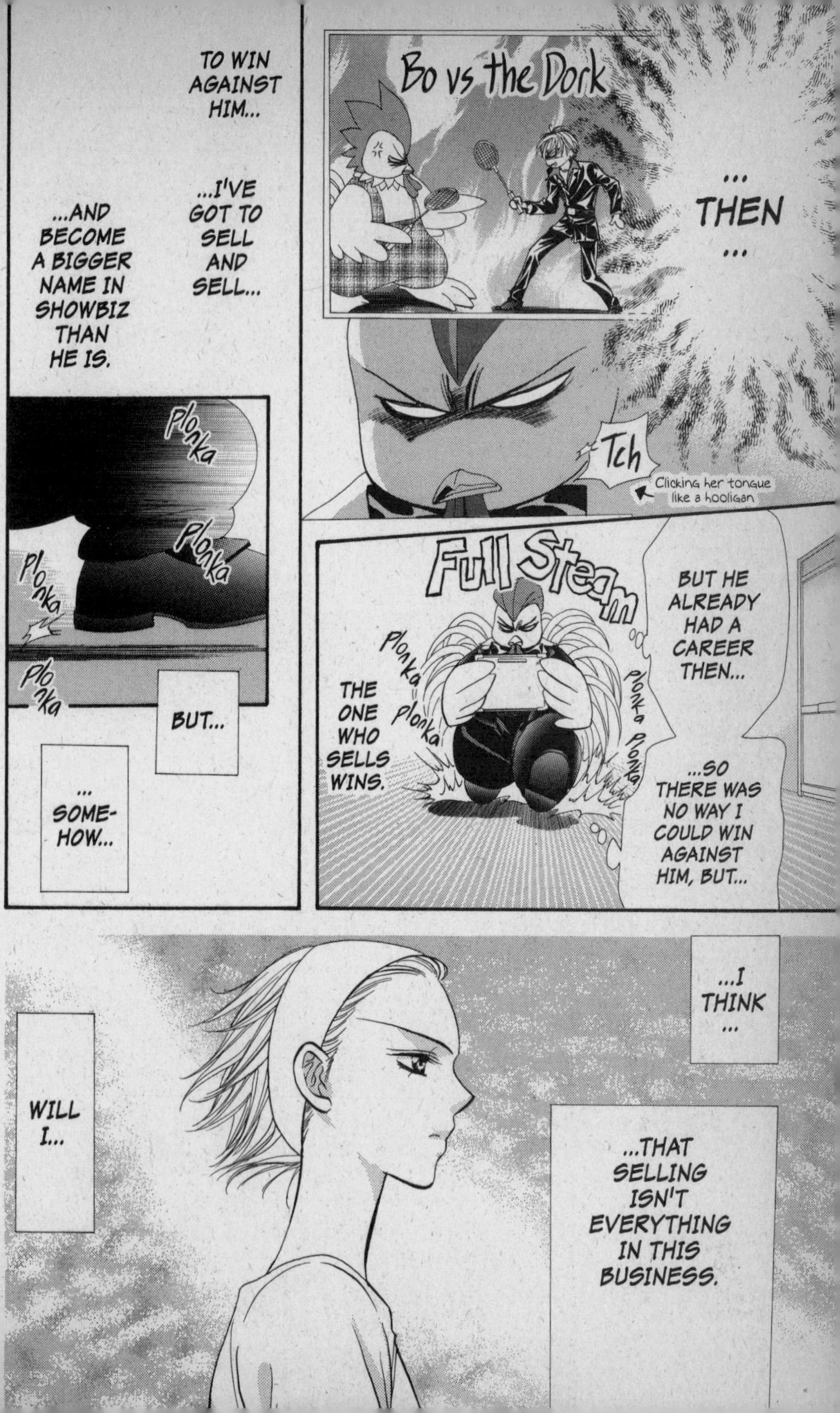
Bo vs the Dork
... THEN ...
Tch
Clicking her tongue like a hooligan
TO WIN AGAINST HIM...
...I'VE GOT TO SELL AND SELL...
...AND BECOME A BIGGER NAME IN SHOWBIZ THAN HE IS.
Full Steam
BUT HE ALREADY HAD A CAREER THEN...
...SO THERE WAS NO WAY I COULD WIN AGAINST HIM, BUT...
Plonka Plonka
THE ONE WHO SELLS WINS.
Plonka
Plonka
Plonka
Plonka
Plonka
Plonka
BUT...
... SOME-HOW...
...I THINK ...
...THAT SELLING ISN'T EVERYTHING IN THIS BUSINESS.
WILL I...

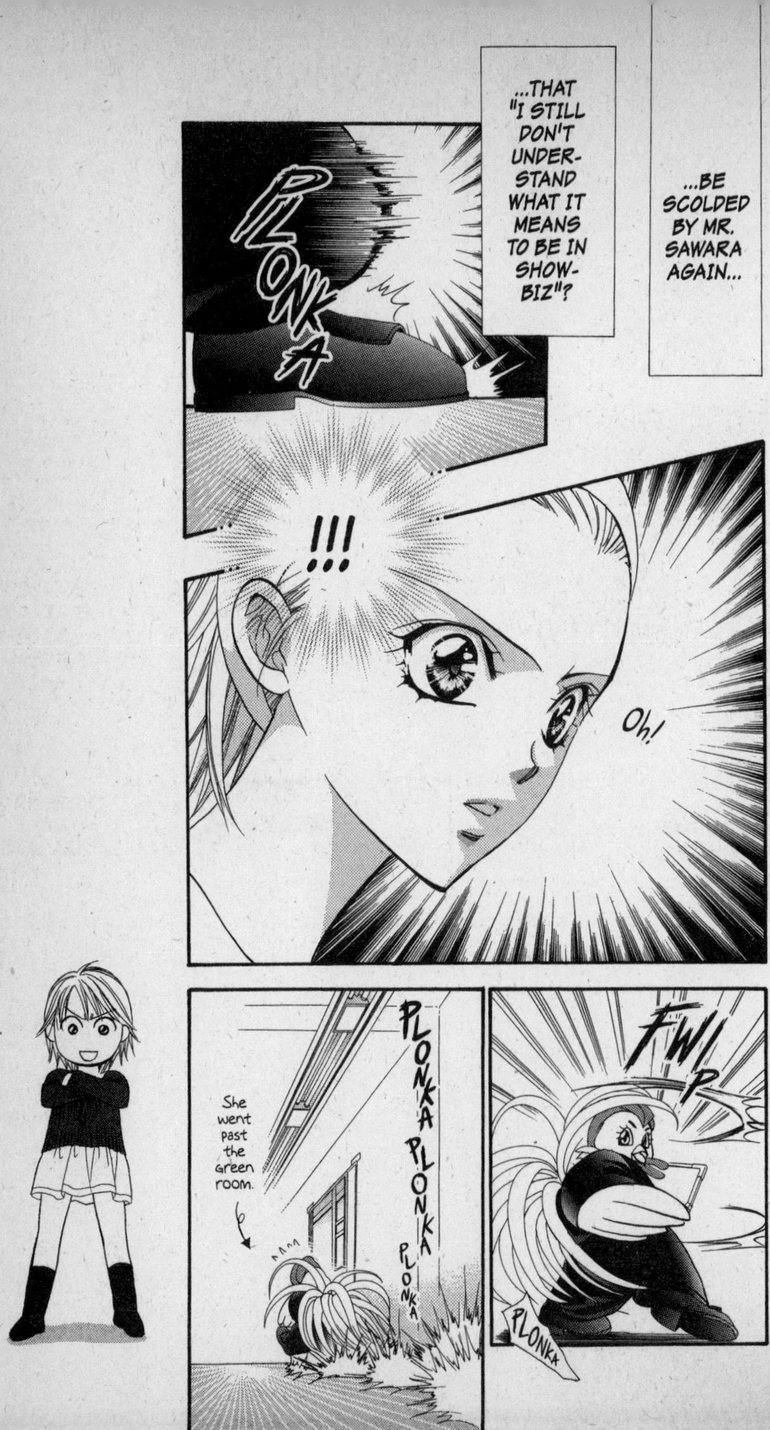
...BE SCOLDED BY MR. SAWARA AGAIN...
...THAT "I STILL DON'T UNDER-STAND WHAT IT MEANS TO BE IN SHOW-BIZ"?
PLONKA
!!!
Oh!
FWIP
PLONKA
PLONKA
PLONKA
PLONKA
She went past the green room.

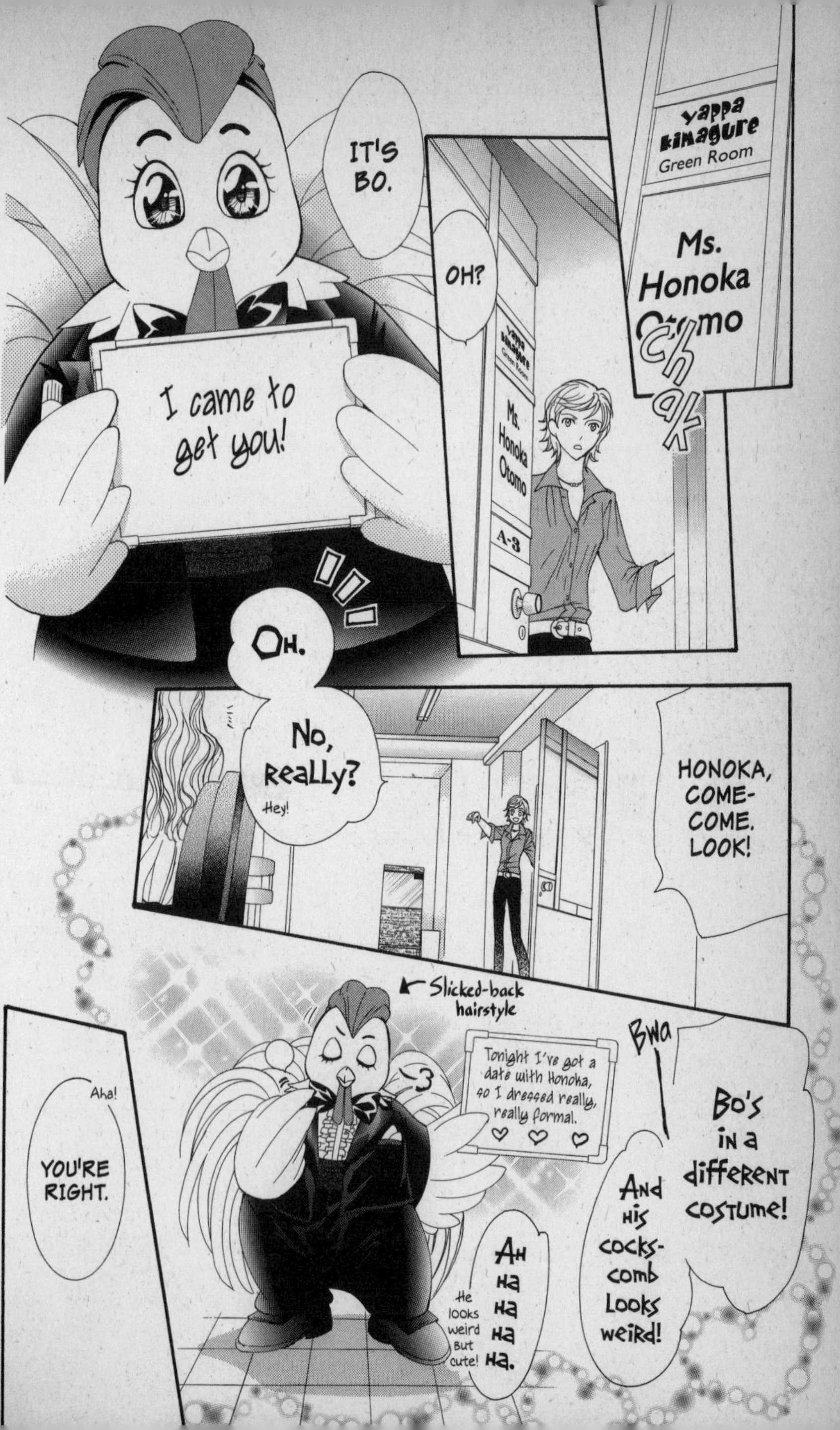
yappa kimagure
Green Room
Ms. Honoka Otomo
Chak
yappa kimagure
Green Room
Ms. Honoka Otomo
A-3
OH?
IT'S BO.
I came to get you!
OH.
HONOKA, COME-COME. LOOK!
No, really?
Hey!
Bwa
Bo's in a different costume!
And his cockscomb looks weird!
Ah ha ha ha ha.
He looks weird but cute!
Slicked-back hairstyle
Tonight I've got a date with Honoka, so I dressed really, really formal.
Aha!
YOU'RE RIGHT.

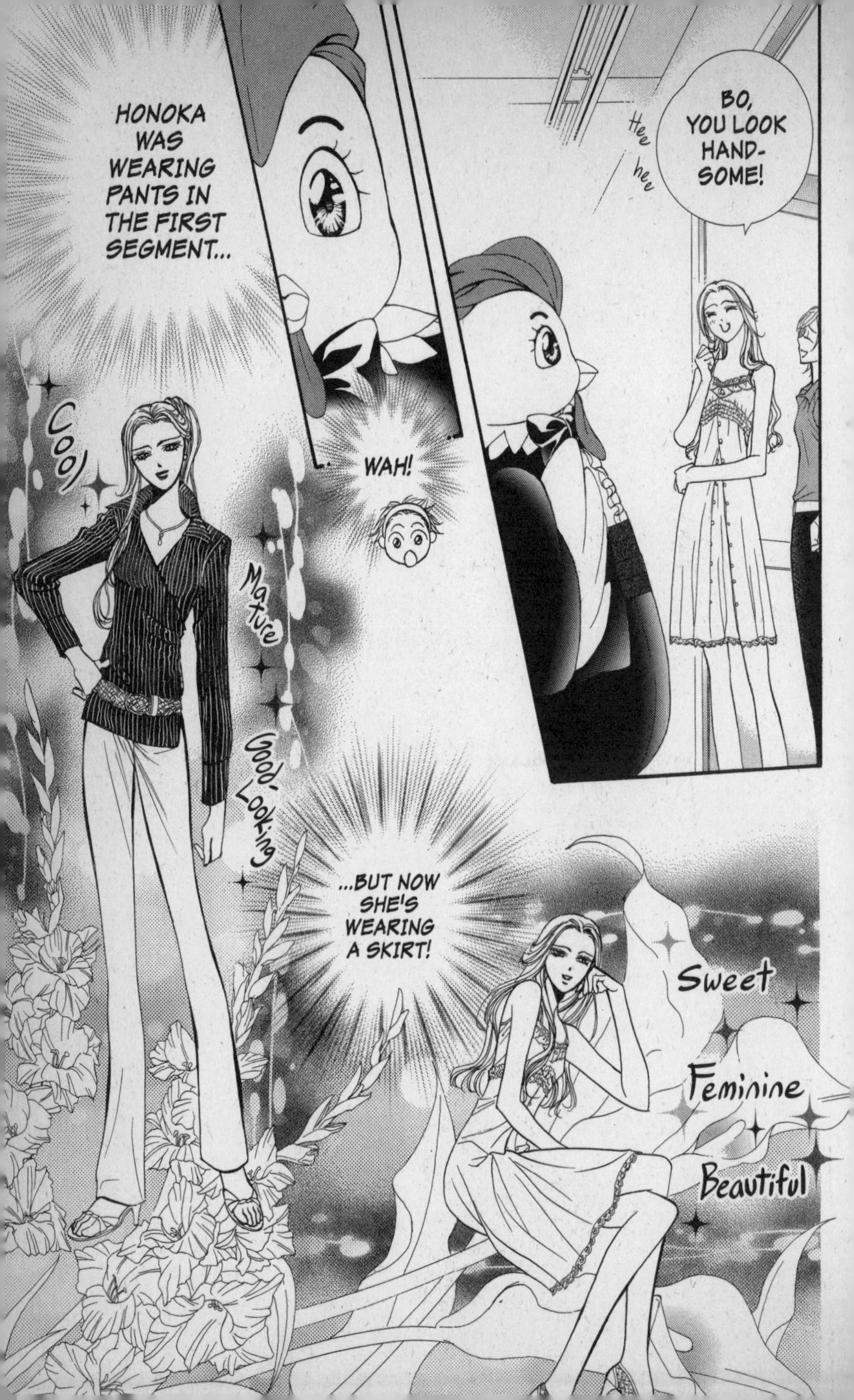
Hee hee
BO, YOU LOOK HAND-SOME!
WAH!
HONOKA WAS WEARING PANTS IN THE FIRST SEGMENT...
Cool
Mature
Good-Looking
...BUT NOW SHE'S WEARING A SKIRT!
Sweet
Feminine
Beautiful

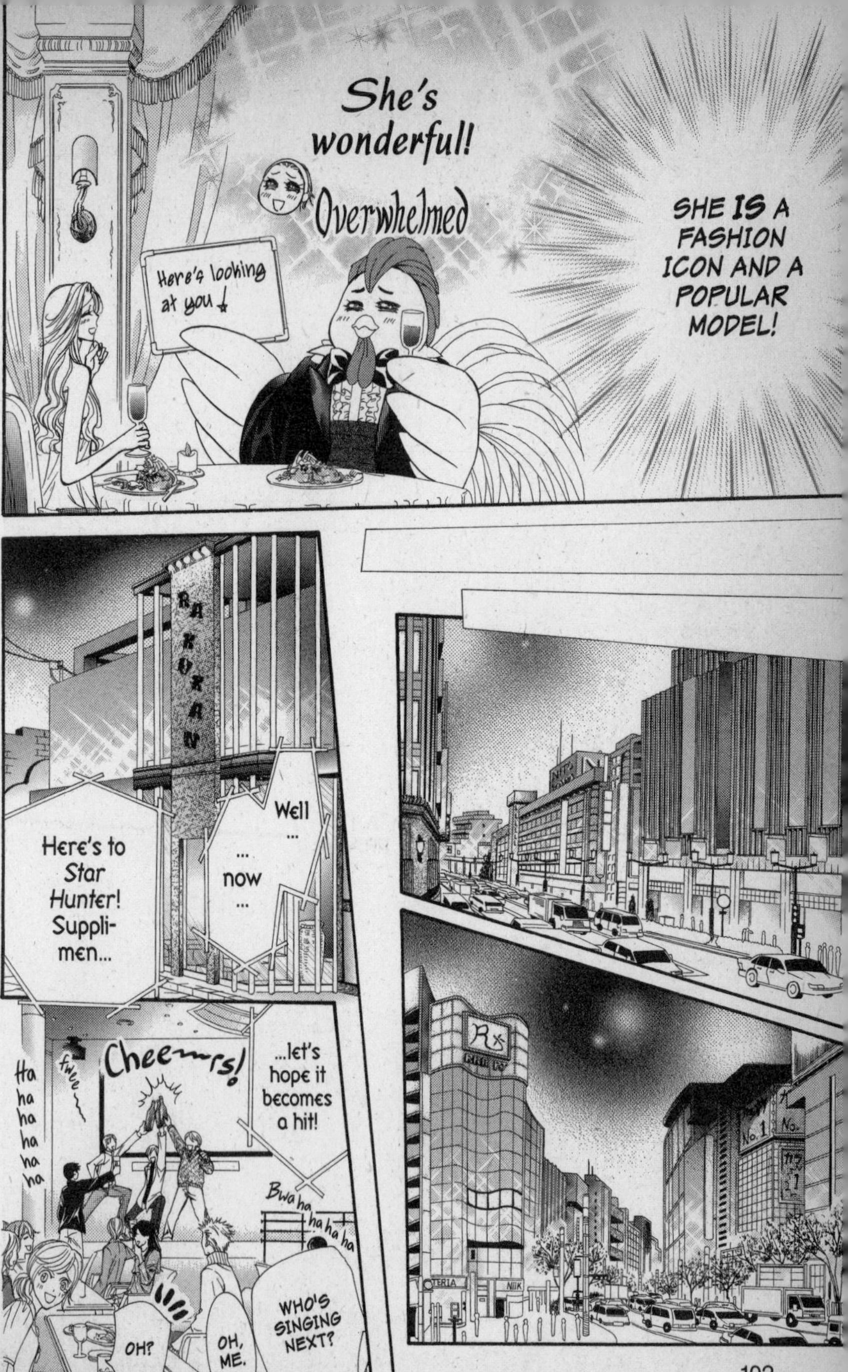
SHE IS A FASHION ICON AND A POPULAR MODEL!
She's wonderful!
Overwhelmed
Here's looking at you
Well ... ... now ...
Here's to Star Hunter! Suppli-men...
...let's hope it becomes a hit!
Cheers!
fwee~
Ha ha ha ha ha ha
Bwa ha ha ha ha ha
WHO'S SINGING NEXT?
OH, ME.
OH?

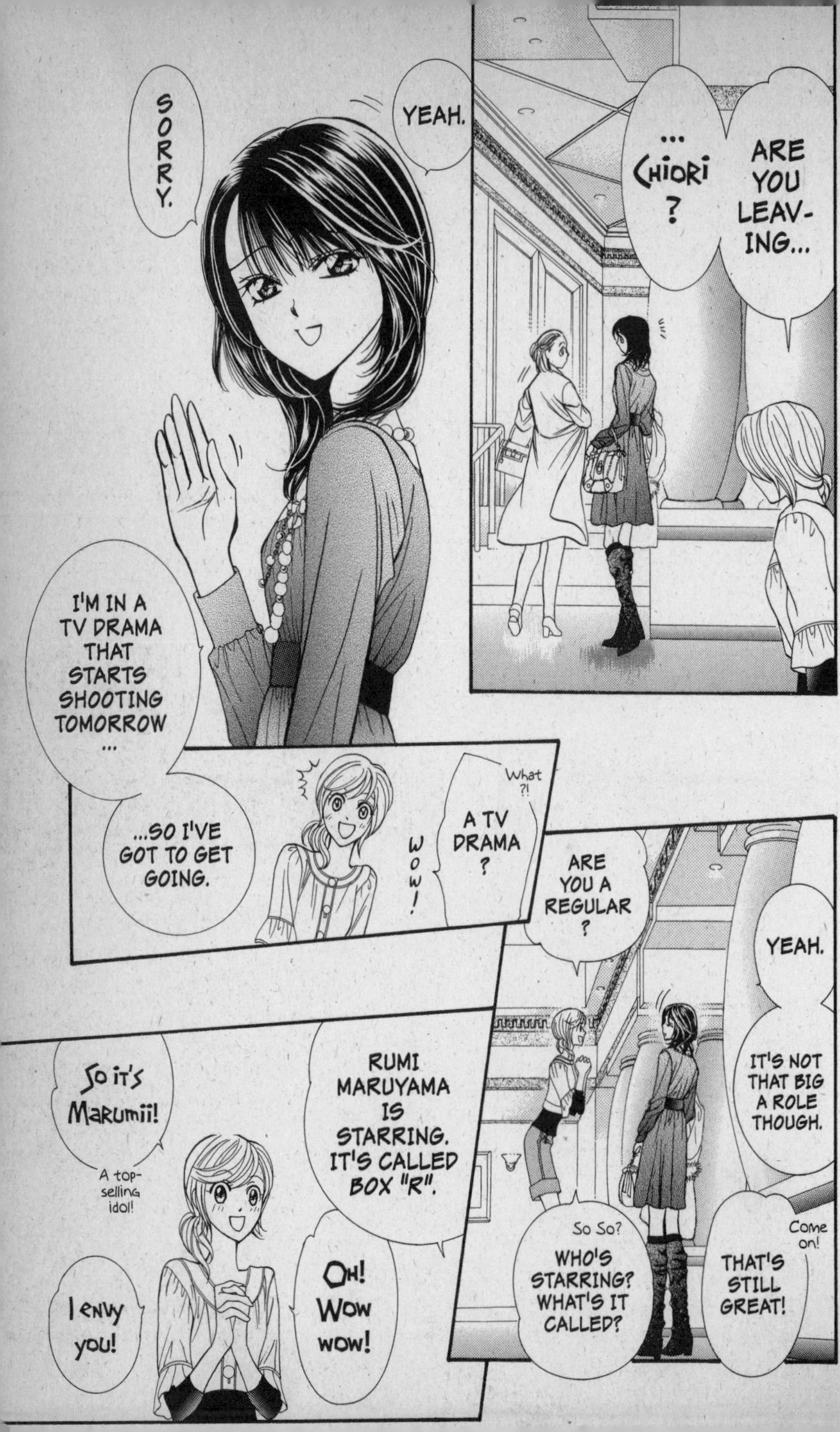
ARE YOU LEAVING...
... CHIORI?
YEAH.
SORRY.
I'M IN A TV DRAMA THAT STARTS SHOOTING TOMORROW...
...SO I'VE GOT TO GET GOING.
What?!
A TV DRAMA?
WOW!
ARE YOU A REGULAR?
YEAH.
IT'S NOT THAT BIG A ROLE THOUGH.
Come on!
THAT'S STILL GREAT!
So So?
WHO'S STARRING? WHAT'S IT CALLED?
RUMI MARUYAMA IS STARRING. IT'S CALLED BOX "R".
So it's Marumii!
A top-selling idol!
OH! WOW WOW!
I envy you!

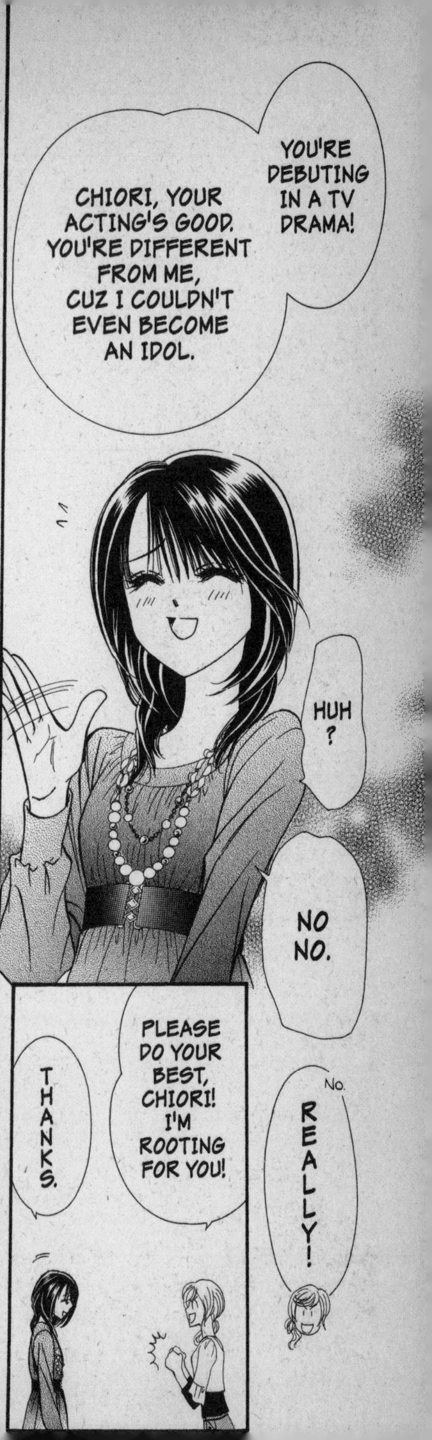
YOU'RE DEBUTING IN A TV DRAMA!
CHIORI, YOUR ACTING'S GOOD. YOU'RE DIFFERENT FROM ME, CUZ I COULDN'T EVEN BECOME AN IDOL.
HUH?
NO NO.
No.
REALLY!
PLEASE DO YOUR BEST, CHIORI! I'M ROOTING FOR YOU!
THANKS.
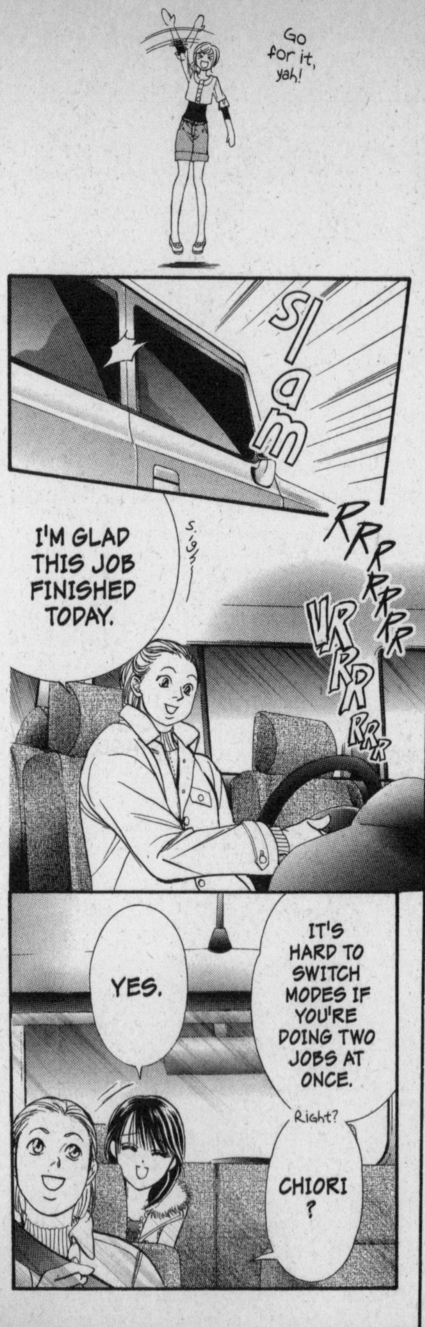
Go for it, yah!
Slam
RRRRRRR
VRRRRRR
I'M GLAD THIS JOB FINISHED TODAY.
IT'S HARD TO SWITCH MODES IF YOU'RE DOING TWO JOBS AT ONCE.
Right?
CHIORI?
YES.

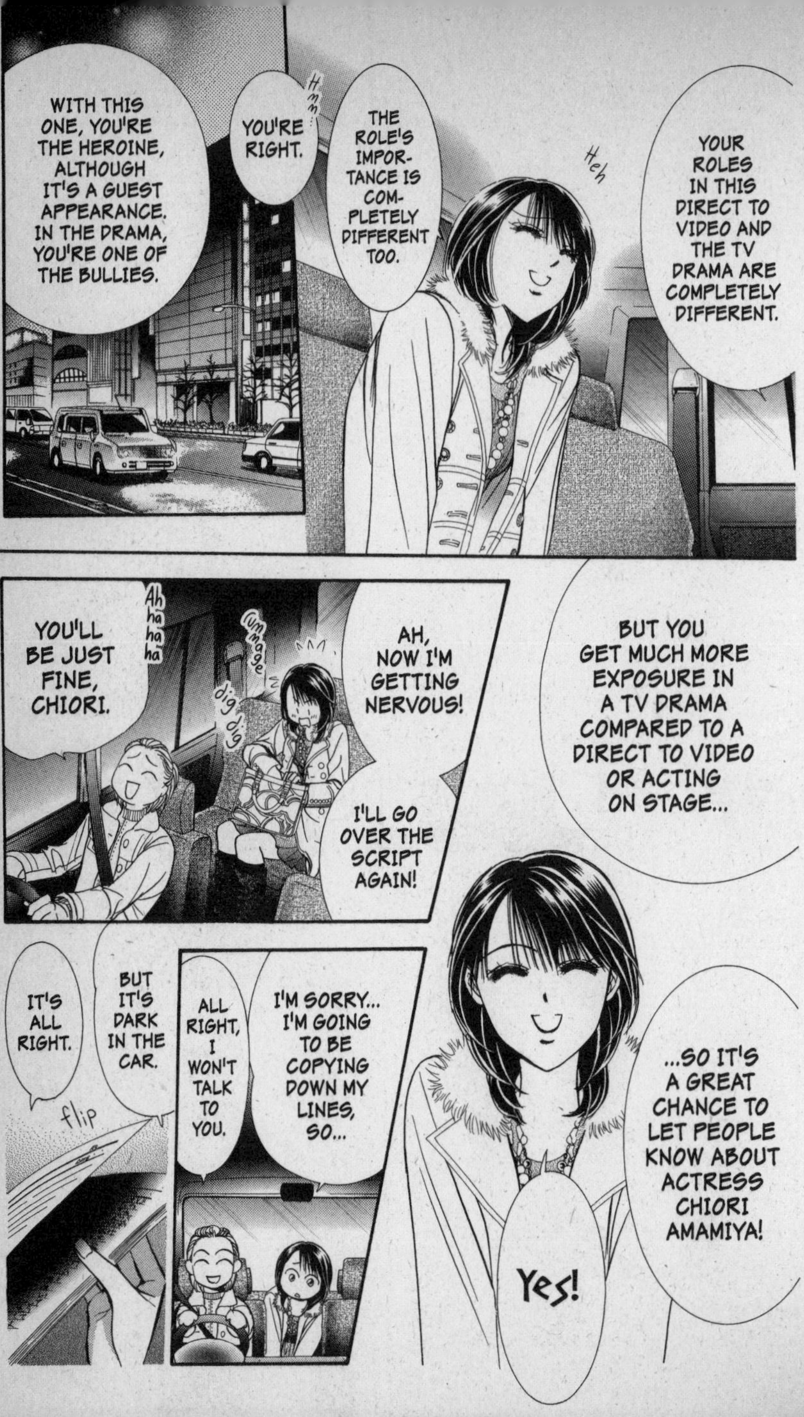
YOUR ROLES IN THIS DIRECT TO VIDEO AND THE TV DRAMA ARE COMPLETELY DIFFERENT.
Heh
THE ROLE'S IMPORTANCE IS COMPLETELY DIFFERENT TOO.
Hmm...
YOU'RE RIGHT.
WITH THIS ONE, YOU'RE THE HEROINE, ALTHOUGH IT'S A GUEST APPEARANCE. IN THE DRAMA, YOU'RE ONE OF THE BULLIES.
BUT YOU GET MUCH MORE EXPOSURE IN A TV DRAMA COMPARED TO A DIRECT TO VIDEO OR ACTING ON STAGE...
...SO IT'S A GREAT CHANCE TO LET PEOPLE KNOW ABOUT ACTRESS CHIORI AMAMIYA!
Yes!
AH, NOW I'M GETTING NERVOUS!
rummage
dig dig
I'LL GO OVER THE SCRIPT AGAIN!
Ah ha ha ha ha
YOU'LL BE JUST FINE, CHIORI.
I'M SORRY... I'M GOING TO BE COPYING DOWN MY LINES, SO...
ALL RIGHT, I WON'T TALK TO YOU.
BUT IT'S DARK IN THE CAR.
IT'S ALL RIGHT.
flip

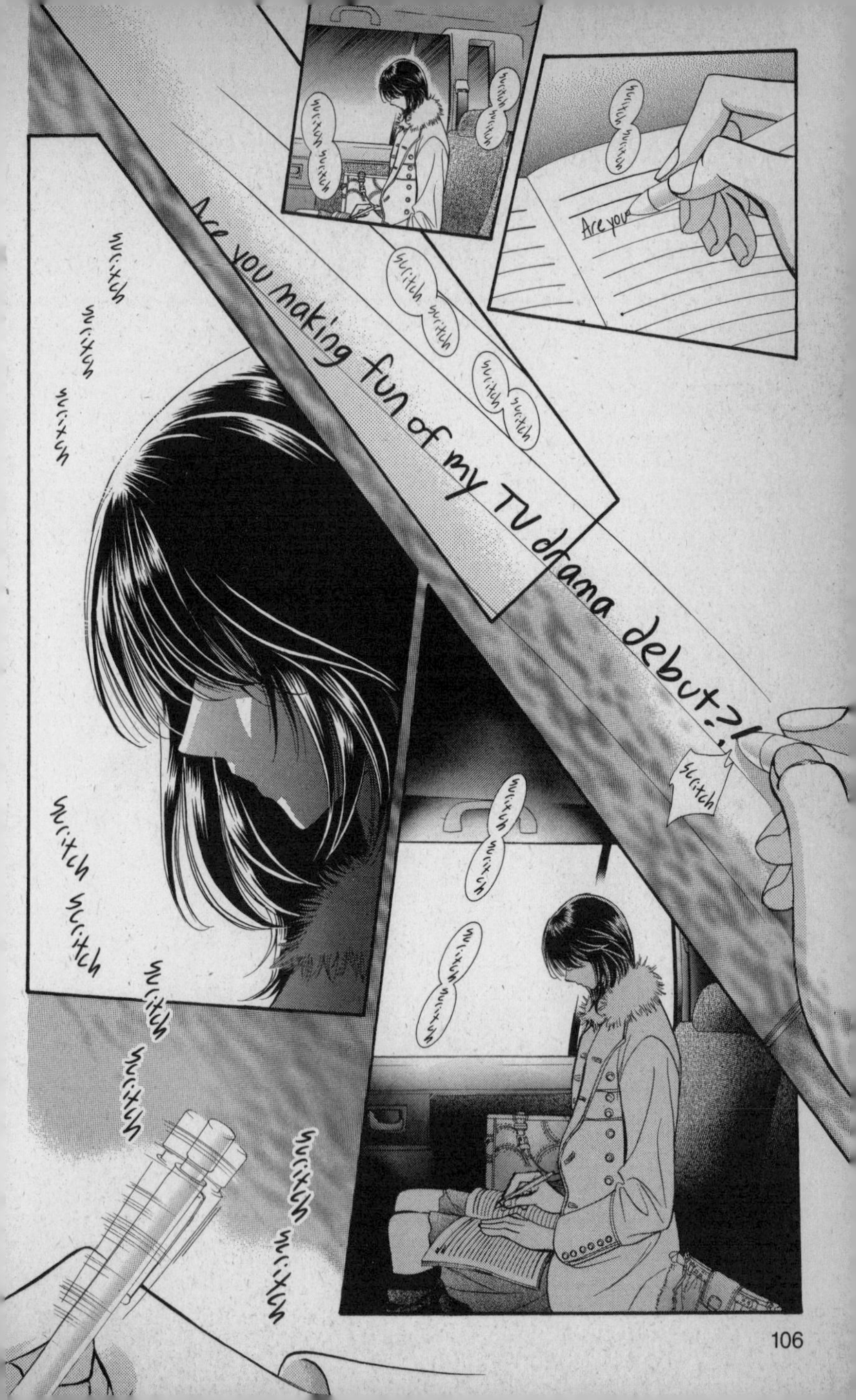
scritch scritch
Are you
scritch scritch
scritch scritch
Are you making fun of my TV drama debut?!
scritch scritch
scritch scritch
scritch
scritch scritch
scritch scritch
scritch
scritch
scritch
scritch scritch
scritch
scritch
scritch scritch

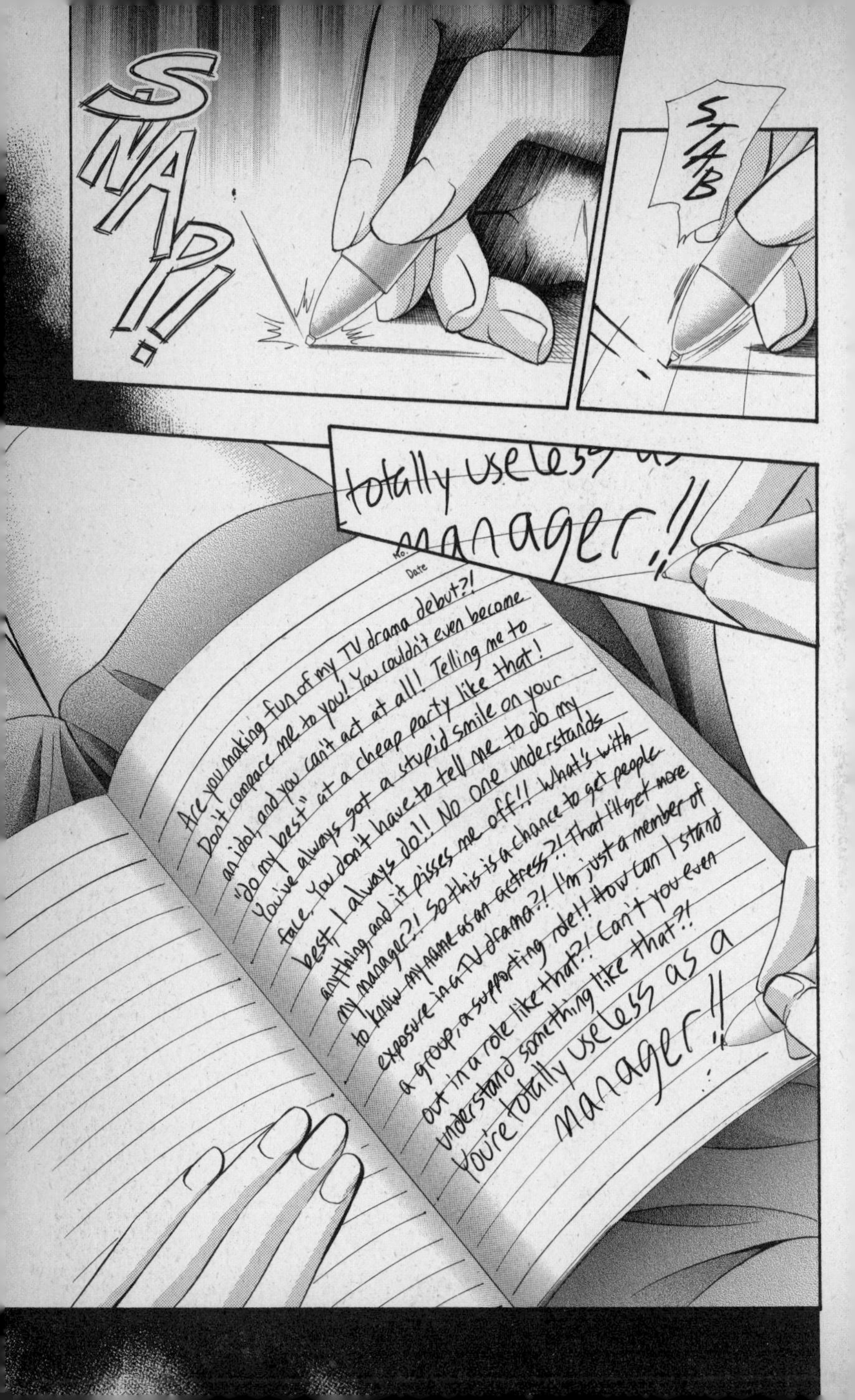
STAB
SNAP!!
totally useless as
manager!!
No.
Date
Are you making fun of my TV drama debut?!
Don't compare me to you! You couldn't even become
an idol, and you can't act at all! Telling me to
"do my best" at a cheap party like that!
You've always got a stupid smile on your
face. You don't have to tell me to do my
best, I always do!! No one understands
anything, and it pisses me off!! What's with
my manager?! So this is a chance to get people
to know my name as an actress?! That I'll get more
exposure in a TV drama?! I'm just a member of
a group, a supporting role!! How can I stand
out in a role like that?! Can't you even
understand something like that?!
You're totally useless as a
manager!!

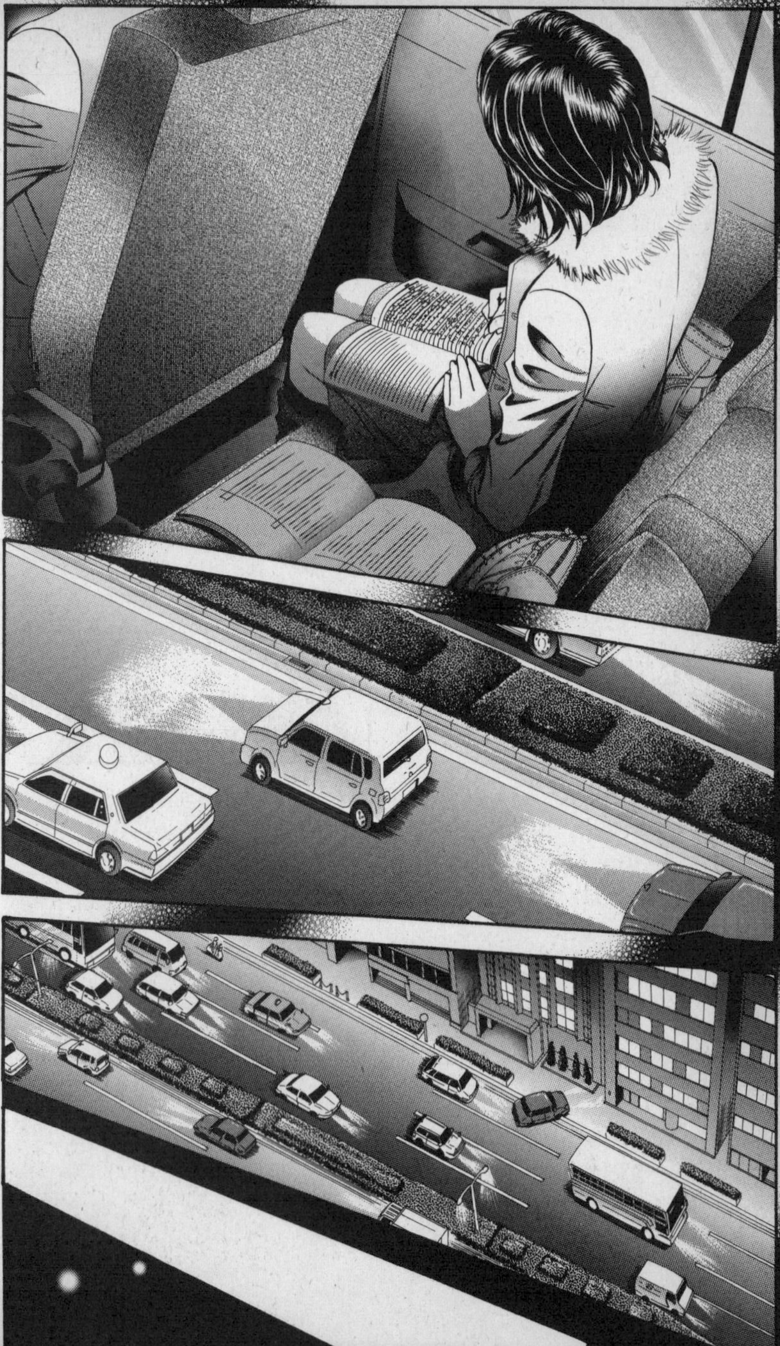

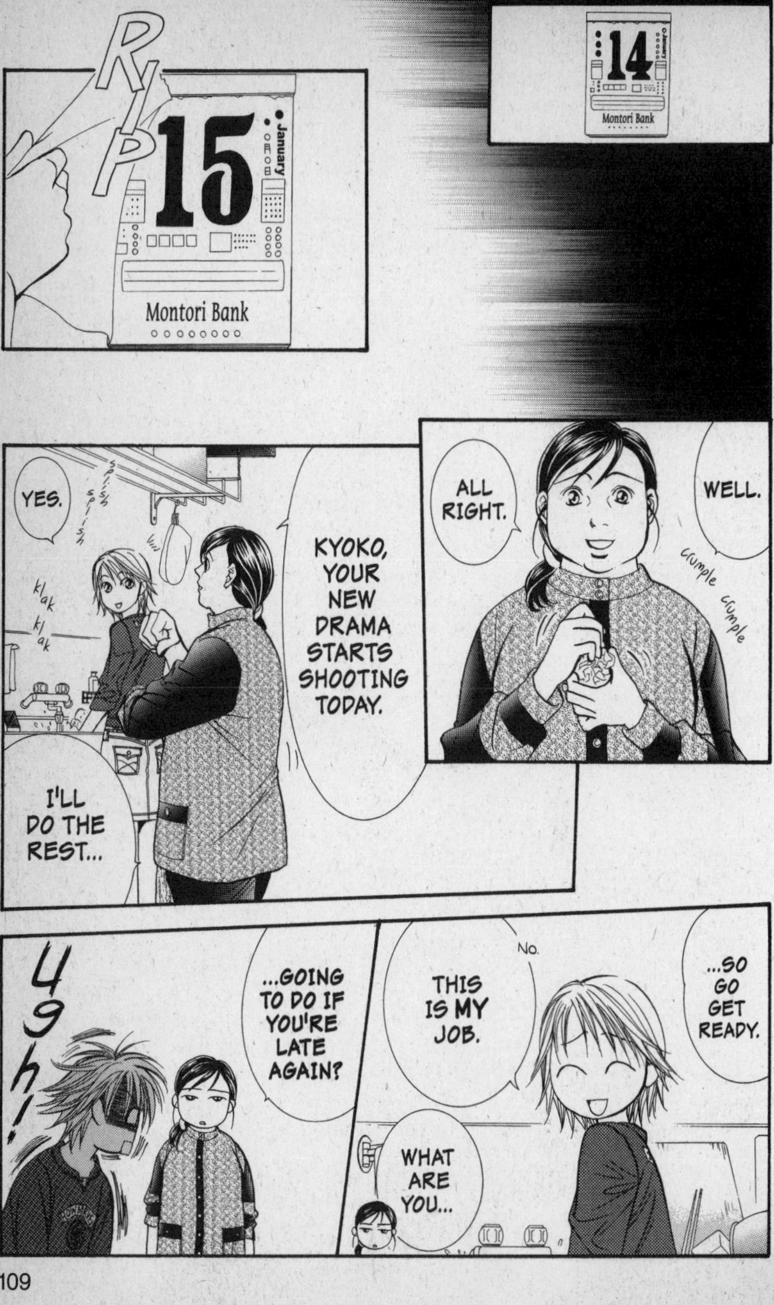
14
January
Montori Bank
RIP
15
January
Montori Bank
WELL.
ALL RIGHT.
crumple crumple
KYOKO, YOUR NEW DRAMA STARTS SHOOTING TODAY.
YES.
spish spish
klak klak
I'LL DO THE REST...
...SO GO GET READY.
No.
THIS IS MY JOB.
WHAT ARE YOU...
...GOING TO DO IF YOU'RE LATE AGAIN?
Ugh!

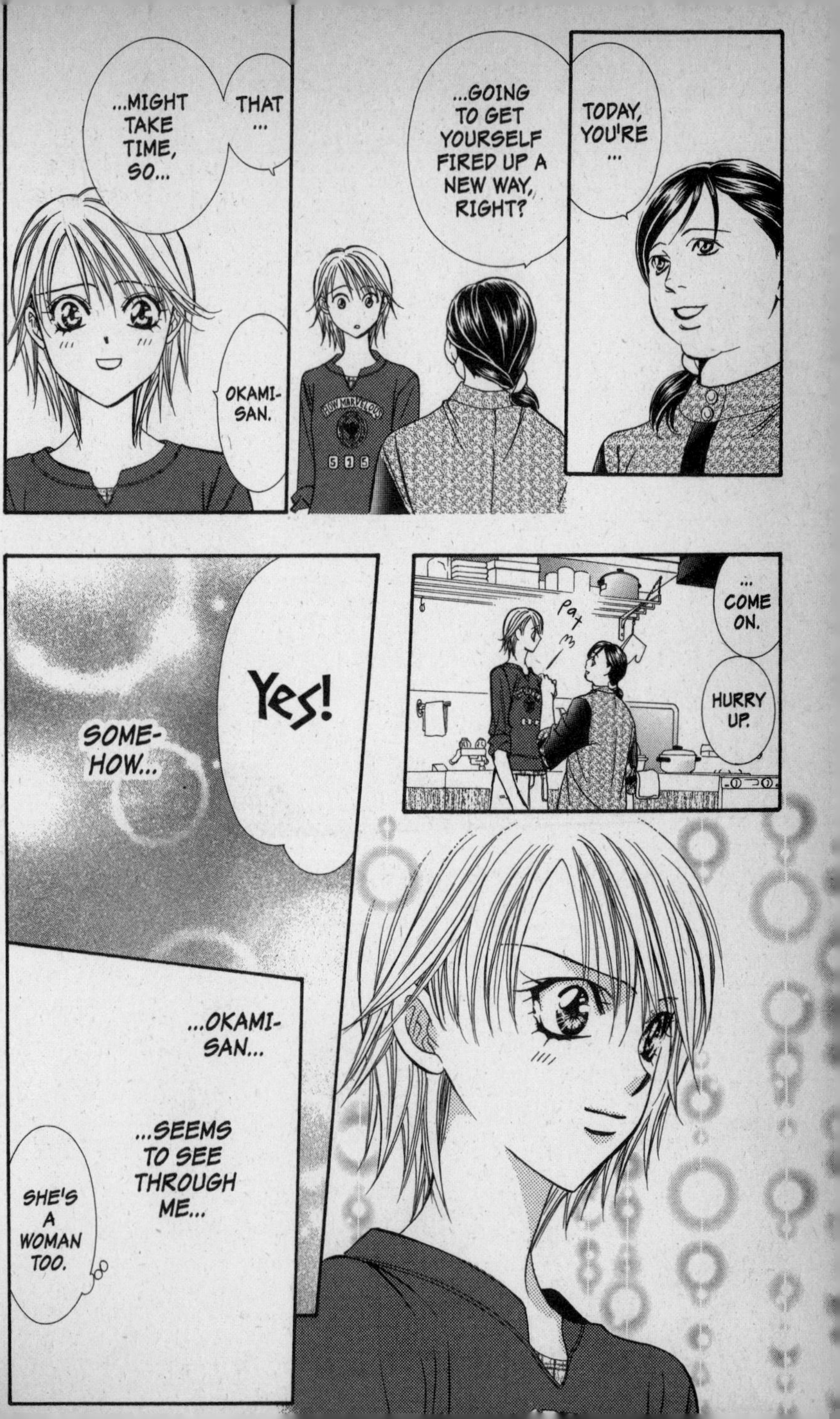
TODAY, YOU'RE ...
...GOING TO GET YOURSELF FIRED UP A NEW WAY, RIGHT?
THAT ...
...MIGHT TAKE TIME, SO...
OKAMI-SAN.
... COME ON.
HURRY UP.
Pat
Yes!
SOME-HOW...
...OKAMI-SAN...
...SEEMS TO SEE THROUGH ME...
SHE'S A WOMAN TOO.

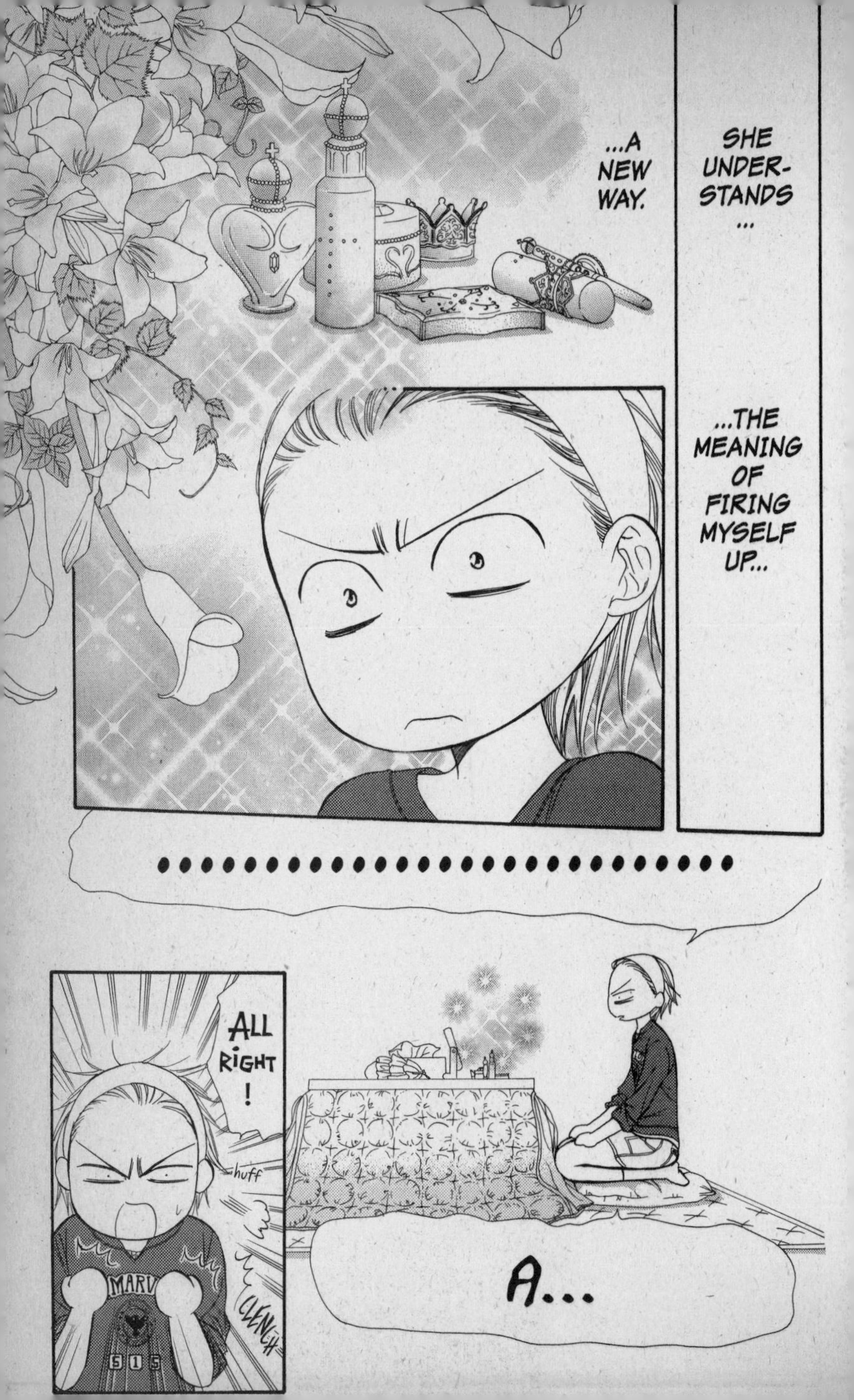
SHE UNDER-STANDS...
...THE MEANING OF FIRING MYSELF UP...
...A NEW WAY.
....
A...
ALL RIGHT!
huff
CLENCH

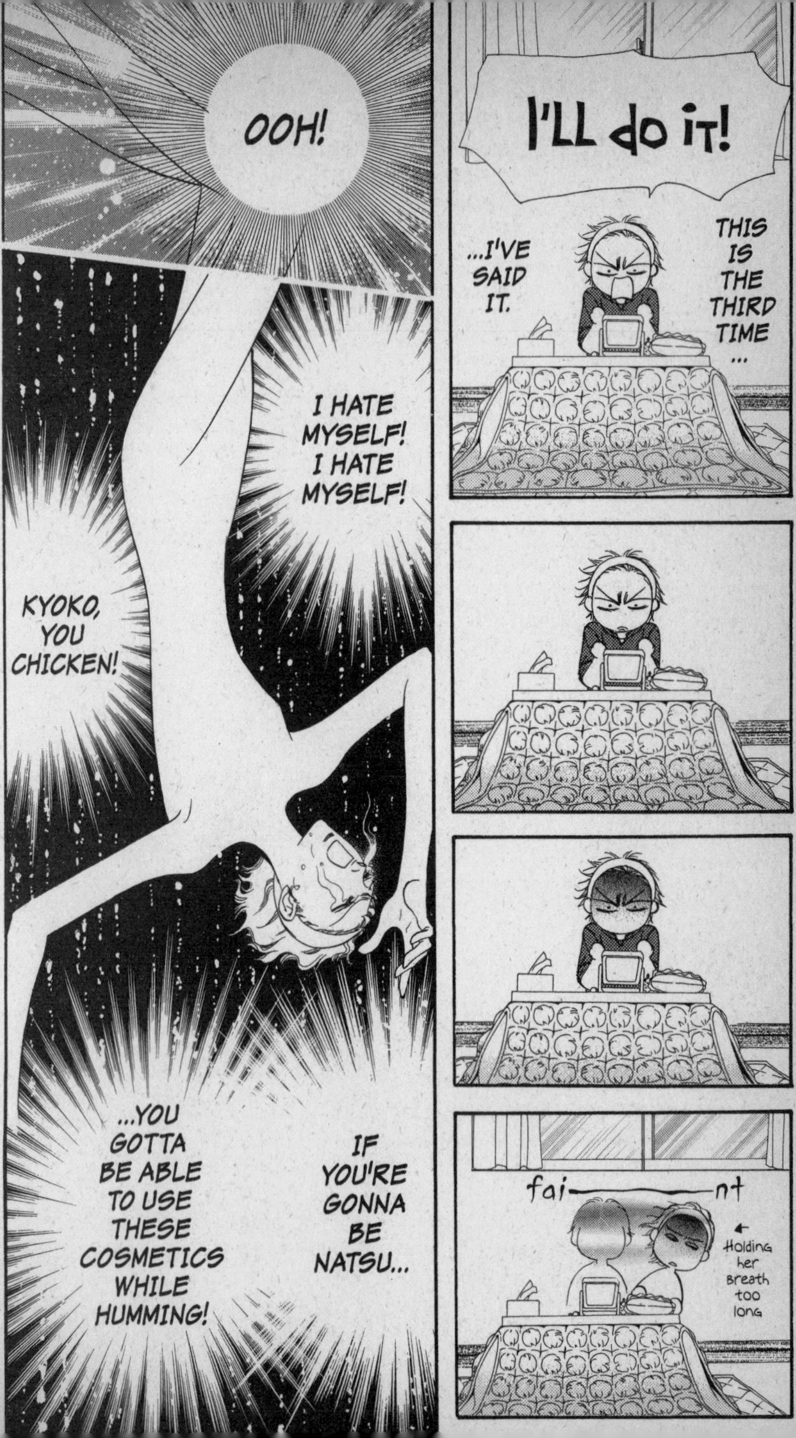
I'LL do it!
THIS IS THE THIRD TIME ...
...I'VE SAID IT.
fai———nt
← Holding her Breath too long
OOH!
I HATE MYSELF! I HATE MYSELF!
KYOKO, YOU CHICKEN!
IF YOU'RE GONNA BE NATSU...
...YOU GOTTA BE ABLE TO USE THESE COSMETICS WHILE HUMMING!

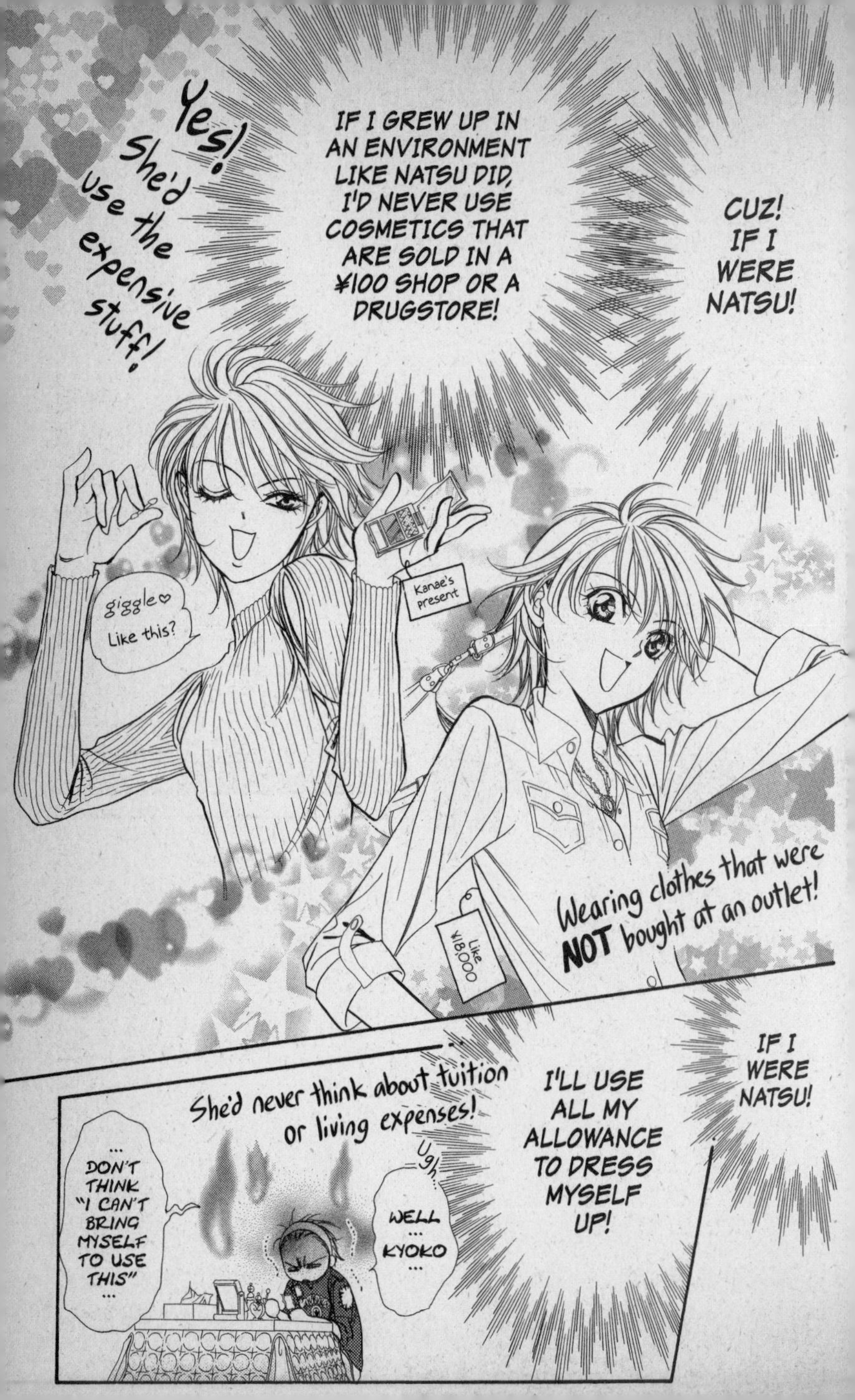
CUZ! IF I WERE NATSU!
IF I GREW UP IN AN ENVIRONMENT LIKE NATSU DID, I'D NEVER USE COSMETICS THAT ARE SOLD IN A ¥100 SHOP OR A DRUGSTORE!
Yes! She'd use the expensive stuff!
Kanae's present
giggle♡ Like this?
Wearing clothes that were NOT bought at an outlet!
Like ¥18,000
IF I WERE NATSU!
I'LL USE ALL MY ALLOWANCE TO DRESS MYSELF UP!
She'd never think about tuition or living expenses!
Ugh...
WELL ... KYOKO ...
... DON'T THINK "I CAN'T BRING MYSELF TO USE THIS" ...

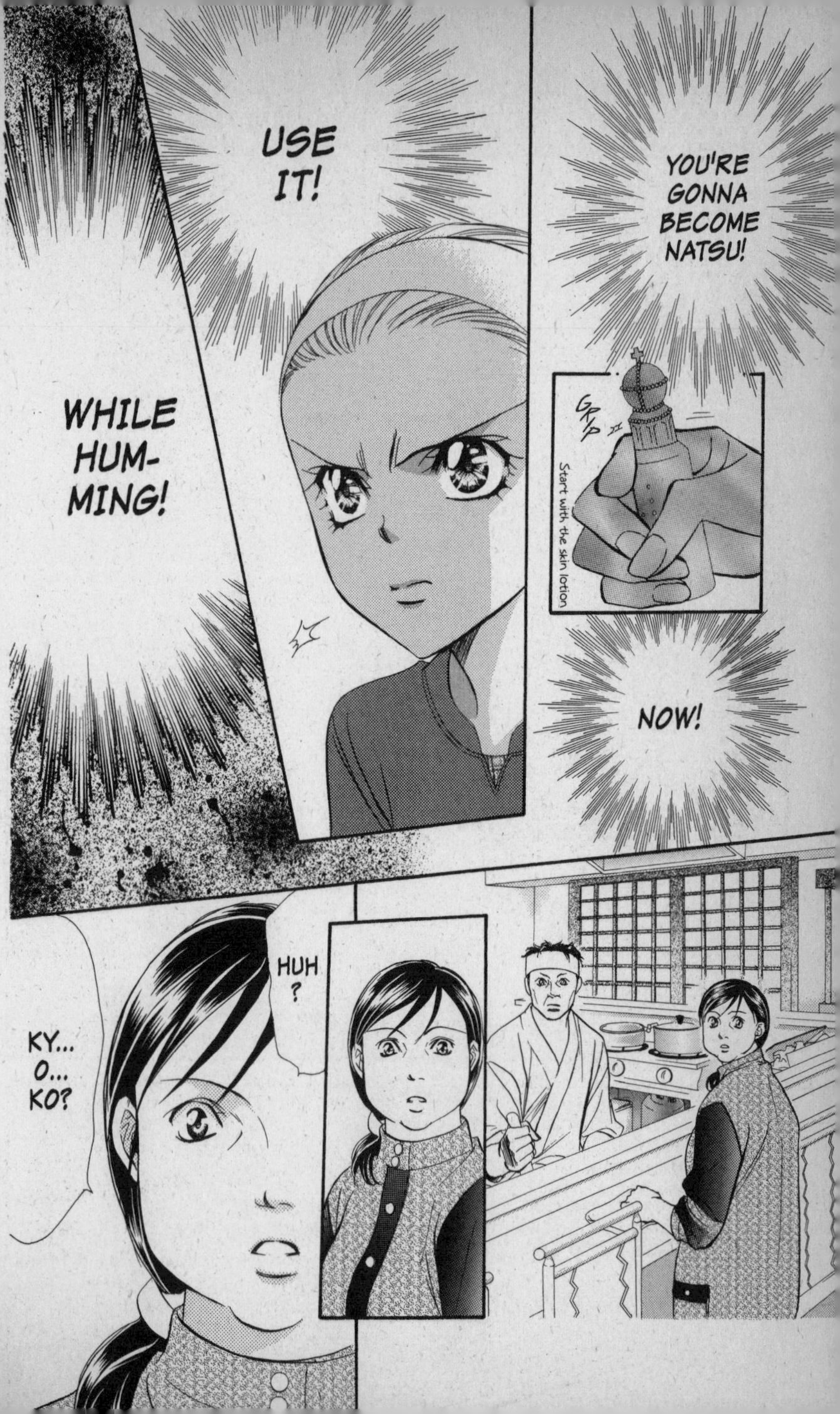
YOU'RE GONNA BECOME NATSU!
Start with the skin lotion
NOW!
USE IT!
WHILE HUM-MING!
HUH?
KY... O... KO?

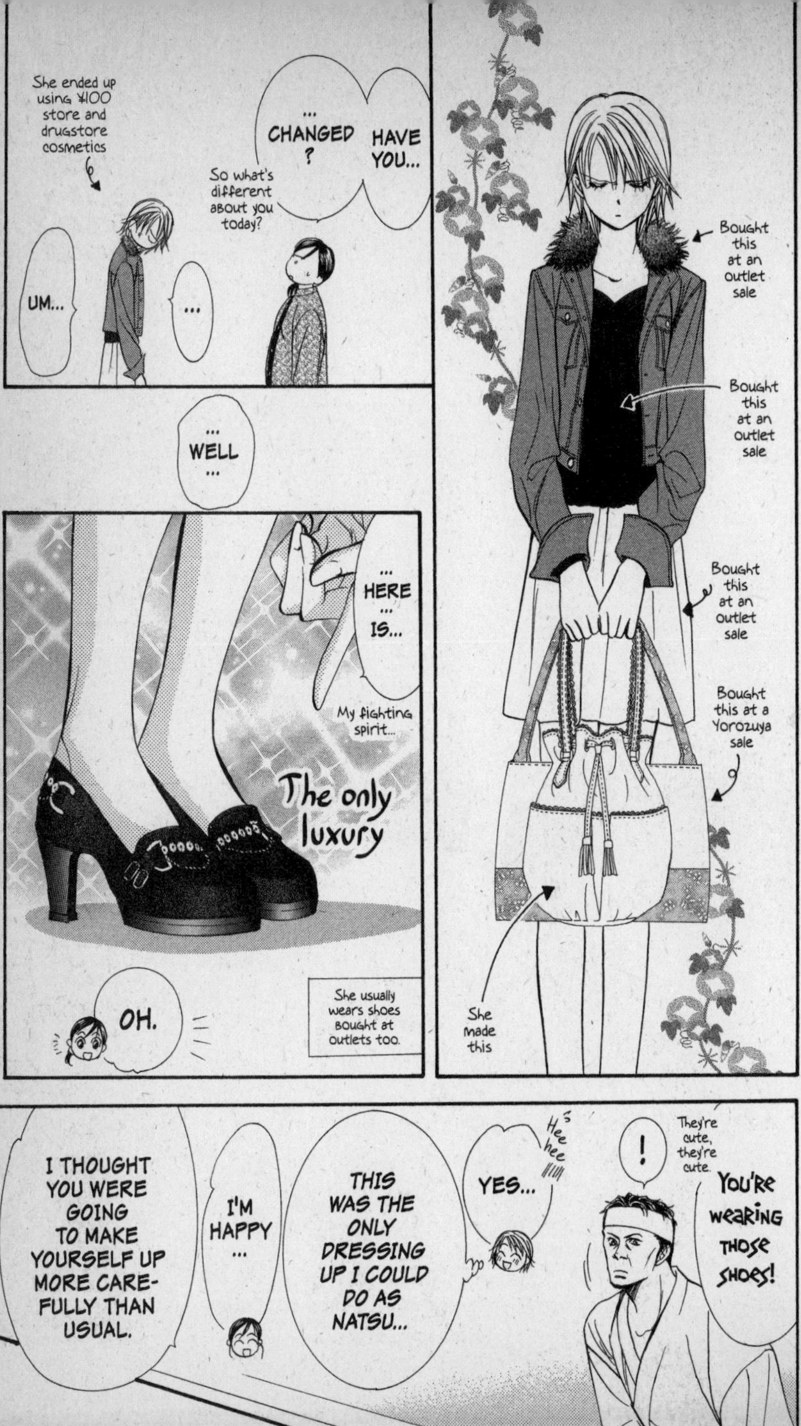
Bought this at an outlet sale
Bought this at an outlet sale
Bought this at an outlet sale
Bought this at a Yorozuya sale
She made this
HAVE YOU...
... CHANGED ?
So what's different about you today?
...
UM...
She ended up using ¥100 store and drugstore cosmetics
... WELL ...
... HERE ... IS...
My fighting spirit...
The only luxury
She usually wears shoes bought at outlets too.
OH.
!
They're cute, they're cute.
YOU'RE WEARING THOSE SHOES!
YES...
Hee hee
THIS WAS THE ONLY DRESSING UP I COULD DO AS NATSU...
I'M HAPPY ...
I THOUGHT YOU WERE GOING TO MAKE YOURSELF UP MORE CARE-FULLY THAN USUAL.

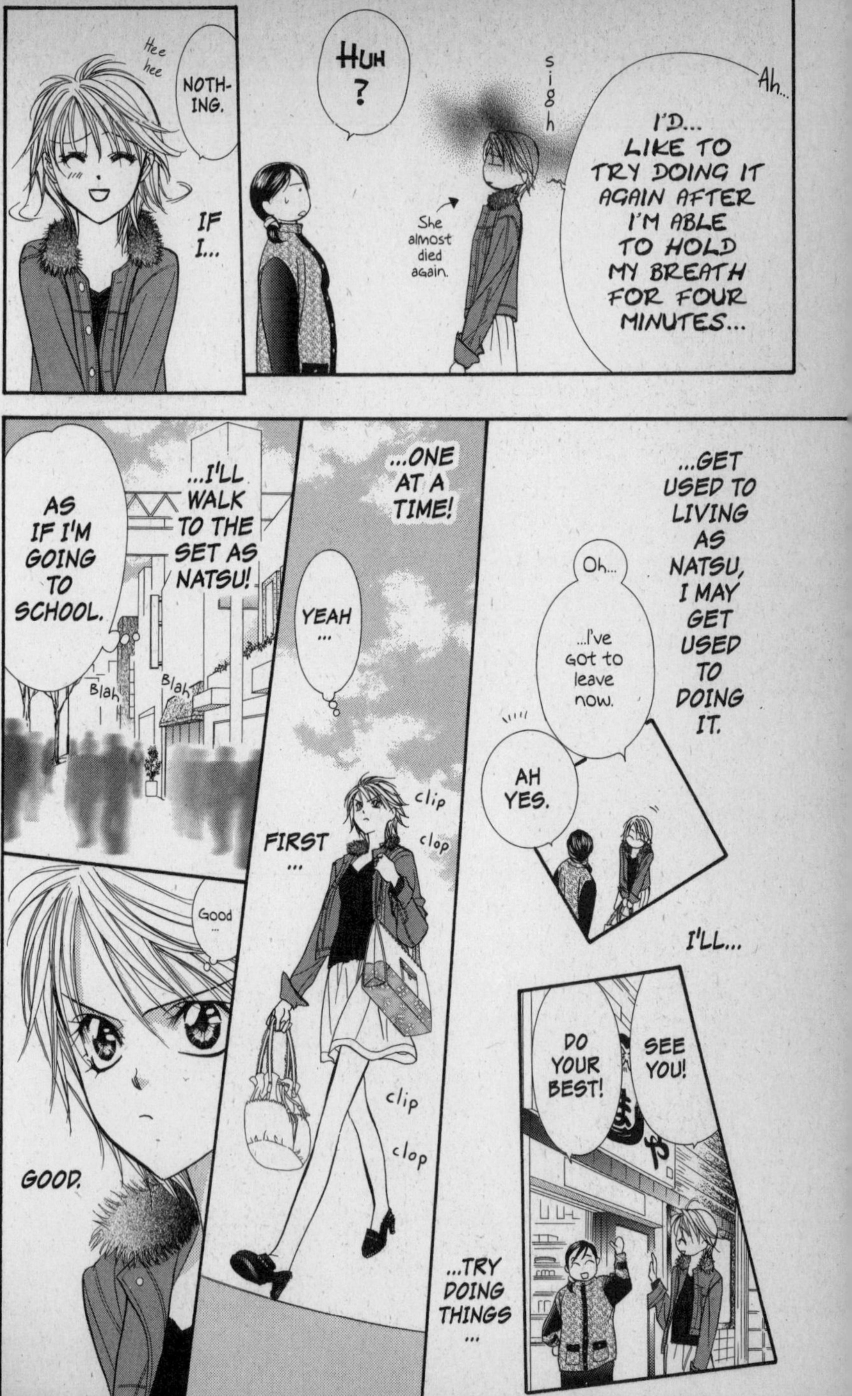
Ah...
I'D... LIKE TO TRY DOING IT AGAIN AFTER I'M ABLE TO HOLD MY BREATH FOR FOUR MINUTES...
sigh
She almost died again.
HUH?
Hee hee
NOTH-ING.
IF I...
...GET USED TO LIVING AS NATSU, I MAY GET USED TO DOING IT.
Oh...
...I've got to leave now.
AH YES.
I'LL...
SEE YOU!
DO YOUR BEST!
...TRY DOING THINGS...
...ONE AT A TIME!
YEAH...
FIRST...
clip
clop
clip
clop
...I'LL WALK TO THE SET AS NATSU!
AS IF I'M GOING TO SCHOOL.
Blah
Blah
Good...
GOOD.

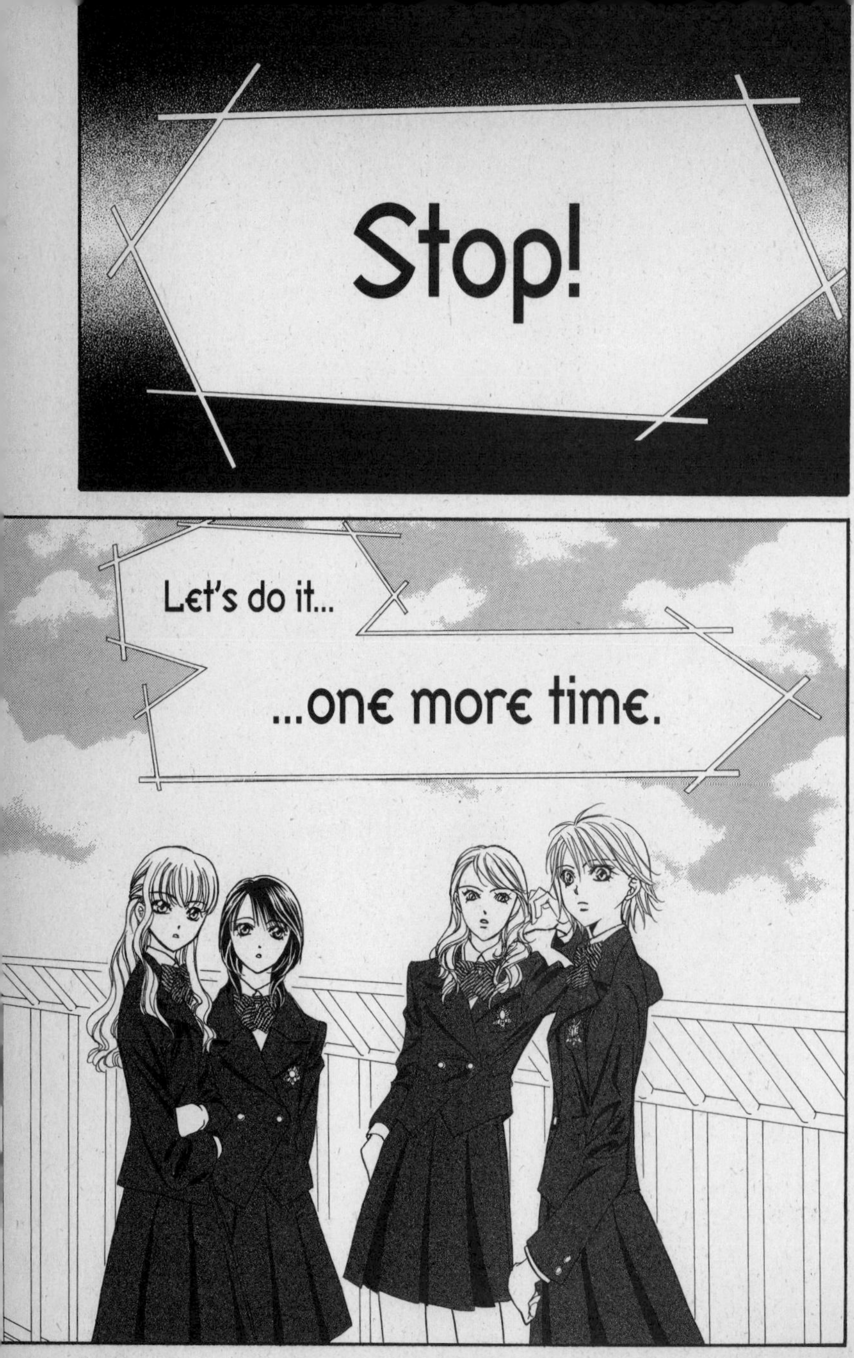
Stop!
Let's do it...
...one more time.

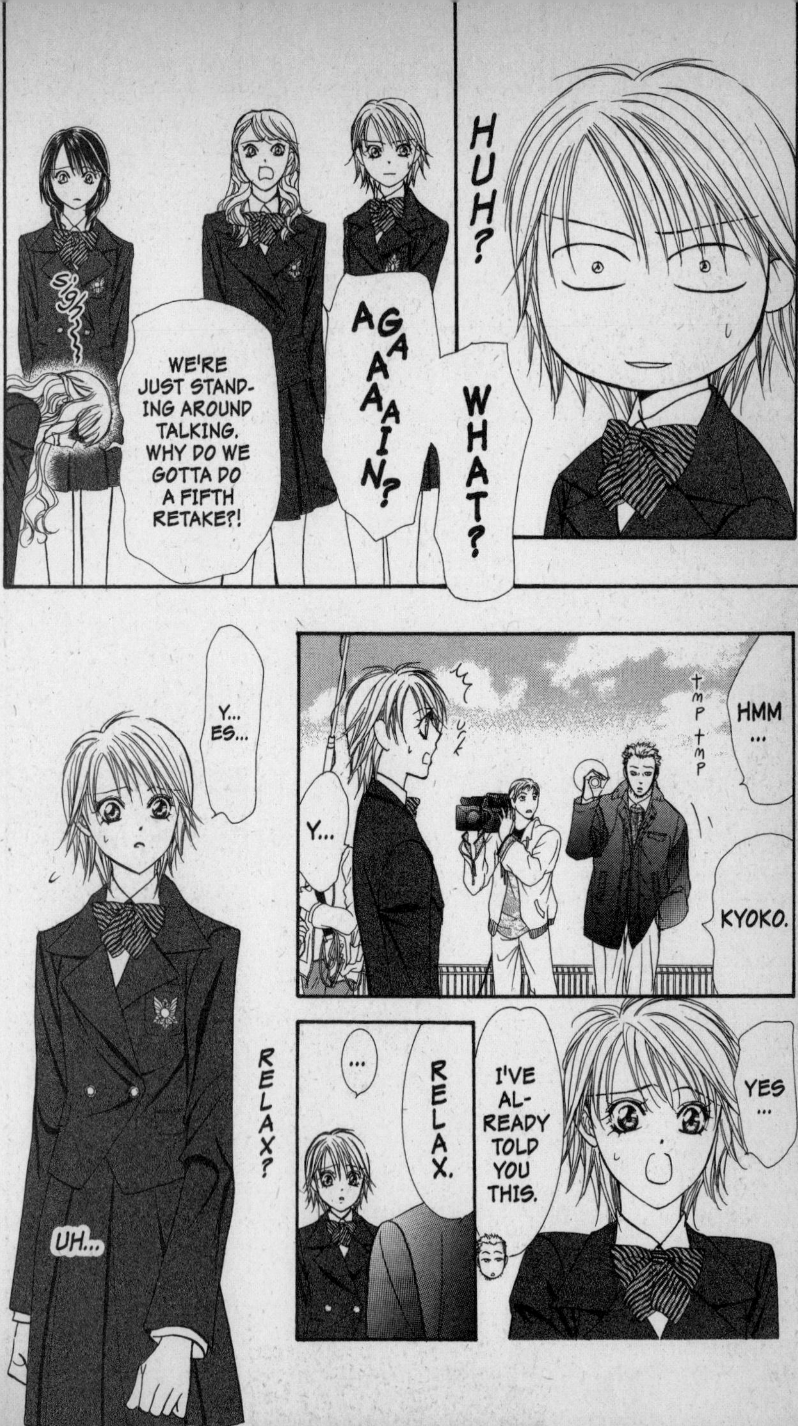
HUH?
WHAT?
AGAAAAIN?
WE'RE JUST STANDING-ING AROUND TALKING. WHY DO WE GOTTA DO A FIFTH RETAKE?!
sigh...
HMM...
tmp tmp tmp
urk
KYOKO.
Y...
YES...
I'VE AL-READY TOLD YOU THIS.
RELAX.
...
Y... ES...
RELAX?
UH...

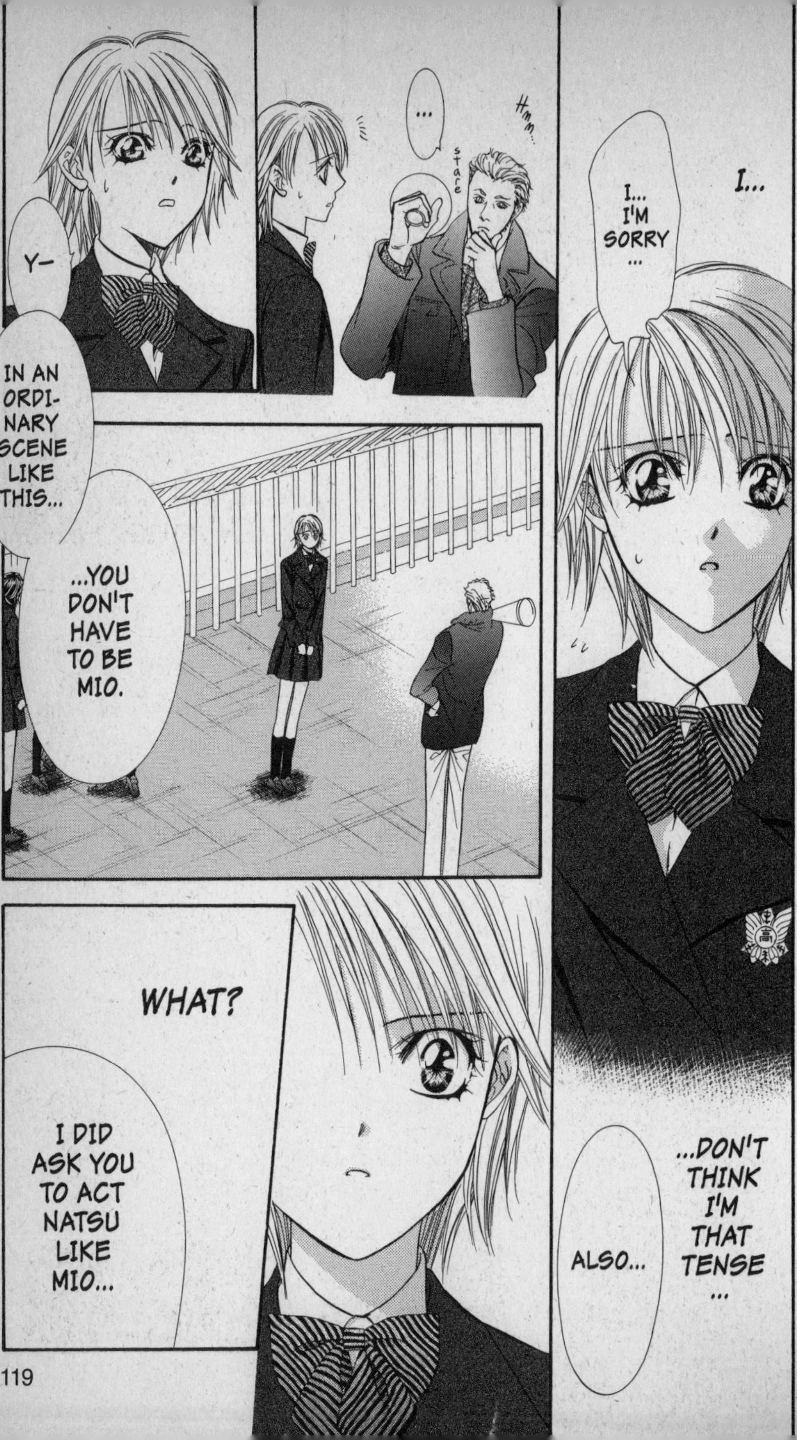
I... I'M SORRY...
I...
...
Hmm...
stare
Y—
IN AN ORDINARY SCENE LIKE THIS...
...YOU DON'T HAVE TO BE MIO.
...DON'T THINK I'M THAT TENSE...
ALSO...
WHAT?
I DID ASK YOU TO ACT NATSU LIKE MIO...

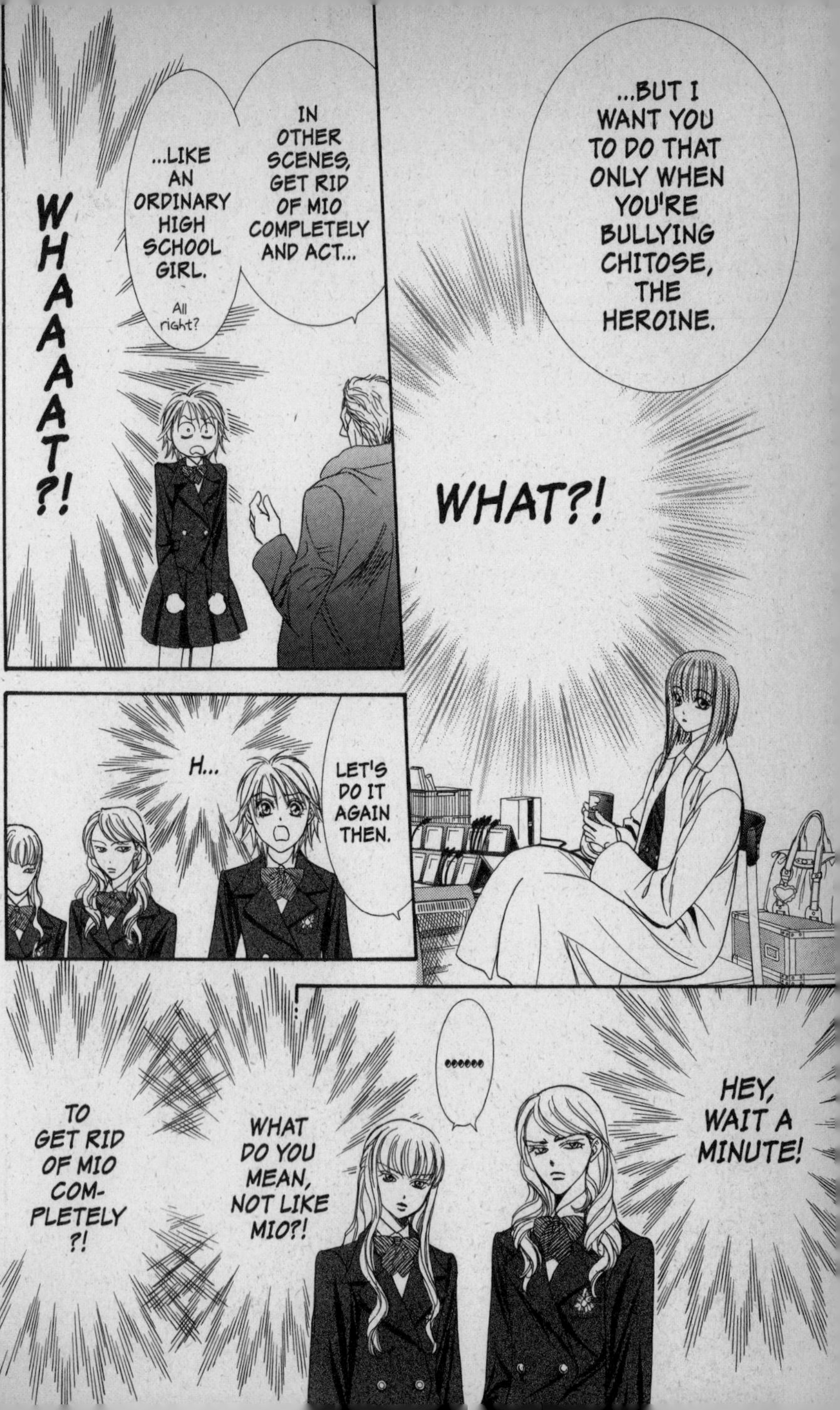
...BUT I WANT YOU TO DO THAT ONLY WHEN YOU'RE BULLYING CHITOSE, THE HEROINE.
WHAT?!
IN OTHER SCENES, GET RID OF MIO COMPLETELY AND ACT...
...LIKE AN ORDINARY HIGH SCHOOL GIRL.
All right?
WHAAAAAT?!
LET'S DO IT AGAIN THEN.
H...
HEY, WAIT A MINUTE!
......
WHAT DO YOU MEAN, NOT LIKE MIO?!
TO GET RID OF MIO COM-PLETELY?!

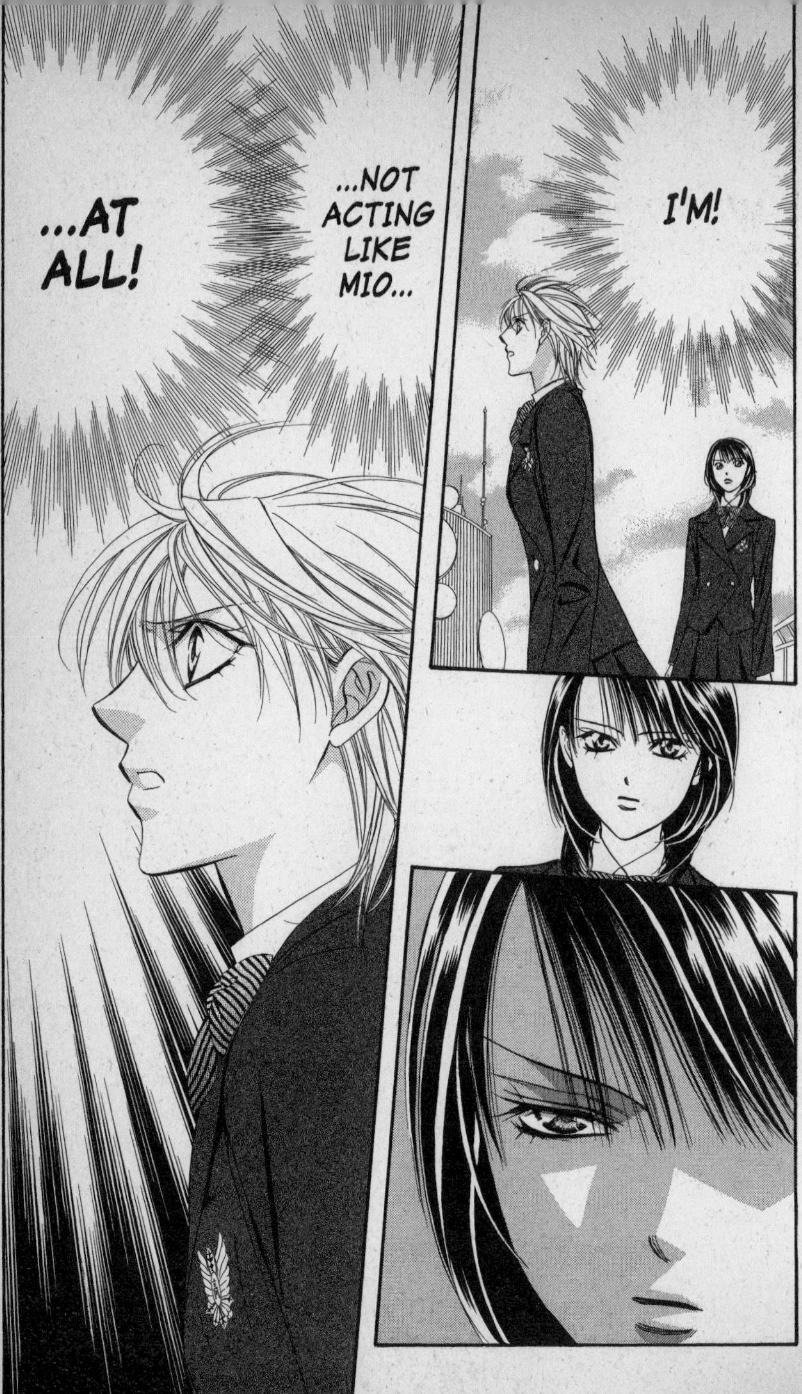
I'M!
...NOT ACTING LIKE MIO...
...AT ALL!

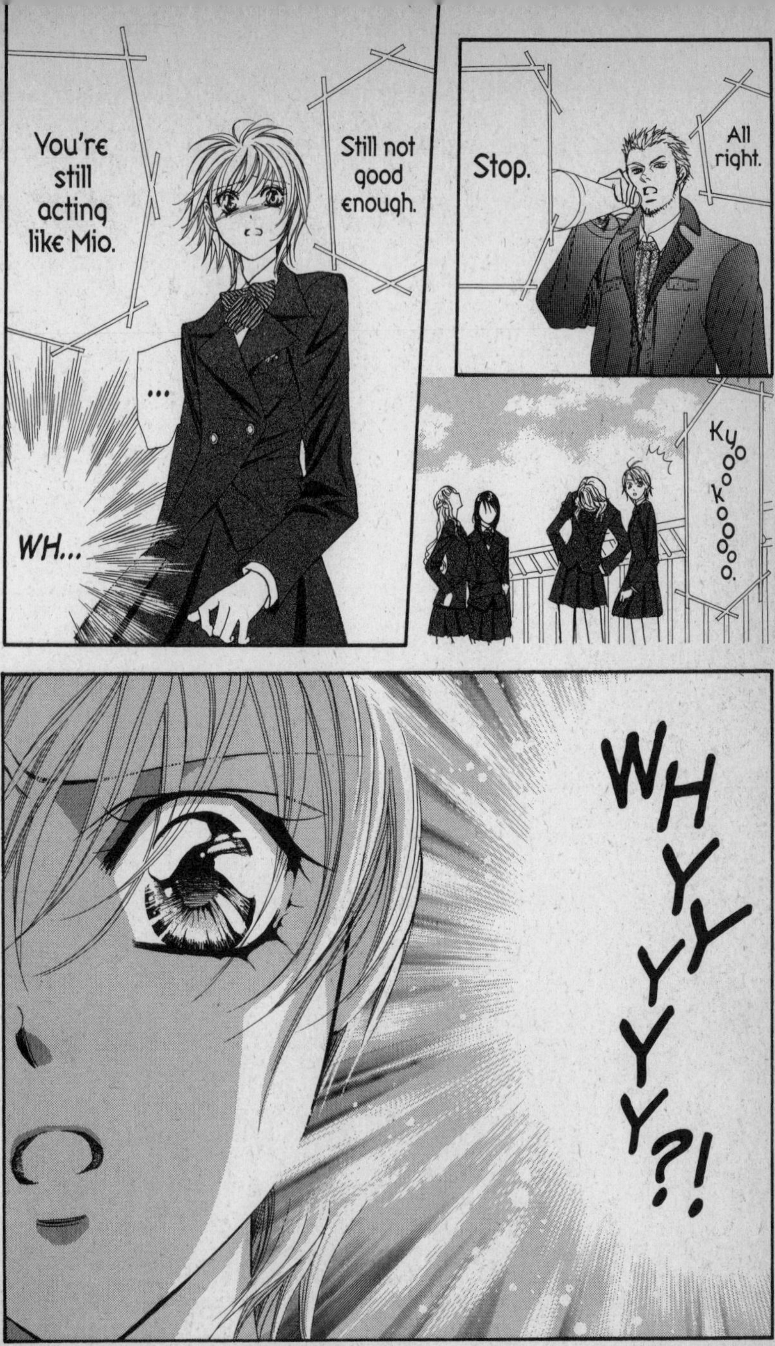
All right.
Stop.
Kyoookooooo.
Still not good enough.
You're still acting like Mio.
...
WH...
WHYYYYYY?!

End of Act 124

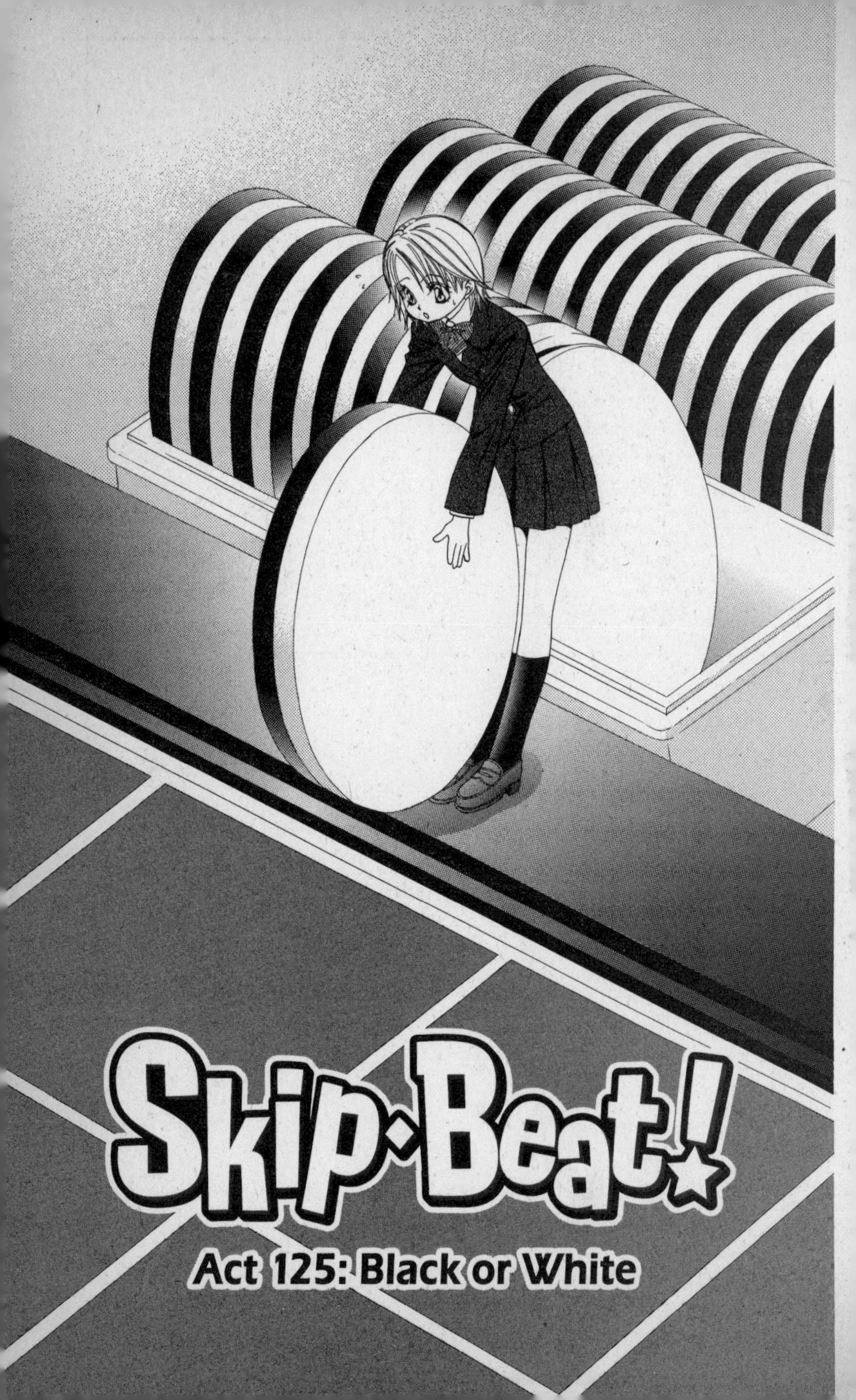
Skip·Beat!
Act 125: Black or White

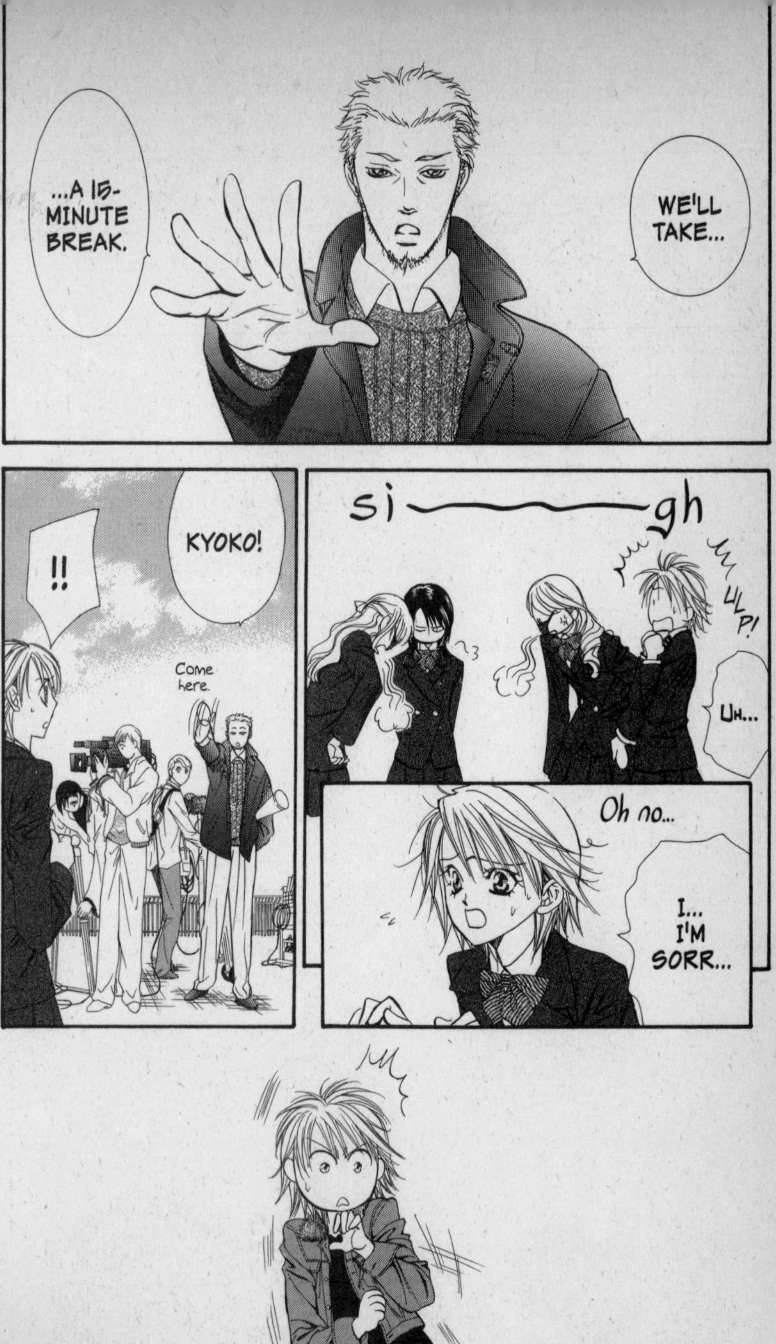
WE'LL TAKE...
...A 15-MINUTE BREAK.
si———gh
ULP!
UH...
Oh no...
I... I'M SORR...
KYOKO!
!!
Come here.

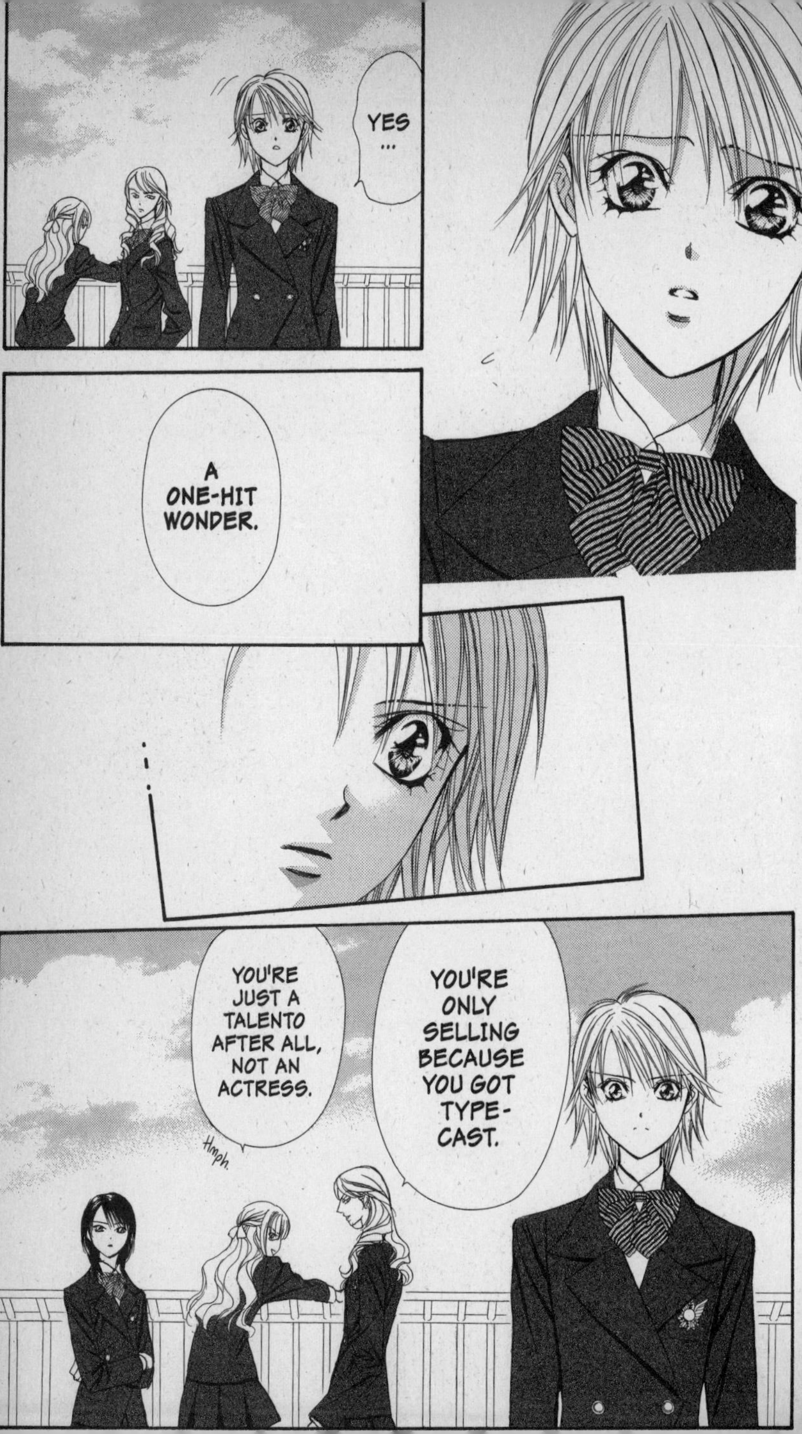
YES ...
A ONE-HIT WONDER.
...
YOU'RE ONLY SELLING BECAUSE YOU GOT TYPE-CAST.
YOU'RE JUST A TALENTO AFTER ALL, NOT AN ACTRESS.
Hmph.

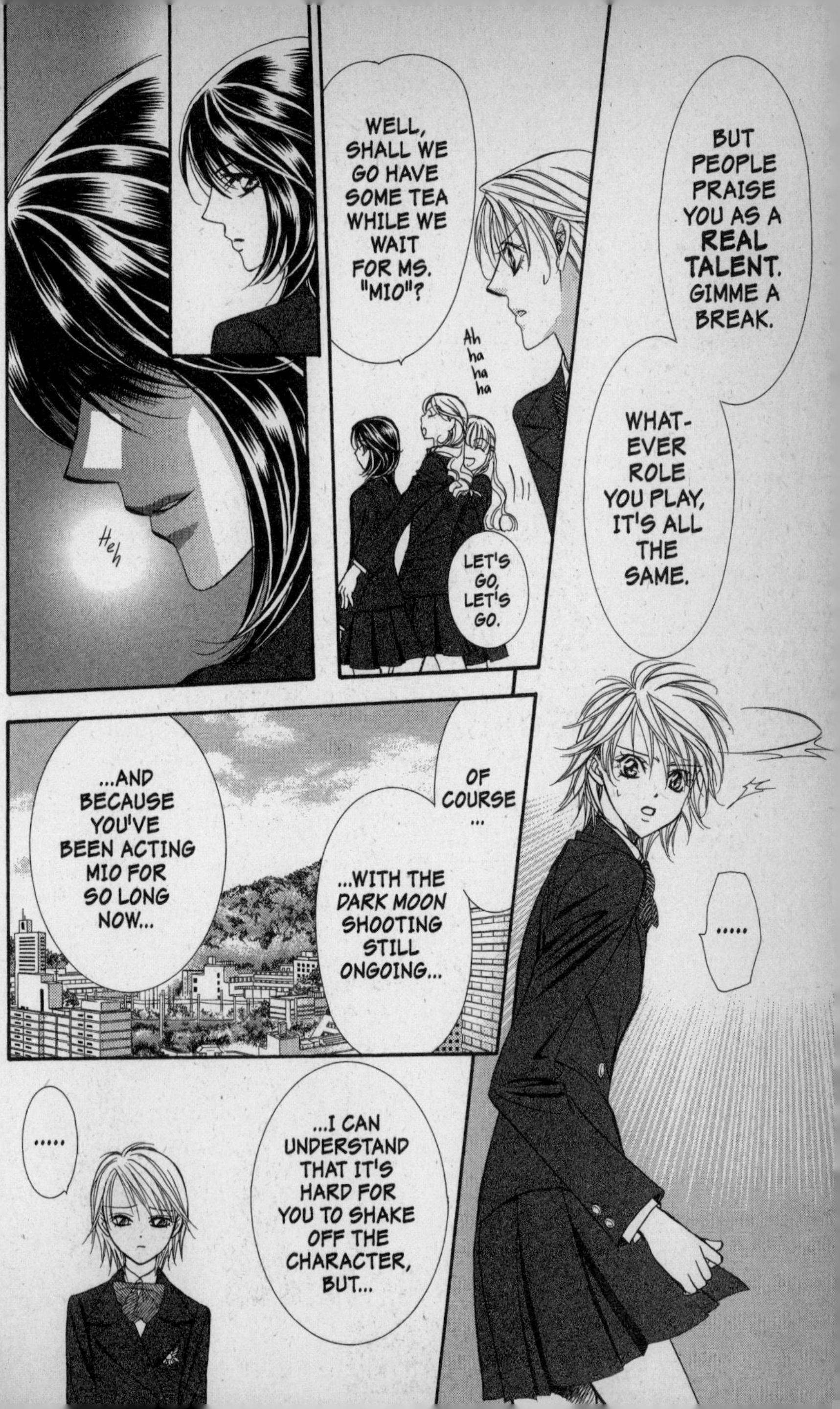
BUT PEOPLE PRAISE YOU AS A REAL TALENT. GIMME A BREAK.
WHAT-EVER ROLE YOU PLAY, IT'S ALL THE SAME.
WELL, SHALL WE GO HAVE SOME TEA WHILE WE WAIT FOR MS. "MIO"?
Ah ha ha ha
LET'S GO, LET'S GO.
Heh
OF COURSE...
...WITH THE DARK MOON SHOOTING STILL ONGOING...
...AND BECAUSE YOU'VE BEEN ACTING MIO FOR SO LONG NOW...
.....
...I CAN UNDERSTAND THAT IT'S HARD FOR YOU TO SHAKE OFF THE CHARACTER, BUT...
.....

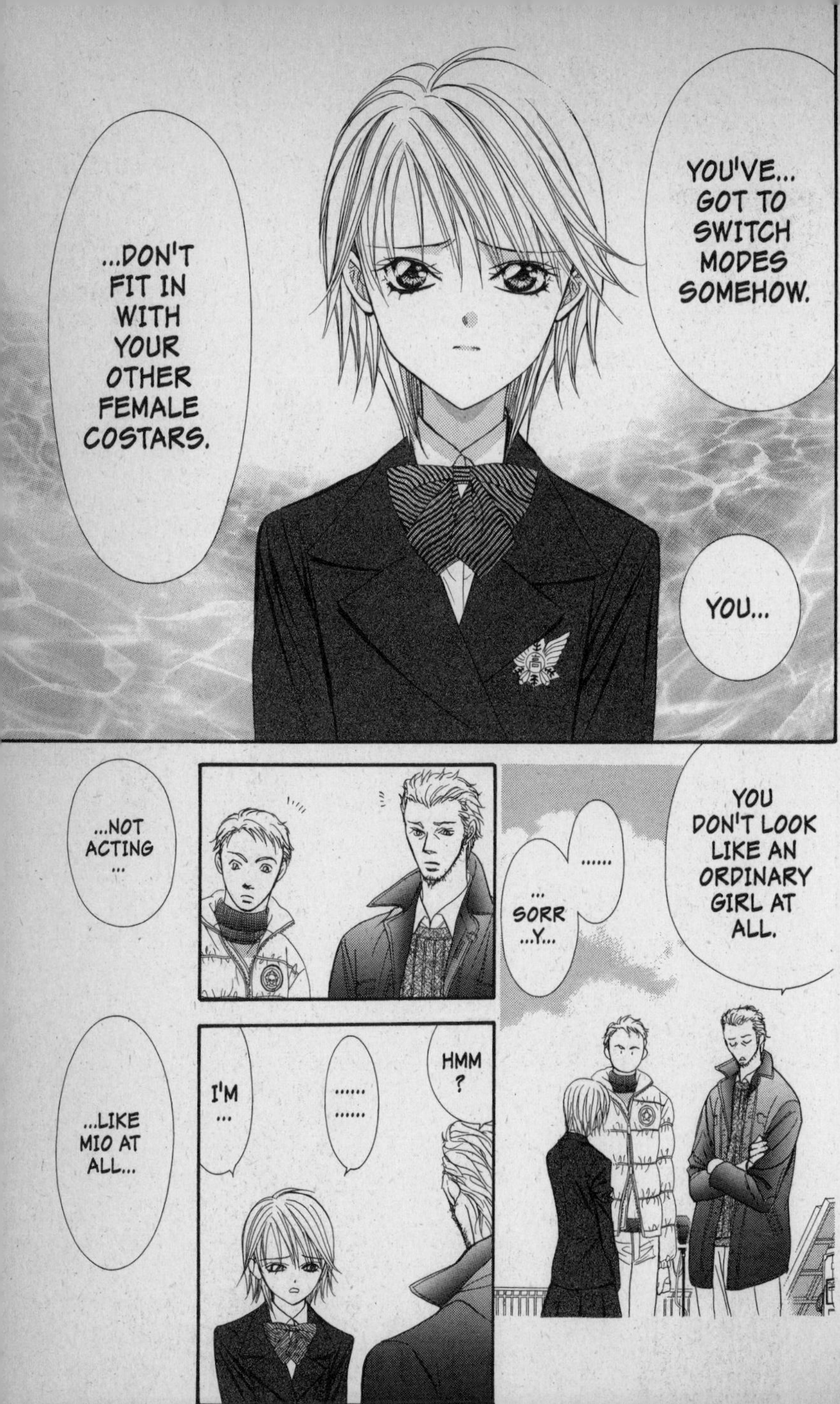
YOU'VE... GOT TO SWITCH MODES SOMEHOW.
YOU...
...DON'T FIT IN WITH YOUR OTHER FEMALE COSTARS.
YOU DON'T LOOK LIKE AN ORDINARY GIRL AT ALL.
......
...SORR...Y...
...NOT ACTING ...
HMM?
....
I'M ...
...LIKE MIO AT ALL...

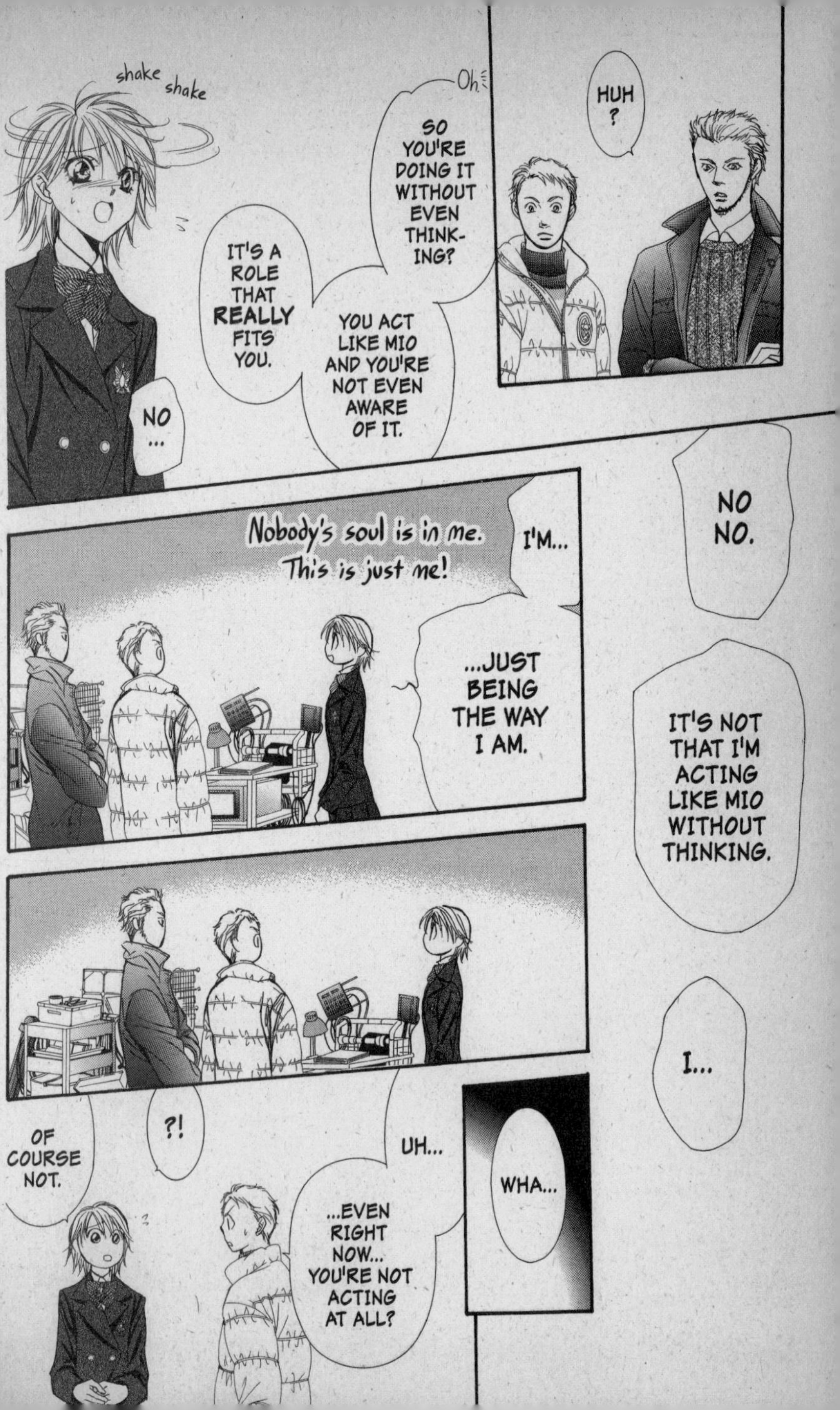
HUH?
Oh
SO YOU'RE DOING IT WITHOUT EVEN THINKING?
YOU ACT LIKE MIO AND YOU'RE NOT EVEN AWARE OF IT.
IT'S A ROLE THAT REALLY FITS YOU.
shake shake
NO...
NO NO.
IT'S NOT THAT I'M ACTING LIKE MIO WITHOUT THINKING.
I...
I'M...
...JUST BEING THE WAY I AM.
Nobody's soul is in me. This is just me!
WHA...
UH...
...EVEN RIGHT NOW... YOU'RE NOT ACTING AT ALL?
?!
OF COURSE NOT.

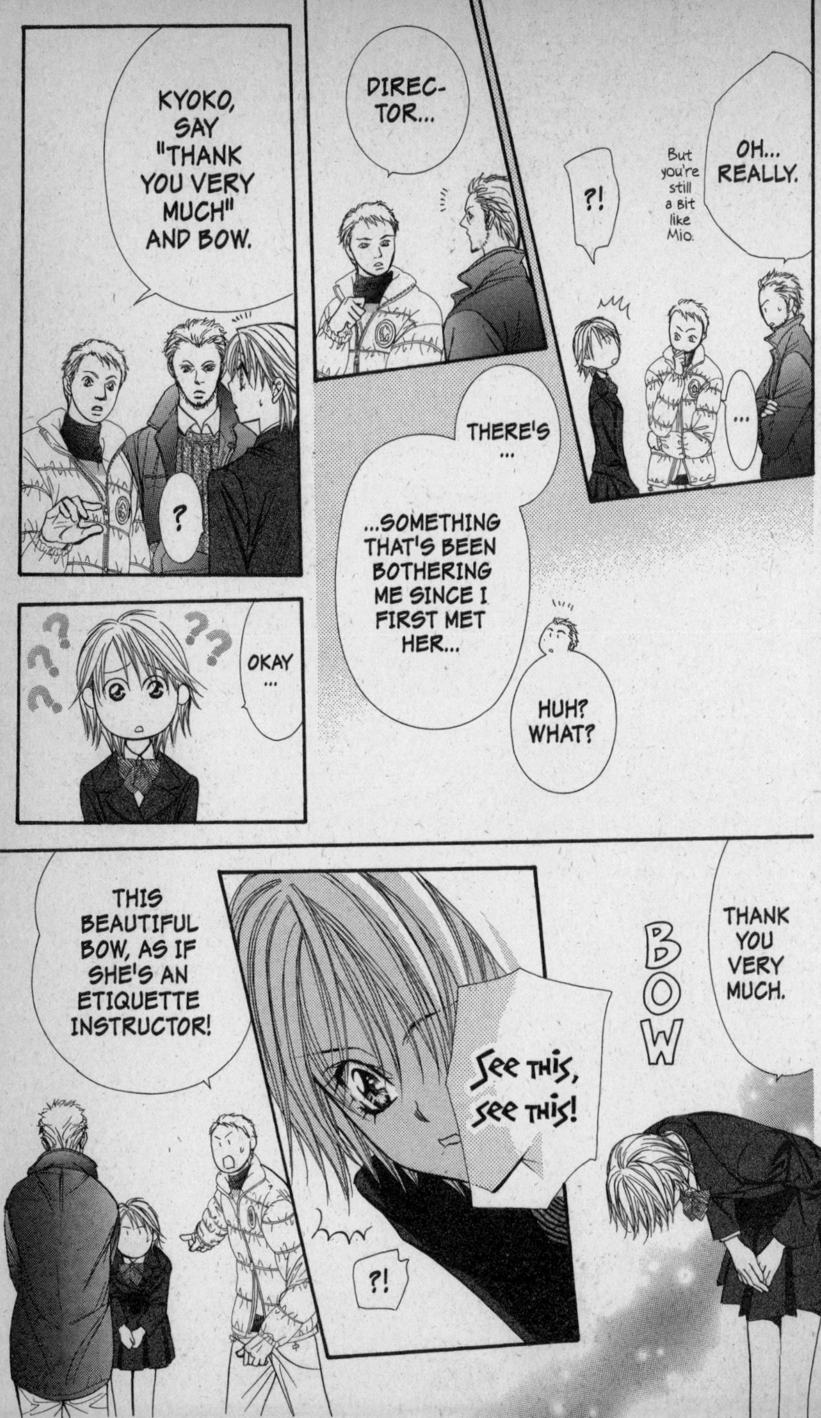
OH... REALLY.
But you're still a bit like Mio.
?!
...
DIREC-TOR...
THERE'S ...
...SOMETHING THAT'S BEEN BOTHERING ME SINCE I FIRST MET HER...
HUH? WHAT?
KYOKO, SAY "THANK YOU VERY MUCH" AND BOW.
?
OKAY ...
THANK YOU VERY MUCH.
BOW
See this, see this!
?!
THIS BEAUTIFUL BOW, AS IF SHE'S AN ETIQUETTE INSTRUCTOR!

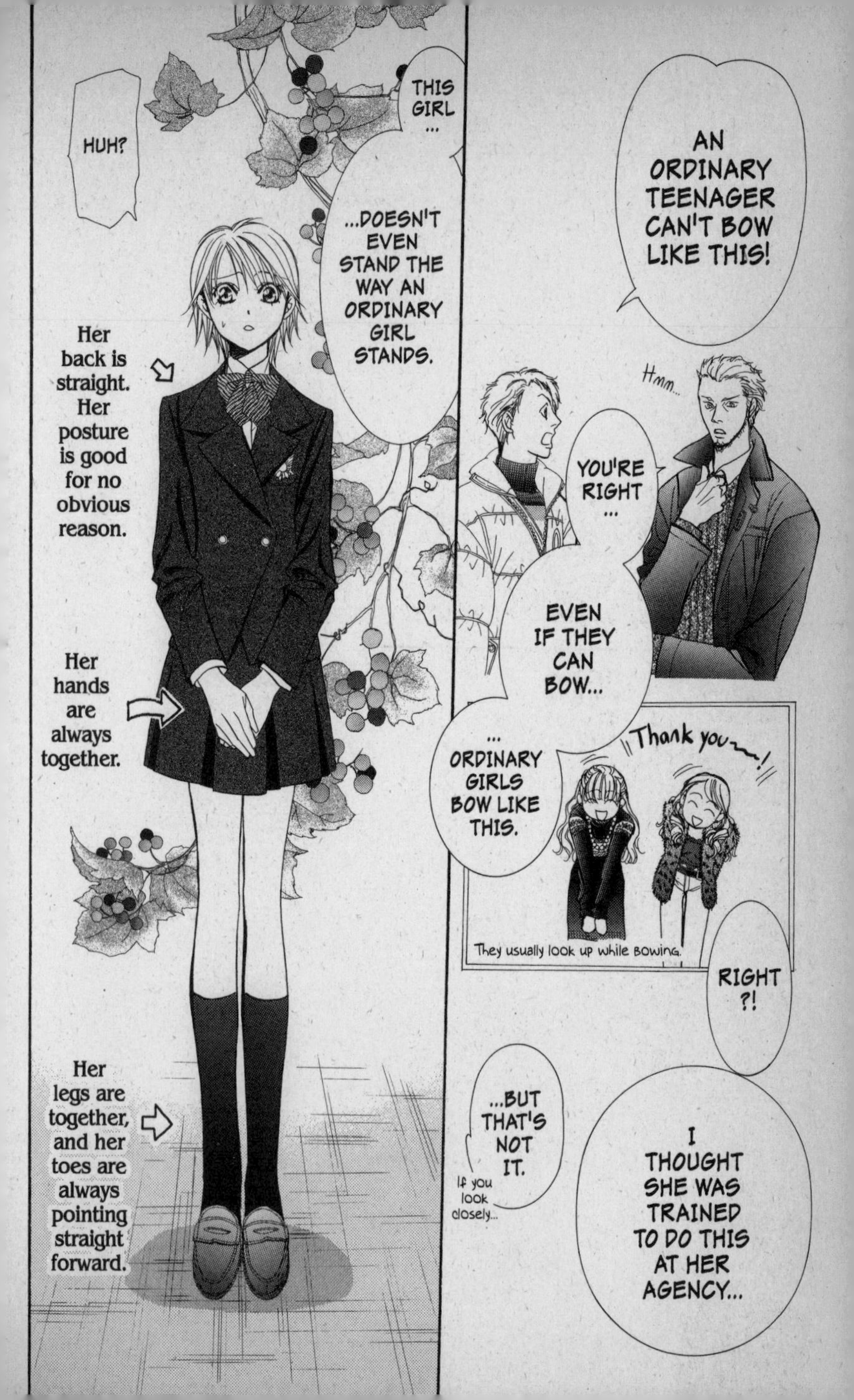
AN ORDINARY TEENAGER CAN'T BOW LIKE THIS!
Hmm...
YOU'RE RIGHT ...
EVEN IF THEY CAN BOW...
... ORDINARY GIRLS BOW LIKE THIS.
Thank you~~!
They usually look up while bowing.
RIGHT ?!
I THOUGHT SHE WAS TRAINED TO DO THIS AT HER AGENCY...
...BUT THAT'S NOT IT.
If you look closely...
THIS GIRL ...
...DOESN'T EVEN STAND THE WAY AN ORDINARY GIRL STANDS.
HUH?
Her back is straight. Her posture is good for no obvious reason.
Her hands are always together.
Her legs are together, and her toes are always pointing straight forward.

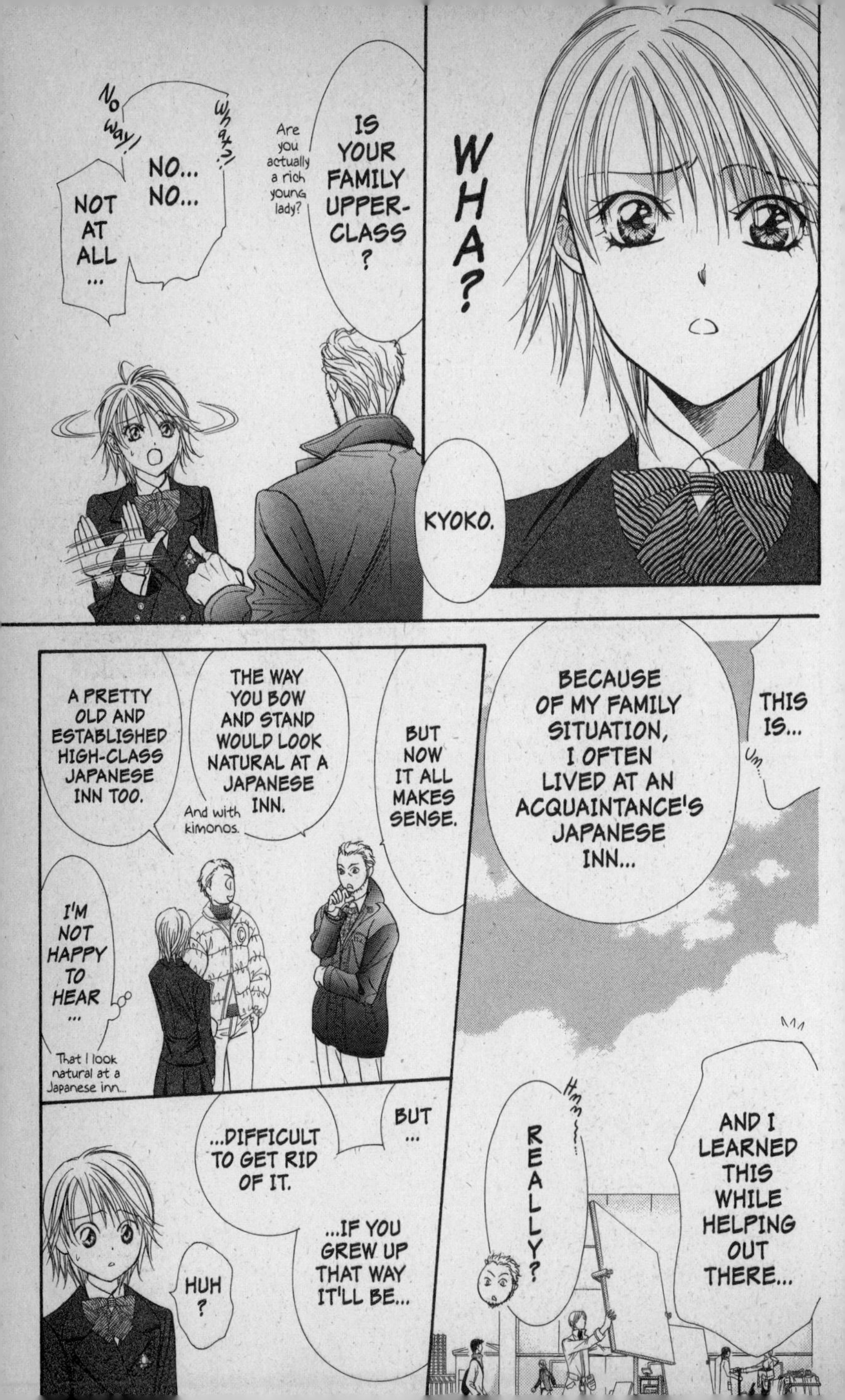
WHA?
KYOKO.
IS YOUR FAMILY UPPER-CLASS?
Are you actually a rich young lady?
What?!
NO... NO...
No way!!
NOT AT ALL...
THIS IS...
Um...
BECAUSE OF MY FAMILY SITUATION, I OFTEN LIVED AT AN ACQUAINTANCE'S JAPANESE INN...
AND I LEARNED THIS WHILE HELPING OUT THERE...
REALLY?
Hmm...
BUT NOW IT ALL MAKES SENSE.
THE WAY YOU BOW AND STAND WOULD LOOK NATURAL AT A JAPANESE INN.
And with kimonos.
A PRETTY OLD AND ESTABLISHED HIGH-CLASS JAPANESE INN TOO.
I'M NOT HAPPY TO HEAR...
That I look natural at a Japanese inn...
BUT...
...IF YOU GREW UP THAT WAY IT'LL BE...
...DIFFICULT TO GET RID OF IT.
HUH?

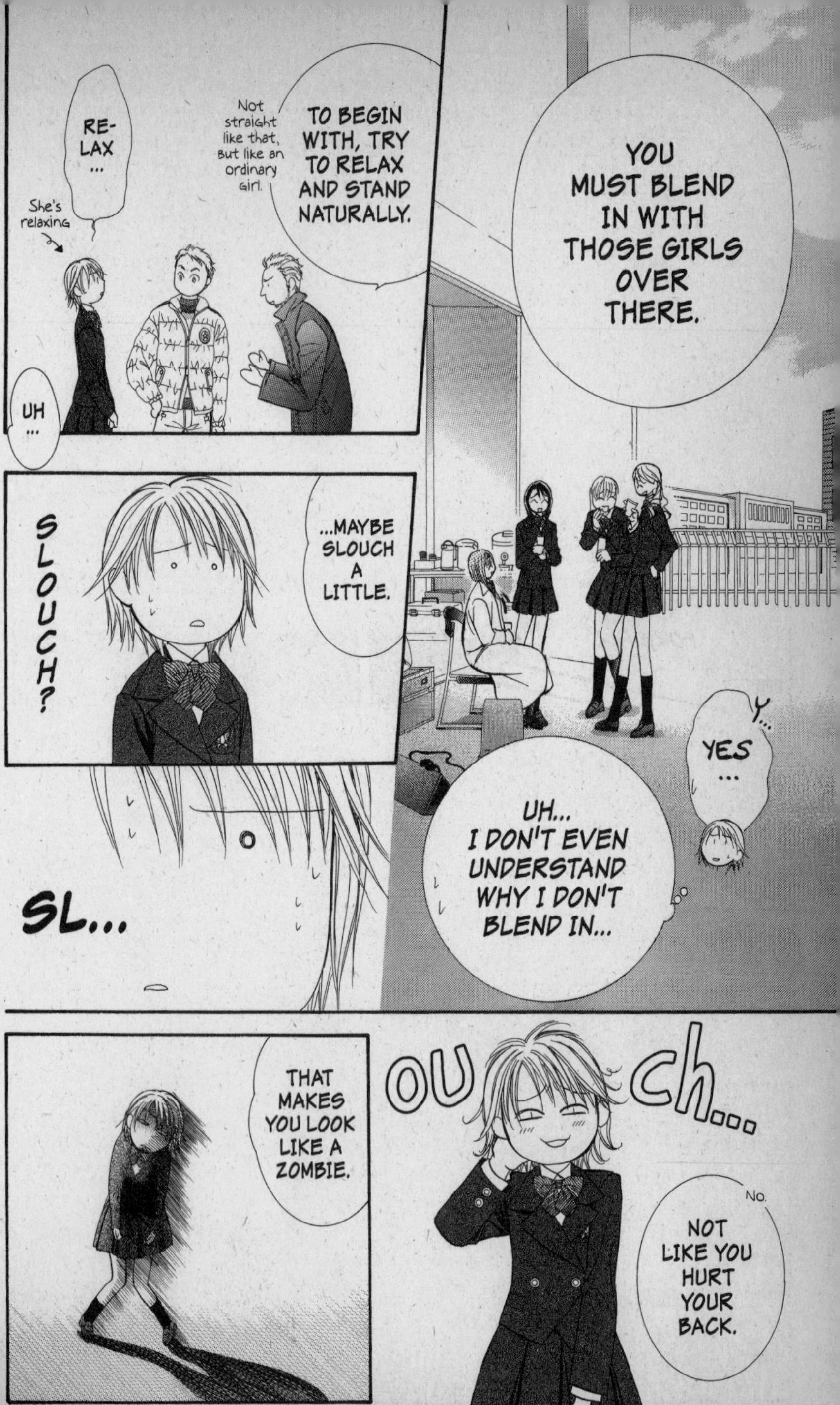
YOU MUST BLEND IN WITH THOSE GIRLS OVER THERE.
Y... YES...
UH... I DON'T EVEN UNDERSTAND WHY I DON'T BLEND IN...
TO BEGIN WITH, TRY TO RELAX AND STAND NATURALLY.
Not straight like that, but like an ordinary girl.
RE-LAX...
She's relaxing
UH...
...MAYBE SLOUCH A LITTLE.
SLOUCH?
SL...
ouch...
NO.
NOT LIKE YOU HURT YOUR BACK.
THAT MAKES YOU LOOK LIKE A ZOMBIE.

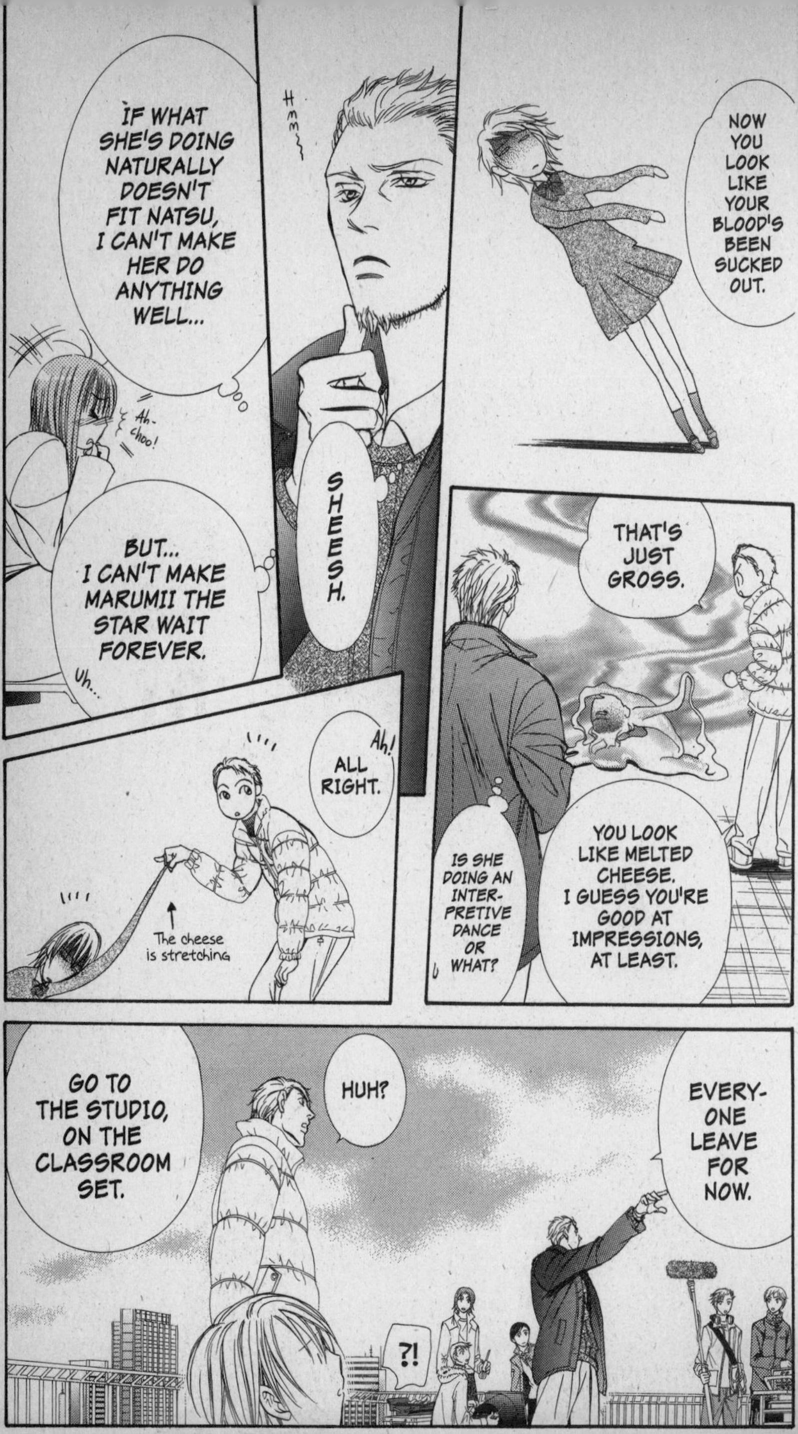
NOW YOU LOOK LIKE YOUR BLOOD'S BEEN SUCKED OUT.
HMM~
SHEESH.
IF WHAT SHE'S DOING NATURALLY DOESN'T FIT NATSU, I CAN'T MAKE HER DO ANYTHING WELL...
Ah-choo!
BUT... I CAN'T MAKE MARUMII THE STAR WAIT FOREVER.
Uh...
THAT'S JUST GROSS.
YOU LOOK LIKE MELTED CHEESE. I GUESS YOU'RE GOOD AT IMPRESSIONS, AT LEAST.
IS SHE DOING AN INTER-PRETIVE DANCE OR WHAT?
Ah!
ALL RIGHT.
The cheese is stretching
EVERY-ONE LEAVE FOR NOW.
HUH?
GO TO THE STUDIO, ON THE CLASSROOM SET.
?!

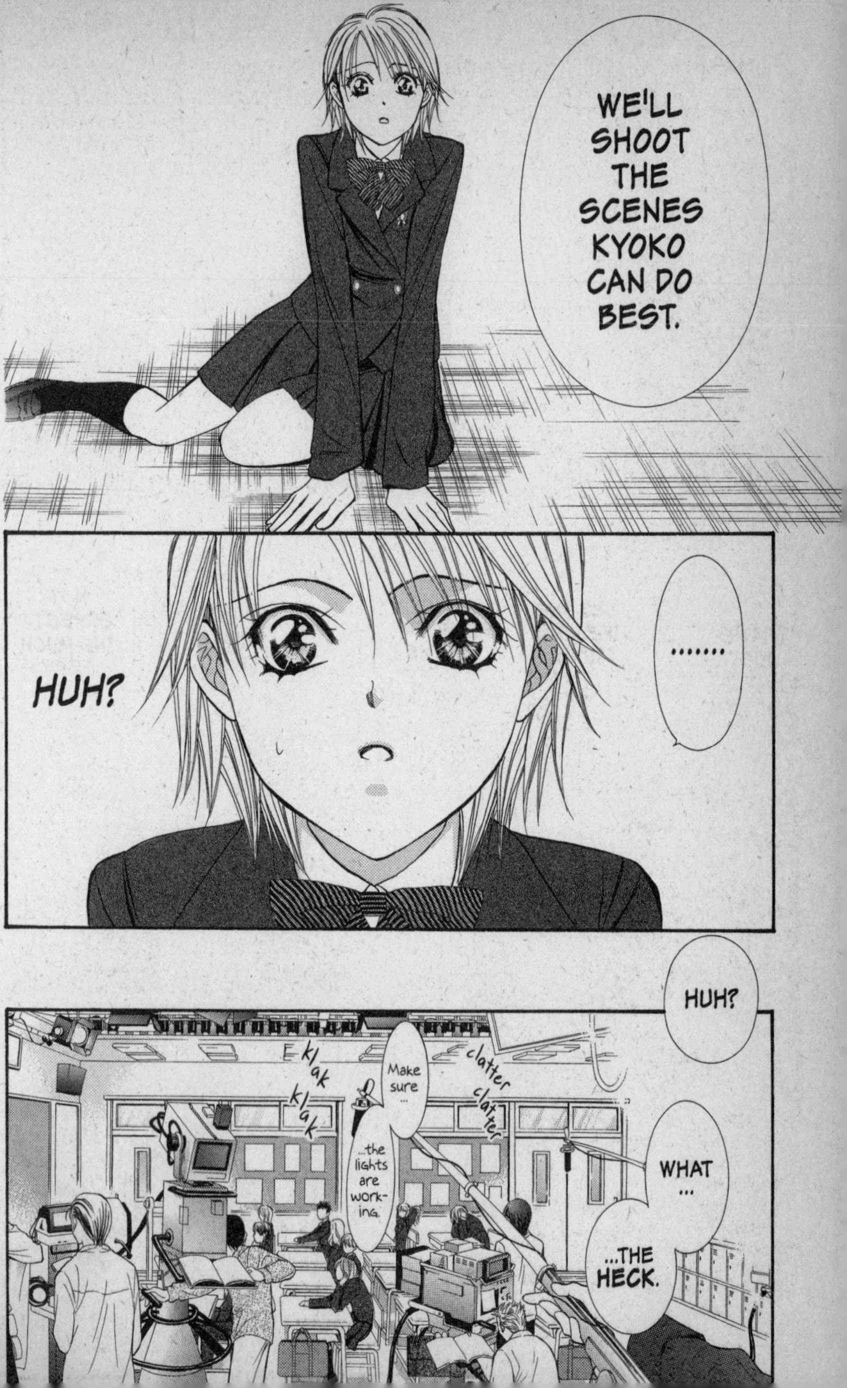
WE'LL SHOOT THE SCENES KYOKO CAN DO BEST.
....
HUH?
HUH?
WHAT ...
...THE HECK.
clatter clatter
Make sure ...
...the lights are work-ing.
klak klak

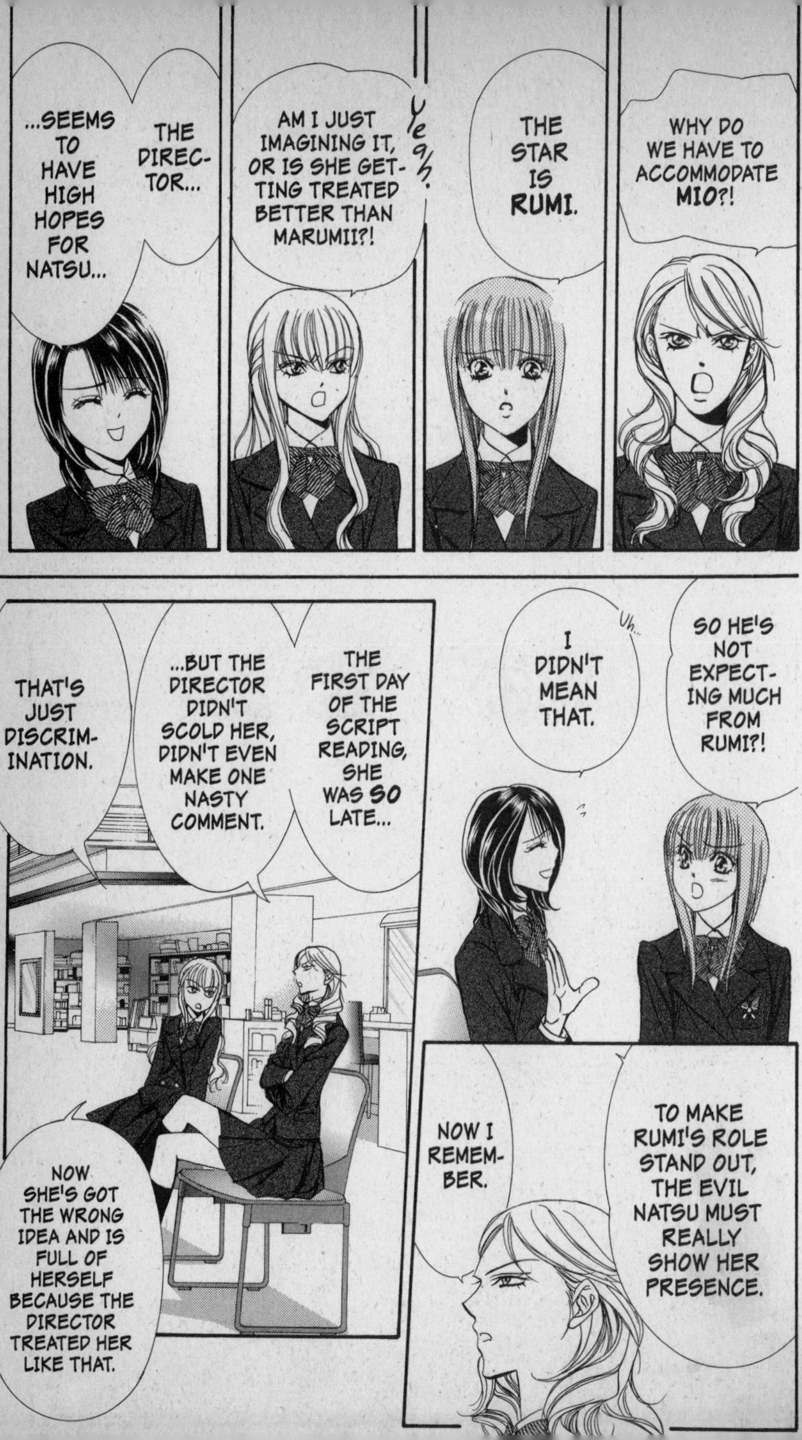
WHY DO WE HAVE TO ACCOMMODATE MIO?!
THE STAR IS RUMI.
Yeah.
AM I JUST IMAGINING IT, OR IS SHE GETTING TREATED BETTER THAN MARUMII?!
THE DIRECTOR...
...SEEMS TO HAVE HIGH HOPES FOR NATSU...
SO HE'S NOT EXPECTING MUCH FROM RUMI?!
Uh...
I DIDN'T MEAN THAT.
TO MAKE RUMI'S ROLE STAND OUT, THE EVIL NATSU MUST REALLY SHOW HER PRESENCE.
NOW I REMEMBER.
THE FIRST DAY OF THE SCRIPT READING, SHE WAS SO LATE...
...BUT THE DIRECTOR DIDN'T SCOLD HER, DIDN'T EVEN MAKE ONE NASTY COMMENT.
THAT'S JUST DISCRIMINATION.
NOW SHE'S GOT THE WRONG IDEA AND IS FULL OF HERSELF BECAUSE THE DIRECTOR TREATED HER LIKE THAT.

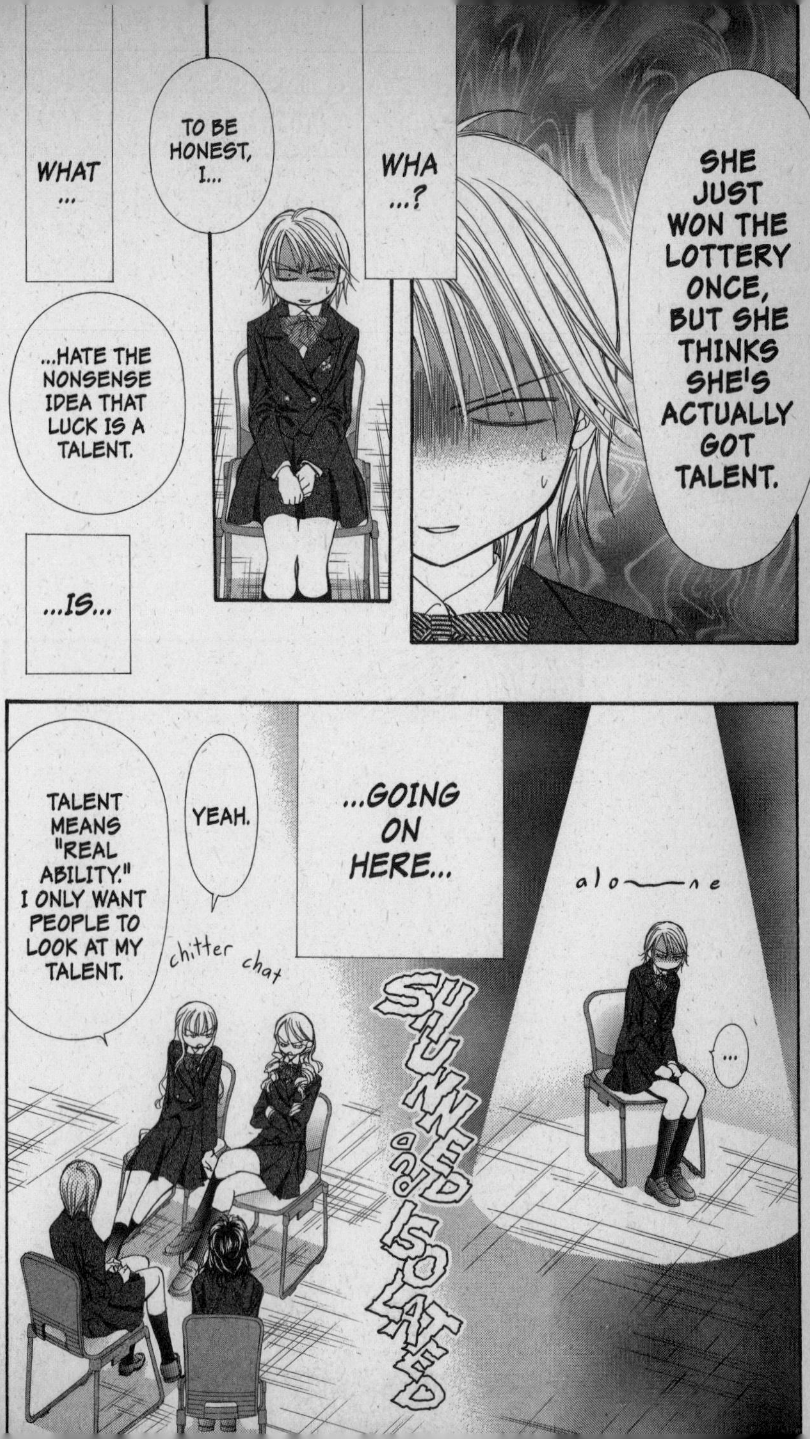
SHE JUST WON THE LOTTERY ONCE, BUT SHE THINKS SHE'S ACTUALLY GOT TALENT.
WHA ...?
TO BE HONEST, I...
...HATE THE NONSENSE IDEA THAT LUCK IS A TALENT.
WHAT ...
...IS...
...GOING ON HERE...
alo—ne
YEAH.
TALENT MEANS "REAL ABILITY." I ONLY WANT PEOPLE TO LOOK AT MY TALENT.
chitter chat
...
SHUNNED and ISOLATED

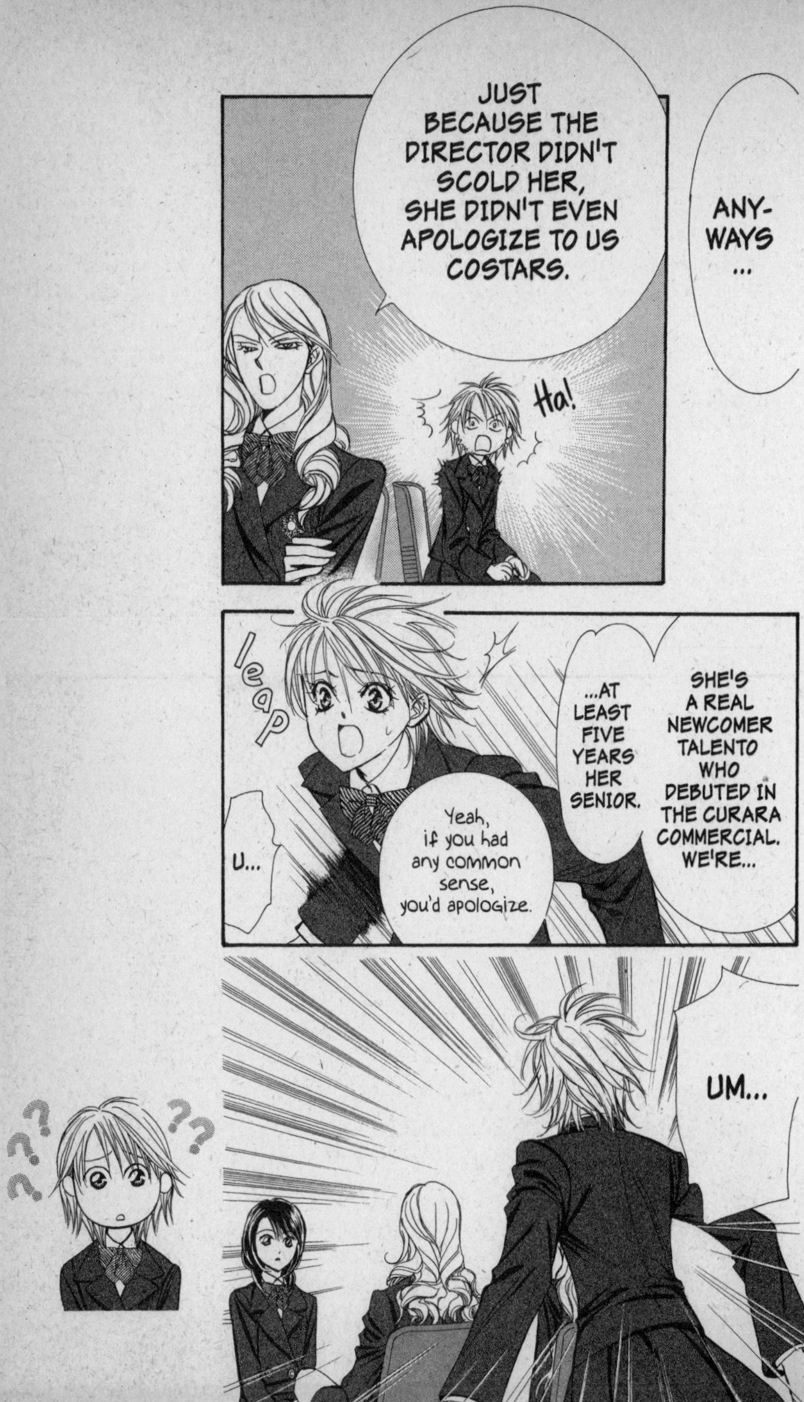
ANY-WAYS ...
JUST BECAUSE THE DIRECTOR DIDN'T SCOLD HER, SHE DIDN'T EVEN APOLOGIZE TO US COSTARS.
Ha!
SHE'S A REAL NEWCOMER TALENTO WHO DEBUTED IN THE CURARA COMMERCIAL. WE'RE...
...AT LEAST FIVE YEARS HER SENIOR.
leap
Yeah, if you had any common sense, you'd apologize.
U...
UM...
??
??
??

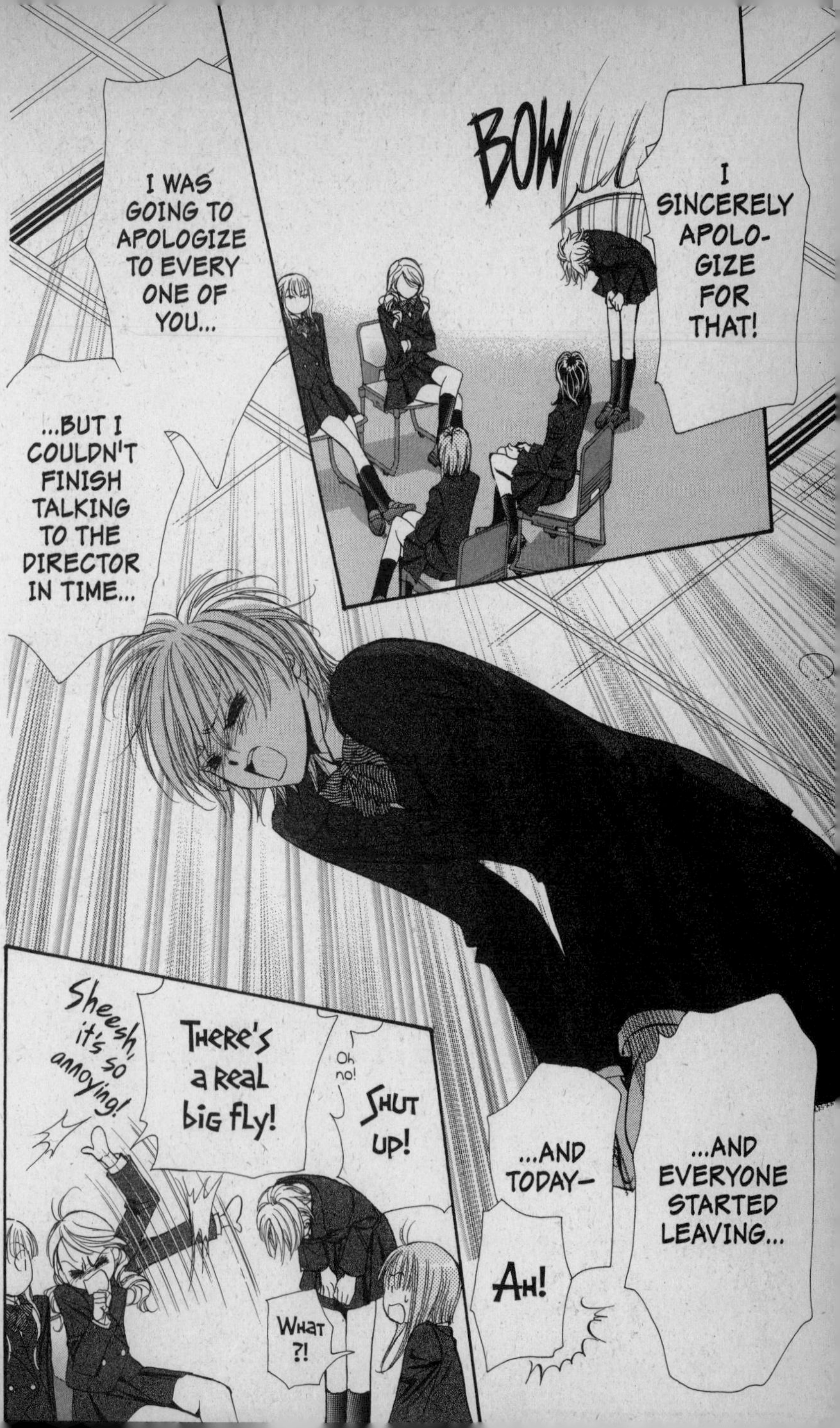
BOW
I SINCERELY APOLOGIZE FOR THAT!
I WAS GOING TO APOLOGIZE TO EVERY ONE OF YOU...
...BUT I COULDN'T FINISH TALKING TO THE DIRECTOR IN TIME...
...AND EVERYONE STARTED LEAVING...
...AND TODAY—
AH!
Oh no!
SHUT UP!
There's a real big fly!
Sheesh, it's so annoying!
WHAT?!

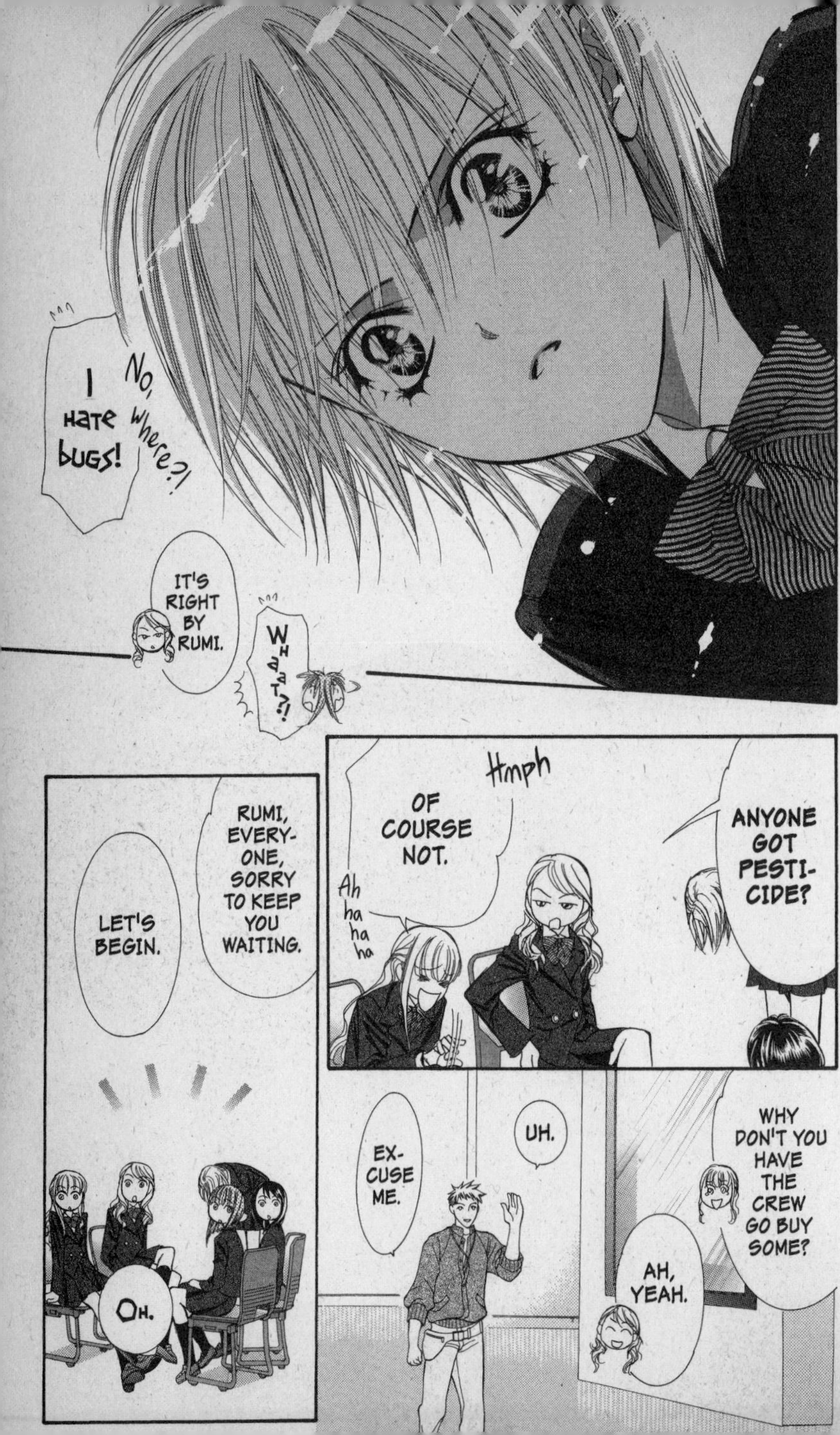
No, where?!
I hate bugs!
Whaat?!
It's right by Rumi.
Anyone got pesticide?
Hmph
Of course not.
Ah ha ha ha
Why don't you have the crew go buy some?
Ah, yeah.
Uh.
Excuse me.
Rumi, everyone, sorry to keep you waiting.
Let's begin.
Oh.

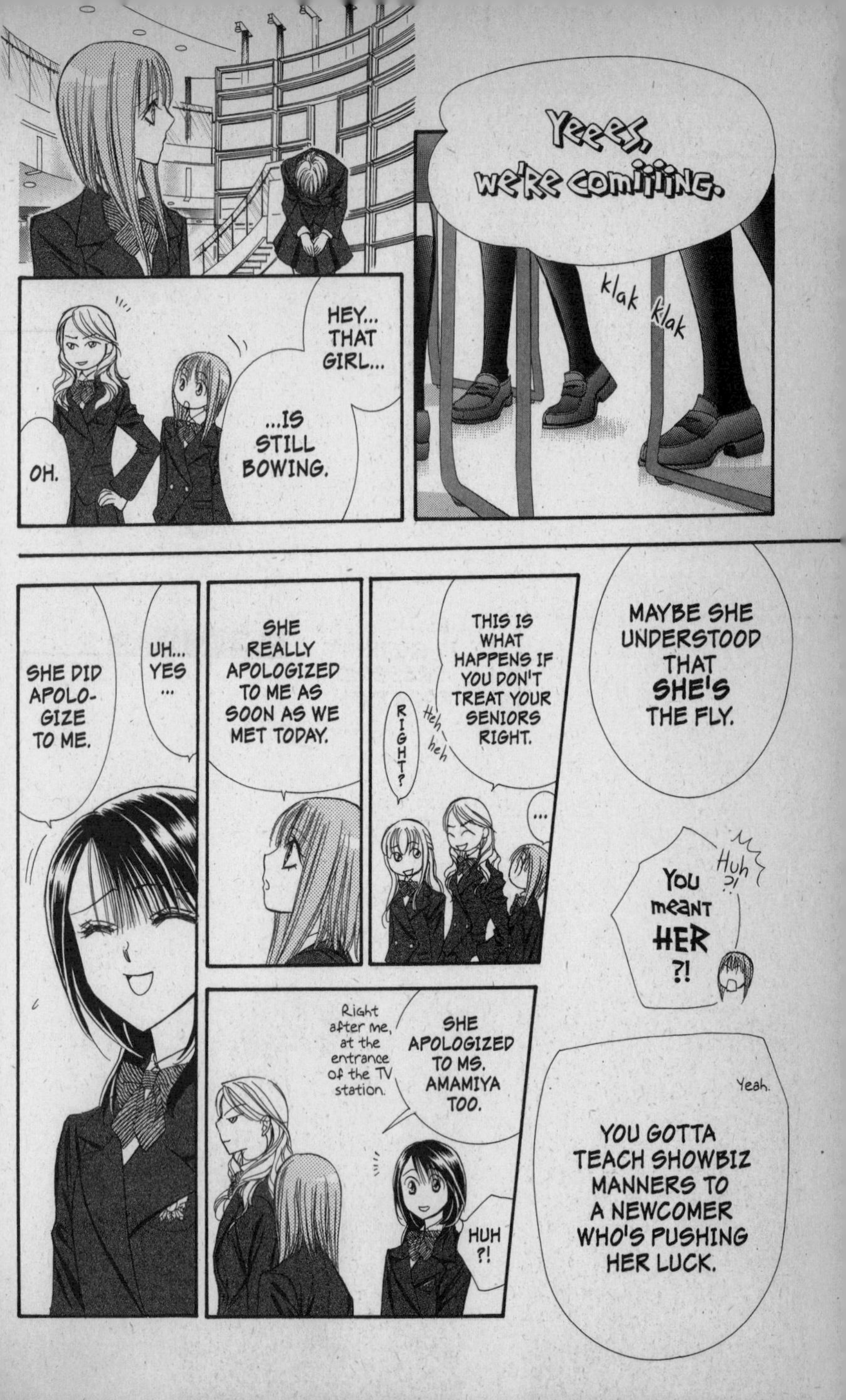

Yeees, we're comiiiing.
klak klak
HEY... THAT GIRL...
...IS STILL BOWING.
OH.
MAYBE SHE UNDERSTOOD THAT SHE'S THE FLY.
You meant HER?!
Huh?!
Yeah.
YOU GOTTA TEACH SHOWBIZ MANNERS TO A NEWCOMER WHO'S PUSHING HER LUCK.
THIS IS WHAT HAPPENS IF YOU DON'T TREAT YOUR SENIORS RIGHT.
RIGHT?
Heh heh
...
SHE REALLY APOLOGIZED TO ME AS SOON AS WE MET TODAY.
UH... YES...
SHE DID APOLOGIZE TO ME.
SHE APOLOGIZED TO MS. AMAMIYA TOO.
Right after me, at the entrance of the TV station.
HUH?!

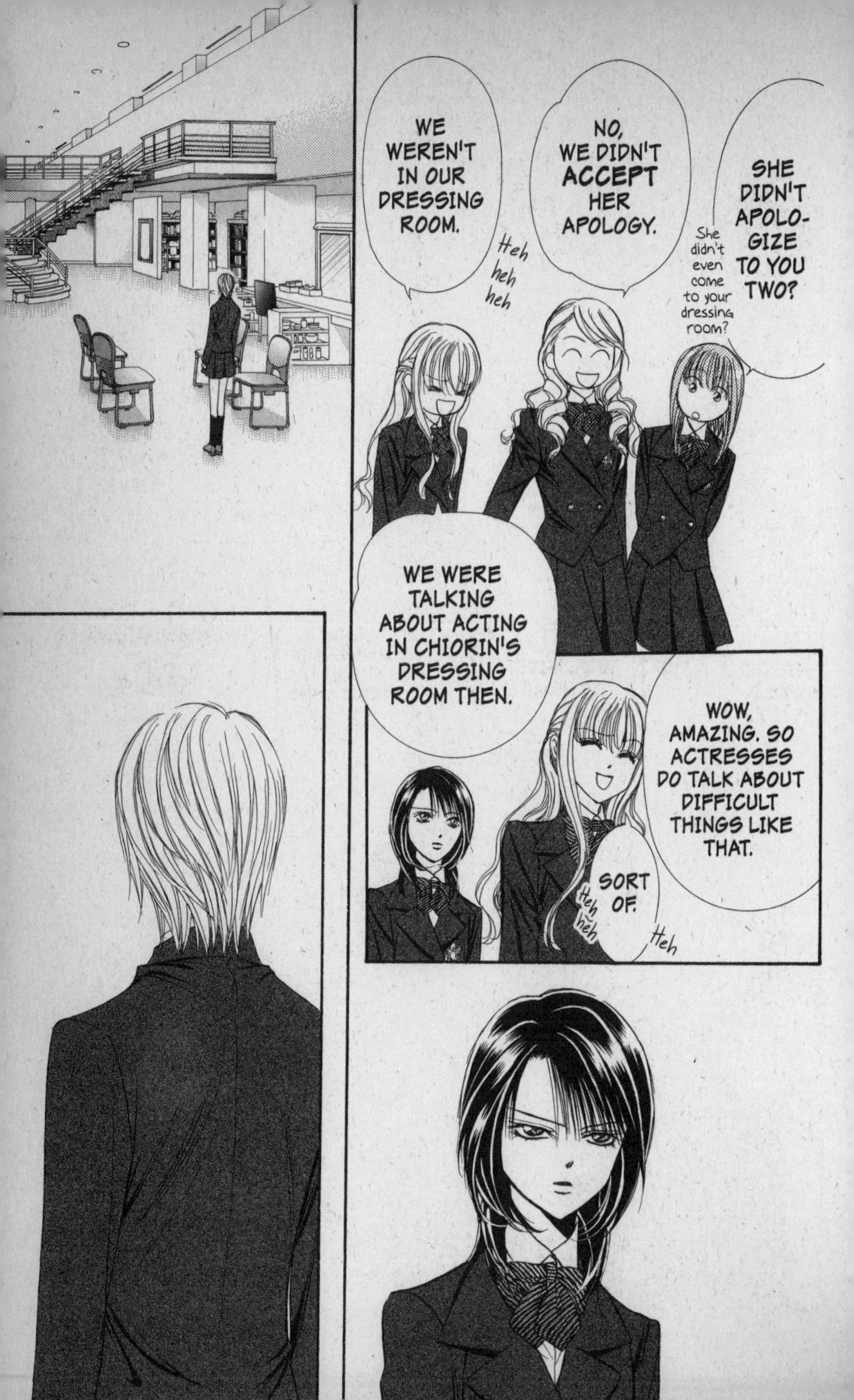
SHE DIDN'T APOLOGIZE TO YOU TWO?
She didn't even come to your dressing room?
NO, WE DIDN'T ACCEPT HER APOLOGY.
WE WEREN'T IN OUR DRESSING ROOM.
Heh heh heh
WE WERE TALKING ABOUT ACTING IN CHIORIN'S DRESSING ROOM THEN.
WOW, AMAZING. SO ACTRESSES DO TALK ABOUT DIFFICULT THINGS LIKE THAT.
Heh
SORT OF.
Heh heh

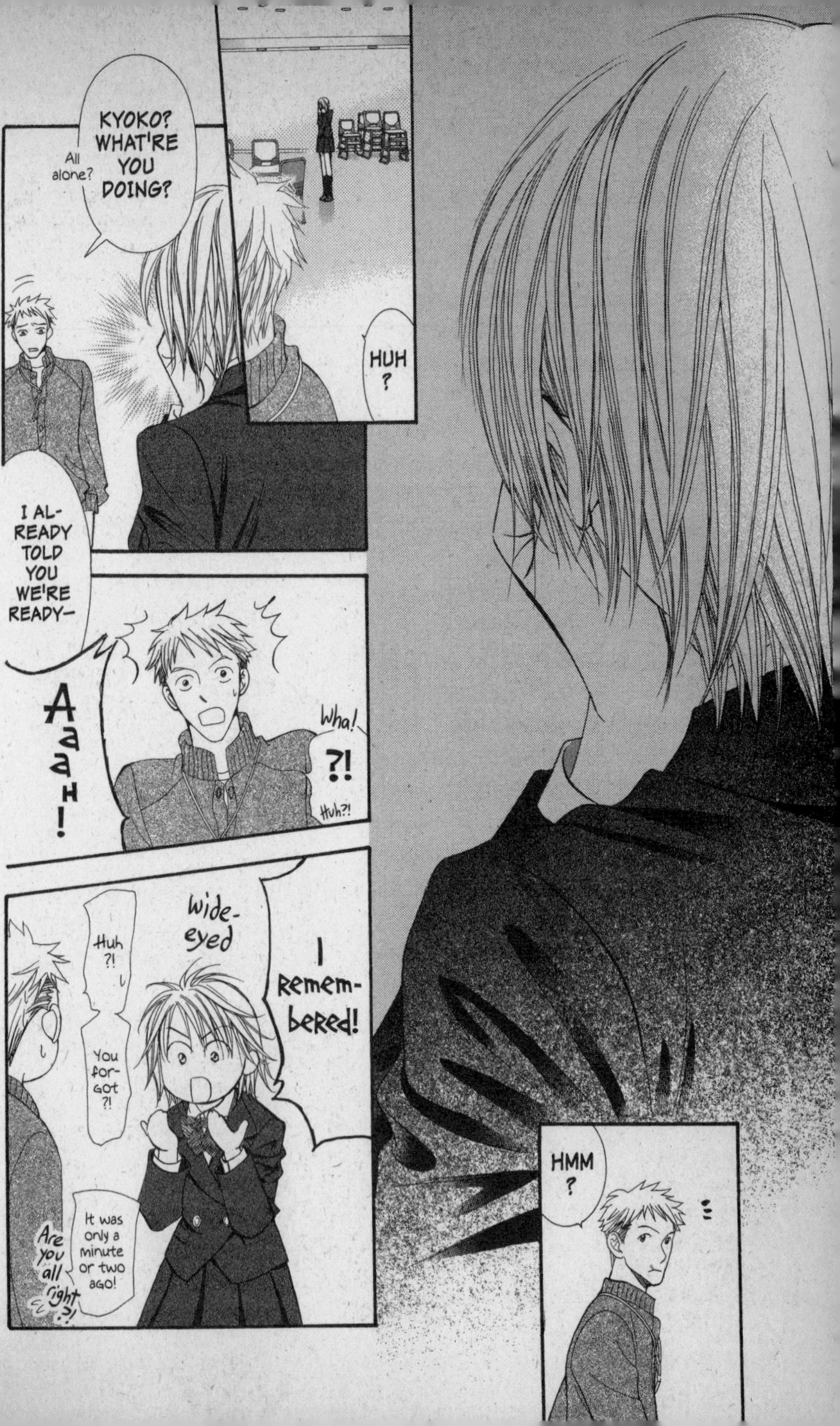
HMM?
...
HUH?
KYOKO? WHAT'RE YOU DOING?
All alone?
I AL-READY TOLD YOU WE'RE READY—
Aaah!
Wha! ?!
Huh?!
I remem-bered!
wide-eyed
Huh?!
You for-got?!
It was only a minute or two ago!
Are you all right?!

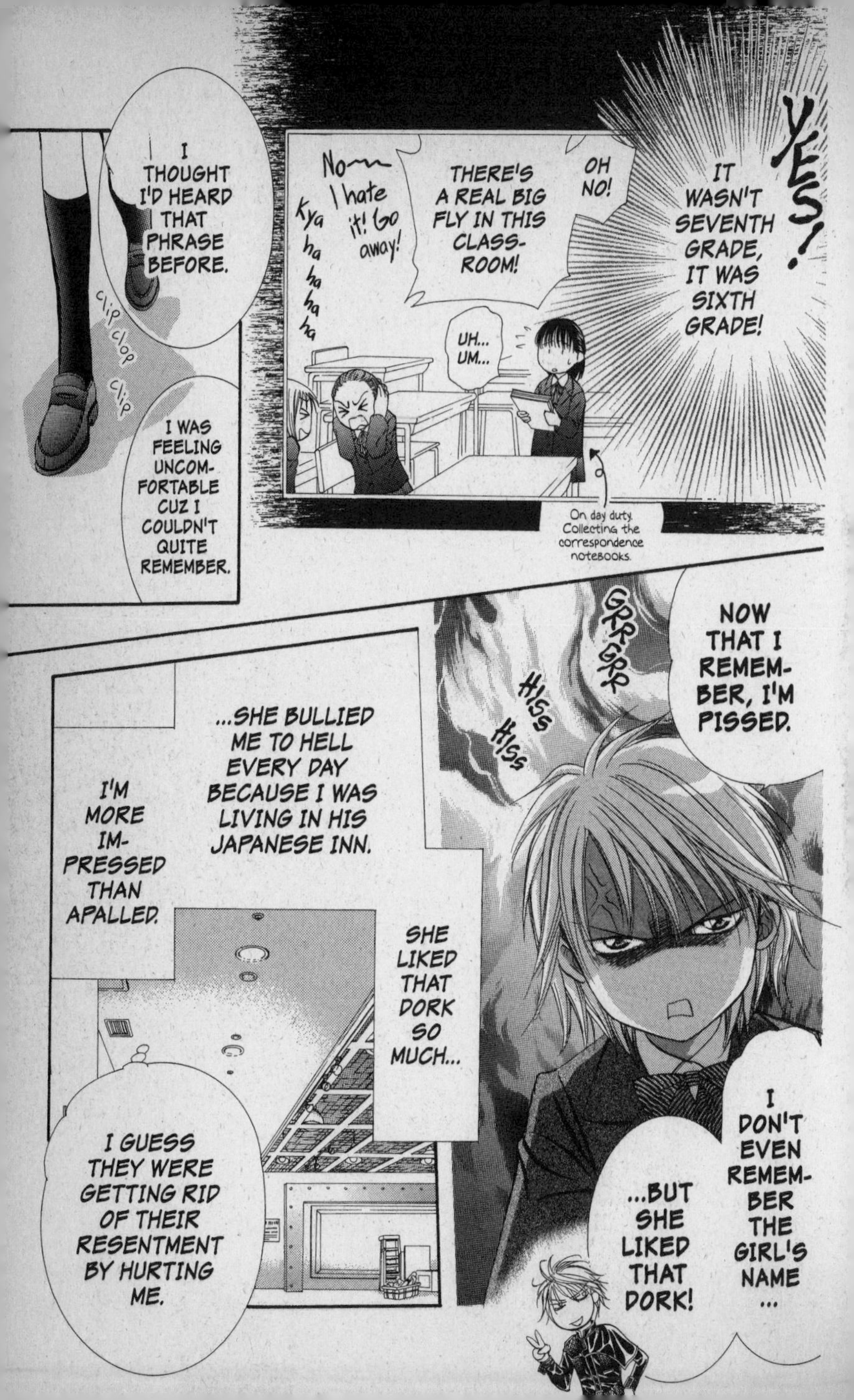
YES!
IT WASN'T SEVENTH GRADE, IT WAS SIXTH GRADE!
OH NO!
THERE'S A REAL BIG FLY IN THIS CLASSROOM!
No~~ I hate it! Go away!
Kya ha ha ha ha ha
UH... UM...
On day duty. Collecting the correspondence notebooks.
I THOUGHT I'D HEARD THAT PHRASE BEFORE.
clip clop clip
I WAS FEELING UNCOMFORTABLE CUZ I COULDN'T QUITE REMEMBER.
NOW THAT I REMEMBER, I'M PISSED.
GRR GRR
HISS HISS
I DON'T EVEN REMEMBER THE GIRL'S NAME ...
...BUT SHE LIKED THAT DORK!
...SHE BULLIED ME TO HELL EVERY DAY BECAUSE I WAS LIVING IN HIS JAPANESE INN.
I'M MORE IMPRESSED THAN APALLED.
SHE LIKED THAT DORK SO MUCH...
I GUESS THEY WERE GETTING RID OF THEIR RESENTMENT BY HURTING ME.

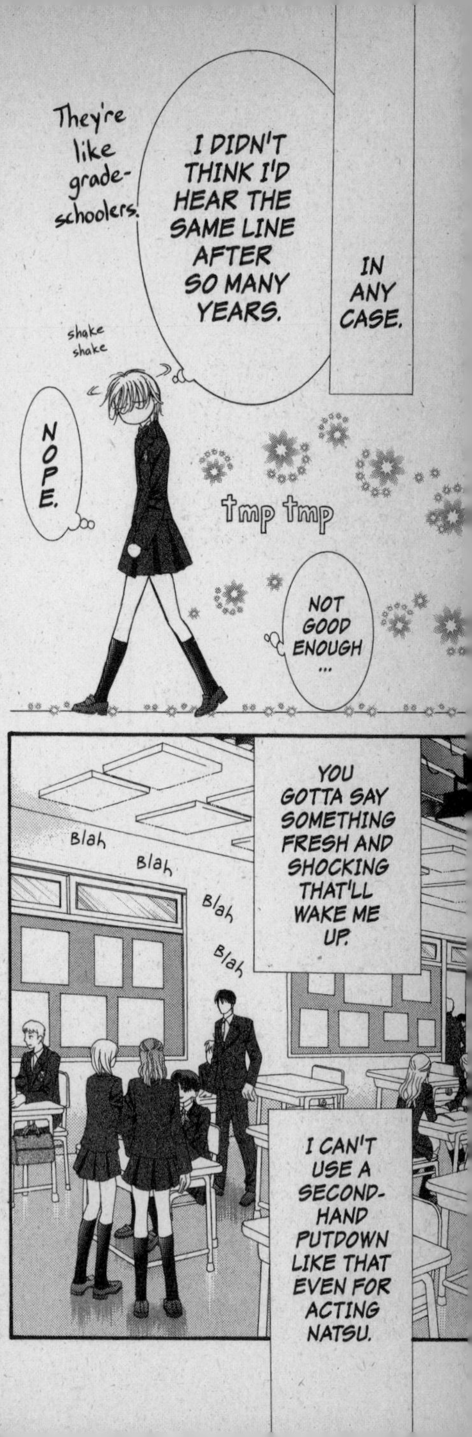
IN ANY CASE.
I DIDN'T THINK I'D HEAR THE SAME LINE AFTER SO MANY YEARS.
They're like grade-schoolers.
shake shake
NOPE.
tmp tmp
NOT GOOD ENOUGH ...
YOU GOTTA SAY SOMETHING FRESH AND SHOCKING THAT'LL WAKE ME UP.
Blah
Blah
Blah
Blah
I CAN'T USE A SECOND-HAND PUTDOWN LIKE THAT EVEN FOR ACTING NATSU.
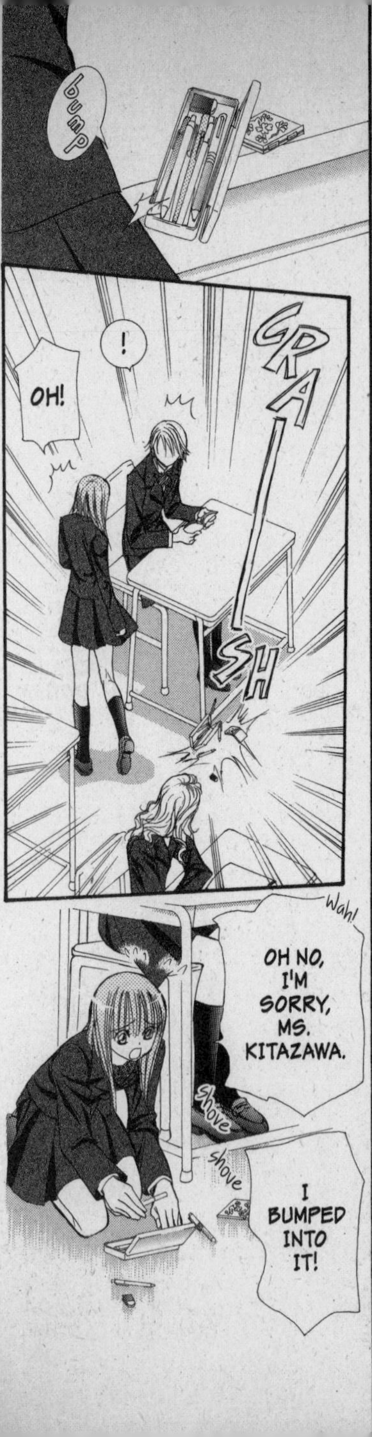
bump
CRASH
!
OH!
Wah!
OH NO, I'M SORRY, MS. KITAZAWA.
shove
shove
I BUMPED INTO IT!

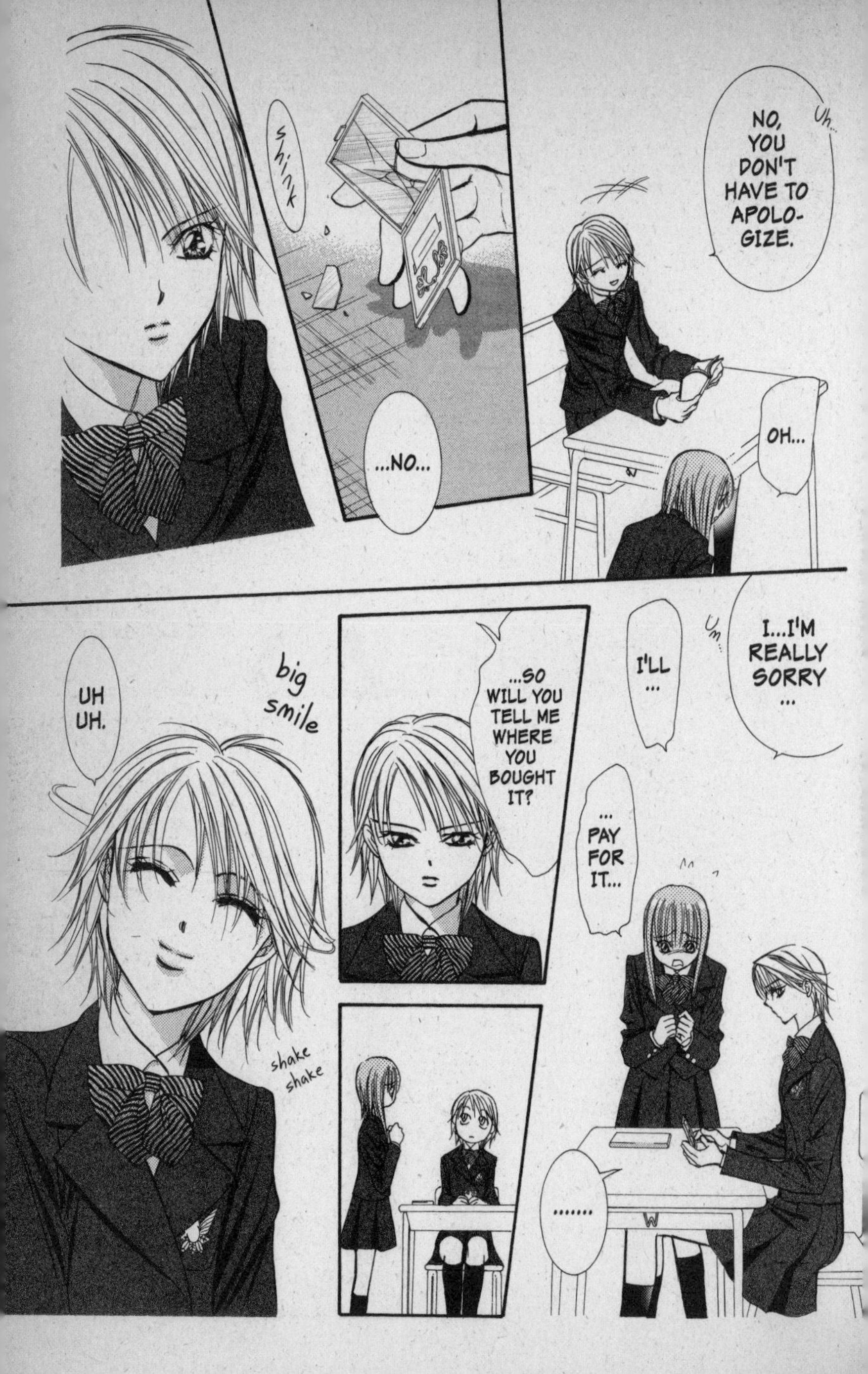
Uh...
NO, YOU DON'T HAVE TO APOLOGIZE.
OH...
shink
...NO...
Um...
I...I'M REALLY SORRY ...
I'LL ...
... PAY FOR IT...
....
...SO WILL YOU TELL ME WHERE YOU BOUGHT IT?
UH UH.
big smile
shake shake

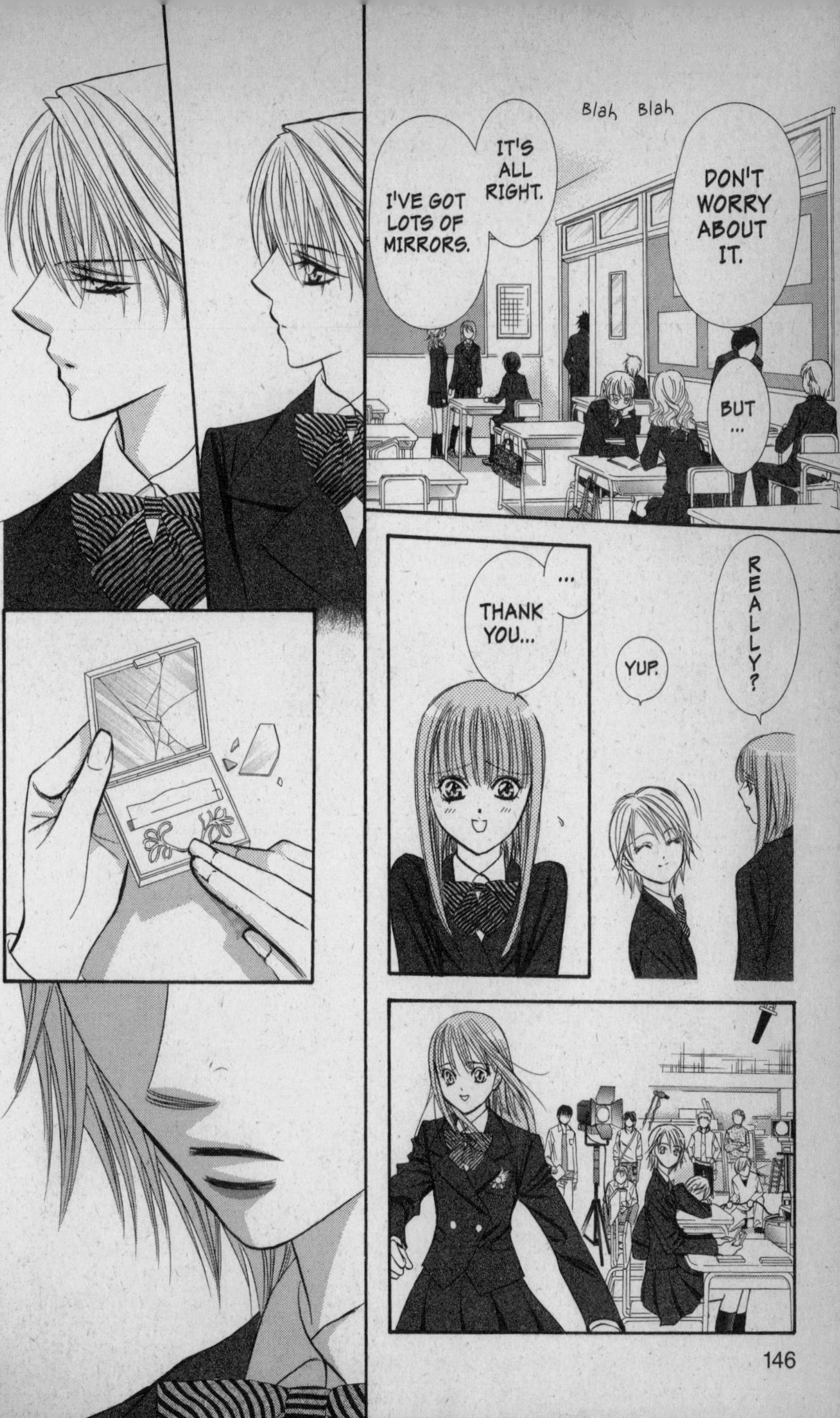
Blah Blah
DON'T WORRY ABOUT IT.
IT'S ALL RIGHT.
I'VE GOT LOTS OF MIRRORS.
BUT ...
REALLY?
YUP.
... THANK YOU...

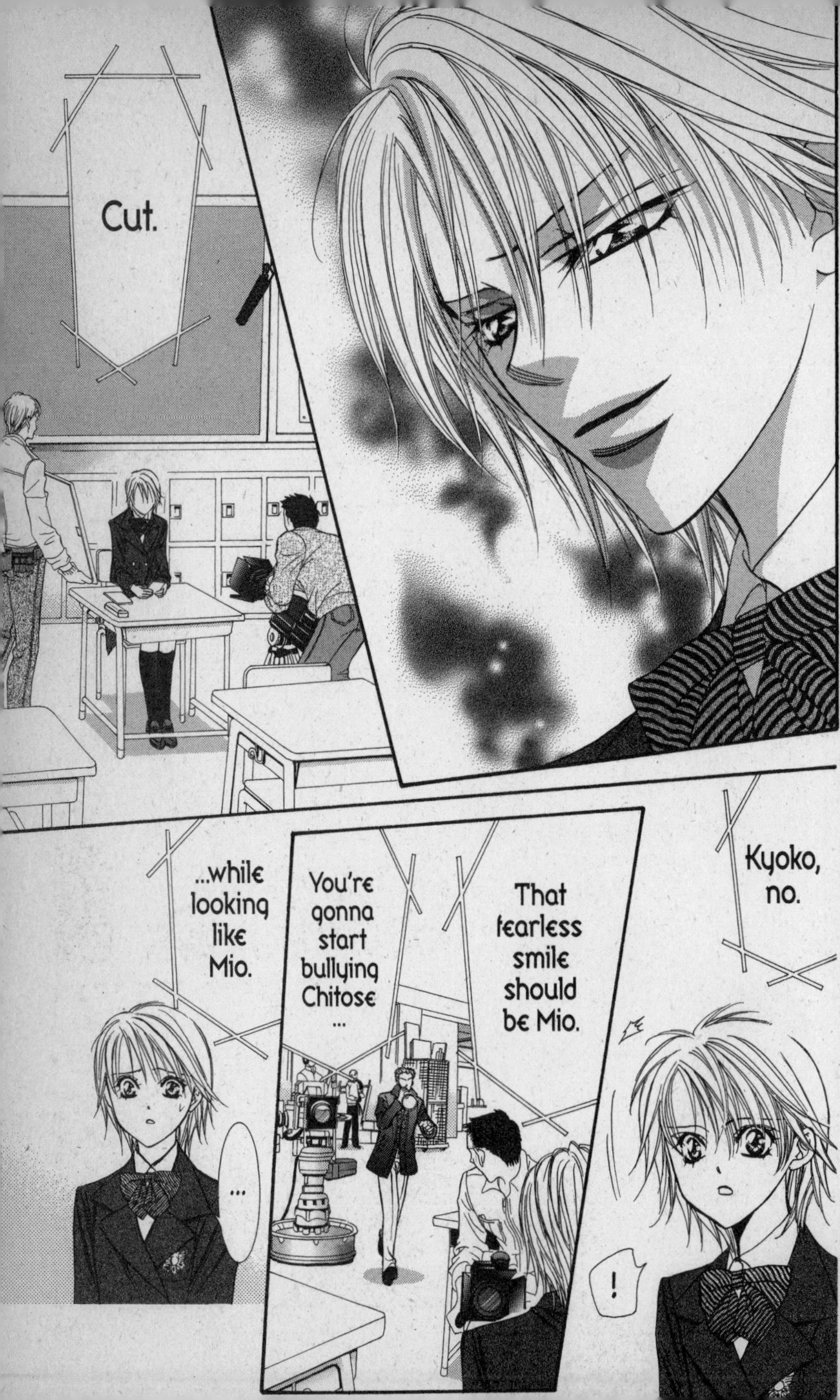
Cut.
Kyoko, no.
!
That tearless smile should be Mio.
You're gonna start bullying Chitose ...
...while looking like Mio.
...

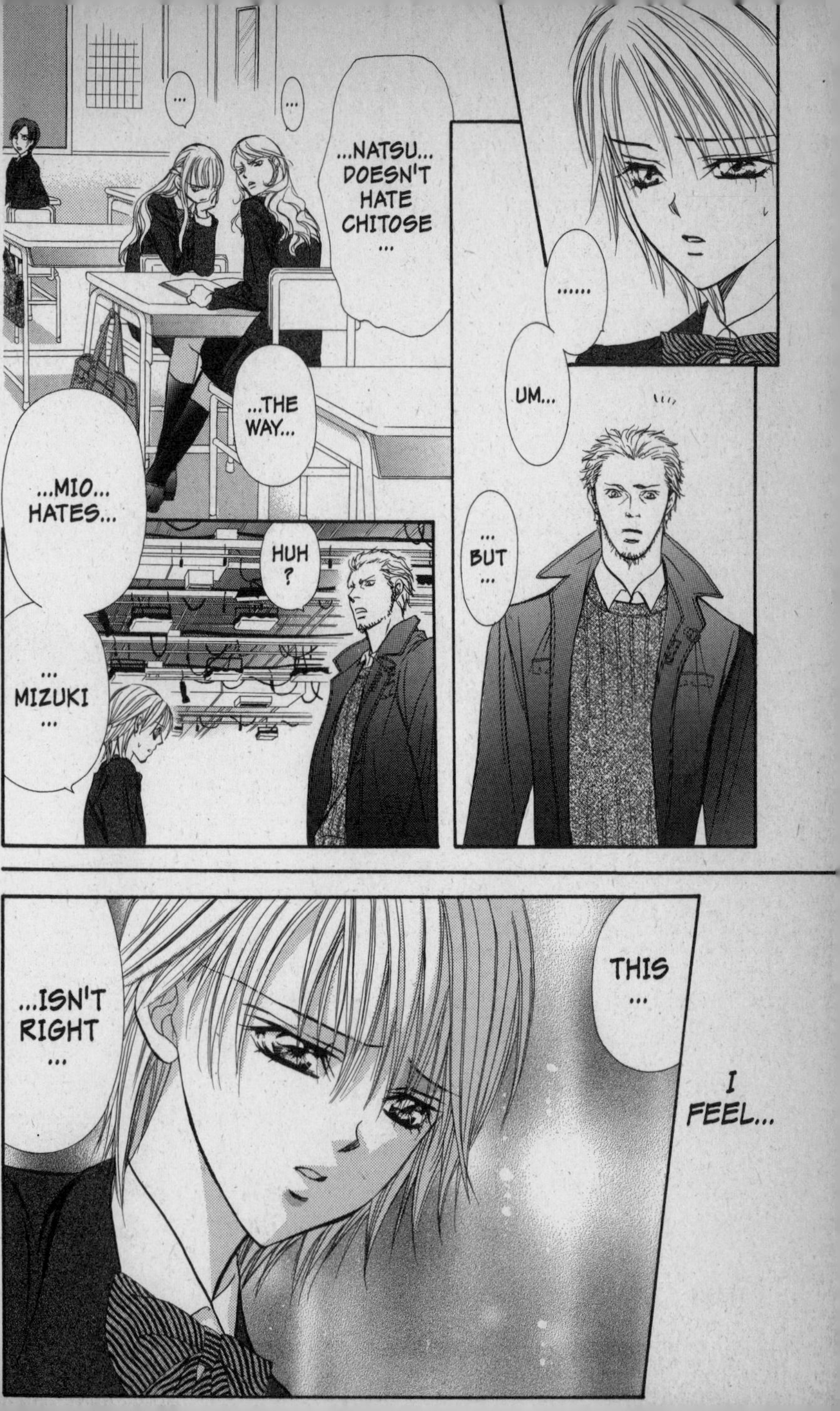

......
UM...
... BUT ...
...
...
...NATSU... DOESN'T HATE CHITOSE ...
...THE WAY...
...MIO... HATES...
HUH ?
... MIZUKI ...
THIS ...
I FEEL...
...ISN'T RIGHT ...

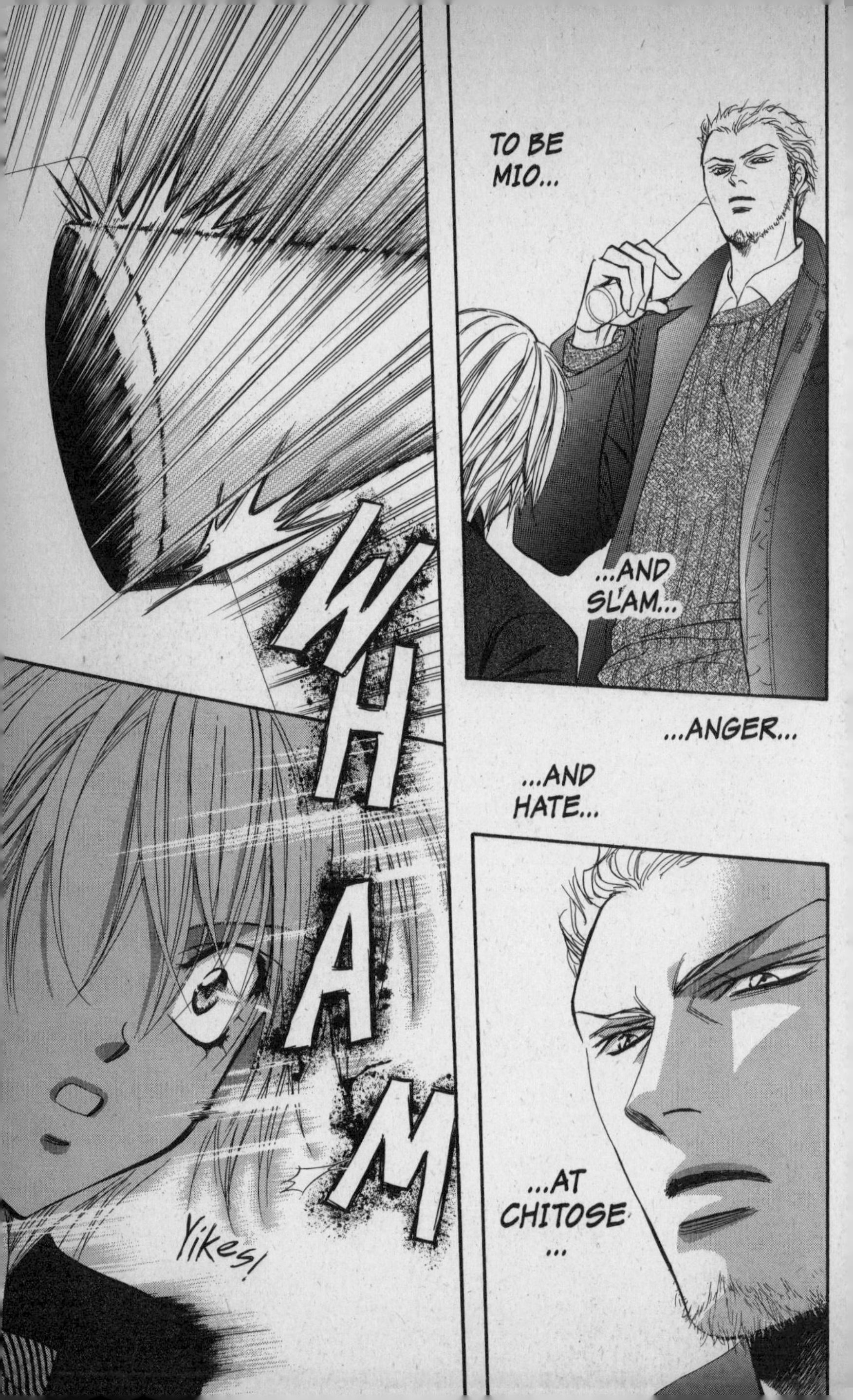
TO BE MIO...
...AND SLAM...
...ANGER...
...AND HATE...
...AT CHITOSE ...
WHAM
Yikes!

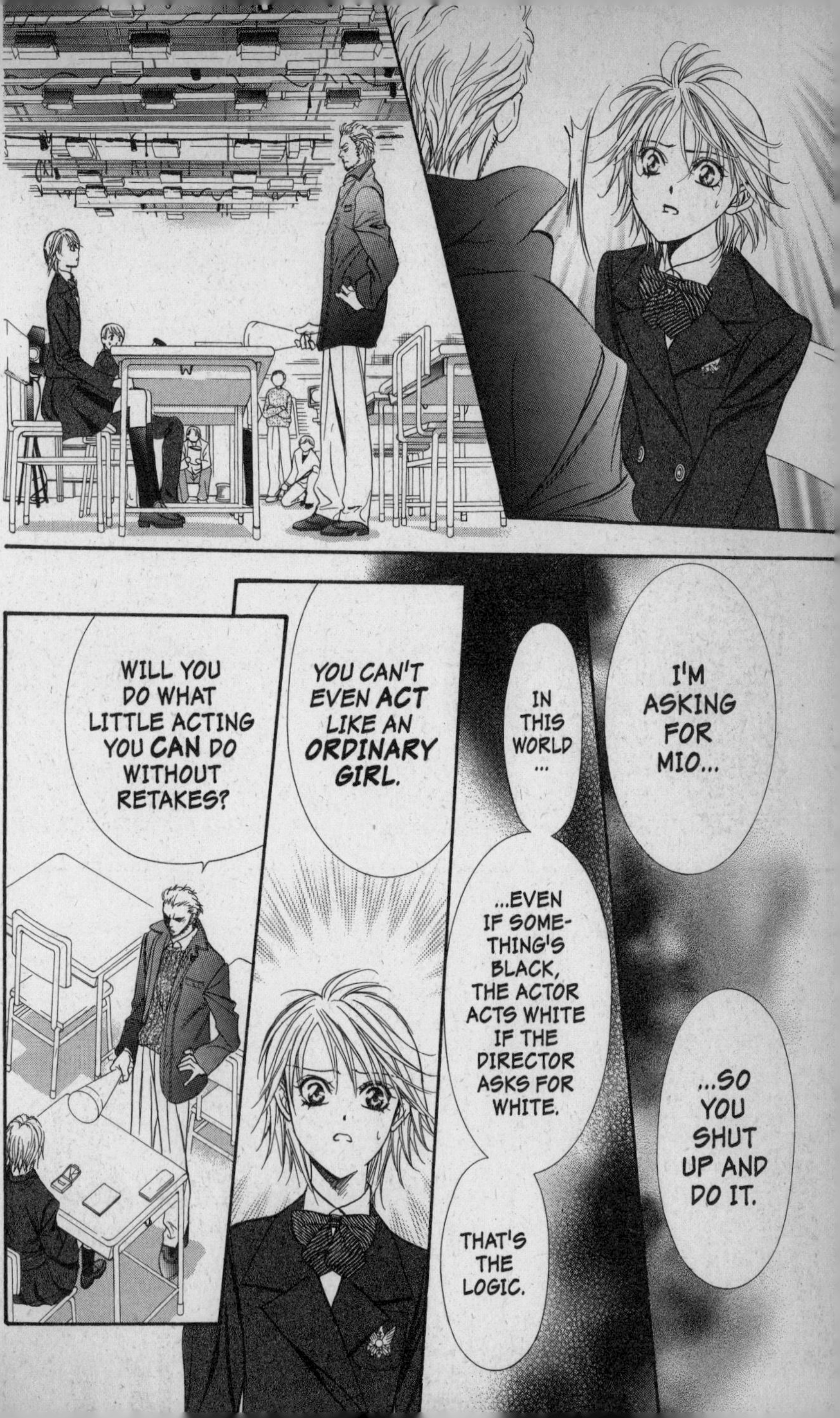

I'M ASKING FOR MIO...
IN THIS WORLD...
...EVEN IF SOMETHING'S BLACK, THE ACTOR ACTS WHITE IF THE DIRECTOR ASKS FOR WHITE.
...SO YOU SHUT UP AND DO IT.
THAT'S THE LOGIC.
YOU CAN'T EVEN ACT LIKE AN ORDINARY GIRL.
WILL YOU DO WHAT LITTLE ACTING YOU CAN DO WITHOUT RETAKES?

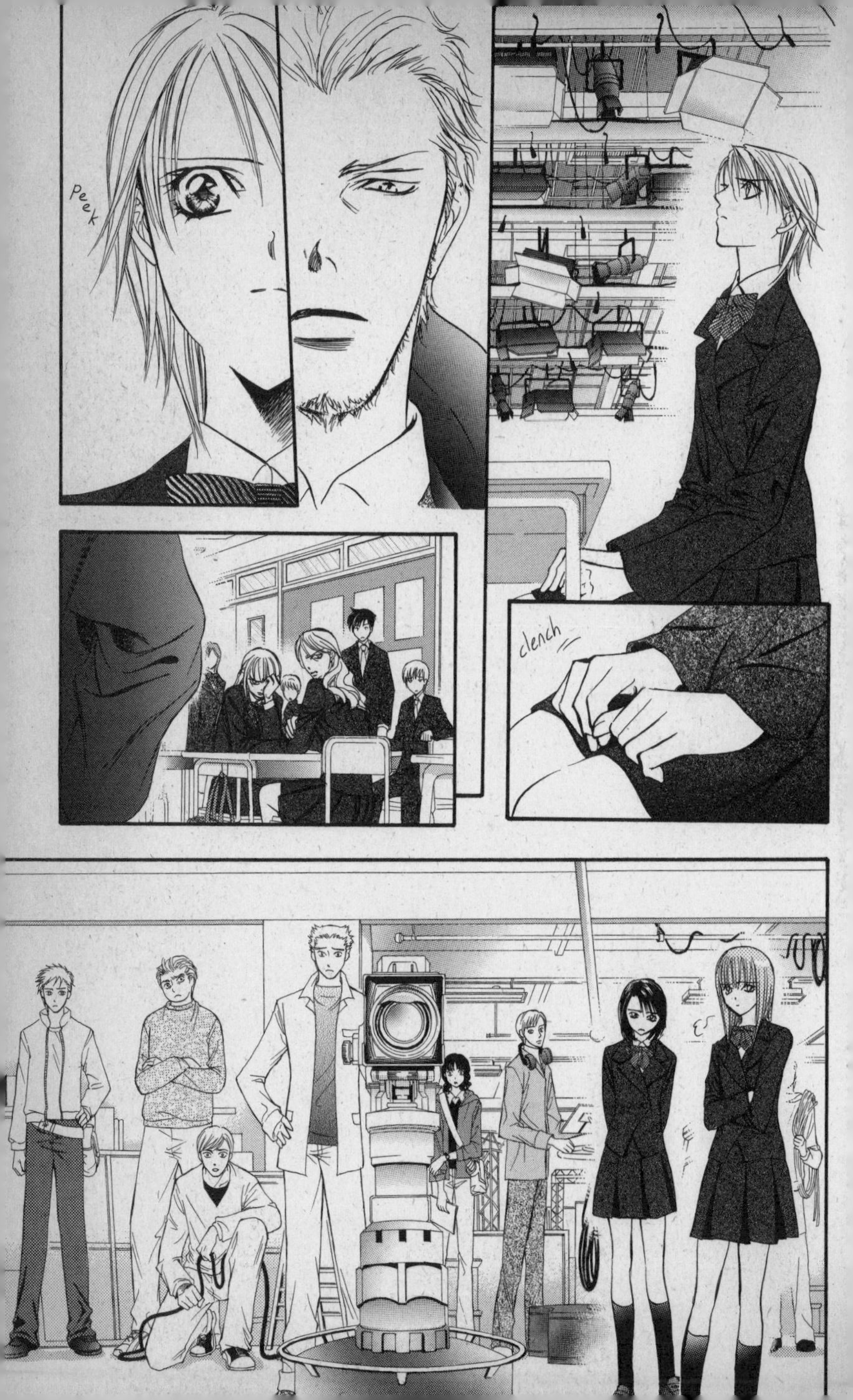
clench
peek

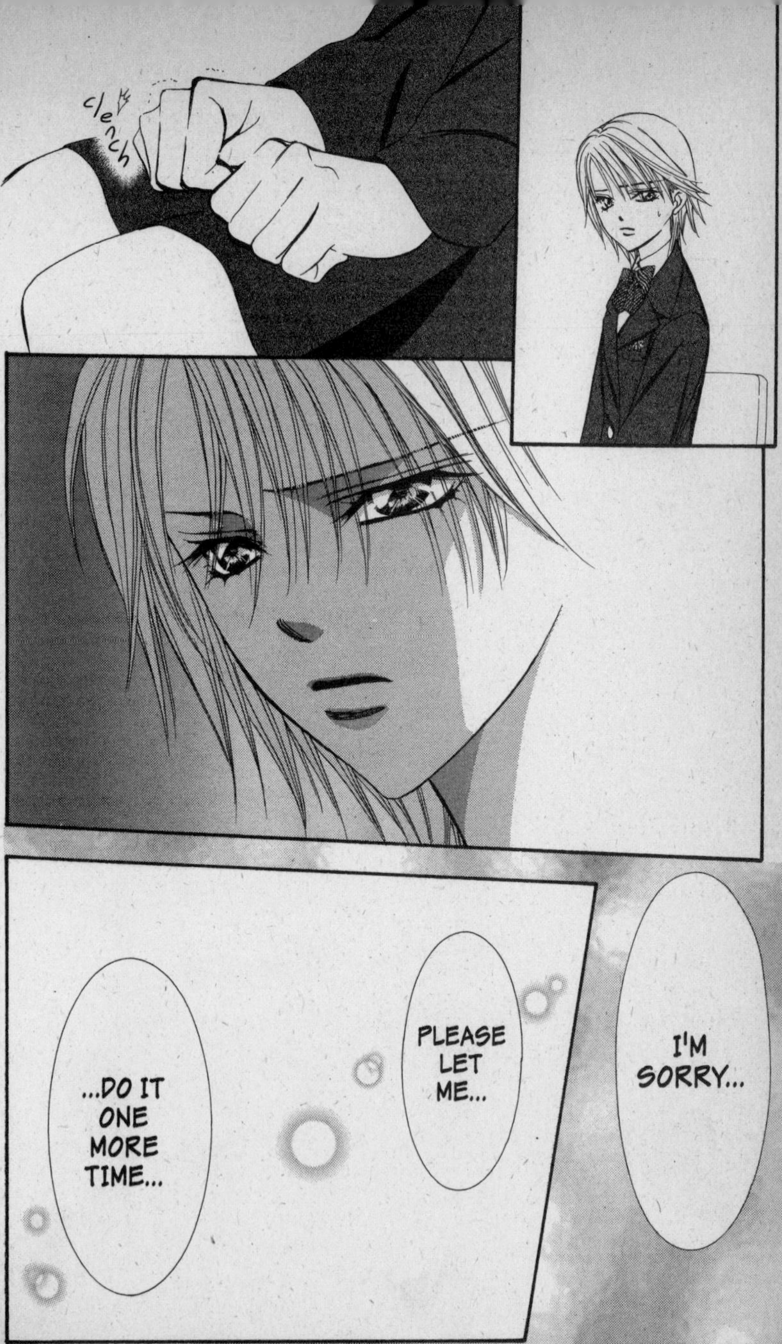
clench
I'M SORRY...
PLEASE LET ME...
...DO IT ONE MORE TIME...

End of Act 125

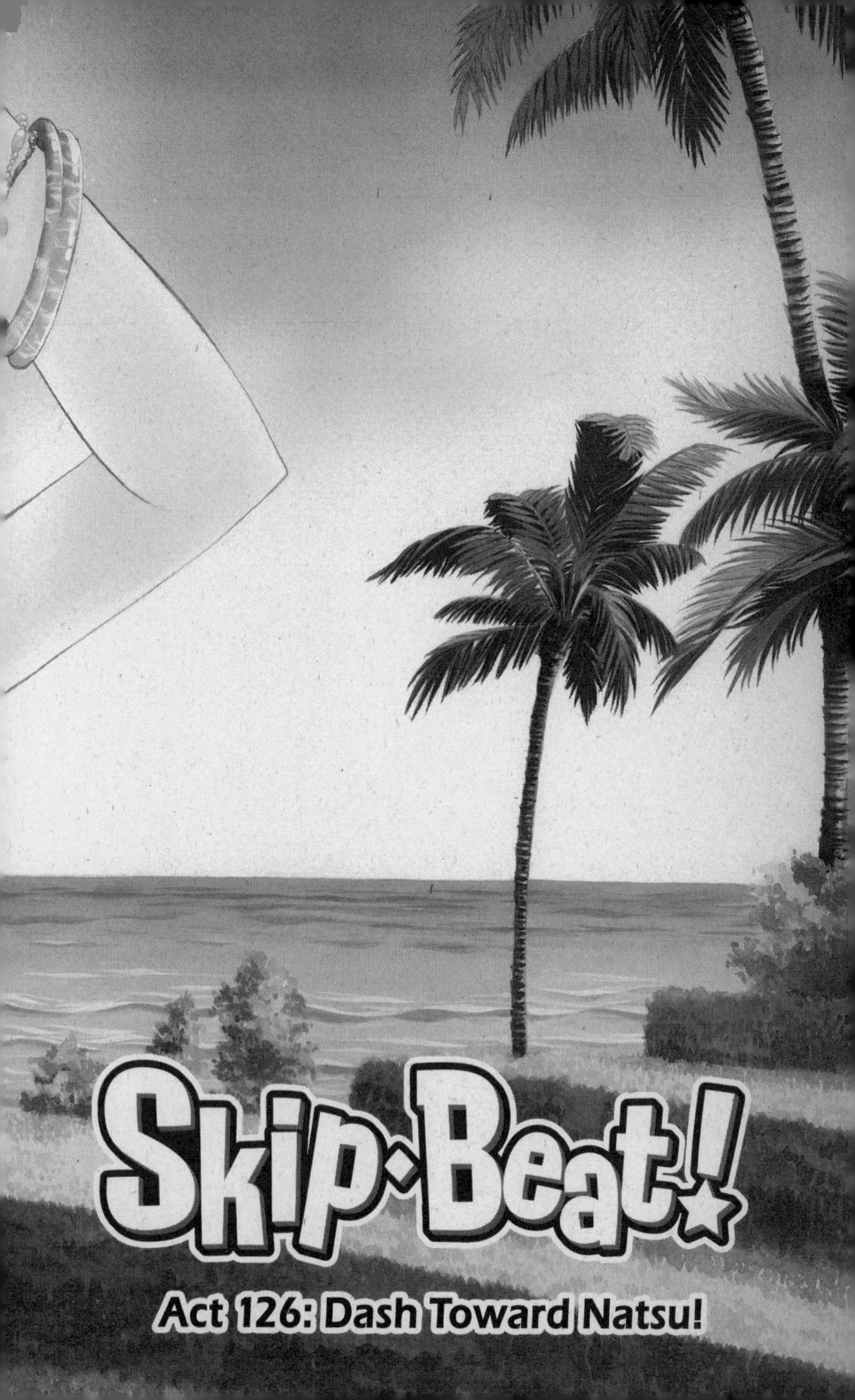
Skip·Beat!
Act 126: Dash Toward Natsu!

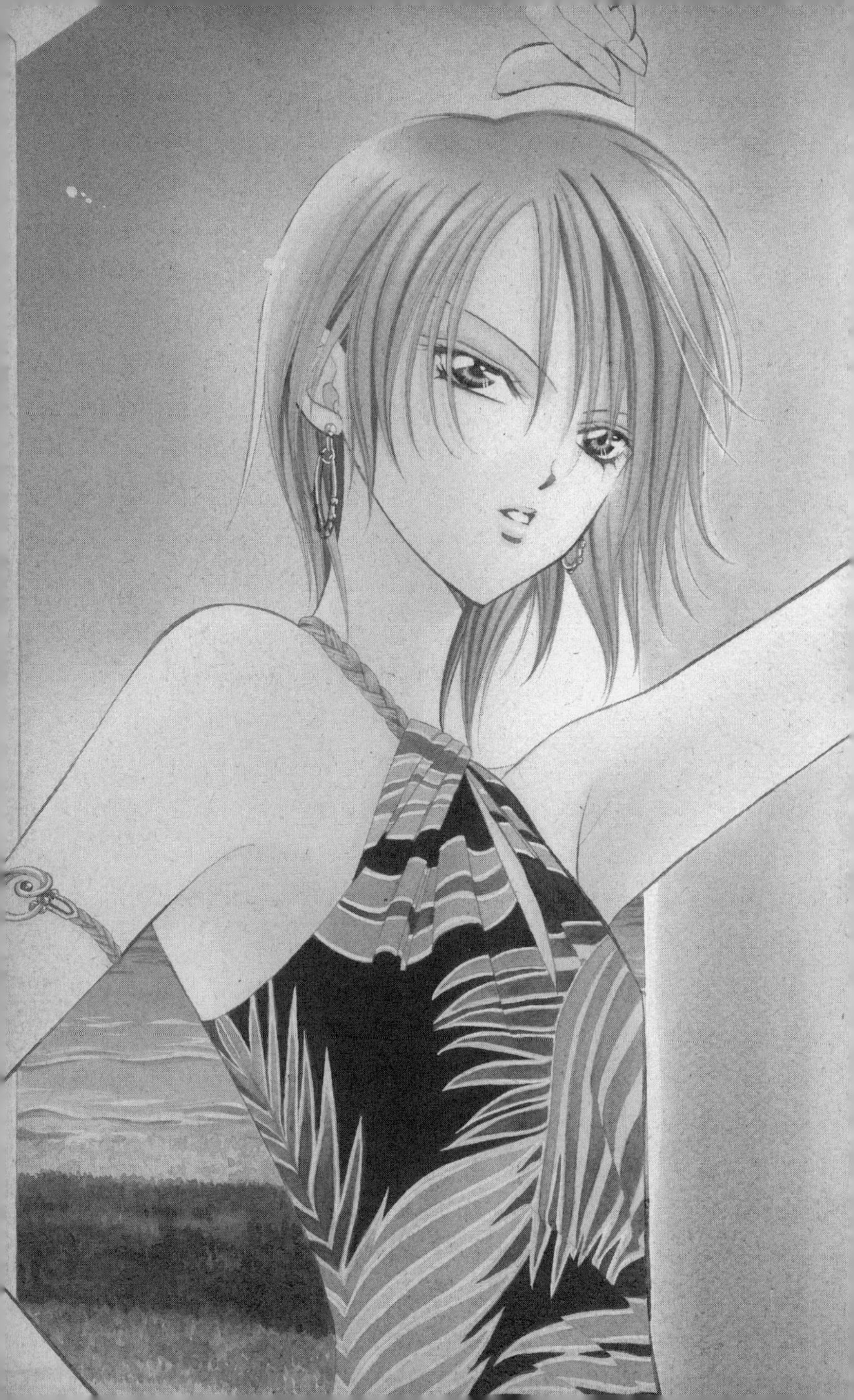

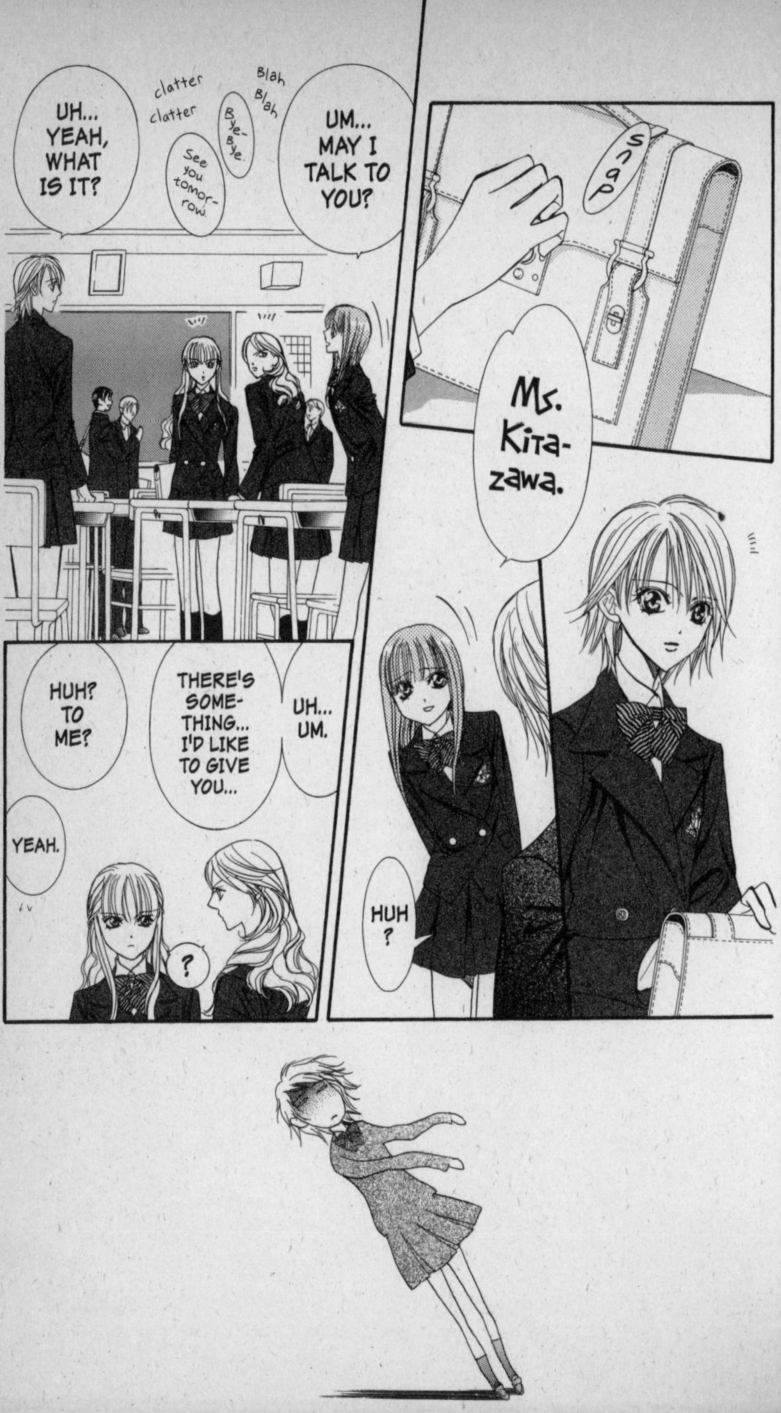

snap
Ms. Kita-zawa.
HUH?
UM... MAY I TALK TO YOU?
Blah Blah
Bye-Bye.
See you tomor-row.
clatter clatter
UH... YEAH, WHAT IS IT?
UH... UM.
THERE'S SOME-THING... I'D LIKE TO GIVE YOU...
HUH? TO ME?
YEAH.
?

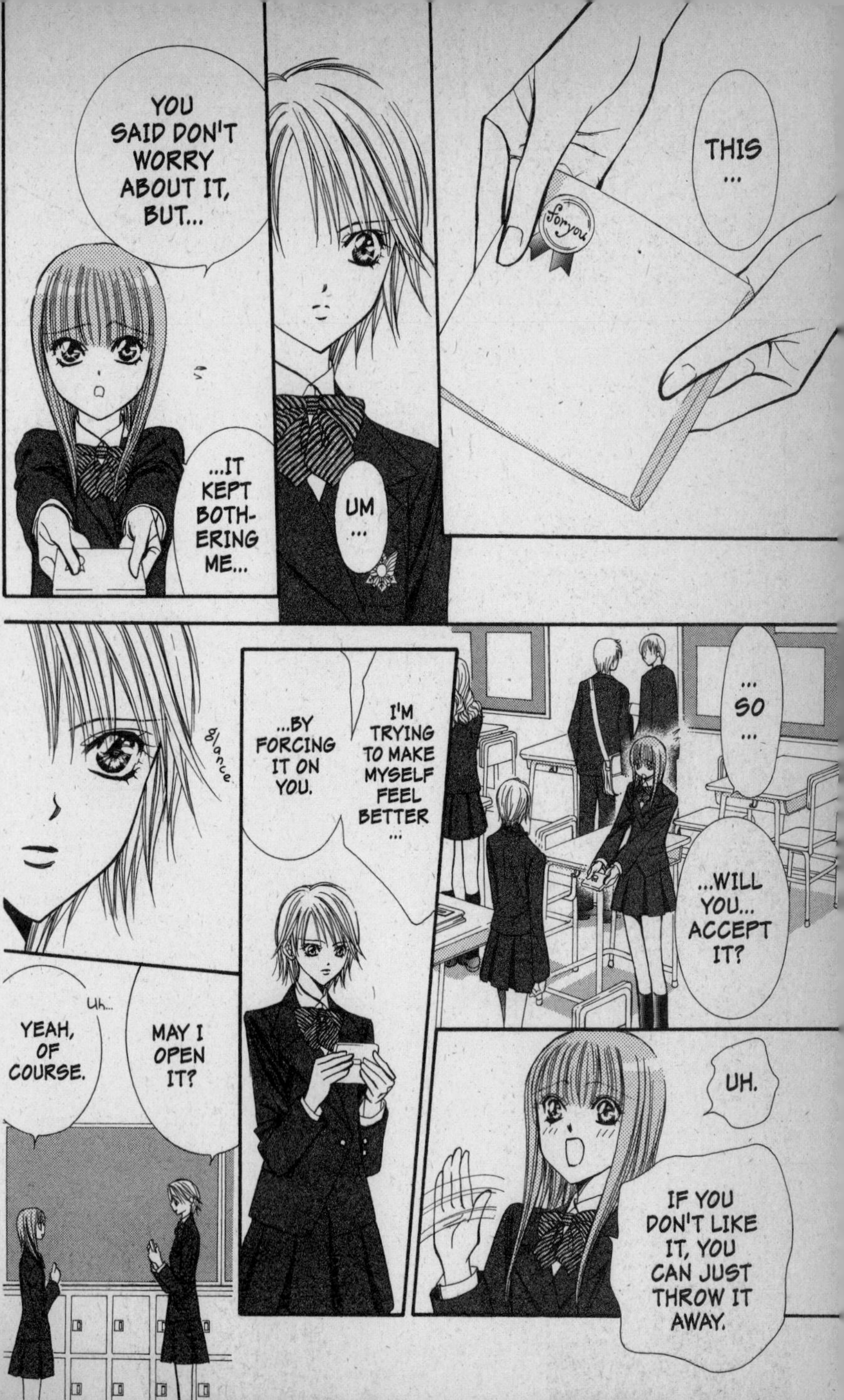
THIS ...
UM ...
YOU SAID DON'T WORRY ABOUT IT, BUT...
...IT KEPT BOTHERING ME...
... SO ...
...WILL YOU... ACCEPT IT?
UH.
IF YOU DON'T LIKE IT, YOU CAN JUST THROW IT AWAY.
I'M TRYING TO MAKE MYSELF FEEL BETTER ...
...BY FORCING IT ON YOU.
glance
MAY I OPEN IT?
Uh...
YEAH, OF COURSE.

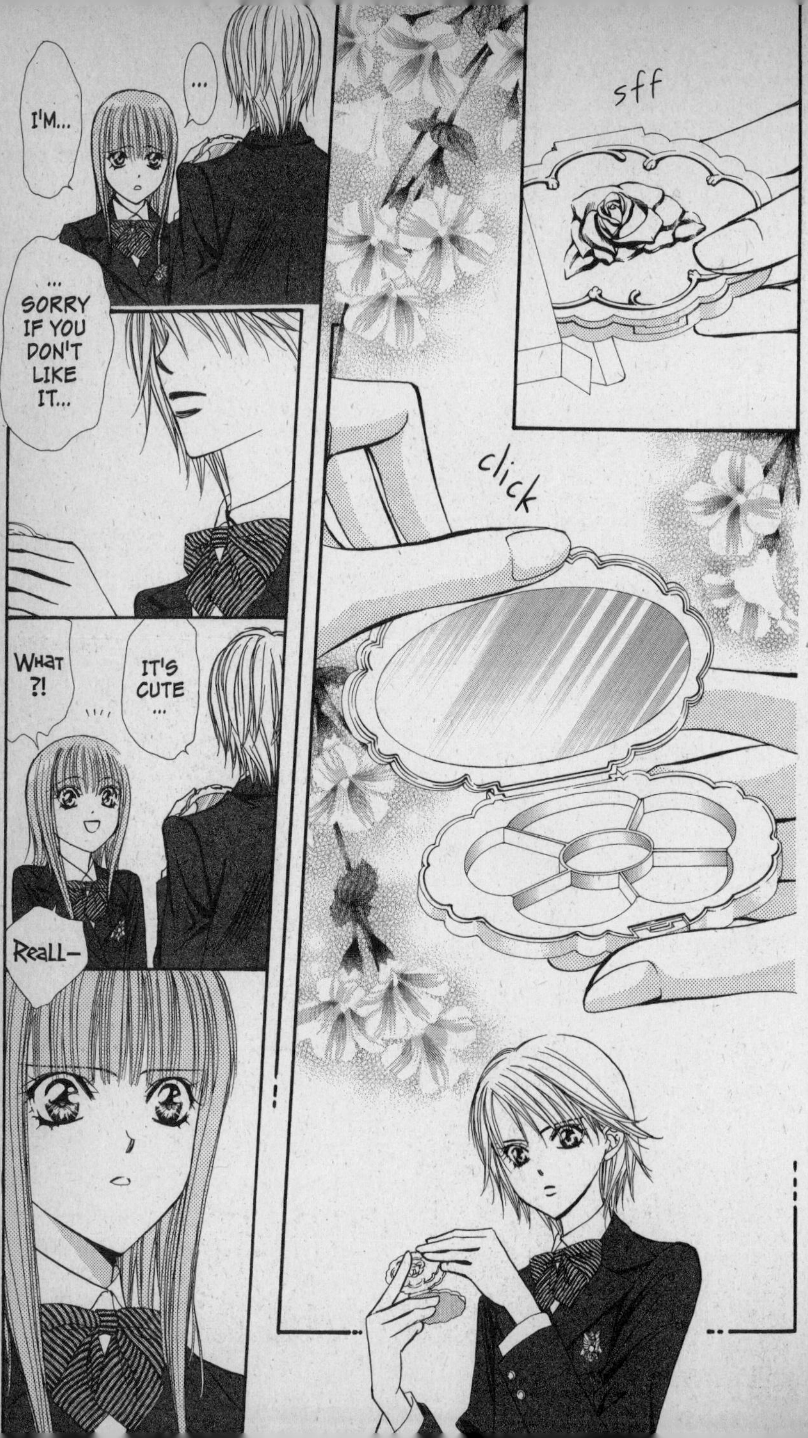
sff
click
...
I'M...
... SORRY IF YOU DON'T LIKE IT...
IT'S CUTE ...
WHAT ?!
ReaLL-

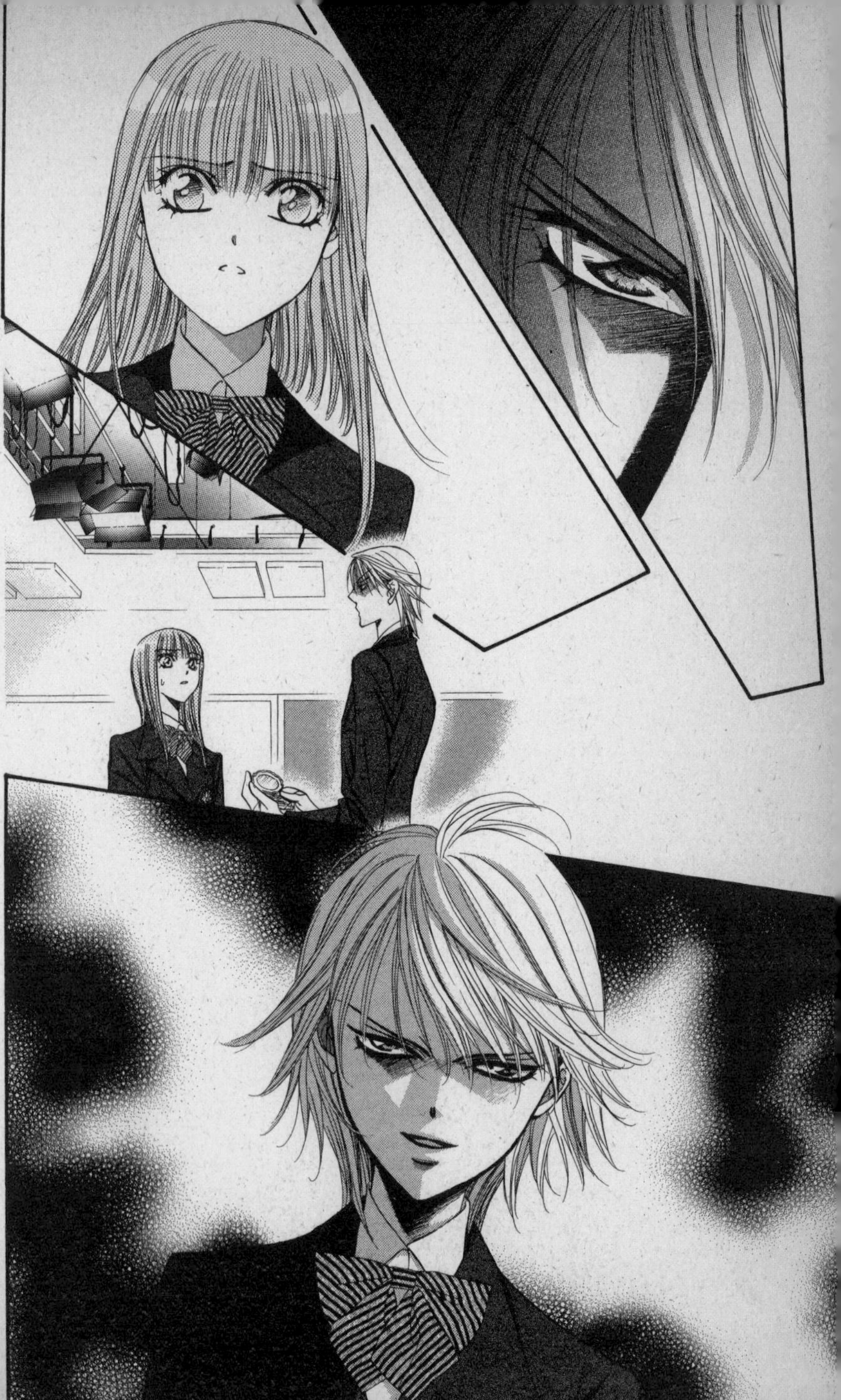

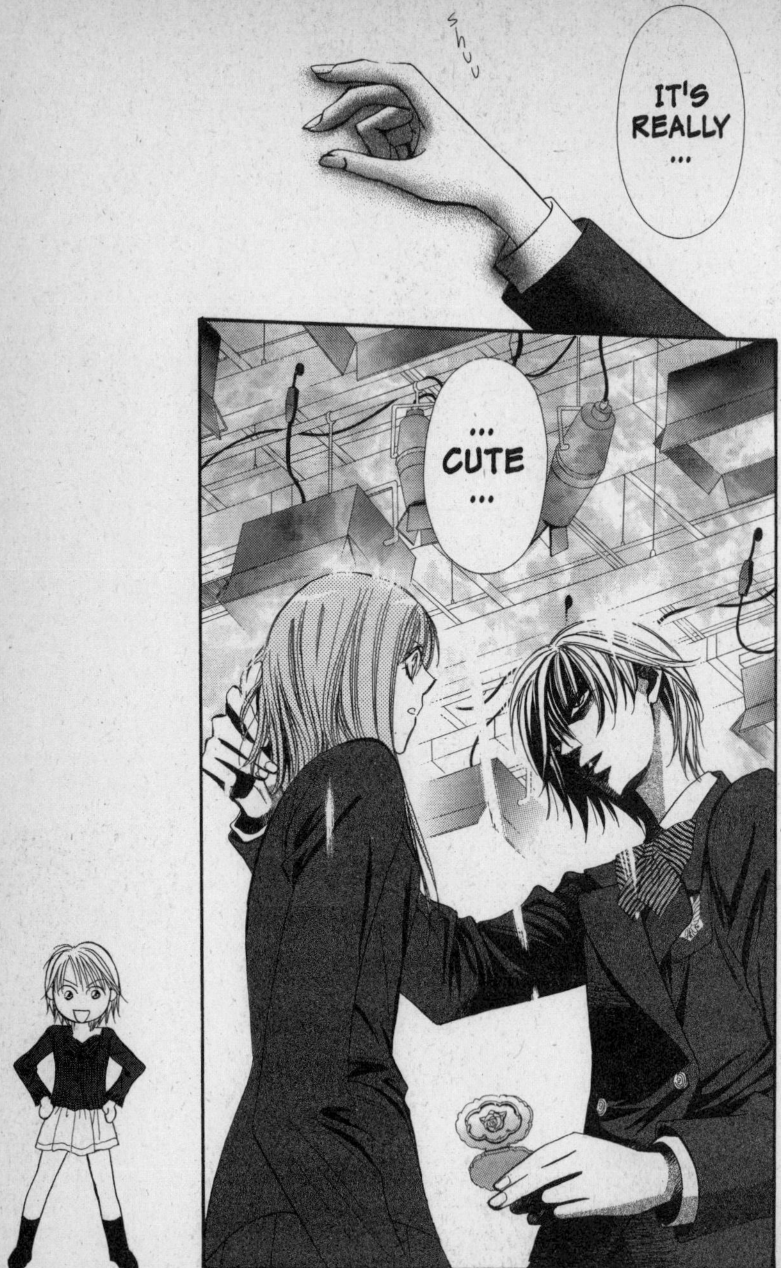
IT'S REALLY ...
SHUU
... CUTE ...

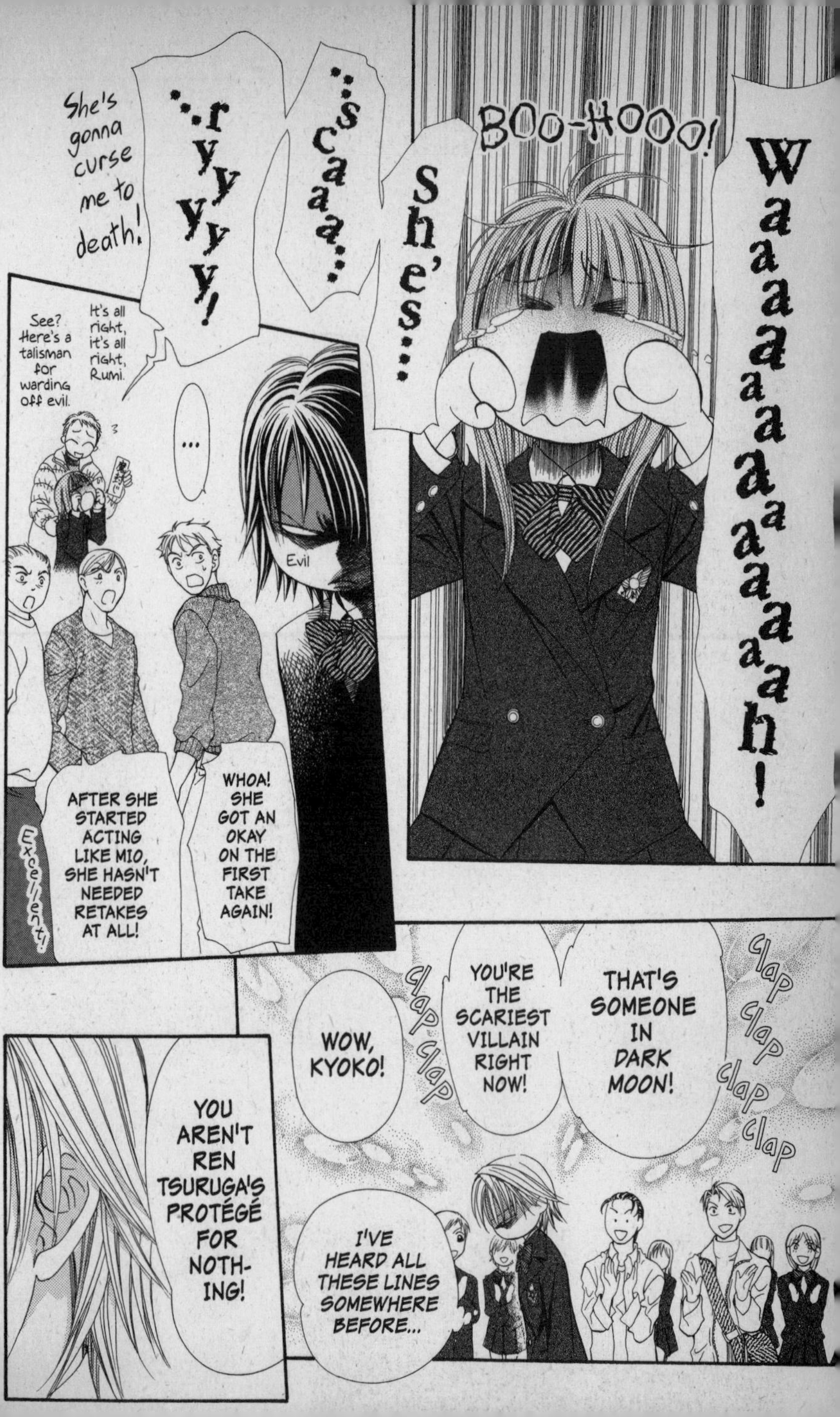
Waaaaaaaaaaaaaah!
BOO-HOOO!
She's...
scaaa...
ryyyyy!
She's gonna curse me to death!
It's all right, it's all right, Rumi.
See? Here's a talisman for warding off evil.
...
Evil
WHOA! SHE GOT AN OKAY ON THE FIRST TAKE AGAIN!
AFTER SHE STARTED ACTING LIKE MIO, SHE HASN'T NEEDED RETAKES AT ALL!
Excellent!
clap clap clap clap
THAT'S SOMEONE IN DARK MOON!
YOU'RE THE SCARIEST VILLAIN RIGHT NOW!
clap clap
WOW, KYOKO!
I'VE HEARD ALL THESE LINES SOMEWHERE BEFORE...
YOU AREN'T REN TSURUGA'S PROTÉGÉ FOR NOTH-ING!

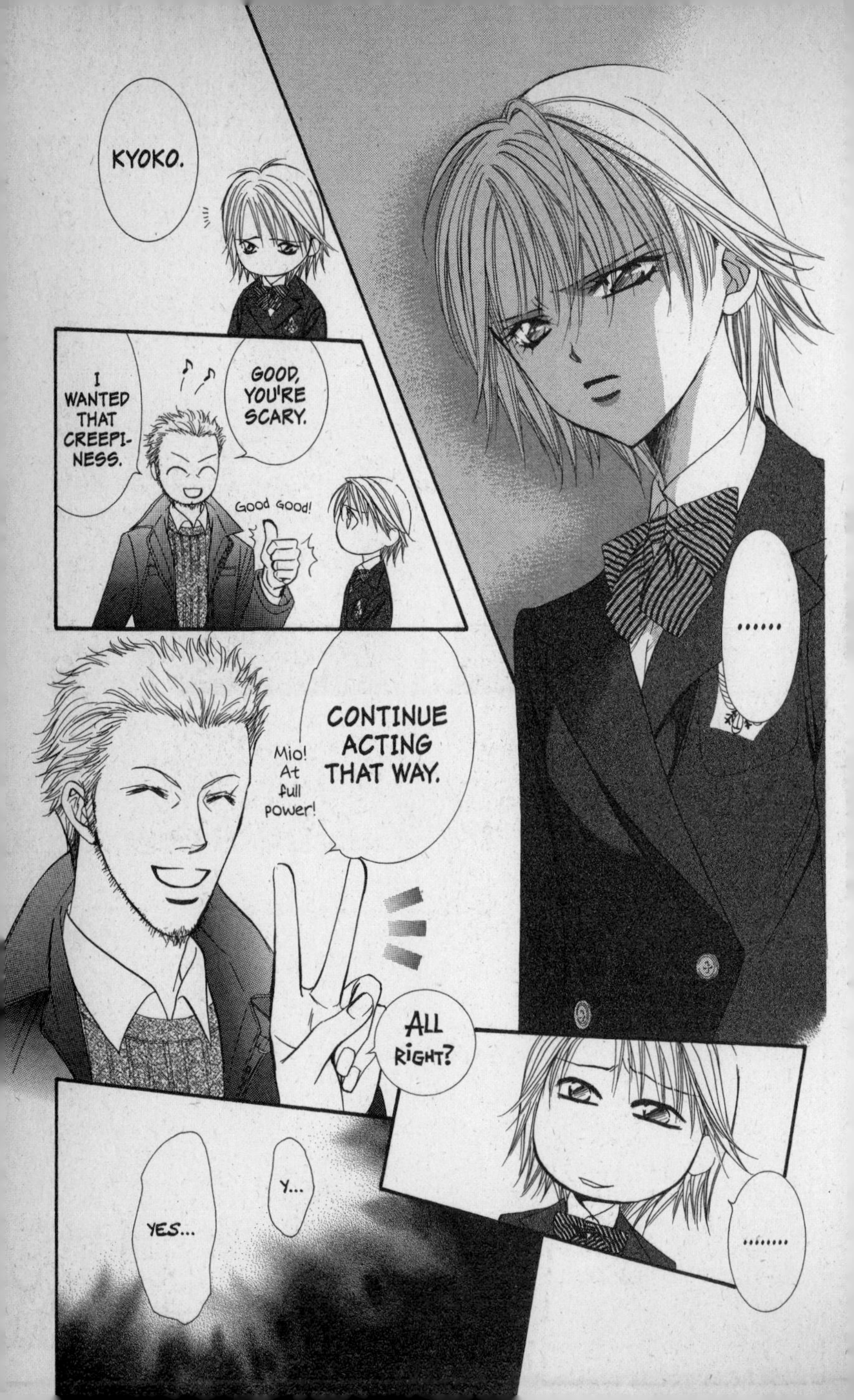

......
KYOKO.
GOOD, YOU'RE SCARY.
I WANTED THAT CREEPINESS.
Good Good!
CONTINUE ACTING THAT WAY.
Mio! At full power!
ALL RIGHT?
....
Y...
YES...

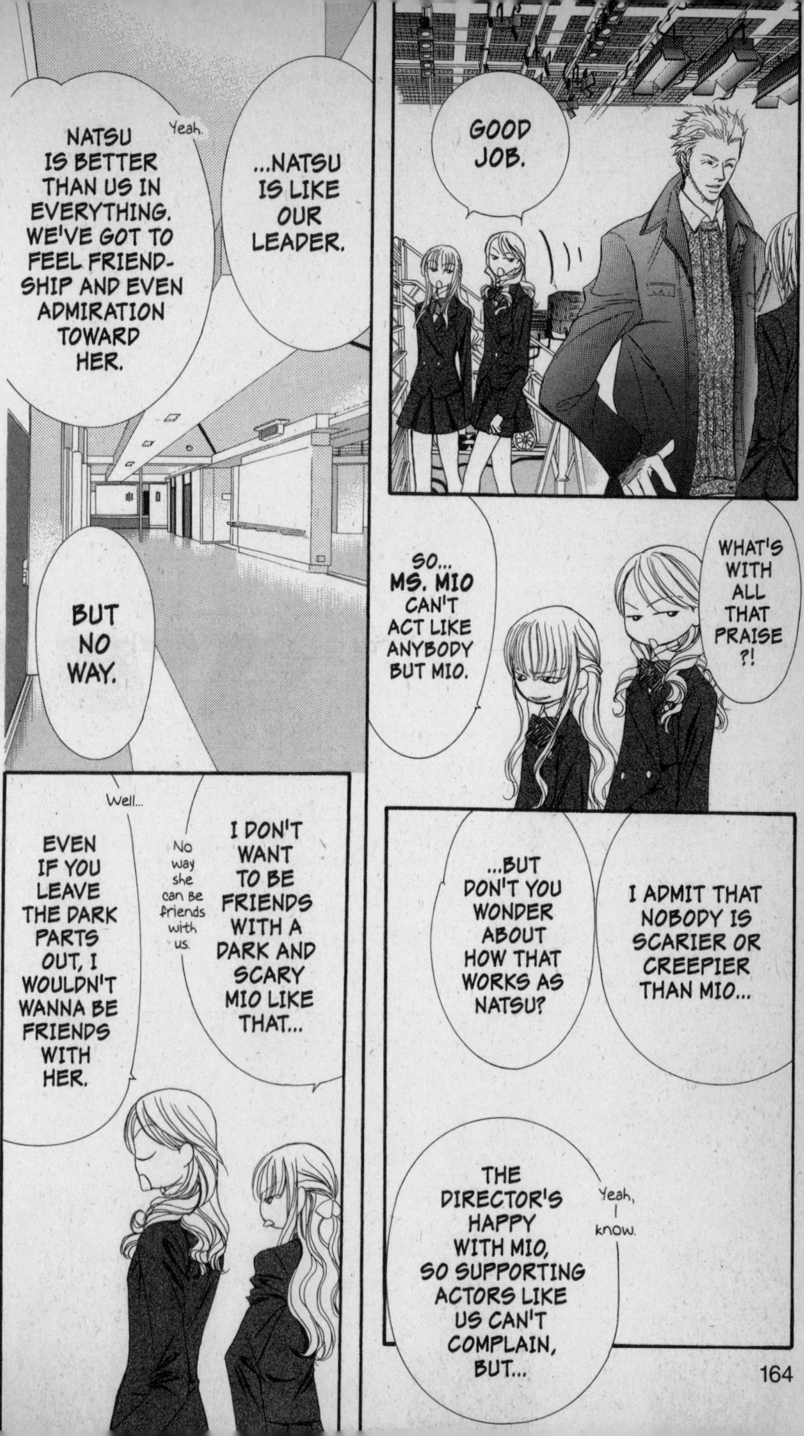
GOOD JOB.
WHAT'S WITH ALL THAT PRAISE?!
SO... MS. MIO CAN'T ACT LIKE ANYBODY BUT MIO.
I ADMIT THAT NOBODY IS SCARIER OR CREEPIER THAN MIO...
...BUT DON'T YOU WONDER ABOUT HOW THAT WORKS AS NATSU?
THE DIRECTOR'S HAPPY WITH MIO, SO SUPPORTING ACTORS LIKE US CAN'T COMPLAIN, BUT...
Yeah, I know.
...NATSU IS LIKE OUR LEADER.
Yeah.
NATSU IS BETTER THAN US IN EVERYTHING. WE'VE GOT TO FEEL FRIENDSHIP AND EVEN ADMIRATION TOWARD HER.
BUT NO WAY.
I DON'T WANT TO BE FRIENDS WITH A DARK AND SCARY MIO LIKE THAT...
No way she can be friends with us.
Well...
EVEN IF YOU LEAVE THE DARK PARTS OUT, I WOULDN'T WANNA BE FRIENDS WITH HER.

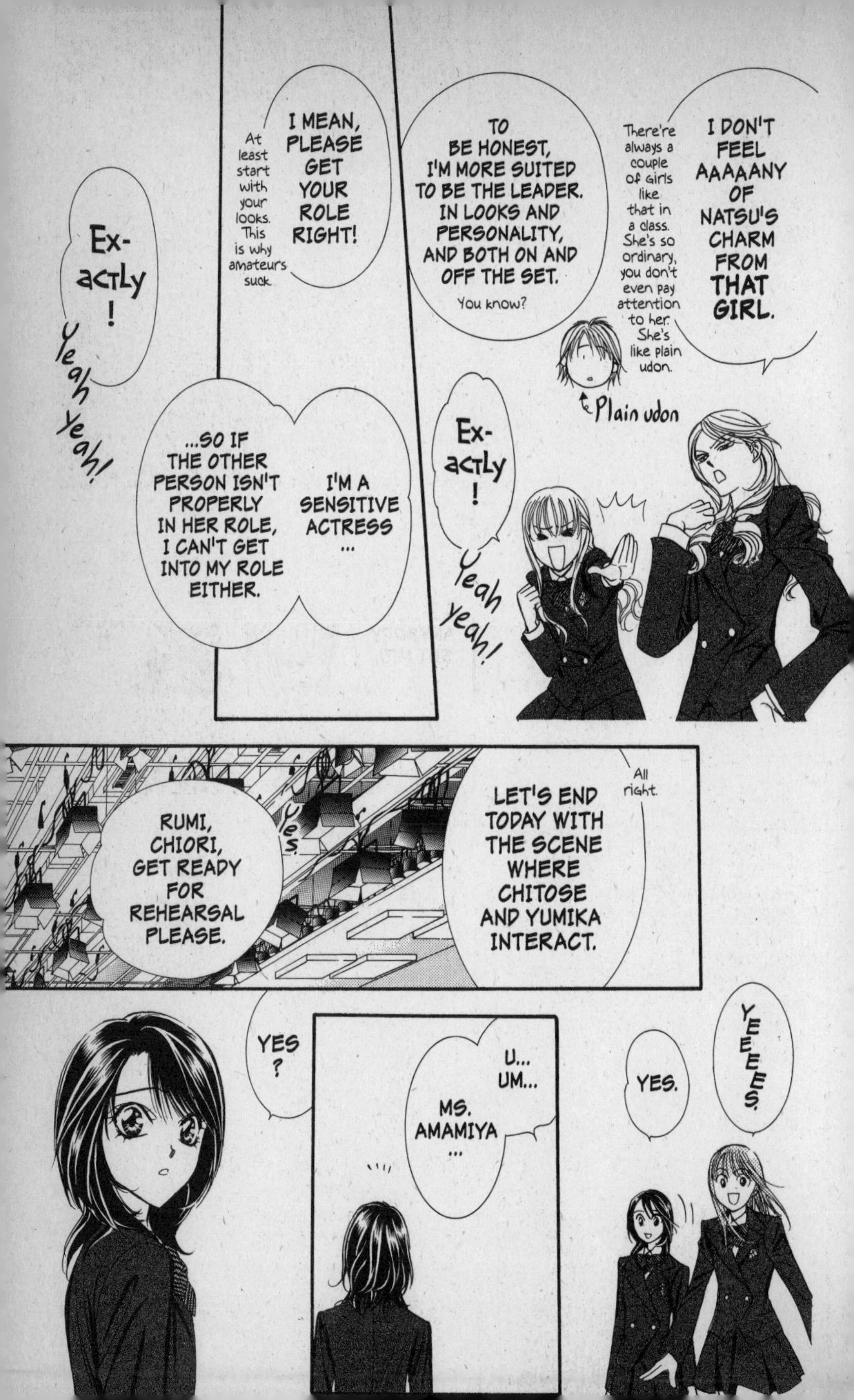

I DON'T FEEL AAAAANY OF NATSU'S CHARM FROM THAT GIRL.
There're always a couple of girls like that in a class. She's so ordinary, you don't even pay attention to her. She's like plain udon.
Plain udon
TO BE HONEST, I'M MORE SUITED TO BE THE LEADER. IN LOOKS AND PERSONALITY, AND BOTH ON AND OFF THE SET.
You know?
Ex-actly!
Yeah yeah!
I MEAN, PLEASE GET YOUR ROLE RIGHT!
At least start with your looks. This is why amateurs suck.
I'M A SENSITIVE ACTRESS...
...SO IF THE OTHER PERSON ISN'T PROPERLY IN HER ROLE, I CAN'T GET INTO MY ROLE EITHER.
Ex-actly!
Yeah yeah!
All right.
LET'S END TODAY WITH THE SCENE WHERE CHITOSE AND YUMIKA INTERACT.
Yes.
RUMI, CHIORI, GET READY FOR REHEARSAL PLEASE.
YEEEES.
YES.
U... UM... MS. AMAMIYA...
YES?

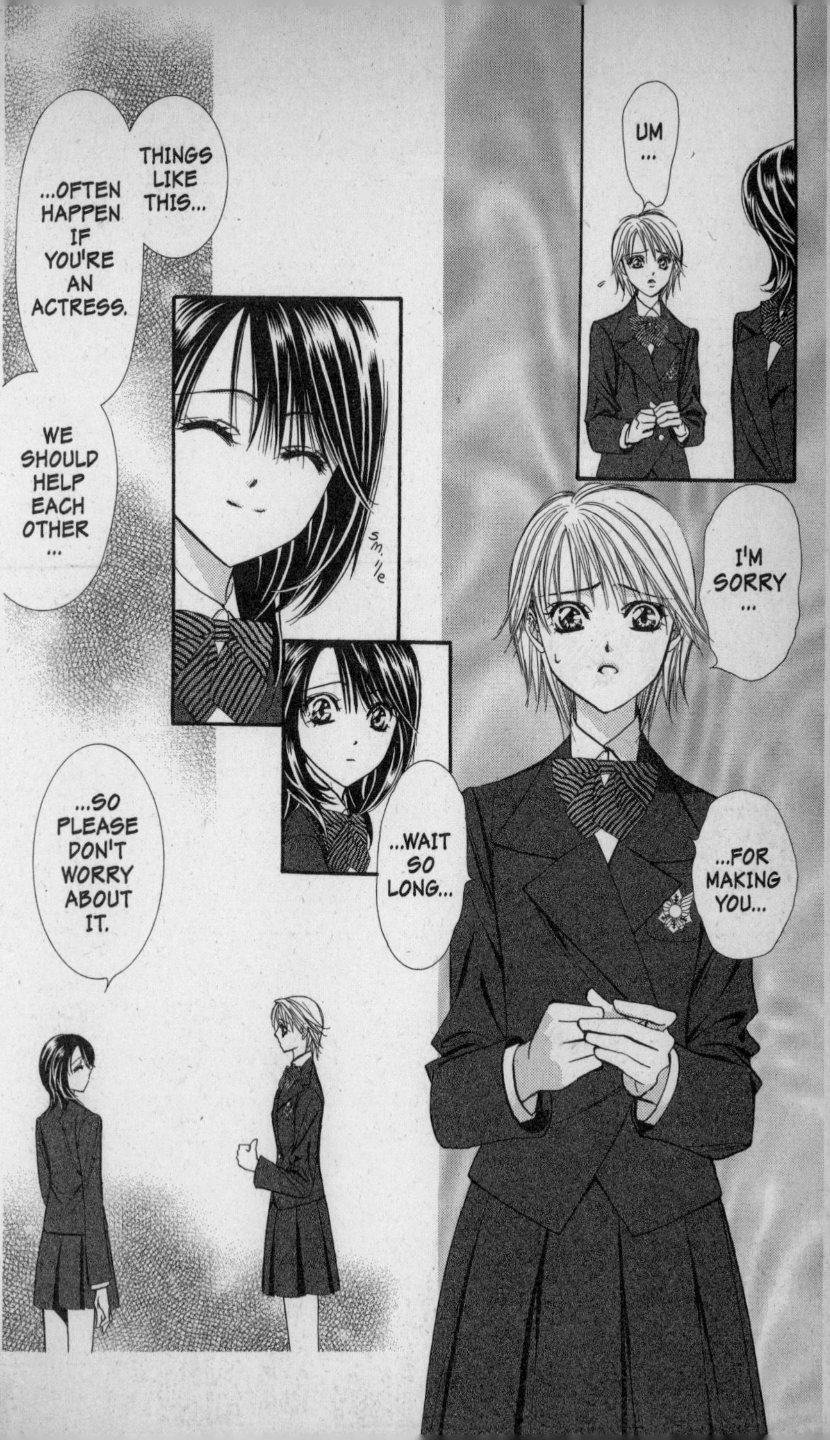
UM ...
I'M SORRY ...
...FOR MAKING YOU...
...WAIT SO LONG...
THINGS LIKE THIS...
...OFTEN HAPPEN IF YOU'RE AN ACTRESS.
smile
WE SHOULD HELP EACH OTHER ...
...SO PLEASE DON'T WORRY ABOUT IT.

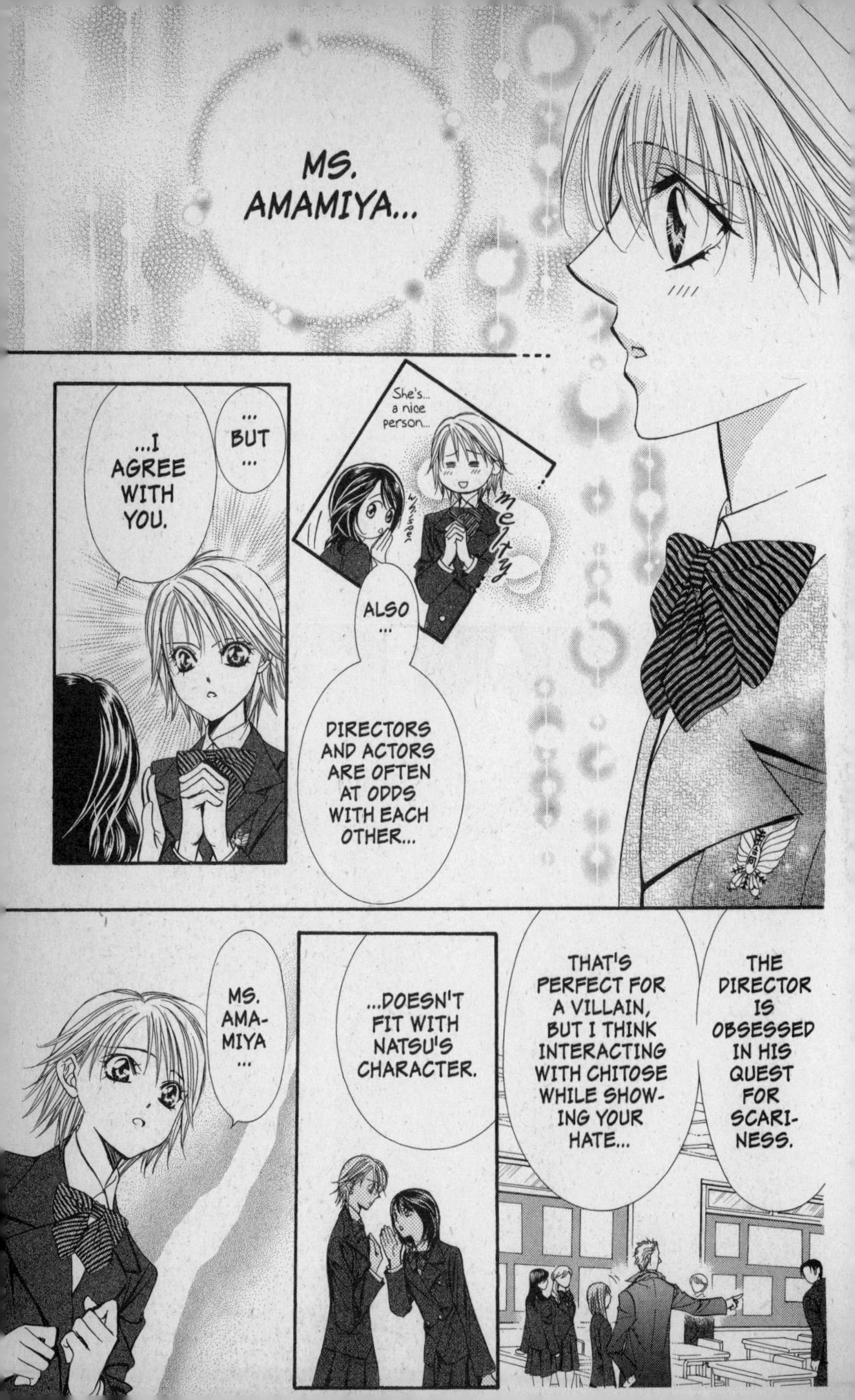
MS. AMAMIYA...
She's... a nice person...
whisper
melty
ALSO...
DIRECTORS AND ACTORS ARE OFTEN AT ODDS WITH EACH OTHER...
...BUT...
...I AGREE WITH YOU.
THE DIRECTOR IS OBSESSED IN HIS QUEST FOR SCARI-NESS.
THAT'S PERFECT FOR A VILLAIN, BUT I THINK INTERACTING WITH CHITOSE WHILE SHOW-ING YOUR HATE...
...DOESN'T FIT WITH NATSU'S CHARACTER.
MS. AMA-MIYA...

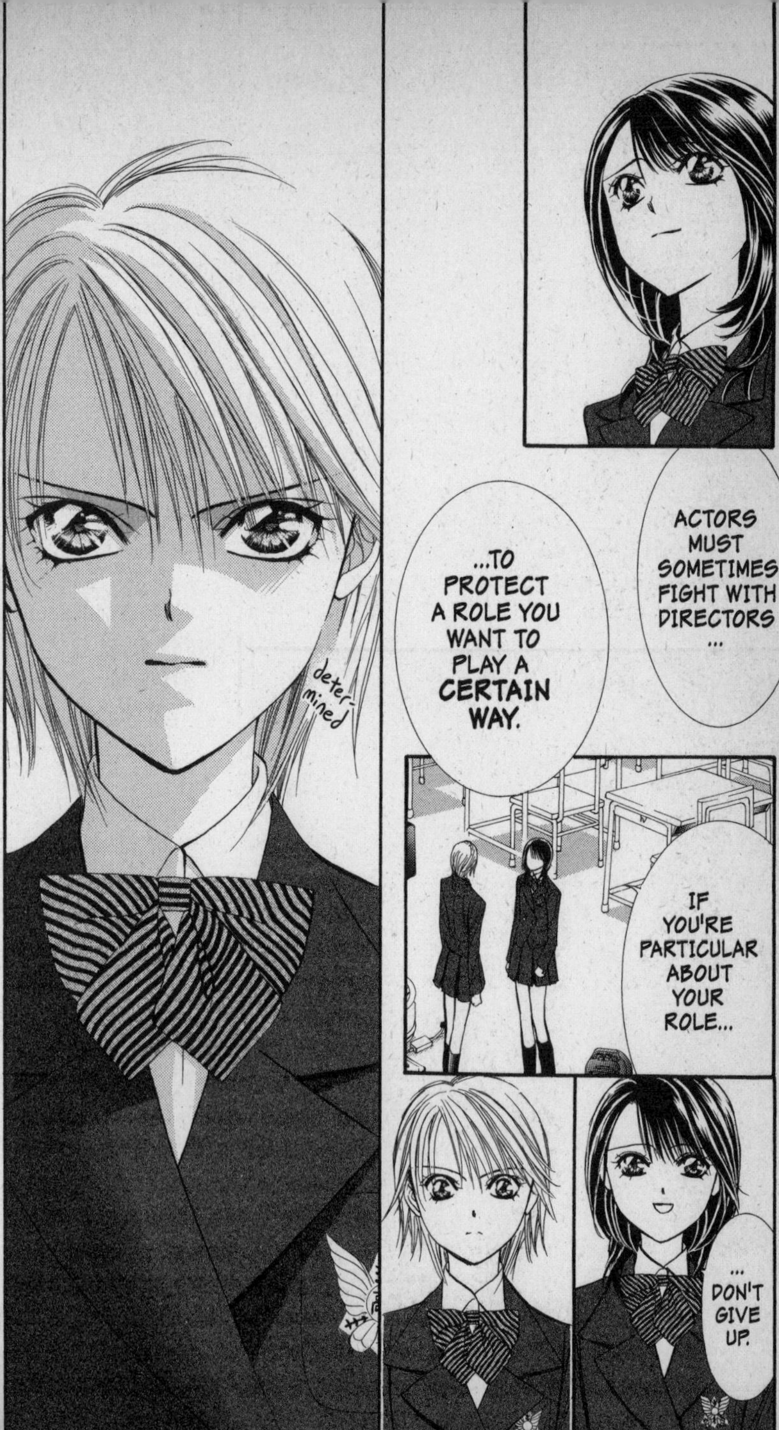
ACTORS MUST SOMETIMES FIGHT WITH DIRECTORS ...
...TO PROTECT A ROLE YOU WANT TO PLAY A CERTAIN WAY.
IF YOU'RE PARTICULAR ABOUT YOUR ROLE...
... DON'T GIVE UP.
determined

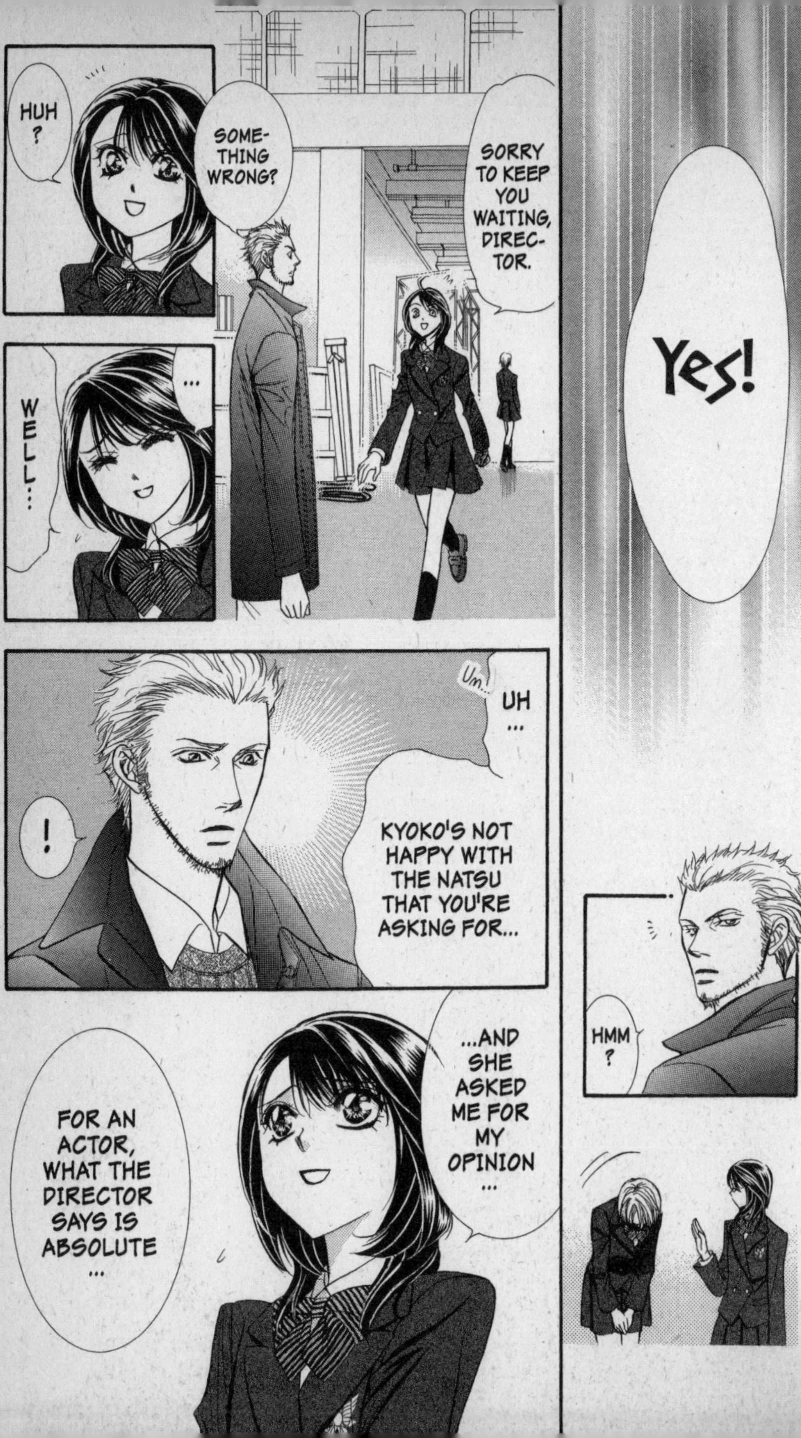
Yes!
HMM ?
SORRY TO KEEP YOU WAITING, DIRECTOR.
SOME-THING WRONG?
HUH ?
...
WELL...
Um!
UH ...
!
KYOKO'S NOT HAPPY WITH THE NATSU THAT YOU'RE ASKING FOR...
...AND SHE ASKED ME FOR MY OPINION ...
FOR AN ACTOR, WHAT THE DIRECTOR SAYS IS ABSOLUTE ...

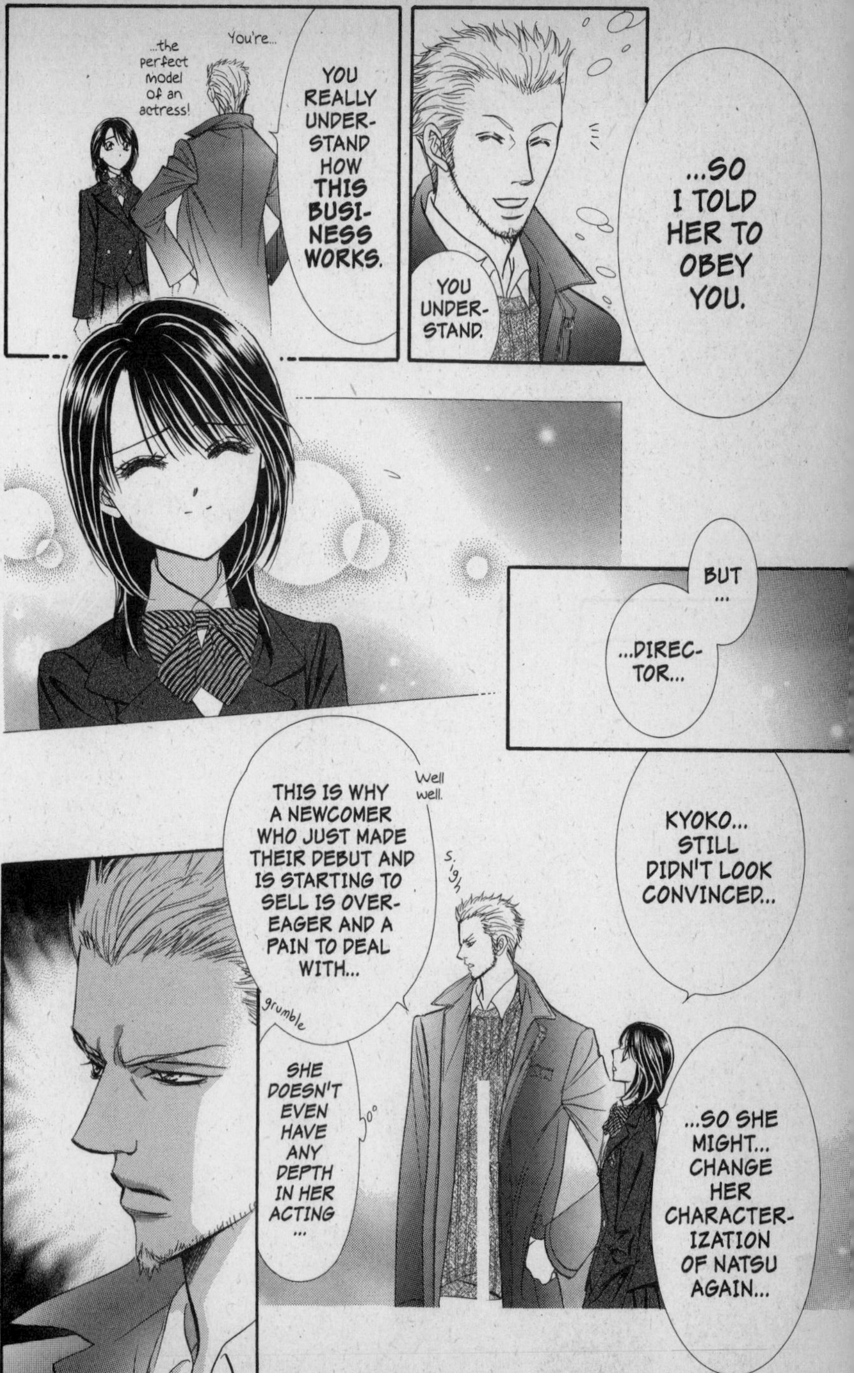
...SO I TOLD HER TO OBEY YOU.
YOU UNDERSTAND.
YOU REALLY UNDERSTAND HOW THIS BUSINESS WORKS.
You're...
...the perfect model of an actress!
BUT...
...DIRECTOR...
KYOKO... STILL DIDN'T LOOK CONVINCED...
Well well.
THIS IS WHY A NEWCOMER WHO JUST MADE THEIR DEBUT AND IS STARTING TO SELL IS OVER-EAGER AND A PAIN TO DEAL WITH...
sigh
...SO SHE MIGHT... CHANGE HER CHARACTERIZATION OF NATSU AGAIN...
grumble
SHE DOESN'T EVEN HAVE ANY DEPTH IN HER ACTING...

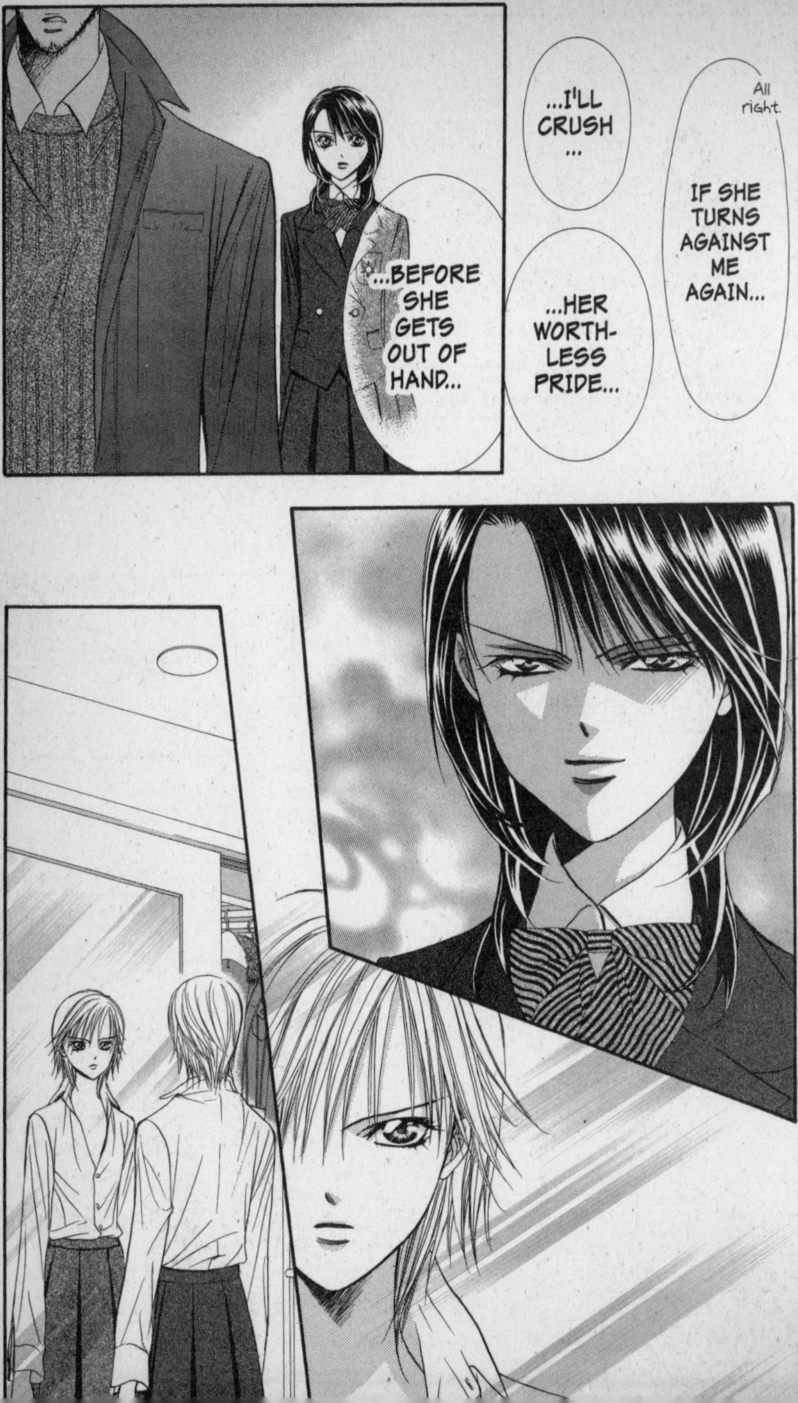
All right.
IF SHE TURNS AGAINST ME AGAIN...
...I'LL CRUSH...
...HER WORTH-LESS PRIDE...
...BEFORE SHE GETS OUT OF HAND...

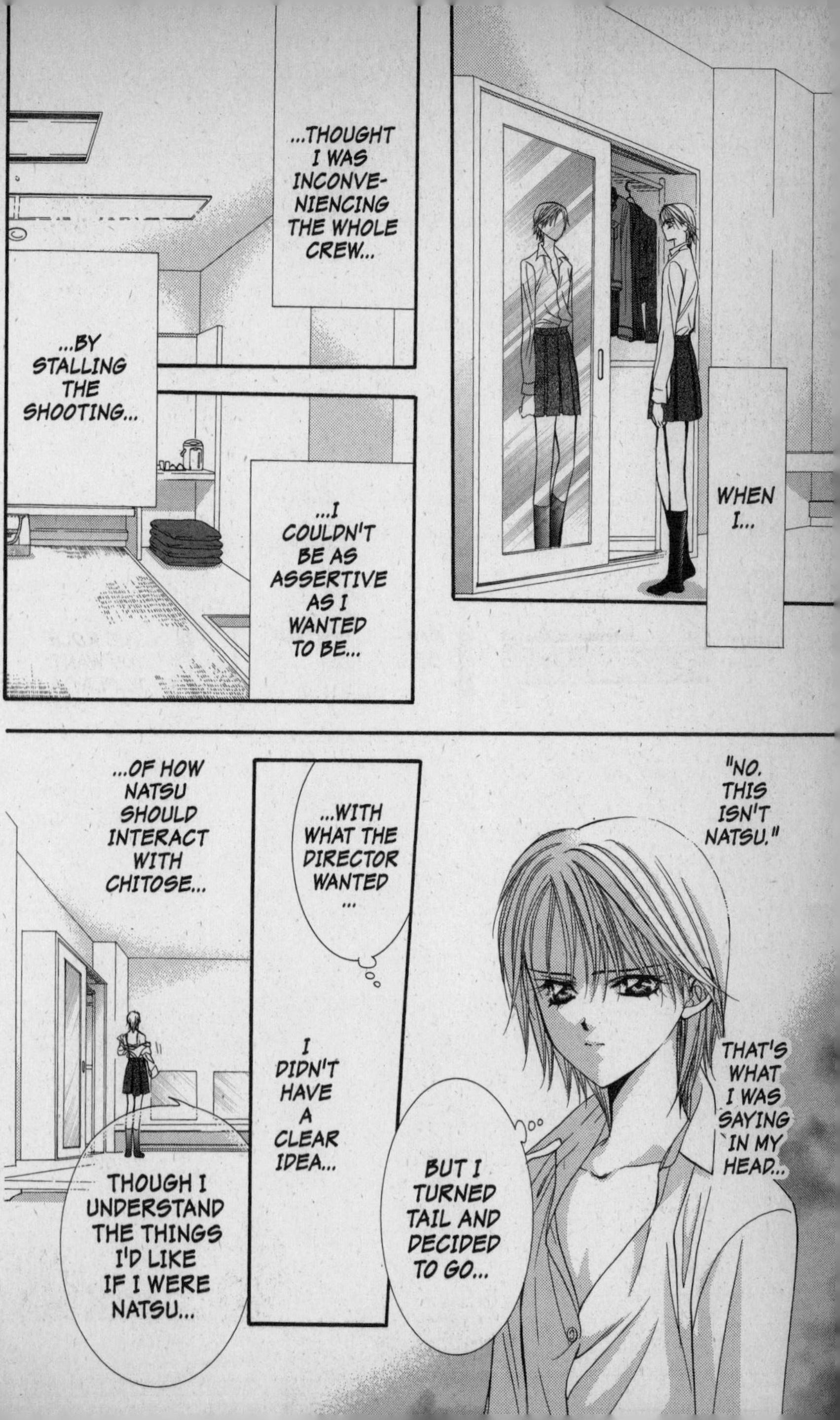
WHEN I...
...THOUGHT I WAS INCONVENIENCING THE WHOLE CREW...
...BY STALLING THE SHOOTING...
...I COULDN'T BE AS ASSERTIVE AS I WANTED TO BE...
"NO. THIS ISN'T NATSU."
THAT'S WHAT I WAS SAYING IN MY HEAD...
BUT I TURNED TAIL AND DECIDED TO GO...
...WITH WHAT THE DIRECTOR WANTED...
I DIDN'T HAVE A CLEAR IDEA...
...OF HOW NATSU SHOULD INTERACT WITH CHITOSE...
THOUGH I UNDERSTAND THE THINGS I'D LIKE IF I WERE NATSU...

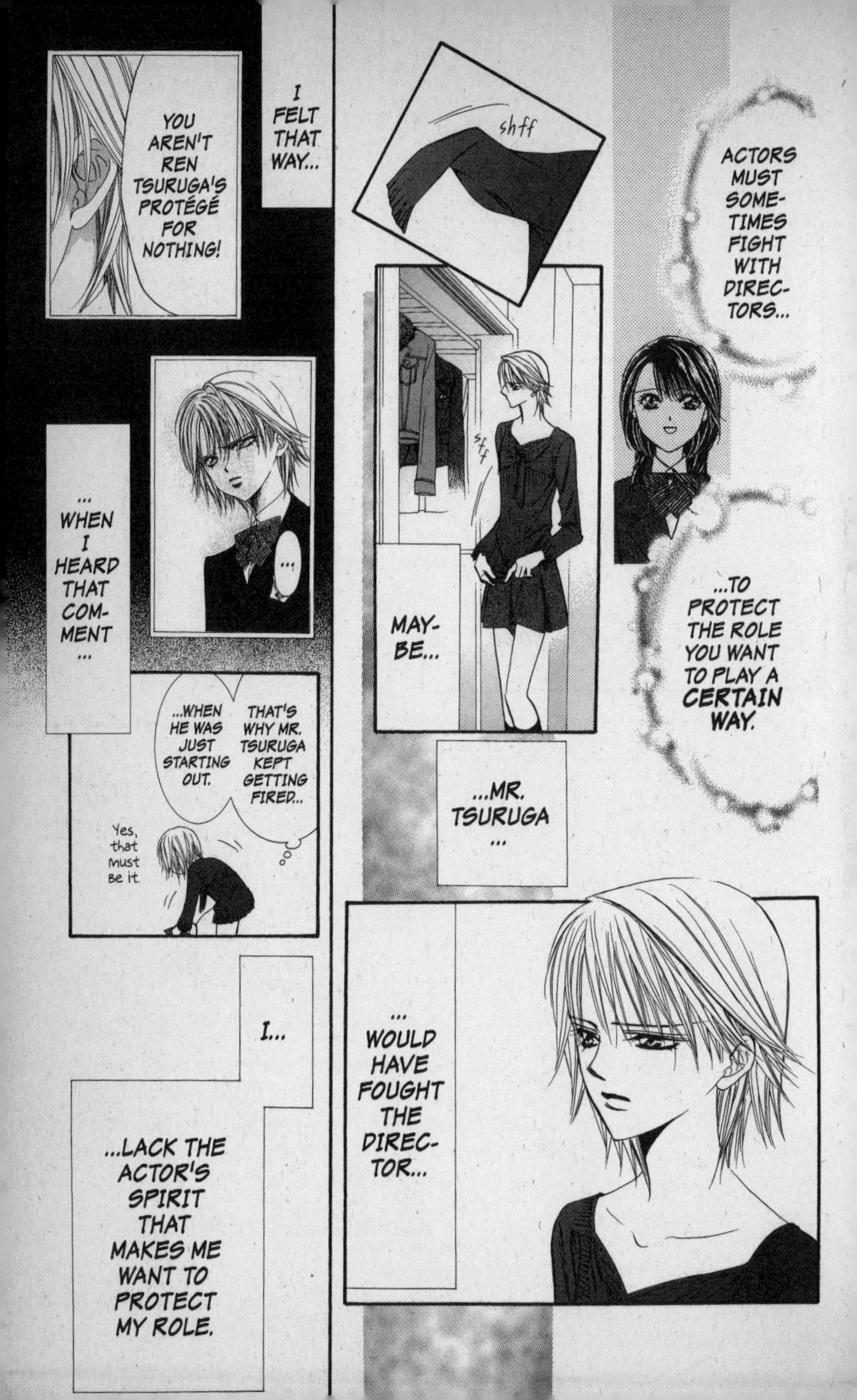
ACTORS MUST SOMETIMES FIGHT WITH DIRECTORS...
...TO PROTECT THE ROLE YOU WANT TO PLAY A CERTAIN WAY.
shff
sff
MAYBE...
...MR. TSURUGA ...
...WOULD HAVE FOUGHT THE DIRECTOR...
I FELT THAT WAY...
YOU AREN'T REN TSURUGA'S PROTÉGÉ FOR NOTHING!
...
...WHEN I HEARD THAT COMMENT...
THAT'S WHY MR. TSURUGA KEPT GETTING FIRED...
...WHEN HE WAS JUST STARTING OUT.
Yes, that must be it.
I...
...LACK THE ACTOR'S SPIRIT THAT MAKES ME WANT TO PROTECT MY ROLE.

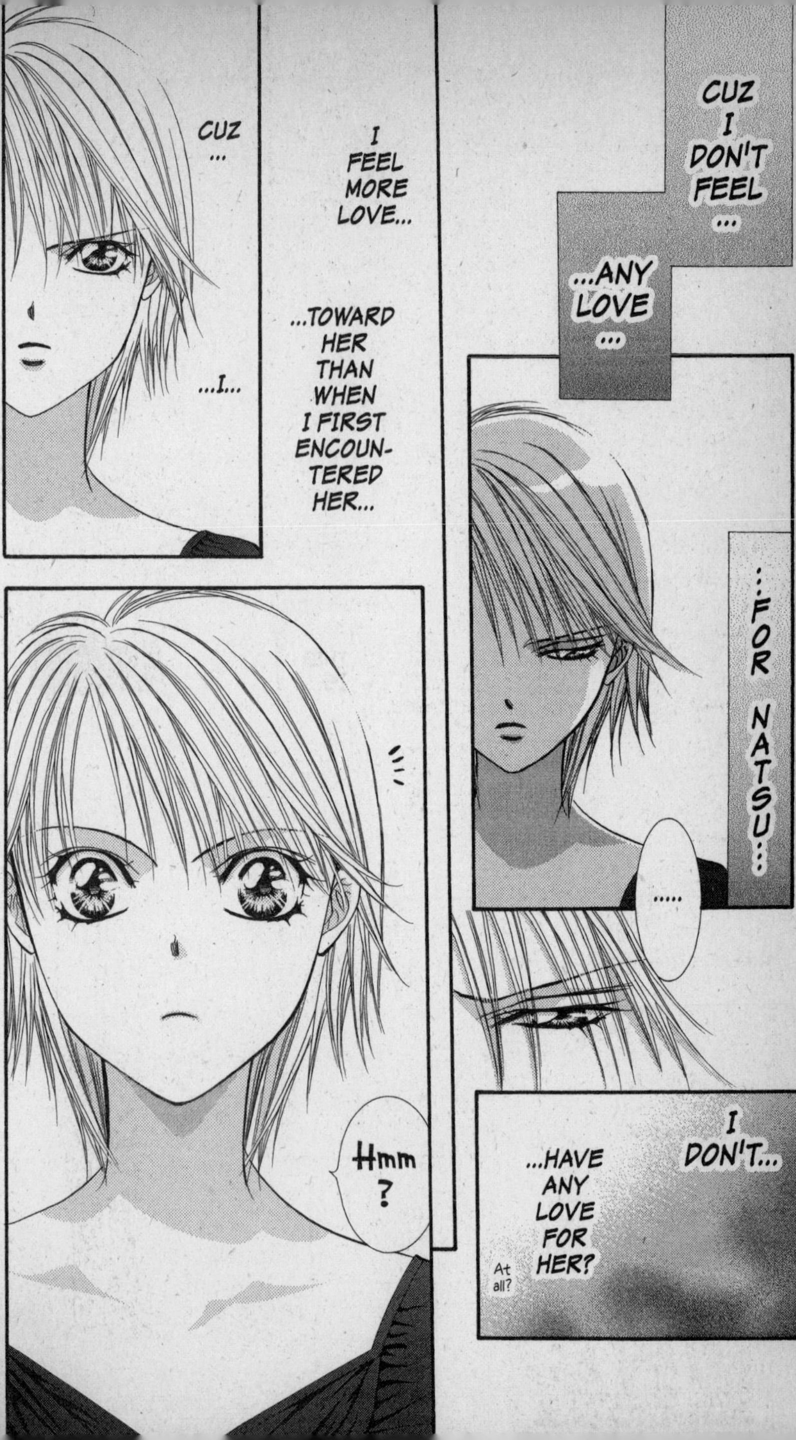
CUZ I DON'T FEEL...
...ANY LOVE...
...FOR NATSU...
.....
I DON'T...
...HAVE ANY LOVE FOR HER?
At all?
CUZ...
...I...
I FEEL MORE LOVE...
...TOWARD HER THAN WHEN I FIRST ENCOUNTERED HER...
Hmm?

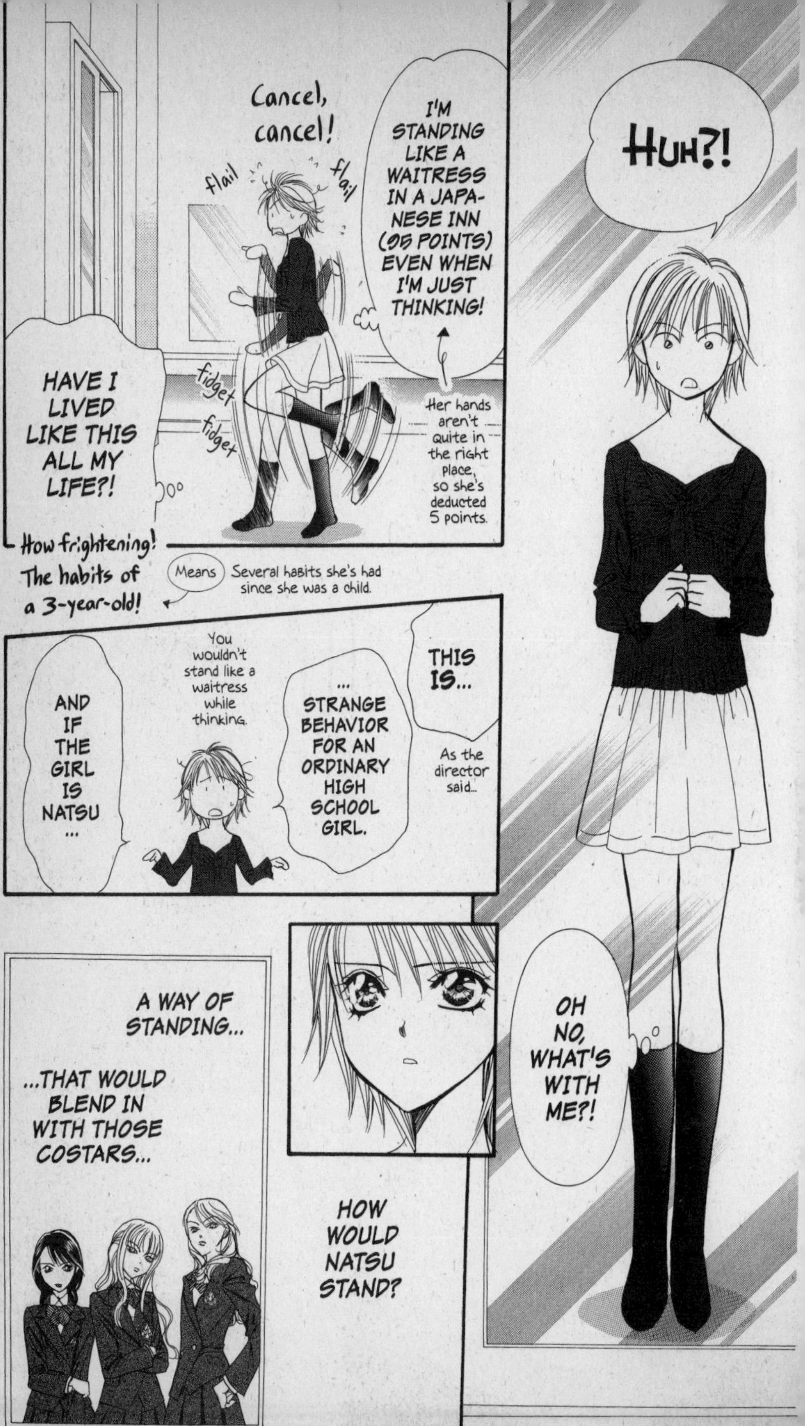
HUH?!
OH NO, WHAT'S WITH ME?!
I'M STANDING LIKE A WAITRESS IN A JAPANESE INN (95 POINTS) EVEN WHEN I'M JUST THINKING!
Cancel, cancel!
flail
flail
Her hands aren't quite in the right place, so she's deducted 5 points.
fidget
fidget
HAVE I LIVED LIKE THIS ALL MY LIFE?!
How frightening! The habits of a 3-year-old!
Means
Several habits she's had since she was a child.
THIS IS...
As the director said...
...STRANGE BEHAVIOR FOR AN ORDINARY HIGH SCHOOL GIRL.
You wouldn't stand like a waitress while thinking.
AND IF THE GIRL IS NATSU...
HOW WOULD NATSU STAND?
A WAY OF STANDING...
...THAT WOULD BLEND IN WITH THOSE COSTARS...

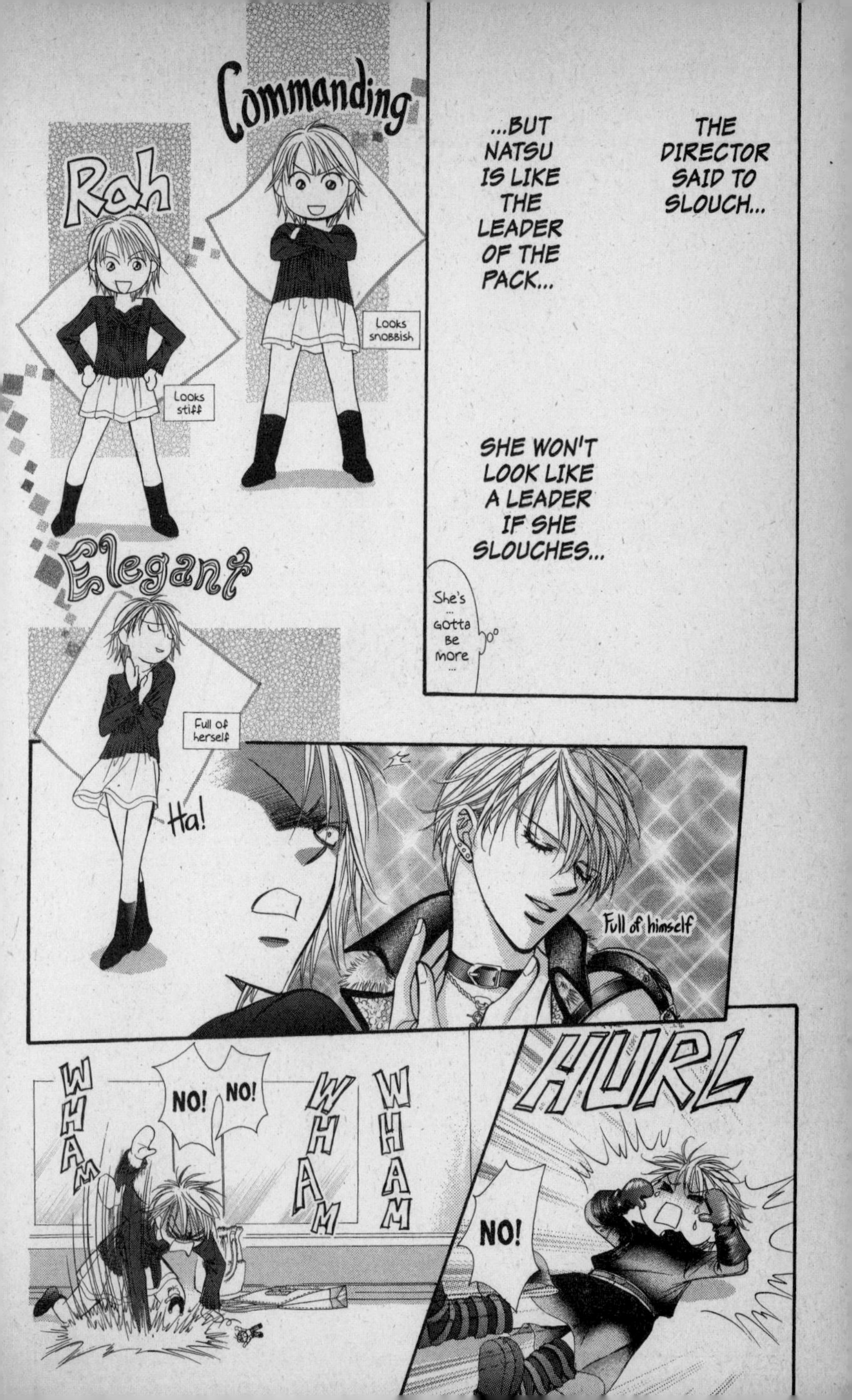
THE DIRECTOR SAID TO SLOUCH...
...BUT NATSU IS LIKE THE LEADER OF THE PACK...
SHE WON'T LOOK LIKE A LEADER IF SHE SLOUCHES...
She's... gotta be more...
Commanding
Looks snobbish
Rah
Looks stiff
Elegant
Full of herself
Ha!
Full of himself
HURL
NO!
WHAM
WHAM
NO!
NO!
WHAM

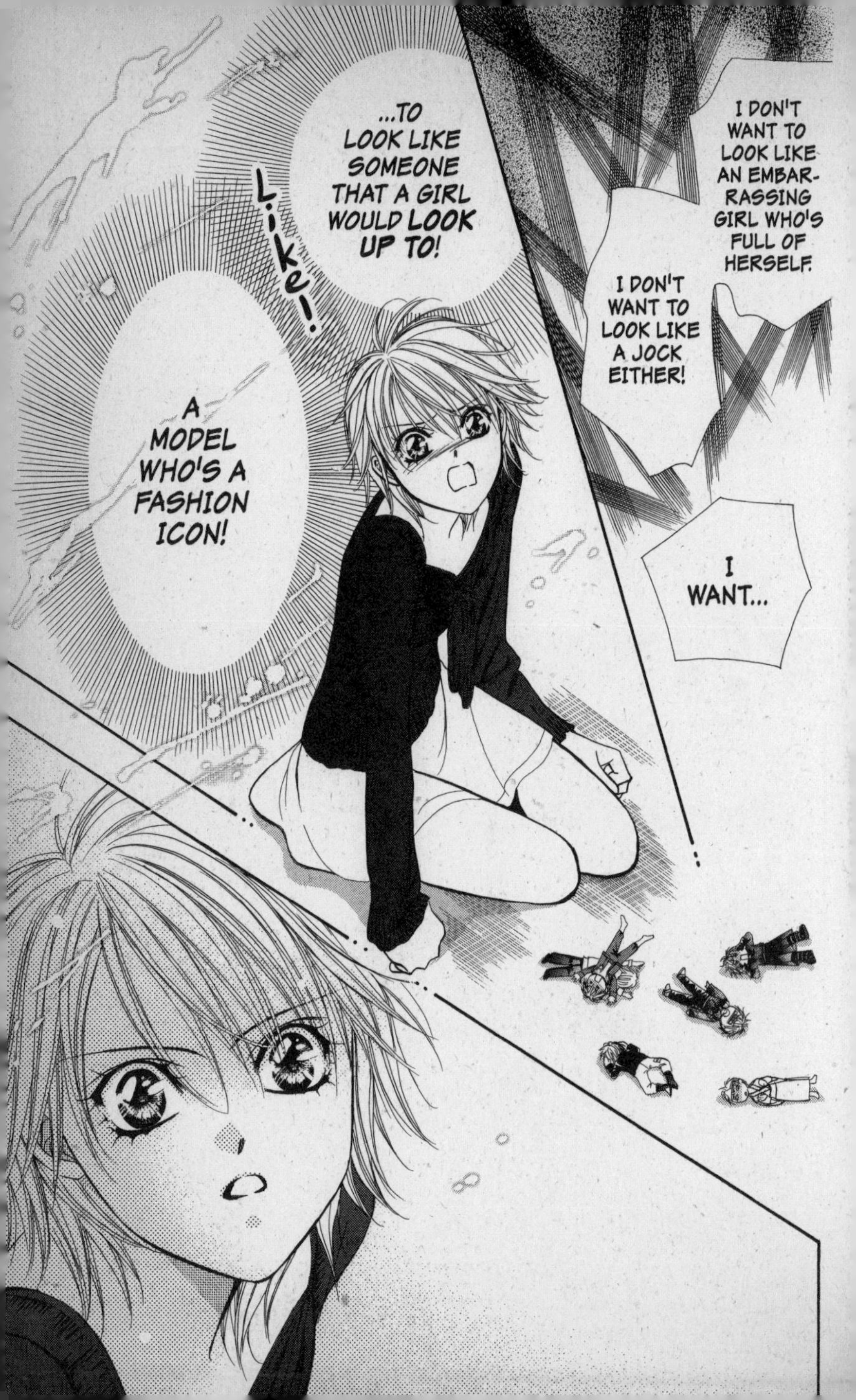
I DON'T WANT TO LOOK LIKE AN EMBAR-RASSING GIRL WHO'S FULL OF HERSELF.
I DON'T WANT TO LOOK LIKE A JOCK EITHER!
I WANT...
...TO LOOK LIKE SOMEONE THAT A GIRL WOULD LOOK UP TO!
Like!
A MODEL WHO'S A FASHION ICON!

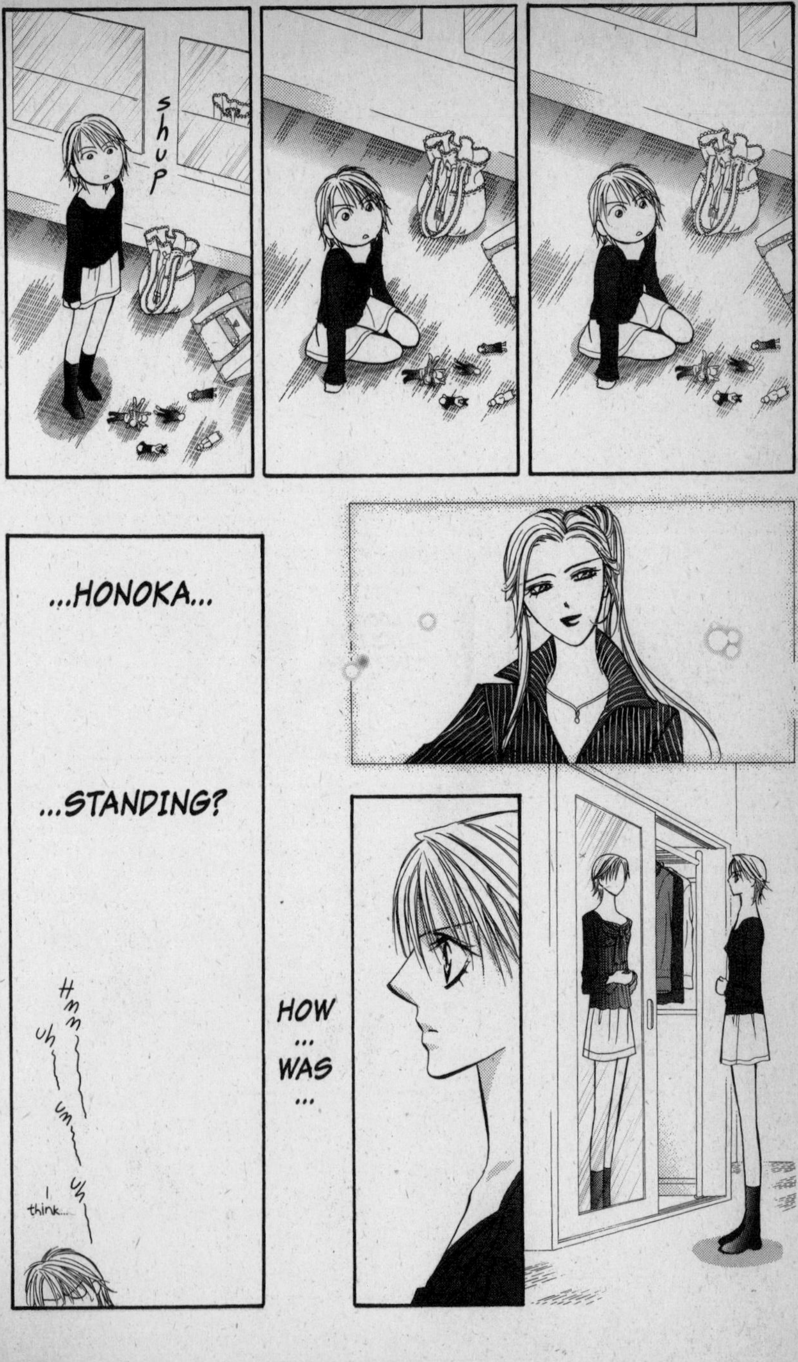
shup
HOW ... WAS ...
...HONOKA...
...STANDING?
Hmm uh um uh
I think...

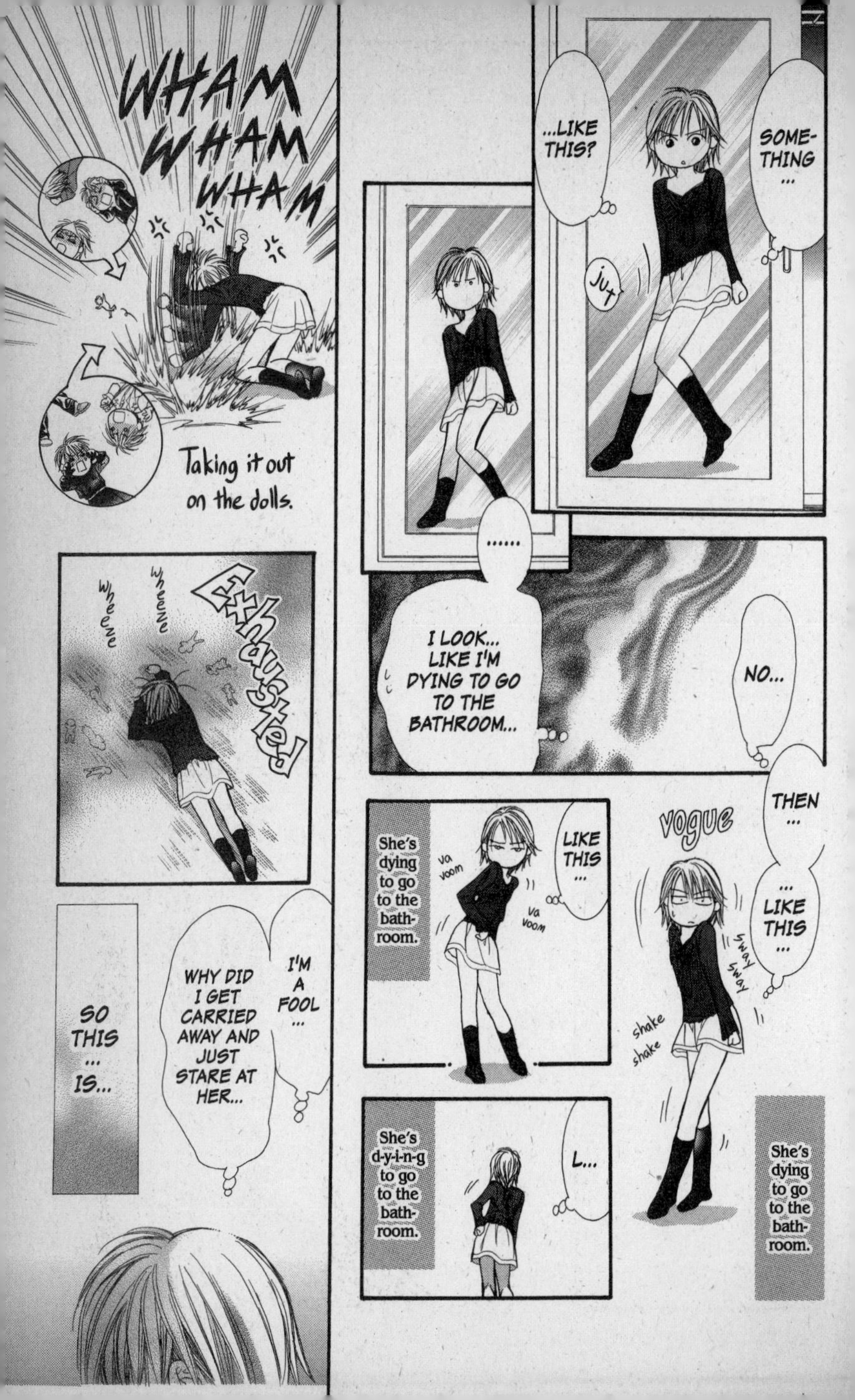
SOME-THING ...
jut
...LIKE THIS?
......
NO...
I LOOK... LIKE I'M DYING TO GO TO THE BATHROOM...
THEN ...
... LIKE THIS ...
vogue
sway sway
shake shake
She's dying to go to the bath-room.
LIKE THIS ...
va voom
va voom
She's dying to go to the bath-room.
L...
She's d-y-i-n-g to go to the bath-room.
WHAM WHAM WHAM
Taking it out on the dolls.
Exhausted
wheeze
wheeze
I'M A FOOL ...
WHY DID I GET CARRIED AWAY AND JUST STARE AT HER...
SO THIS ... IS...

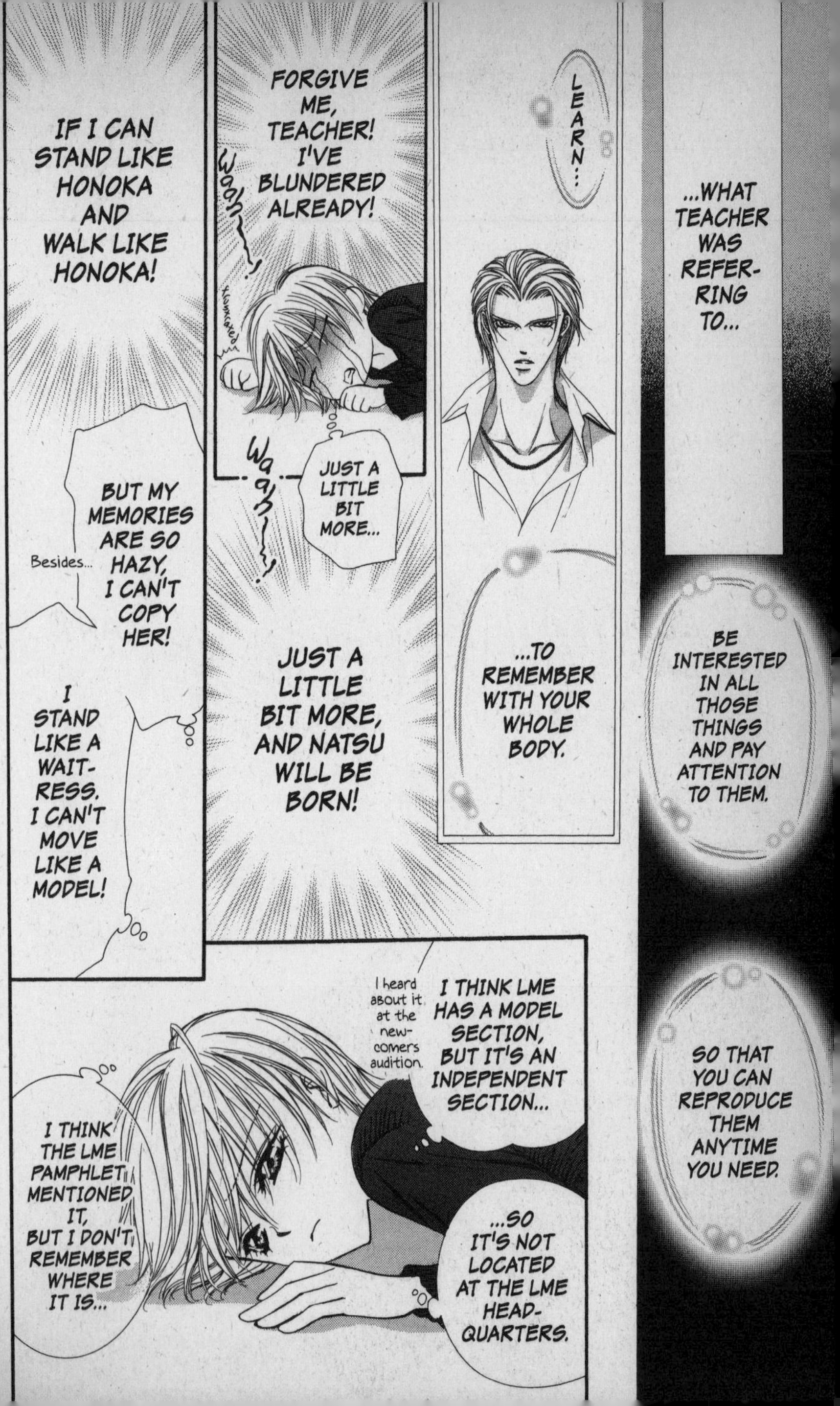
...WHAT TEACHER WAS REFERRING TO...
BE INTERESTED IN ALL THOSE THINGS AND PAY ATTENTION TO THEM.
SO THAT YOU CAN REPRODUCE THEM ANYTIME YOU NEED.
LEARN...
...TO REMEMBER WITH YOUR WHOLE BODY.
FORGIVE ME, TEACHER! I'VE BLUNDERED ALREADY!
Waah—!
JUST A LITTLE BIT MORE...
Waah—!
JUST A LITTLE BIT MORE, AND NATSU WILL BE BORN!
IF I CAN STAND LIKE HONOKA AND WALK LIKE HONOKA!
Besides...
BUT MY MEMORIES ARE SO HAZY, I CAN'T COPY HER!
I STAND LIKE A WAITRESS. I CAN'T MOVE LIKE A MODEL!
I heard about it at the newcomers audition.
I THINK LME HAS A MODEL SECTION, BUT IT'S AN INDEPENDENT SECTION...
...SO IT'S NOT LOCATED AT THE LME HEADQUARTERS.
I THINK THE LME PAMPHLET MENTIONED IT, BUT I DON'T REMEMBER WHERE IT IS...

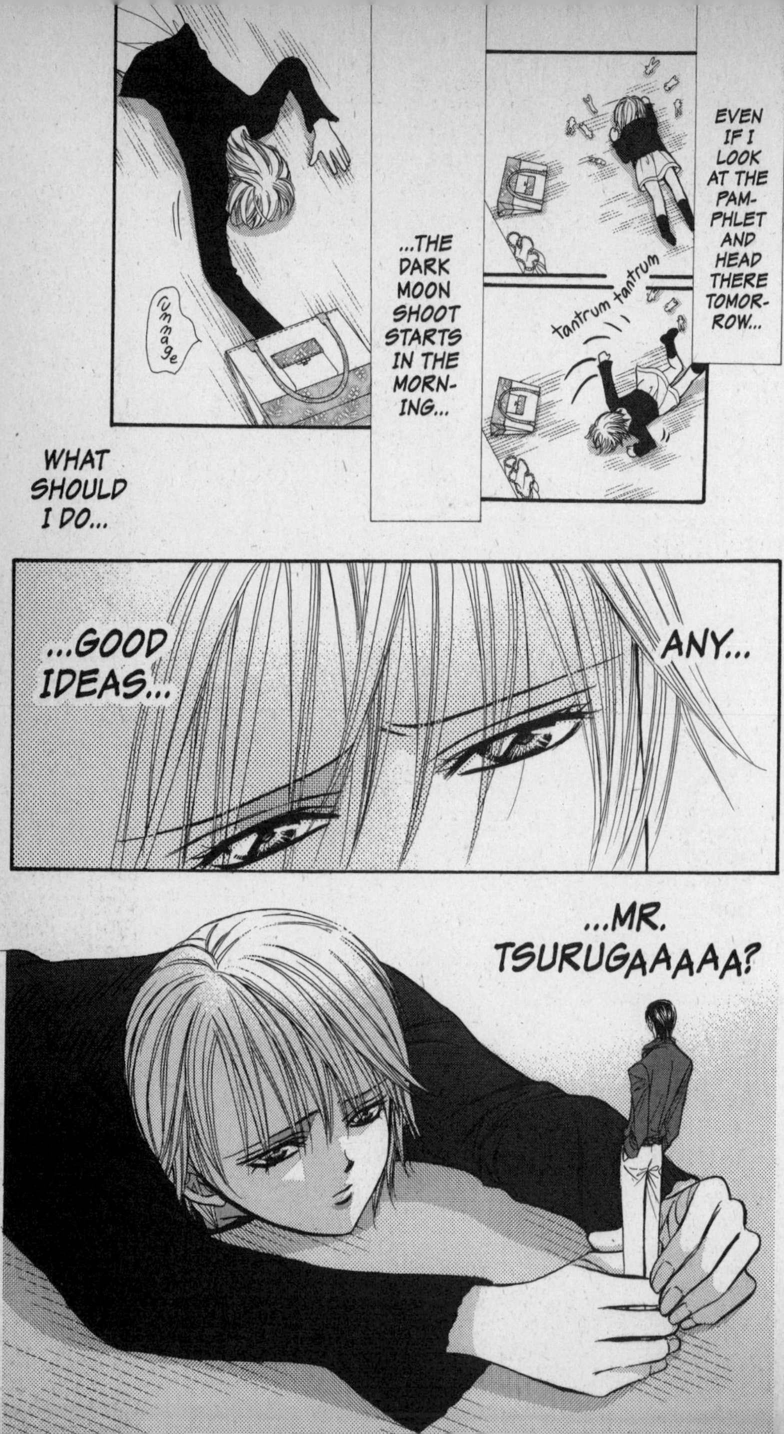
EVEN IF I LOOK AT THE PAMPHLET AND HEAD THERE TOMORROW...
tantrum tantrum
...THE DARK MOON SHOOT STARTS IN THE MORNING...
rummage
WHAT SHOULD I DO...
ANY...
...GOOD IDEAS...
...MR. TSURUGAAAAA?

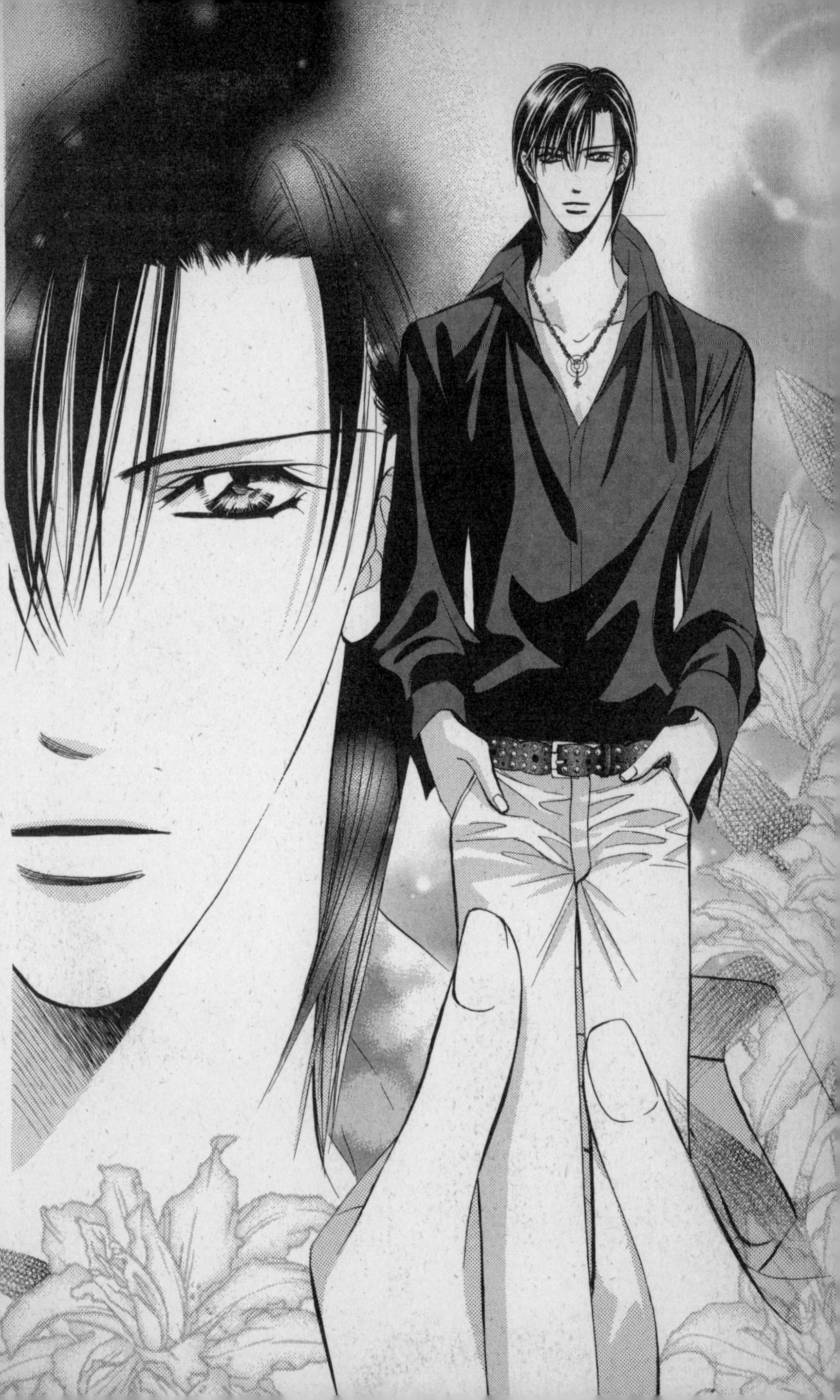

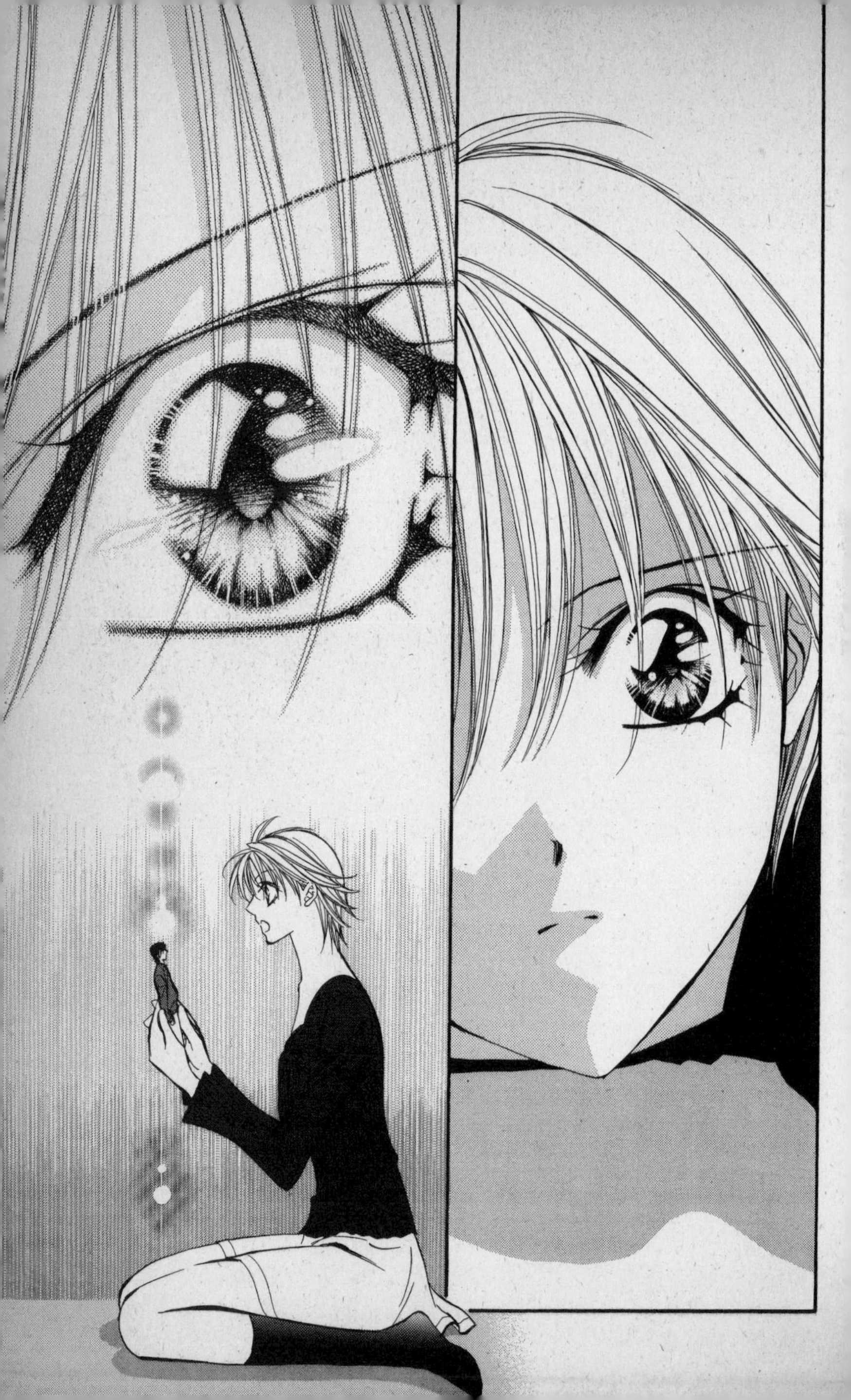

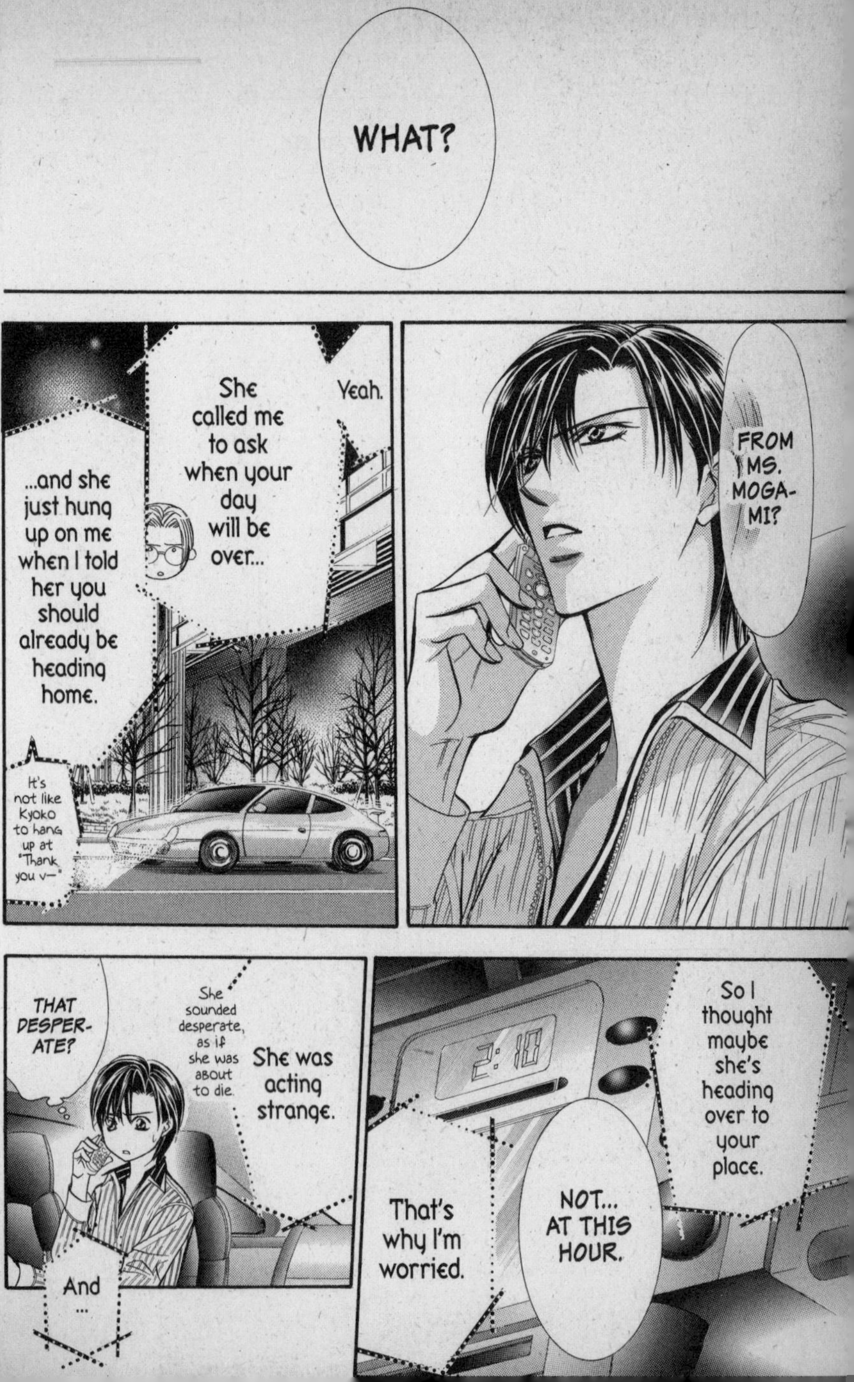
WHAT?
FROM MS. MOGAMI?
Yeah.
She called me to ask when your day will be over...
...and she just hung up on me when I told her you should already be heading home.
It's not like Kyoko to hang up at "Thank you v—"
So I thought maybe she's heading over to your place.
2:10
NOT... AT THIS HOUR.
That's why I'm worried.
She was acting strange.
She sounded desperate, as if she was about to die.
THAT DESPERATE?
And ...

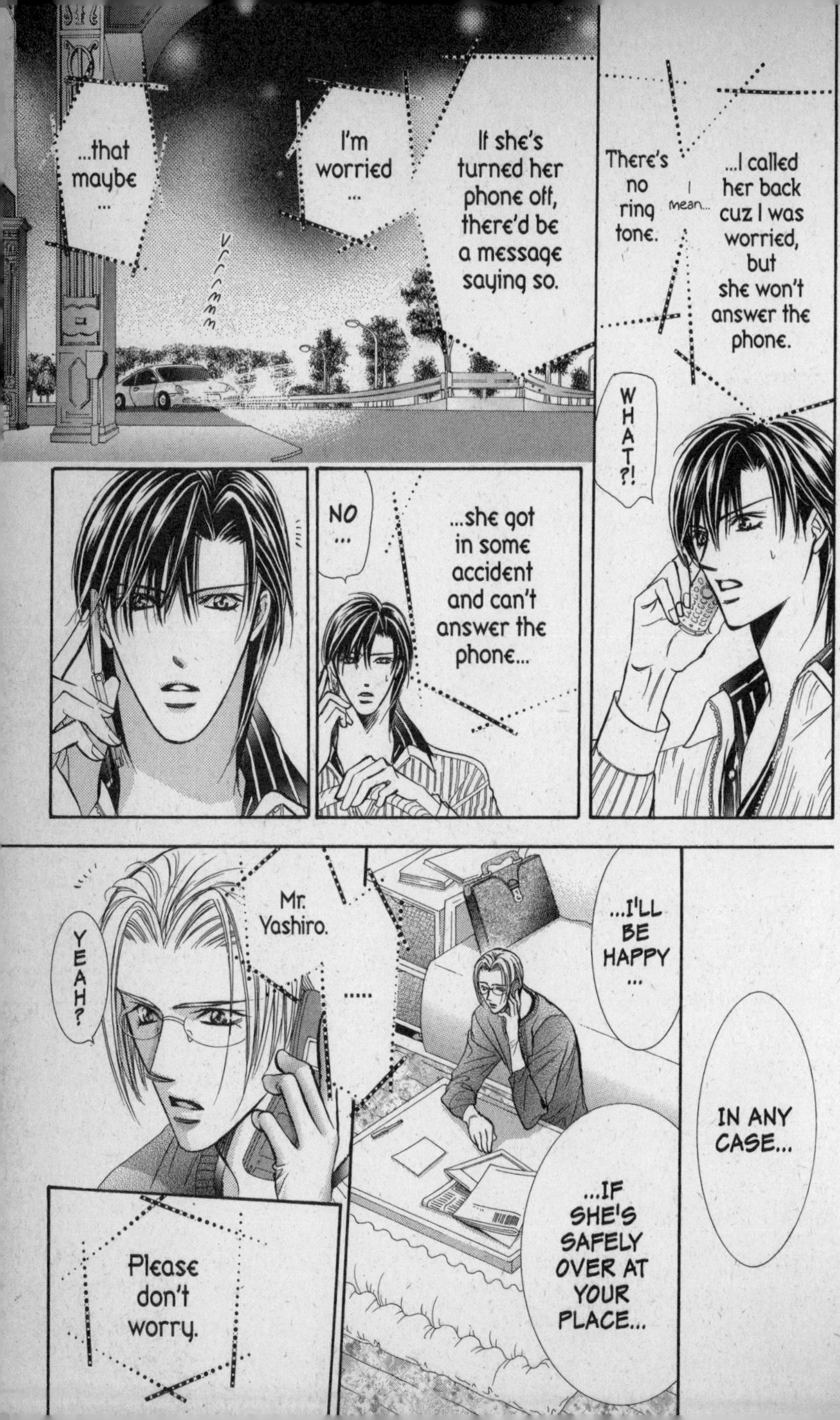
...I called her back cuz I was worried, but she won't answer the phone.
I mean...
There's no ring tone.
WHAT?!
If she's turned her phone off, there'd be a message saying so.
I'm worried...
...that maybe...
Vrrrmmm
...she got in some accident and can't answer the phone...
NO...
IN ANY CASE...
...IF SHE'S SAFELY OVER AT YOUR PLACE...
...I'LL BE HAPPY...
....
Mr. Yashiro.
YEAH?
Please don't worry.

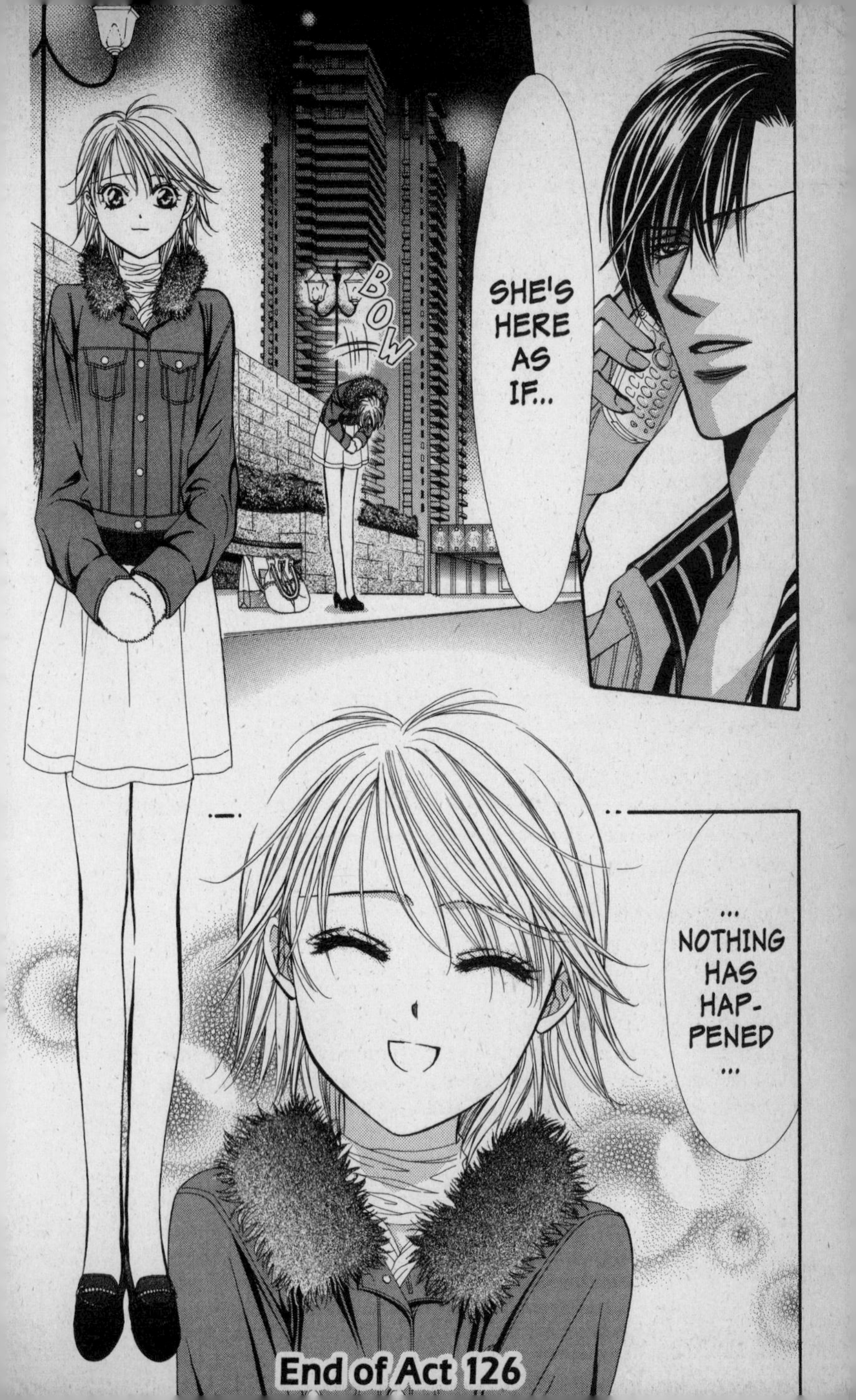
SHE'S HERE AS IF...
... NOTHING HAS HAP-PENED ...
BOW
End of Act 126

Skip·Beat! End Notes
Everyone knows how to be a fan, but sometimes cool things from other cultures need a little help crossing the language barrier.

Page 5, panel 2: Okamisan
In traditional Japanese restaurants, the female manager is called "Okamisan."

Page 11, panel 4: More letters
In hiragana Chiorin (ちおリン) and Chiririn (ちりリン) have the same number of characters.

Page 13, panel 1: (Calm down) Depreeeeeeeeessed
In the original Japanese, the kanji translated as "calm down" and "depressed" can both be read as "chin."

Page 41, panel 2: Yorozuya
Yorozuya means "a dealer in all sorts of articles," and tends to refer to a general store, but here is the name of the store.

Page 64, panel 1: Talento
A "talento" in Japan usually appears on various TV shows and other mass media outlets. They often sing, star in commercials and write for print media as well.

Page 88, panel 1: Doves, beans
In Japanese there is an expression "to look as if a dove got hit by a peashooter," which refers to a puzzled look or a blank look.

Page 105, panel 1: Direct to video
Called V Cinema in Japan, they are low-budget flicks that are made mainly for the video rental market and rarely get shown in theaters. Many V Cinema movies feature the underground world, such as the yakuza.

Page 143, panel 1: Correspondence notebooks
Used for communication between students, teachers and parents.

Page 165, panel 1: Plain udon
Udon in hot broth with minimal toppings, if any.

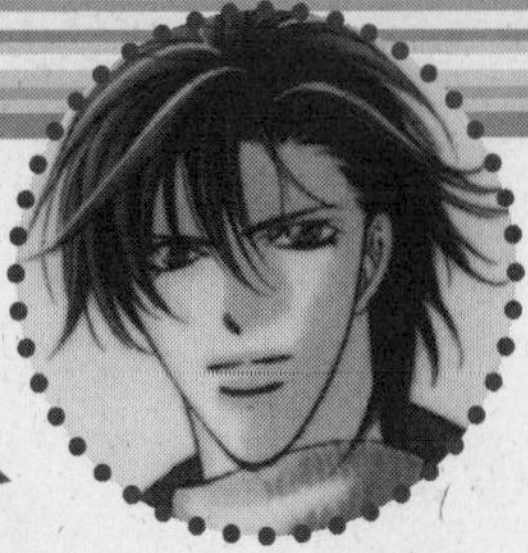

Yoshiki Nakamura is originally from Tokushima prefecture. She started drawing manga in elementary school, which eventually led to her 1993 debut of *Yume de Au yori Suteki* (Better than Seeing in a Dream) in *Hana to Yume* magazine. Her other works include the basketball series *Saint Love, MVP wa Yuzurenai* (Can't Give Up MVP), *Blue Wars* and *Tokyo Crazy Paradise*, a series about a female bodyguard in 2020 Tokyo.

SKIP·BEAT!
Vol. 21
Shojo Beat Edition

STORY AND ART BY YOSHIKI NAKAMURA

English Translation & Adaptation/Tomo Kimura
Touch-up Art & Lettering/Sabrina Heep
Design/Ronnie Casson
Editor/Pancha Diaz

VP, Production/Alvin Lu
VP, Sales & Product Marketing/Gonzalo Ferreyra
VP, Creative/Linda Espinosa
Publisher/Hyoe Narita

Skip-Beat! by Yoshiki Nakamura © Yoshiki Nakamura 2009.
All rights reserved. First published in Japan in 2009 by HAKUSENSHA, Inc., Tokyo.
English language translation rights arranged with HAKUSENSHA, Inc., Tokyo.

Printed in Canada

Published by VIZ Media, LLC.
P.O. Box 77010
San Francisco, CA 94107

10 9 8 7 6 5 4 3 2 1
First printing, August 2010

www.viz.com

www.shojobeat.com

PARENTAL ADVISORY
SKIP·BEAT! is rated T for Teen and is
recommended for ages 13 and up. This
volume contains a grudge.
ratings.viz.com

curtain call

Honey Hunt

BY Miki Aihara! THE CREATOR OF
HOT GIMMICK AND TOKYO BOYS & GIRLS!

Growing up in the shadow of her famous parents, Yura's used to the pressure of being in a celebrity family. But when the spotlight starts to shine directly on her, will Yura have the courage—and talent—to stand on her own?

Find out in the *Honey Hunt* manga— **on sale now!**